The Causes of Economic Growth

Rick Szostak

The Causes of Economic Growth

Interdisciplinary Perspectives

 Springer

Dr. Rick Szostak
Department of Economics
University of Alberta
Tory Building 8-14
Edmonton, Alberta T6G 2H4
Canada
rick.szostak@ualberta.ca

ISBN 978-3-540-92281-0   e-ISBN 978-3-540-92282-7

DOI 10.1007/978-3-540-92282-7

Library of Congress Control Number: 2008943996

Cover design: WMXDesign GmbH, Heidelberg, Germany

Printed on acid-free paper

9 8 7 6 5 4 3 2 1

springer.com

Contents

      6.4.3 The Course of Technological Innovation (Endogeneity) 163
      6.4.4 Clustering, General Purpose Technologies............................. 167
      6.4.5 Research and Growth 169
      6.4.6 Product Versus Process Innovation 170
      6.4.7 Technology Transmission.. 171
      6.4.8 Links to Technological Innovation 174
      6.4.9 Technology and Social Structure 185
  6.5 Geography 186
      6.5.1 Climate and Location.. 186
      6.5.2 Resources 187
      6.5.3 Country Size.. 188
      6.5.4 Regional Clusters 189
      6.5.5 Environment.. 190

7 The Causes of Economic Growth: Institutions.............................. 191
  7.1 Institutions and Growth.. 191
      7.1.1 Institutions and Investment... 195
      7.1.2 Institutions and Infrastructure 196
  7.2 Which Functions?... 198
      7.2.1 Ownership (Property Rights) 198
      7.2.2 Exchange... 199
      7.2.3 Finance 199
      7.2.4 Production 200
  7.3 Which Institutions? 200
      7.3.1 Property Rights 202
      7.3.2 Financial Institutions.. 204
      7.3.3 Labor Markets and Work Effort 204
  7.4 Institutional Change 207
      7.4.1 Economics Approaches... 207
      7.4.2 Economic History 209
      7.4.3 Sociological Institutionalism 214
      7.4.4 An Insight from Anthropology 217
      7.4.5 Institutions and Psychology 217
      7.4.6 Politics and Institutions.. 218
      7.4.7 Business History 223
      7.4.8 Integrating These Approaches 224
      7.4.9 Democracy 229

8 The Causes of Economic Growth: Cultural and Social Determinants ..233
  8.1 Culture.. 233
      8.1.1 Culture and Institutions... 233
      8.1.2 The Nature of Culture 235
      8.1.3 Cultural Change 236
      8.1.4 Culture and Growth... 238

Acknowledgments

This book combines the two key strands of my research career: as an economic historian studying the causes of economic growth (and decline) and as an inter-disciplinarian exploring the theory and practice of interdisciplinarity itself. As such it provides a useful opportunity to thank the two people who have played the greatest role in shaping my career. Joel Mokyr supervised my dissertation a quarter-century ago, and has remained a mentor and friend ever since. Bill Newell, longtime executive director of the Association for Integrative Studies (and also coincidentally an economic history PhD), has patiently read many of the books and articles I have written in the last decade and given me copious advice. Both are characterized by genuine intellectual curiosity and an immense breadth of knowledge, and I am lucky to have known them both.

I have had two main academic communities over the last decade as I formulated the ideas for this book: on the one hand the Association for Integrative Studies (whose Board I have served on with pleasure for much of that time) and kindred organizations such as the Association for General and Liberal Studies; and on the other the economic historians I have interacted with at conferences of the Canadian Network for Economic History, Economic History Association, Cliometric Society, and European Historical Economics Society. I thank my many friends and colleagues in both communities for a lifetime of intellectual exchange. Given the deep roots that this book has in my previous research, I must eschew the temptation to thank by name all those who have informed and encouraged me along the way.

Much of the present book was drafted while I was a Visiting Fellow at European University Institute in Florence, Italy, during the 2006-7 academic year. I thank Giovanni Federico for making that visit possible, productive, and enjoyable. I thank Rita Peero for finding me that great office with a sweeping view of Florence. And I thank the EUI more generally for its great library, all-too-tempting seminar series, and much-needed computer support services. And I thank the staff of the local children's hospital for taking such good care of my sons when they somehow managed to contract serious cases of pneumonia.

Elements of the present book were presented to annual conferences of the Canadian Economics Association, Association for Integrative Studies, and European Historical Economics Society, and also to the Twelfth World Congress of Social Economics and the Second International Conference on Interdisciplinary Social Science. A short paper, "An Interdisciplinary Analysis of Economic Growth" was published in the *International Journal of Interdisciplinary Social Science* 2:3, after the latter conference. Presentations were also made to the Socio-Economics Forum at the University of West Indies (Trinidad campus; February, 2008) and as the First Annual STS Lecture at the University of Alberta in April of 2008. I thank participants at all of these venues for helpful comments. I thank the anonymous referees of that paper and this larger project. Bill Newell has characteristically read this entire manuscript; it is much better as a result of his sage advice. Allen Repko read parts of the manuscript and also provided useful advice. I used the draft manuscript as the text for my course "ECON 222: Technology, Institutions, and Economic Growth" during the Winter of 2008 at the University of Alberta. I thank the students in that course for both their patience and helpful advice. Research on this project has been supported by a grant from the Social Sciences and Humanities Research Council of Canada for which I am extremely grateful.

Last but far from least I thank my children, Mireille, Julien, and Theo. Even though I have not followed their advice to write shorter books with pictures of animals, they proved willing to occasionally let me use our computer while in Italy in order to set these words down. And they gave me the immense pleasure of seeing Europe through their eyes (even if I continue to believe that Stonehenge is more than 'just rocks'). Writing books, teaching good students, and playing with my children has been a pretty sweet life.

List of Tables

1 Interdisciplinarity and Economic Growth

1.1 Applying Interdisciplinary Analysis to the Study of Growth

What are the causes of economic growth? There is perhaps no more important question in all of human science. Billions of people live in abject poverty and their hopes for the future rely on sustained economic growth. Economic growth may be of less critical importance for those who are already comfortable, but here too the achievement of an environmentally sustainable and capability-enhancing future hinges on an understanding of the causes of growth. There is also perhaps no more complex question in human science, for it is clear from contemporary scholarship that a very wide array of phenomena at least potentially influences rates of economic growth. Many of these phenomena are economic in nature, but many are not. Thus the question lends itself to interdisciplinary exploration. We will arguably gain our best understanding of economic growth if we integrate the understandings of economists, political scientists, sociologists, anthropologists, and others. If this is so, then it follows that we will want to follow 'best-practice' strategies for interdisciplinary analysis in exploring economic growth. Fortunately, the scholarship of interdisciplinarity has suggested how interdisciplinary research should best proceed. The contribution of this book is to follow a twelve-step process for interdisciplinary analysis in exploring the causes of growth.

Interdisciplinarity: It is increasingly advocated by university presidents, government research granting agencies, and public intellectuals. Pressing social problems, we are told, do not come in tidy disciplinary bundles but require the combined insights of many scholarly communities. This argument regarding the complexity of social policy reflects recent developments in natural science and technology, where it is likewise felt that advances in biotechnology, nanotechnology, or information technology require interdisciplinary approaches. Yet at the same time that interdisciplinarity is advocated widely there is a deep skepticism within academia as to whether interdisciplinarity is desirable or even possible. The vast majority of academics has a narrow graduate training in one discipline or subdiscipline, and has spent their careers examining even narrower questions. They naturally wonder how scholars, even in groups, can master enough of the detail of multiple disciplines in order to perform quality interdisciplinary research.[1] Less

---

[1] Dogan (1998, 98) raises a common concern that it is simply impossible to master two or more disciplines, and thus 'the idea of interdisciplinary research is illusory.' Yet Dogan urges integration across subfields of disciplines. This book relies on a more general argument that powerful integrative analysis is possible without having a practitioner level of mastery in each field addressed. As Newell (2001) argues, the interdisciplinarian must only have a general sense of the overall disciplinary perspective of a discipline and of the theories and methods relevant to the question at hand. Even specialized researchers need not 'master' their entire discipline in the sense of being able to reproduce the works they cite, but need only to comprehend the

R. Szostak, *The Causes of Economic Growth*,
DOI: 10.1007/978-3-540-92282-7_1, © Springer-Verlag Berlin Heidelberg 2009

laudably, many academics think that their discipline holds to superior practices or standards, and thus fear mingling with others.

Many scholars pretend to interdisciplinarity only when drafting grant applications. Many others proudly claim to be interdisciplinary but hardly reflect on what this means or how interdisciplinary research is best performed. At its worst, such 'un-self-conscious' interdisciplinarity can be terribly superficial: one book in sociology is read to provide sociological insight, or a long-discredited theory is borrowed from psychology, or a biased reading of works in many disciplines is used to justify some grand theory.

Happily, as interdisciplinary research and teaching have grown in importance, many scholars have examined – both theoretically and empirically – how interdisciplinary analysis should best proceed. Such analyses can potentially encourage scholars to both more actively entertain interdisciplinary research and achieve qualitatively better insights when they do so. But it must first be established that research following these recommended practices is both viable and valuable. Only then will the skeptics truly embrace interdisciplinary research. In pursuing an interdisciplinary examination of economic growth this book not only consolidates our understanding of growth but simultaneously establishes the viability of certain 'best-practice' techniques for interdisciplinary analysis. These, while the result of generations of scholarship, have not previously been applied explicitly to a research question of this scope.

This book proceeds through several steps in interdisciplinary analysis, and asks what insight each of these provides for our understanding of the causes of economic growth. Of course, no one book can be expected to provide the complete and final answer to such a broad question. The hope, rather, is that this book can achieve two goals with respect to our understanding of economic growth: provide a better understanding of the causes of economic growth than is possible within the confines of any one discipline, and identify promising paths for future research that are not presently implicated by the research programs of any one discipline. If successful in these ways the book will have established that scholars collectively know more than we realize, but that the relevant knowledge has not been integrated properly. We can thus in turn appreciate what has been lost through a narrow approach.

The starting premise of this book is simple, and hopefully obvious: *Economic growth is a complex process, involving the causal interaction of numerous phenomena.* Several implications follow from this (and we will see in what follows that many but not all scholars, in economics and elsewhere, accept these implications):

---

underlying theory and method. Notably Dogan a few pages later bemoans the tendency of competing theories to evolve in isolation both within and across disciplines: 'But there must be debate' (105). Surely one task of interdisciplinary research is to identify such disagreements, and suggest avenues of rapprochement? Dogan also applauds the ability of area studies scholars to borrow eclectically from various disciplines in order to study topics of special importance to a particular area (117).

- Since many of these phenomena are non-economic, insights from disciplines that study these other phenomena are likely to be invaluable.
- Due to the number of complex interactions among these various phenomena, our understanding of economic growth (at least in the foreseeable future) will involve a complex amalgam of complementary theories rather than one theory of everything.
- Less obviously but importantly, we shall see (especially in chapter 3) that different theories and different phenomena are best investigated with different methods. Moreover, scholarly confidence in any theoretical proposition should be strongest when evidence from multiple methods and data sources can be marshaled in its support. Thus we will want to carefully evaluate various methods and types of evidence in what follows.

Many economists working with formal growth models appreciate that these serve to identify only (some of) the 'proximate' causes of growth: countries that invest more, develop or borrow better technology, and develop superior infrastructure (education, health, transport) will tend to grow faster on average. Such insights beg the more difficult questions of why some countries invest more, innovate more, and develop better schools than others (and also why some countries get better results from doing so than others).[2] 'No one would claim that we now have a really good causal account of either technological and organizational progress or of the accumulation of human capital in all of its various forms' (Solow 2005, 7). Economists disagree about such questions more than is the case in most/all other fields of economic inquiry. Economists increasingly recognize that the answers to these questions involve differences in political and economic institutions (that is, formal rules and organizations) across countries. Many economists venture even farther afield to speculate that differences in culture, social structure (family forms, gender relations, ethnic diversity, and so on), geographical environment, and political practices are also of key importance. The economics literature is thus characterized at present by a variety of models that each stresses different causal relationships (though these tend to have broadly similar theoretical roots). The goal here, then, is not to supersede economic analysis but to place this appropriately within a broader structure of complementary theories and methods applied to a much wider range of causal links.[3]

---

[2] Baumol (2000, 13) appreciates that technological innovation cannot mostly/entirely be explained by the variables included in endogenous growth models (which purport to explain technology endogenously). He urges detailed micro-level analysis of the causes of innovation. 'Economic growth is notoriously the blackest of the many black boxes in economics ... attempts to account for [the stylized facts of growth] in a single theory have had mixed results at best' (*Economist* March 6, 1999, 72).

[3] Paul Romer, the endogenous growth theorist, has remarked that modeling is a long-term exercise, but that growth is a pressing public policy issue. Thus even if it is imagined that economic theory will one day encompass all that needs to be known about economic growth, it makes sense in the short run to combine existing scholarly analyses. Moreover, the insights of other

Variables representing aspects of culture or politics or geography are often inserted into the models that economists test statistically, but few economists read widely in the literatures of disciplines that take culture or politics or geography as their focus. The logic of their own research program has brought (many) economists to the edge of the abyss: they sense that the insights of other disciplines may be important but are unsure of how best to incorporate those insights into a more comprehensive understanding of growth.[4] The fact that these other disciplines use different terminology, theories, and methods makes the process of borrowing both more difficult and more suspect.

Scholars in other disciplines only rarely directly address 'the causes of economic growth.' They often, though, address the related question of 'development' and even more often discuss various proximate causes of growth: technology, institutions, and so on. The fact that scholars in different disciplines ask quite different research questions often means that the research of one is less useful to the other than it could be, even though they address causally related phenomena. Just as economists can benefit from a greater understanding of relevant literatures in other disciplines, so too can scholars in other disciplines benefit from an enhanced understanding of the potential connections across disciplinary research programs.

A book with multiple aims serves multiple audiences. This book should be of interest to all who care about economic growth. For economists, it is hoped that this book will show them both what can be learned from other disciplines and how to do so. For those in other disciplines, it will highlight how important their insights may be to the study of growth, and how these can be integrated with insights from other disciplines. The book will be written in a jargon-free style in order to reach these different audiences.[5] One of the challenges of interdisciplinary analysis is simply communicating in a meaningful way across disciplinary boundaries: this book thus seeks to illustrate that careful analysis can be undertaken without recourse to jargon. The book should equally be of interest to scholars of interdisciplinarity, even those with no particular interest in economic growth (though given that economic growth in turn powerfully affects almost all aspects of our lives such a disposition may be rare). It is, as noted above, the first explicit application of a detailed process for interdisciplinary analysis to a research question of broad scope.

---

disciplines can feed into theorizing in economics. Robert Solow among others has argued that modelers should draw upon a wide range of insights.

[4] 'Some of the most interesting thinking on economic growth is to be found on the borders of political science and sociology' (Temple, 1999, 146). He notes that the former receive more attention because they are more easily quantified.

[5] One important cost of such an approach is that this book cannot then guide the reader to appreciate the terminology of scholarly communities whose works it encourages them to read. However, providing an overview in plain English of the key arguments of various communities should facilitate the task of mastering jargon. In some important cases, such as 'social capital,' careful definitions are provided of terms widely used.

Jargon serves many purposes in academia. At its best it facilitates communication within scholarly communities by attaching a simple term to a carefully defined concept. At its worst jargon allows scholars to make banal statements appear more insightful than they really are. This book in pursuing clarity of expression cannot hide behind unnecessary jargon. The integrative insights presented here must stand on their own merits.

By eschewing jargon, and by moving beyond formal models to embrace non-formal analyses and a wider range of phenomena, the book facilitates teaching about growth. Given the importance of economic growth in human lives, its limited role in university curricula is stunning: at most universities neither economics departments nor interdisciplinary programs offer dedicated courses on the subject. Yet there is obvious pedagogical value in teaching such material early, given the range of economic topics (trade, industrial organization) and non-economic topics (democracy, international relations, consumerism) that are better understood in a growth context. This curricular reality is beginning to change: a handful of texts now exist that allow the economic aspects of the issue to be readily taught to junior undergraduates (economic growth having previously been one subject addressed briefly in senior courses addressing business cycle theories). Such books, as can well be imagined, provide an accessible guide to the proximate causes (investment, innovation, education) outlined above but stumble when it comes to institutions or the sources of innovation or culture. This book, it is hoped, will permit a more comprehensive coverage of this complex question.[6] And by integrating across the sometimes contradictory insights of different disciplines, it follows the advice of Graff (1992) to 'teach the conflicts' rather than encourage students to ignore the existence of scholarly disagreement.

1.2 Authorship

Given the twin goals of this book to advance our understanding of both economic growth and the process of interdisciplinary analysis, some notes on authorship are perhaps warranted. I am an economic historian – and we shall see that this quasi-interdisciplinary subfield of economics is best treated as a separate discipline for the purposes of this book. My research as an economic historian tended to focus on the big questions – the causes of the Industrial Revolution, the causes of the Great Depression, always with an eye to more general insights involving growth

---

[6] I created such a course at my own university (ECON 222: Technology, Institutions, and Economic Growth), and moved from assigning a collection of readings to use Weil (2005), which I quite liked, but supplemented with a great deal of interdisciplinary material. Like most economics texts, Weil focuses on issues for which equations and diagrams can be marshaled, and precise answers given; it seemed to me that more important but contentious issues are downplayed. I used a draft of the present manuscript when I taught the course in 2008, and found this much more suitable to the needs of the course.

(or decline) itself – and thus I have long pondered the sorts of interdisciplinary connections outlined above. Early in my career I became interested in methodological issues. The field of economic methodology is often misunderstood by economists as a frontal attack on disciplinary practices. I, like most economic methodologists, objected not to the theory and method that dominate economic analysis but to the reliance on only one theory and method.[7] That is, I did not object to economists doing (most of) what they do but to the profession only doing so. These methodological concerns both reflected and reinforced my interdisciplinary leanings. Yet in looking at other disciplines, I readily appreciated that while these had strengths that compensated for some of the limitations of the practices of economists, these other disciplines had shortcomings as well.

When it is argued that more attention should be paid to alternative theories or methods, a natural response is to ask what we would know if this had been done. But there is an unintentional unfairness here, for it is simply impossible to say what thousands of economists (or those in other disciplines) using alternative methods or theories might have discovered over the years. One can appeal to the insights of a heterodox minority in any discipline, but such insights tend naturally to be less well-developed than those worked out by the much larger mainstream. Interdisciplinarity allows a different response, for one can outline what other large communities of scholars using different methods and theories have indeed discovered. Fortunately, economic historians, political scientists, sociologists, and others have indeed performed much valuable research, and this is poorly integrated into formal economic analysis of growth. Unfortunately, as noted above, these other disciplines not only have their own limitations but have generally asked a quite different set of research questions.

Interdisciplinary research is also far from perfect at present. Many scholars do interdisciplinary research and teaching without reflecting much on what it means to be interdisciplinary. This I think is a dangerous state of affairs. Disciplines (and increasingly sub-disciplines) take their strength from shared understandings of how research in that field should proceed. Interdisciplinary research not guided by any shared understanding of the essence of interdisciplinarity can all too easily be shallow and idiosyncratic. I have thus in recent years devoted much of my scholarly attention to contributing to the literature on the nature and best-practice techniques of interdisciplinarity.

I have in a series of books (especially Szostak 2004) and articles investigated the strengths and weaknesses of different methods and theory types utilized in the academy, and mapped the subject matter of the human sciences. I have shown that there are only about a dozen distinct methods used by scholars, and that the types of theories used by scholars can usefully be classified in a simple five-dimensional typology. I have identified the key strengths and limitations of each method and

---

[7] This, I might note, is also a common attitude of other social scientists pondering economic questions. See for example Swedberg and Granovetter (2001, 2). They thus argue that the theories and methods of their disciplines can complement those of economics.

theory type, and shown that different theory types and methods have *compensating* strengths and limitations: they are thus *complementary*. I have also developed a 12-step process for interdisciplinary analysis, which draws heavily on these classifications (2002). This process drew on the previous work of other scholars, and has since been further synthesized with the efforts of Newell (2007) and others in the important work of Repko (2008). This book will be structured around the process outlined in Szostak (2002), revised to reflect the insights of these later works.

1.3 The Relationship Between Interdisciplinarity and Disciplines

This book is respectful but critical in its approach to insights from all disciplines. This approach reflects most of all the belief that there should be a symbiotic relationship between interdisciplinary research and specialized research. This is a book of synthesis and is only possible because of the concerted efforts of thousands of scholars across all social science disciplines. Yet none of these insights can be taken for granted: each must be carefully evaluated, and compared and contrasted with alternatives. It is hoped in turn that this work informs specialized researchers of how they can benefit from an enhanced understanding of the insights of other disciplines. In doing so, it follows the advice of Coleman, who carefully distinguishes constructive from malicious criticism in economics, and argues that 'integration is a mark of rational criticism' (2002, 232).

Interdisciplinary analysis is often mistakenly viewed as a challenge to the specialized research that characterizes disciplines. Nothing could be further from the truth. Interdisciplinary and specialized research are complements (see Szostak 2004). There are good reasons for the existence of specialized communities of researchers: by sharing common assumptions, definitions of key concepts, and theoretical and methodological understandings, they are able to communicate readily. Interdisciplinary research integrates the insights of this specialized research. In doing so it provides an invaluable but under-appreciated feedback. The obvious danger of specialized research is that – since the assumptions being used and theories and methods applied need not be carefully justified each time – the scholarly community comes to take its practices for granted, and assumes that these are the only or best way to proceed. Interdisciplinary research as in this book can usefully remind specialized researchers:

• That (and how) their research fits into a broader whole[8]

---

[8] 'Disciplines legitimate our necessarily partial knowledge. They define what it is permissible not to know' (Abbott, 130). While disciplinary scholarship benefits from specialization, disciplinary scholars should arguably be 'interdisciplinary' enough to appreciate how their shared research agenda fits into the broader world of scholarship.

- That there may be phenomena lying outside their usual gaze that could usefully be included in their analyses
- That research using alternative theories and methods can produce valuable insights that they can usefully be aware of in their own research (and perhaps even pursue). Note in this respect that such insights may be valuable even if they spur the community in question to compile argument and evidence *against* these
- In turn to look more closely at their own insights if these are inconsistent with the insights of other communities. Specialized researchers can usefully join interdisciplinarians in seeking to identify the source of such disagreements, and generating common ground across disciplines, *but only if these disagreements are both known and properly understood*
- More generally to be more aware of the unspoken assumptions that guide their research
- That the purpose of research is not (at least in the short term) to identify the one true theory of everything, but to assemble complementary theoretical insights that together provide the best understanding of complex events or processes.

Of course sketching a list of potentially useful contributions from interdisciplinary research does not prove that it should be an essential part of the scholarly landscape: one must weigh the costs and benefits. Yet the costs are small. Specialized research can continue, albeit hopefully in a more outward-looking (and ironically also introspective) manner. And the benefits may be huge: the history of science suggests that most major breakthroughs in understanding came from synthesizing ideas from multiple disciplines.[9] The ideal balance between specialized and integrative research is difficult to estimate, but it seems likely that the overall productivity of the scholarly enterprise could be enhanced by shifting some resources from the former toward the latter. With respect to economic growth in particular we have seen that economists themselves recognize that their theories alone provide a limited understanding of why some countries grow faster than others. As Hayek (1956, 463) famously said, 'The economist who is only an economist is likely to become a nuisance if not a positive danger.' Kenneth Boulding, the interdisciplinary economist, has argued that interdisciplinarity can be conceived in terms of economic trade theory: it involves the exchange of ideas between specialized communities of scholars, and can thus benefit all (in Gasper 2004). This analogy has not yet won the hearts of all economists.

---

[9] Benoit Mandelbrot, the developer of fractal geometry attributes his success to an interdisciplinary education and working environment. He worries about the increasing specialization of science (In *The Economist*, December 6, 2003, 35-6). More generally see Root-Bernstein (1989).

1.4 Starting Assumption

What if we start with an assumption that no community of scholars has been entirely wasting its time over the last decades or centuries? Like any assumption, we should be ready to abandon it if it seems inappropriate in certain circumstances. And it should in no way stop us from the important task of evaluating the insights of different academic communities. But the assumption nevertheless guides us to expect that our best understanding of economic growth will come through integrating insights from multiple sources. Given the complexity of the growth process, the assumption leads us to expect that understandings of different elements of the growth process can be found in many different parts of the academy. These insights deserve to be brought together. Since these understandings have come from different theories and methods, they cannot be combined through recourse to some grand theory or method. Fortunately, we shall see that by using the classifications mentioned above it is possible to organize these various insights into a coherent whole without recourse to grand theory or method.

1.5 A Critical Insight Regarding the Complexity of the Growth Process

Economic growth is a complex process. Both theoretically and (especially) empirically, growth-oriented economists have devoted much of their effort in recent decades to identifying which phenomena are most important for economic growth: does technological innovation matter more than investment or education?; does culture or social structure or political stability have an important effect? These efforts are valuable but have tended by their very nature to downplay the *interactions* among the causes of growth. The effect of investment on growth depends on how well that investment is deployed, and this in turn depends on the state of technology, availability of skilled labor, political decisions, and a host of other influences. Likewise the ability of a country to employ superior technology depends on its educational system, access to funds for investment, and many other variables. Economists are not unaware of these interactions, as we shall see, but nevertheless policy advice from economists has often been erroneous precisely because these were ignored (as when the World Bank for decades set investment targets for poor countries in order to achieve desired levels of growth without addressing the conditions for optimal deployment of investment). Policies to enhance growth can benefit from an appreciation of the general importance of education, investment, and innovation, but will be even more effective if grounded in a detailed appreciation of the various other circumstances conducive to these (and other) growth-inducing factors achieving their maximum effect. To this day many economists imagine that the same simple prescription applies to all countries in the world, whereas an appreciation of interactions guides one to expect that a country with a poor educational system may need to have different priorities from one with good schools but lousy banks (this point is made in a slightly different way by Sachs 2005). And thus one crying need in the study of growth is for a *more nuanced understanding of the interactions among the causes of growth.* This book can in the first instance serve this need by extending the analysis of growth across a much wider set of phenomena than is usually engaged in the literature. And it can then discuss how these phenomena interact with each other and with those more usually studied (as well as how those interact with each other). This step is trickier because each discipline tends to study different sets of phenomena, and the links across such sets are thus seriously understudied. Nevertheless the path to enhanced understanding is often quite clear.

1.6 Motivation (Is Growth Good?)

While this book is about the causes rather than consequences of economic growth, a few words on the desirability of growth itself seem called for. It is after all common these days to call for an end to economic growth. The case in favor of growth is most easily made for the poorest countries where billions of people live in extreme poverty: not getting enough food to eat, having levels of infant mortality of hundreds per thousand live births compared to the developed country average of four, suffering many diseases long eradicated from the developed world, often lacking access to decent schools or roads or health services, and living in sometimes quaint but cramped and unhealthy shacks or huts. 800 million people are undernourished in the world, over a billion lack reliable access to clean water, and two billion lack sewer service. Economic growth can dramatically increase the quality of life of such people. While income distributions may worsen in the early stages of economic development, they never worsen enough such that the poorest do not benefit (on average) from growth in their countries. And the more general result is that the incomes of the poorest quintile grow as fast as the country average. Economic growth translates directly into poverty reduction.

Social scientists (and especially economists) have had a couple of golden opportunities to encourage economic growth in poor countries: in the early postwar decades when developed countries wished (at least officially) to foster growth in Africa, Asia, and Latin America, and at least some governments in those regions were open to policy advice (though often this was twisted to serve their self-interest). A second came in the 1990s when politicians in both East and West wanted advice regarding the transition in Eastern Europe toward a more market-based economy. In both cases the dominant advice given was simplistic and in important ways misguided. With hindsight, most scholars can now imagine superior and more nuanced advice that might have been given. In both cases one can find examples of scholars at the time who urged appropriate cautions regarding the advice being given. In both cases the human suffering that has resulted from suboptimal advice is simply immense. The economic decline of many transition economies – including Russia itself – is greater in both depth and temporal extent than was the experience of the Depression of the 1930s in the West (but is the subject of relatively little scholarly attention in the West). The failure of Africa and Latin America (and parts of Asia until recently) to catch up to rich countries means that hundreds of millions (if not billions) of people are less healthy and secure than they might have been. A book such as this cannot guarantee that the next golden opportunity is not missed so egregiously, but can at the very least bring different scholarly assessments of the causes of growth to the fore, and thus set the stage for less simplistic advice in the future. Poor countries are too often the recipients of vague and contradictory policy advice; this book aspires to do better by integrating the insights of all relevant disciplines.

If one were born in 1820, one had an 85 percent chance of earning less than the equivalent of $1 US (2000) per day. Today, the probability is only 20 percent. Given the quintupling of human population over that time, the numbers of very poor is still unconscionably large. But it is a fraction of what it would have been without centuries of economic growth (though of course population would likely have grown much slower in at least some countries if food output had not increased).

In richer countries the case for growth is harder to make. Survey evidence suggests that people in developed countries are no happier on average than they were decades ago.[10] The fact that those with higher incomes in these countries are happier than those with lower incomes can thus be attributed to the vices of pride and jealousy rather than to any beneficial effect of income on wellbeing. Yet I have argued elsewhere (2005a) that some sorts of growth are beneficial: increases in basic goods access for the rich countries' own poor, goods that replace undesirable home labor, and goods or services that enhance social interaction.[11] I would

---

[10] Admittedly, there are problems with this evidence. Respondents are asked to say how happy they are on a three or five point scale. It is possible that people might become happier but not enough to adjust their score. And people may always judge their happiness in relative terms; if so average reported happiness within a reference group could never rise.

[11] People want human relationships more than anything, and much consumption of music and sports serves mainly to provide a common basis for human conversations. I take a much more benign view of growth than the negative emphasis of Douthwaite (1999); he stresses, for example, increased rates of certain stress-related maladies rather than increases in life expectancy. He makes a similar argument to me, though, in urging us to focus on beneficial types of growth (336). He urges societal decisions here, while I see a key role for individual choice. (Ellis 1998 makes a compelling ethical argument for valuing 'needs' more than 'wants' and discusses how these can be distinguished empirically). With respect to resource depletion, humanity has for many decades discovered new resources faster then it has used these up. In the very long run any positive rate of use of non-renewable resources is unsustainable, but we simply do not know how close we might be to exhausting resources. I concur with Douthwaite (1999, 320) that the discount rates appropriate to individuals are inappropriate for societies (or future generations fall out of economic calculations), and thus that we likely exhaust resources faster than is societally optimal.

hope that growth in rich countries is increasingly channeled in those directions, and away from items of conspicuous consumption. I would also emphasize the value of increased leisure time (and the opportunities for increased interaction with friends and family, increased appreciation and pursuit of art, volunteer work, and other valuable pursuits that this allows), and would indeed encourage us to think of growth on a per hour worked rather than per person basis (and note that we have seriously underestimated past rates of economic growth on this account).[12] There has been no general trend in income equality within countries over the last couple of centuries, but rather periods of movement in each direction; I would hope that future growth will be channeled toward the poor (and indeed would be applied to the reduction of all types of social inequality).[13] I would note in this respect that economic growth is almost inevitably associated with some new economic opportunities, and thus increased opportunities for social mobility. I also argued that it is both possible and desirable to have growth without certain undesirable cultural attributes associated with it, such as a belief that selfish behavior is always acceptable, or that individual responsibility is a substitute for rather than complement to social responsibility, or that somehow a life gains meaning just through earning money and buying stuff.[14] In the latter respect I share Easterlin's concern that economic growth has encouraged a cultural pre-ference toward wanting more for its own sake (2004, 53). With respect to the envi-ronment, I recognize that while economic growth has created challenges it has also been associated with increased environmental concern (and improvements in some but not all sorts of environmental quality), and thus believe that eco-nomic growth need not and should not be incompatible with improvements to the

---

[12] Fogel (2004) notes very positive trends in terms of leisure time (which he notes is a form of consumption), and also in terms of work done because it is rewarding relative to work done out of necessity. The latter ratio in the United States was 4:1 in 1880, 2:3 today, and Fogel foresees 1:3 in 2040. With respect to the former, there is survey evidence that many workers in developed countries would happily reduce income and working hours. Fogel predicts that humanity will finally face the challenge of earthly self-realization in the next century, as the time needed for work plummets. This idea is supported by the research of Ronald Ingelhart and other political scientists and sociologists who suggest that as economic security has increased people in the West increasingly value self-expression, freedom, equality, and quality of life (see Dalton 1998, 342).

[13] Offer (2006) urges us not to focus on growth for the majority in rich countries, but to improve income distribution and reinvigorate personal relationships. He also recommends enhanced investment in youth and improved care for the mentally disabled.

[14] McCloskey (2006, ch. 9) asserts that capitalism has not encouraged an increase in selfishness (nor has it caused us to lead fragmented lives). But earlier she notes that a (misguided) belief that markets depend on selfish behavior can be self-fulfilling. In Part 2, McCloskey argues that eco-nomic growth encourages the virtues of faith (in our abilities) and hope (for a better life). Her argument that modern economies are not driven by greed (chapter 43) is unconvincing. Near the end of the book she notes that she has been arguing that the ethical effect of capitalism has been 'not entirely bad' (480). I wish McCloskey had stressed the possibility of a much more ethical economy. In Szostak (2005) I stressed the need to celebrate economic activity that benefits others while disdaining income earned at the expense of others.

environment.[15] We should, nevertheless, stress types of economic growth with limited environmental side-effects, and be especially wary of irreversible environmental damage such as the destruction of aquifers or topsoil.

Emile Durkheim, one of the founders of modern sociology, worried a century ago that economic growth was no longer viewed as a means to an end, but had become the predominant goal of human societies. Humans thus downplayed the value of friends, family, and social responsibility in the selfish pursuit of money and things. While I value growth, I would join Durkheim in urging us all to appreciate that it is merely a means to other ends.[16]

As may be clear from the foregoing, I share with many scholars misgivings about the use of Gross Domestic Product (GDP) as *the* standard by which growth is measured. I am well aware that many utility-enhancing activities (think of friendship or volunteer work) are not captured by GDP while many utility-reducing activities are (GDP goes up with efforts to clean up after an environmental disaster). Recognition of these flaws in GDP measures should not be conflated with a critique of growth itself. As Amartya Sen has said many times, economic growth can and should mean an increase in the human ability to be freed from want in order to live the good life. We will return to the question of how best to measure growth in the next chapter.

The preceding analysis has been largely consequential in orientation: growth is judged to be good because it has good consequences. Once one moves beyond a focus on GDP to a stress on particular types of growth, then it is straightforward to justify growth as good with respect to the other four major types of ethical analysis. Greater provision of basic goods to the poor, for example, is virtuous, intuitively appealing, indicates respect for individual rights, and accords with the general tendency of all human societies to attempt to alleviate the suffering of the poor (see Szostak 2005a for a detailed discussion both of the five types of ethical analysis and their application to economic growth).

Small differences in annual rates of economic growth can have huge cumulative impacts over time. And thus a governmental policy that increases growth even slightly will have a greater impact on wellbeing in the very long run than policies that tackle more pressing but transitory social problems.[17] This does not mean that governments should focus exclusively on growth but that growth should always be one of their priorities.

---

[15] On the whole, pollution that is local and visible has decreased markedly in developed countries in recent decades (though smog has worsened in areas of rapid industrialization despite increased controls). The most serious environmental problems today involve pollution that crosses borders and/or has less obvious effects.

[16] Fevre (2003) also cites Durkheim favorably. But Fevre feels that sociologists should criticize efforts to increase labor productivity (231-3), and thus fails to appreciate how growth can improve our lives.

[17] Baumol (2000, 16) appreciates that economic growth is more important than the issues of static efficiency that dominate research in the economics discipline.

Scholars too should thus make the pursuit of economic growth one of their priorities. But this has hardly been the case. As we will see in Chapter 4, economic growth has been a topic of limited research in economics – and almost disappeared from the journals in the 1980s. Even today courses on economic growth are rare in economics departments. Economic historians might claim that the study of economic growth is their primary purpose (a point made in Szostak 2006), but in practice do not: we shall see that economic history has a great deal to teach us about economic growth, but economic historians have generally not attempted to combine their various insights. Other disciplines are even less likely to directly address the subject of economic growth, though they too can provide important insights into many pieces of the growth puzzle. It is hoped that this book will encourage a greater and more coherent scholarly investigation of the subject.

Of course, at some point in the future growth may become either impossible or undesirable. Larsson (2004) argues that there is a limited range of human wants, and thus of goods and services that can be provided; there is also a limit to how fast and cheap goods and services can be provided. At some point, then, growth must end. Even before such a point, humanity may decide that it collectively has enough, and focus its energies elsewhere. Nor is this a bad thing: as should already be clear I view economic growth as a means to other desirable ends rather than an end in itself. But economic growth is a very important means to other ends for the foreseeable future. And even if/when growth ends, society will need to understand it well to transition smoothly into a no-growth future.

This discussion of motivation has an important implication for our study of the causes of growth, and an implication that has often been neglected by economists. Economists often take for granted that individuals everywhere respond to economic incentives and are willing to expend additional effort in order to increase their income. Yet the preceding discussion suggests that individual agents need not equate 'more' with 'better.' Two thousand years ago Aristotle warned against the danger that 'making money' could be seen as an end in itself rather than a means to the end of purchasing goods and services that supported the good life (a point stressed by Gudeman 2001, 10).[18] Growth will be much more likely in a society in which agents draw this connection than in a society in which they do not. The former view accords with a sense that GDP is an accurate measure of economic wellbeing, the latter with a recognition that some goods and services are more important in our lives (and others less) than their price indicates. Economic growth as generally measured will tend to occur faster in societies with an outlook that Aristotle would view as unethical.[19] More generally, the possibility that some of the causes of growth may be 'bad' needs to be appreciated.

---

[18] This line of argument was first brought to my attention in an excellent Economics Honours Essay written under my supervision by Aaron Braaten.

[19] Gudeman argues that exchanges within traditional communities focus naturally on end-use [and the symbolic value of exchanges]; market exchange can do so as well but is much more likely to support an emphasis on making money for its own sake. The marketization of an economy may be necessary for (both good and bad kinds of) economic growth to occur, but it may

1.7 The Integrative Process

The key elements of the approach to interdisciplinary analysis that will be pursued in this book have already been hinted at in the foregoing. Given that terms such as 'interdisciplinarity' and 'integration' receive different definitions in the wider literature, it is useful here to both emphasize and clarify the key elements of the approach:

1. We will seek to identify and understand the causal links among the phenomena of importance to the process of growth (including interactions between causes), but also emergent properties arising from complex interactions within systems of phenomena. We will be broadly inclusive with respect to phenomena, examining those with a notable effect not just on growth itself but also on the proximate causes of growth. We nevertheless neglect phenomena that appear to have at best a minimal and highly indirect effect on growth, for the simple reason that this description applies to literally hundreds of phenomena. In understanding causal links, our focus will be on identifying the causal mechanisms at work and discussing their likely importance. Identifying parameter values is of secondary importance, in part as these generally vary across time and place, and in part because the existing literature is far from establishing clear results of this type (perhaps inevitably).[20]
2. Here and elsewhere we must be careful not to be captured by the extant literature: a link may be important but have received little attention.
3. We are primarily interested in disciplinary 'insights': what particular disciplines have to say about particular links or emergent properties.
4. These insights can only be understood fully within the context of the discipline's theories, methods, subject matter, and overall 'disciplinary perspective.' It cannot be stressed too much that disciplines 'choose' a mutually compatible set of theories, methods, and phenomena: methods that are good at investigating their theory, and phenomena that lend themselves to the application of that theory and method. The material in chapters 1 through 5 on theories, methods, and disciplinary perspectives thus sets the stage for the causal analyses of chapters 6 through 9.
5. By integrating the insights that flow from different disciplines we can obtain a more holistic understanding. The value of integrating across different theories and methods is illustrated by Rothstein (1998, 156-60). Rational choice theories suggest that political institutions solve collective action problems. But selfish

---

tend to encourage bad sorts of growth more than good. The link between culture and incentives is addressed in more detail in Chapter 7.

[20] With respect to the 'persistence of disagreement about parameters' in macroeconomics, Solow (2000) argues that 'the precise location of the right answer to some of the perennial vexed questions may shift from time to time, as attitudes, experiences, folk theories, institutions and policies out in the real world themselves change.'

rational actors would never bother developing such institutions for these agents will benefit even if others agents do so (unless they perceive their interests to be unique). So we need historical analyses of institutional change, and alternative cultural or psychological theories as well. Greif (2006) makes a very similar argument.

6. Integration does not mean just adding together disciplinary insights. It involves first a critical evaluation of those insights, and then a careful effort to achieve some 'common ground' among conflicting insights. With respect to evaluation, this book follows philosophers of science in thinking that no insight, theory, or method is beyond reproach: human judgment must be exercised with respect to every scholarly insight.[21] There are several strategies for achieving common ground, such as scrutinizing the terminology used in different disciplines, adjusting disciplinary assumptions, or restricting the range of applicability of insights (see Newell 2007).

7. While there is no guarantee that common ground can be achieved in every case for which a scholar looks for it, this book is guided by a belief that disciplinary insights are potentially complementary, as opposed to a belief that disciplines are different worlds capable of being understood only from the inside.[22]

> In the past, interaction among scholars using different perspectives has tended to emphasize their seeming irreconcilability, as if Kuhn's 'competing paradigms' provides the unique program for interaction among different approaches in the social sciences. In recent years an alternative program has emerged, emphasizing the complementarities among different approaches. This new program acknowledges differences not as competing paradigms but as potentially complementary approaches to complex phenomena. This suggests a more fruitful interaction among scholars of different approaches, where not only the tools and techniques of the other become relevant, but so too do the phenomena under study (Weingast, 1998, 183).

8. The outcome may be some tidy overarching theory (and indeed interdisciplinarity in its earliest manifestations tended to involve the pursuit of grand theory) such as Maxwell's electromagnetic theory which unified previously separate fields. Indeed, the greatest discoveries in natural science came from those with knowledge of diverse fields (Root-Bernstein 1989, 384), who were operating outside a narrow paradigm (357).[23] But in the case of a complex issue like

---

[21] Blanchard (2000) in describing the course of macroeconomic theory over the preceding century notes that it would be easy but wrong to think that macroeconomists started from scratch each time a new theory came along. Rather, the most outrageous claims of new theories and old tend to be discarded while the best elements of these 'get bastardized and then integrated' (1375). This process internal to economic theory is in this book extended to a wider range of insights, but the logic is the same. Understanding advances best when competing views are compared, contrasted, and integrated.

[22] The latter view is associated with certain versions of postmodernism. See Szostak (2007a) for a discussion of the relationship between interdisciplinarity and postmodernism.

[23] While most scientists are conformist and narrowly focused, Root-Bernstein (316) argues that the most successful have broad interests and are practical, persistent, independent, and energetic.

economic growth holistic insight is more likely to comprise a messy collage of overlapping theories.[24] [Note that if it is true that grand new ideas generally come from interdisciplinarity, one standard by which the scientific credentials of a field might be judged is whether it is open to ideas from outside – yet Hausman 1992 has argued that there are often penalties in Economics for importing ideas from other disciplines.]

9. Gasper (2005) notes that cumulative interdisciplinary research requires some sort of organizing device. Otherwise successive researchers cannot see past the complexity of the overall problem. If grand theory is rejected as the organizing device, an alternative is necessary. This book will organize its insights around the classification of phenomena introduced in chapter 2.

10. The focus of the book is on answering a question: what are the causes of economic growth? This approach is typical of interdisciplinary research: 'Much interdisciplinarity is in response to life-problem situations … Such work may sometimes then not be tidy or conventionally scientific rewarding, but it requires sophisticated skills of judgment, selection, and synthesis.' (Gasper 2004). This orientation distinguishes this work from much research in social science that has as its primary goal testing a particular theory. Rule (1997) warned of the costs of the tendency of social scientists to test theories rather than try to explain events or processes. He stressed the wastefulness of this practice: once a particular theory goes out of vogue, the research done in support of that theory is forgotten. I have applied the Rule distinction between theory-driven and explanation-driven approaches to the study of the Great Depression (Szostak, 2005b), and argued that our understanding of that event, and of economic growth and fluctuations more generally, has been limited by a theory-driven approach. To be sure, scholarly understanding only progresses through the development and testing of theories. But faced with apparent limitations in a theory's ability to explain some event or process scholars should not *only* seek to refine their favored theory. They should also be open to alternate theories

---

They are more willing to tackle bigger and more fundamental problems (407). They often had a deep understanding of the philosophy and history of science. He notes (353-4 and elsewhere) the importance of having multiple paradigms [that is, theories and methods] in order to avoid becoming intellectually boxed in. In social science, Dogan and Pahre (1990, 1) argue that 'innovation in the social sciences occurs more often and with more important results at the intersection of disciplines.'

[24] In the terminology used by Thomas Kuhn, interdisciplinarity need not be (though it can be) revolutionary science, but can proceed as normal science: identifying weaknesses in existing insights, searching for compensating insights from other disciplines, and striving to overcome disagreements between disciplinary insights. Notably, normal science within disciplines proceeds because of the shared understandings that revolutionary science transcends; normal science in interdisciplinary analysis will also be aided by shared understandings of how to proceed, but these must not constrain interdisciplinarians from revolutionary thought. Notably, Rule (1997) suggests that scientific revolutions would be rarer if we sought out insights from various theoretical perspectives and unabashedly put together such scraps of insight.

that may provide complementary explanations. And they should not ignore aspects of the event or process in question that their theory has nothing to say about (as economists determined to use macroeconomic theory to explain the Depression have ignored the very unusual technological experience of the Depression): empirical observations that cannot be explained theoretically should be the focus of discussion, but in reality tend to be ignored. Note that if scholarly research is framed in terms of explanation rather than theory, then the work still has value even if the theory(ies) applied later loses appeal. Interdisciplinary research in particular is more fruitful when organized around questions rather than theories.

11. The idea that we seek a complex amalgam of theories, rather than one perfect theory, is a simple idea. Nor would many theorists object: we have already seen that many economists do not expect formal growth theory to explain everything (some may cling to a hope that it will eventually do so but recognize that progress in this respect is likely to be slow).[25] Rodrik (2003) notes that research in economic growth theory at present is characterized by a variety of models tailored to different situations. Yet the implications of the idea are profound. Economists should not *only* refine their own theories but seek to identify complementary theories elsewhere. The same guideline applies to all disciplines. Again, this strategy is implied if scholars see their purpose as understanding processes or events rather than clarifying theory: if they see theory as a means to an end rather than the end in itself.

12. Academia advances by scholars putting forward hypotheses and (ideally) providing supporting argument and evidence, and then other scholars disagreeing with some or all of the hypothesis and providing countervailing argument or evidence. When consensus is observed in social science, it often reflects the fact that relatively little research has been done, and thus original hypotheses have not been subjected to detailed scrutiny. In other cases, consensus may reflect the ideological or methodological preferences of a particular scholarly community. But if different scholarly communities concur on the value of a particular hypothesis we can be confident (though not perfectly so) that the hypothesis has merit. (Szostak 2005a makes a similar argument regarding ethical statements). We will thus celebrate in what follows occasions where such consensus appears to exist.

Integration can proceed in a variety of ways, depending on the degree of disagreement between disciplinary insights:

- When no discipline has examined a particular causal link, or some aspect of a causal link, further research can be recommended

---

[25] John Hicks, the popularizer of Keynes, said that 'no one theory can answer all our questions.' Samuels (2004) goes on to note that we need different theories not only for different topics but also for different aspects of one topic.

- When disciplines study different but related causal links, or different aspects of the same causal link, disciplinary insights can be added (after being critiqued).
- If the relative strength of these sorts of complementary insights is unclear, further research which explicitly compares these, or tests one against another, may be recommended.
- When disciplinary insights disagree, common ground will be sought: perhaps by changing the assumptions of one or more theories, or limiting the range of applicability of one or more theories, or showing that some insights are misguided or exaggerated given the weaknesses in argument and evidence, or (best of all) developing a more holistic assessment that incorporates the best elements of each.

These various strategies are themselves complementary. In other words, when disciplinary insights are complementary, they can – if each is grounded in reasonable theory and empirics – be added. When disciplinary insights disagree, then each must be carefully critiqued in the search for common ground. Interdisciplinarity requires a combination of analytic (either/or) thinking when reviewing the insights of any discipline and synthetic (both/and) thinking when drawing links between disciplinary insights.

1.8 Plan of Book

The chapters of the book are largely organized around the twelve steps for interdisciplinary analysis outlined in Szostak (2002). These have been revised to reflect the insights of Newell (2007) and Repko (2008), as well as my experience in writing this book.[26] There is, I should stress, a huge overlap across these three approaches; I tend to emphasize evaluation more than Newell, while he in turn stresses achieving common ground. But each process engages in turn with framing an interdisciplinary question, gathering relevant insights but also information on the disciplinary perspectives that shape them, evaluating the insights, integrating these into a holistic view, reflecting on the results (ideally testing these), and communicating these in a widely accessible manner.

Each of these approaches also stresses that the process is iterative. The steps around which this book is organized are never pursued in monotonic order. Scholars will leap ahead as their curiosity takes them, and should then backtrack to fill in intervening steps. Discoveries in later steps call for re-thinking of earlier results: more disciplines or theories or methods or phenomena may need to be

---

[26] The order of Chapters 4 and 5 has been reversed in this book from the order of steps in Szostak (2002). The old Step 8 (comparing and contrasting insights) has been combined with the old step 6 (evaluating insights) in chapter 6 through 8; the old step 7 is covered in Chapter 9. A new Chapter 10 focused on emergent properties has been put in place; this had previously been part of step 6.

investigated. The task of actually integrating is never left to the end by even the most patient of interdisciplinarians (who would have thus to do an awful lot of work before gaining any sense of how interesting their results might be) but occurs as the interdisciplinarians thinks of the implications of every bit of argument and evidence they encounter.

1. The remainder of chapter one discusses and defines the nature of our research question, and addresses whether it is suitably interdisciplinary.
2. Chapter two discusses the range of phenomena that should be embraced in this study.
3. Chapter three identifies and addresses the strengths and weaknesses of relevant theories and methods.
4. Chapter four identifies the key disciplines to be surveyed and discusses the nature of relevant disciplinary perspectives.
5. Chapter five discusses how relevant literature should be and was identified.
6. Chapter six evaluates and integrates disciplinary insights along several key causal links. So many causal links are addressed in turn that this step in integrative analysis is continued through chapters seven and eight.
7. Chapter nine identifies and discusses important causal relationships that have been neglected by all disciplines.
8. Chapter ten explores emergent properties of the system of causal links identified in chapters 6 and 7.
9. Chapter eleven establishes common ground with respect to the role of government in economic growth.
10. Chapter twelve reflects on the results of the four preceding chapters
11. Chapter thirteen discusses how these results might be tested.
12. Chapter fourteen summarizes and communicates the results.

Notably, in chapter three we will see that standard research practice in economics deviates from the 'official' research practice as outlined in econometrics textbooks: whereas economists are supposed to deduce a model and test this against the data (and most articles are written as if this is what happened), in practice economists move back and forth between theory and data, adjusting their theory to fit the data against which it is tested. Nor is this a bad thing entirely for science advances best through a mixture of deduction and induction. However, there are advantages to constraining a scholar to a pre-designed research strategy: it limits the ever-present temptation to gloss over or ignore weaknesses in the analysis. The fact that this book is organized around a pre-existing research process forces the author to engage each step in the analysis seriously.

1.9 The Nature of the Guiding Question

The guiding question for this book has been selected: 'What are the causes of economic growth?' An alternative wording of this question is 'Why does growth occur faster in some times and places than others?' The interdisciplinarian must ask if their guiding question is suitably interdisciplinary. It was suggested earlier in this chapter that this question is indeed interdisciplinary in nature. A more detailed investigation is worthwhile here. Can economic growth be understood by relying only on the insights of one discipline? Or does our understanding increase markedly if the insights of many disciplines are integrated? While this last question is best answered at the end of the book, there are good reasons to think at the outset that the answer will be affirmative.

Economic growth must in the first instance involve an increase in the resources devoted to production – broadly labor, capital, and natural resources (including land itself) – and/or the productivity with which these resources are combined to generate output. These four variables – labor, capital, natural resources, and productivity – are all economic variables, and economists (and economic historians) dominate the study of the question of which of these is most important in driving particular episodes of economic growth. As we shall see, the community of economists is far from achieving consensus on this basic question involving what are commonly termed the *proximate* causes of growth. Even if such consensus were achieved, economists have long appreciated that this question then invites a more complicated set of questions, such as:

• Why is labor more skilled in some countries than others?
• Why is (saving and) investment higher in some countries than others?
• Why do some countries use resources more carefully than others?
• Why do some countries innovate more than others?
• Why is productivity higher in some countries than others?

These questions tend naturally to invite interdisciplinary speculation. How does a society's culture or social structure or politics influence its educational attainment, work effort, saving rate, or environmental policy? Scholars in other disciplines investigate political, social, and especially cultural issues to a much greater extent than do economists.

Special mention might be made here of *institutions* and *technology*. The formal rules of a society – its legal system, economic regulations, firm structure, and so on – likely have a profound influence on its economic performance, and yet such institutions arguably (see chapter 7) emerge from a historical process involving political, social, and cultural influences. Likewise, common sense suggests that technological innovation is an important source of (at least modern) economic growth, and again it seems likely that the rate of innovation in a society might well be influenced by a host of non-economic factors.

While study of the proximate causes of growth is dominated by economists (and economic historians), the study of these deeper causal influences is pursued across the human sciences (see chapter 4). Even the statistical analyses of economists point toward an interdisciplinary treatment. Political, institutional, and even social variables are often found to be important in cross-country regressions of postwar growth experience (Snowdon, 2002, 97-99) – and this despite the twin facts that such variables are often hard to measure and likely exert their effects over a very long time frame. Surveying this evidence and the widely divergent growth experiences of postwar economies more generally, Snowdon (2002, 100) concludes that:

> To understand why some countries have performed so much better than others with respect to growth it is therefore necessary to go beyond the proximate causes of growth and delve into the wider fundamental determinants. This implies that we cannot hope to find the magic bullet by economic analysis alone.

So far, the argument for the interdisciplinarity of our guiding question has proceeded primarily in terms of the wide range of phenomena implicated. This line of argument will be fleshed out further in chapter 2. In chapter 3 two equally powerful arguments will be added: that a range of both theories and methods should be employed in the study of economic growth. These theories and methods are each commonly employed in different disciplines. Chapter 4 will add a less obvious argument: that each discipline brings a set of preferences/biases to its study of (aspects of) economic growth, and that these work in different directions. The preferences of one discipline can thus serve as an antidote to the preferences of others.

While economists have in recent years embraced the necessity of looking beyond proximate causes, this was not always the case. The economics literature for decades was dominated by the analysis of proximate causes. In other words, the profession had effectively defined our guiding question in a disciplinary manner: if only proximate causes were to be investigated then only economic analysis might be necessary. Notably even this argument only holds in terms of phenomena: we shall see that diverse theories, methods, and disciplinary perspectives are valuable even in the investigation of the proximate causes of growth.

In particular, the proximate causes of growth are studied in quite different ways by economic historians than by other (generally macro-) economists. For the purposes of this book, economic history will be treated as a separate discipline. As will be discussed in more detail in chapter 4, there is some institutional warrant for this: while most North American economic historians are housed in Economics departments, an important minority is historians, and in other parts of the world separate programs of economic history are still common. More importantly, economic history is characterized not only by a greater attention to historical detail than mainstream economics but also by a greater openness to evolutionary theory and case study methods.

There is of course a certain logic in the economics profession first striving to nail down the way that proximate causes determine growth before proceeding to examine the sources of the proximate causes themselves. Yet as Paul Romer, the formal growth theorist, has often noted, formal growth theorization is a long-term process, and the pressing need for good policy advice means that economists should look far beyond such models in understanding the causes of growth. Economic historians and development economists have done precisely that, but their efforts have been viewed with suspicion by the mainstream – in part because they used non-formal methods and spoke of things like culture, and in part because the earliest policy advice proffered by development economists was often misguided in important respects. Yet the point remains: scholars of growth need to understand a diversity of causal relationships and how these interact.

Chapter 3 will address the concerns of Rule (1997) that social scientists too often emphasize the refinement of theory over explanation of real-world processes. In their treatment of economic growth until very recently, economists have seemed to be more interested in refining a set of theoretical models than in understanding the complexity of growth processes. As Rule would predict, they simply ignored empirical observations regarding institutions or culture because these were not variables appreciated in their models. Rule does not emphasize interdisciplinarity, but it must seem that an opening toward interdisciplinarity might have occurred decades earlier if the profession had an explanation-driven as opposed to a theory-driven orientation to the study of growth. This book, it cannot be stressed too much, sees theory as the handmaiden of explanation, and is thus willing to engage any theory that might add to our understanding of the causes of economic growth. More importantly, it is not presumed at the outset that one grand theory can encompass all that needs to be understood about economic growth but rather that a messy collage of theories will be needed.

The interdisciplinarian should always stand ready to revise their guiding question as they proceed through later steps. They should be conscious of why they do so and wary of doing so merely for convenience. If the question is changed because more material was found that was relevant to an alternative question, the interdisciplinarian should communicate this fact to the reader. The reader can then judge to what extent the revised question reflects 'disciplinary capture': the analysis only of questions found of interest by previous disciplinary researchers. Both author and reader can also reflect on what might be done to facilitate research along the lines of the original question. In our case, no such revisions were necessary. The question of 'What are the causes of growth?' guides the entire work.

1.10 Defining Economic Growth

Before continuing to later steps it is useful to clarify the guiding question as much as possible. First of all, it must be stressed that the concern here is with the causes of growth rather than the effects. The effects were addressed briefly in section 1.6. They are important and diverse enough to merit a book of their own. For our purposes, the discussion of effects might lead us to prefer some types of growth over others:

- Growth that has limited negative environmental impacts
- Growth that benefits primarily the poorest people in the world
- Growth that is devoted to increased leisure, and the consumption of goods and services that support an ethical and caring life rather than to articles of conspicuous consumption
- Growth that is disassociated from negative cultural attitudes that emphasize selfish over compassionate behavior.

These distinctions will only rarely be made in the pages that follow for a simple reason: once growth occurs, it can be shaped by individual actions, government policies, institutions and/or culture to take various forms. That is, we can to a considerable degree separate the causes of growth from the effects of growth. This book celebrates growth, but hopes that wise societies will choose better forms of growth. There are times, of course, when the causes are not so easily separated from the effects. A government might for example reap a short term increase in measured growth rates by increasing the length of the work week, but this would not yield the most desirable form of growth.

Economic growth can be defined as an increase in the output of goods and services in a society. As the previous paragraph suggests, care should be taken in how growth is measured. Newspapers often report growth in aggregate GDP. But this may grow simply because population has grown, and thus may not reflect any increase in individual incomes.[27] It generally makes more sense to track measures of per capita GDP. As population starts to fall in some developed countries, such a measure may incorrectly suggest economic decline even when per capita incomes are rising.[28] Decreases in the length of the work week will cause output and output per capita to fall, but may well have a positive effect on output per hour worked (if as is often imagined refreshed workers work harder). Cross-country comparisons are also affected: GDP per capita is 26 percent higher in the United States than Germany, but GDP per hour may only differ by 6 percent. Citizens of both countries would be well advised to pay most attention to the latter number in judging how well their economy is doing. Of course, hours worked is harder to

---

[27] Economic historians distinguish 'extensive growth' resulting from output rising with population from 'intensive growth' when per capita output rises. Our preferred measure here is a type of intensive growth. This is not to say that extensive growth is bad: the world would be a much poorer place if output had not (more than) kept pace with increases in population over the last millennia. And extensive growth often precedes intensive growth.

[28] Economic growth in the United States occurred at an annual rate of 2.9 percent 2002-7, but 2.1 percent in Japan. Since Japan's population was stagnant, but America's was rising by over one percent per year, a per capita comparison favors Japan: 2.1 percent over 1.9 percent. Indeed if recessions were defined as a decline in per capita GDP, the United States would have been judged to be in a recession in late 2007 when annualized growth in GDP fell to .6 percent.

measure in practice than is population, but the principle is worth applauding even if difficult to implement.

Problems abound in the measurement of economic output itself. The standard measure, Gross Domestic Product, captures much that is not good, and ignores much that is. Environmental damage and resource use are excluded: when oil is pumped out of the ground and sold no deduction is made for the fact that there is less oil left for future generations. Some have calculated that Indonesia's rate of growth falls from 5 percent to 2 percent when this simple adjustment is made. For most developed countries the effect is much smaller. But adjustments for the cost of dirty air and water might loom much larger. So-called 'defensive expenditures' – undesired in their own right but necessitated by economic activity – such as crime prevention or commuting costs, are included, and thus GDP can grow just because people spend more time in traffic jams. GDP does not account for leisure, working conditions, unemployment, or income distribution. Moreover it emphasizes only market transactions: famously the value of cleaning my house goes into GDP only if I hire someone else to do it, not if I do it myself. Increases in GDP can thus reflect increases in economic specialization rather than any actual increase in output. The GDP of poor countries is seriously underestimated as a result, for poor people produce many goods and services for themselves that are bought in the market in richer countries.

One can devote many pages to the problems in GDP calculations. The first point to stress here is that there are dangers in focusing upon an imperfect measure: such measures guide us to celebrate (and thus governments to support) types of 'growth' that are in fact not beneficial to people. We can to some extent sidestep this issue in this book for the reason noted above: that the causes of growth can to a large degree be separated from the precise shape that growth takes. Nevertheless on occasion it will be necessary to note in what follows that a particular strategy will cause a sort of growth not readily captured by GDP statistics.

While difficulties in calculating GDP are important, there are more fundamental criticisms of the measure. The basic assumption underlying GDP measures is that market prices are the appropriate basis for weighting the value of different goods and services. But does society really place the same value on a $50,000 SUV as it does on $50,000 worth of school lunches for undernourished inner city children? Economic theory itself suggests otherwise: that individuals derive more utility from the first dollars they spend (which are devoted to necessities) than the last. But economists argue that we have no way of comparing utility across individuals: the rich just might enjoy spending more than the poor. We can thus not be sure that the purchaser of an SUV does not get as much benefit as do hundreds of hungry children from a good meal. Most people, though, if given a choice would likely prefer growth that benefited the poor over growth that benefited the rich, or growth devoted to basic needs over growth devoted to luxury goods.

Aware of the limitations of GDP measures, the United Nations has long popularized the idea of a Human Development Index. This index adds to standard GDP measures statistics on life expectancy and literacy. It is felt that GDP alone misses items that have a major impact on a society's health and its population's self-realization. While the HDI provides a useful antidote to the stress elsewhere on GDP, and has likely encouraged some governments to devote more attention to their health and education systems, it relies on an arbitrary equal weighting of the three types of measure. Other measures exist that add even more variables (levels of crime or income distribution, and so on) into the calculation.

All such measures suffer from the necessity of attaching arbitrary weightings to different variables. In the end, though, societies have to choose how much they value the environment or equality or safety, and this is best done by comparing GDP growth rates with changes in these other measures: society can then ask whether they need to and should sacrifice some growth in the pursuit of these other goals. In other words, there is no one best measure of economic growth, but rather public debate should focus on the ideal tradeoff among different measures of economic wellbeing. Environmental side effects and resource depletion can at least potentially be 'priced' and thus adjustments for these readily incorporated into GDP, but legitimate concerns regarding income distribution or health cannot. Where necessary, we will note in what follows if particular growth-enhancing strategies have (necessarily) negative side effects of these various types.

1.11 Defining 'Causes'

Economists are much more comfortable speaking about 'causes' than are scholars in other disciplines, especially in the humanities. The word tends to have a minimalist meaning in economics: if it is said that A causes B, this means only that A exerts some influence on B. It is not at all presumed that only A exerts such an effect. This sort of definition fits well with the statistical analysis favored by economists: regressions generally find that several variables combine to explain movements in another. Scholars in other disciplines react negatively to the word, feeling that it implies that only A exerts an effect on B, and thus reflects an overly simplistic view of the world. The word 'causes' is maintained in this manuscript, but should be interpreted as being equivalent to 'influences.'

Even at that some scholars would object to the very idea of speaking of one thing influencing another. They instead prefer a holistic approach where the world is seen as such a complex amalgam of interacting variables that these cannot be distinguished from each other. That is, we cannot really separate the economic from the political realm because they are inter-woven. I will not engage such concerns in detail here (see Szostak 2004). I will simply note that the vast bulk of scholarship does in fact proceed in terms of discussing how one or more phenomena influence one or more others (indeed even among many scholars who proclaim that this is impossible). This book does accept that everything is inter-related, but takes the common scholarly view that the best way to understand these inter-relationships is as causal relationships among distinct phenomena.

2 The Key Phenomena that Potentially Cause Growth

What are the causes of economic growth? One interdisciplinary approach to answering this question would involve investigating in turn which causes different disciplines think to be important. Such an approach runs the risk of missing causes that have escaped the attention of any discipline. This is a particular danger with respect to the study of economic growth: as noted in the introductory chapter, this topic has only been *explicitly* addressed by one or two disciplines. A much better strategy, then, involves surveying the *entire list of human science phenomena*, and asking in each case whether there seems to be a likely causal relationship to economic growth. This strategy not only insures against being 'captured' by existing disciplinary research programs but provides guidance on what causal links to investigate across disciplines.

Is such a strategy viable? Most of this chapter will argue that it is, and show how the strategy can be pursued in this case. It is first desirable, however, to speak more generally to the advantages of the causal link approach pursued in this book.

2.1 The Causal Link Approach

'The problem with history is the almost infinite multitude of events, all of which have to be classified, described, and analyzed. A simplifying theoretical framework is essential and inevitable' (Freeman and Louca 2001, 123). We have argued in the introductory chapter against seeking integration through some simplifying theory. And thus we must have recourse to a different strategy. The key is the classification of the phenomena that human scientists examine. With this in place it is then possible to evaluate theories along relevant causal links among phenomena.[1] That is, it then becomes feasible to *organize* our insights around a large but finite set of causal links among a large but finite set of phenomena. The argument made by Katznelson and Miller (2002, 2) regarding political science, 'that the eclecticism of the discipline can most effectively produce political knowledge by becoming self-conscious about the limited but compelling set of questions it has addressed' can be applied to human science more widely. Only by identifying the various causal links explored by human science can we intelligently first juxtapose and then integrate the varied insights of human scientists.

---

[1] The economic historian Landes (2004) concludes his book by arguing that modern economic growth is a complex process. He thus pleads for scholars to strive to understand diverse causal links rather than oversimplify through the use of some overarching and deterministic structure.

R. Szostak, *The Causes of Economic Growth*,
DOI: 10.1007/978-3-540-92282-7_2, © Springer-Verlag Berlin Heidelberg 2009

This book will not only seek to identify the full range of causal links appropriate to the study of economic growth but will seek to study each of them in turn. The second step need not follow from the first. Indeed, many research strategies – including the statistical analyses of the economist, the narrative of the historian, and the participant observation of the anthropologist or sociologist – tend naturally to engage a variety of causal links together. It can often be extremely difficult to disentangle various causal links in the reports of such studies. One unfortunate side effect is that it is then hard to perform comparative research, for the precise same set of causal factors is not often duplicated in human history (or even in scholarly research).

The approach pursued here, of examining different causal links in turn (but not losing sight of their interactions, nor of emergent properties of systems), is different enough from the standard practice of examining several links at a time that it deserves some comment. We shall see in chapter 4 that there are difficulties in applying the methodology of models to open systems – ones which are clearly linked causally to phenomena outside the model. While it will be argued that these problems do not destroy the model-building exercise, it is nevertheless true that such models rely on an unrealistic assumption that the relationships observed in such a system can remain fixed through time. Lawson (1997) argues that the economy is clearly an open system, for the economic variables that economists analyze are obviously causally related to a host of non-economic phenomena. As a result, Lawson stresses the search for underlying causal mechanisms rather than empirical regularities. Lawson argues that the results of econometric analysis are rarely robust because of the mass of excluded variables (70). That is, if the relationship between A and B is conditioned by realizations of C and D, but D is not in our equations, then we will find different correlations between A and B in different studies, and will not know how to explain these differences. Since there are never empirical regularities between any two variables because of such extraneous influences, we must understand qualitatively the relationship in question (30).[2] This means that we must make careful causal arguments rather than just report statistical indications of causation. Lawson also stresses the importance of interdisciplinary linkages. He (270-1) argues that human science proceeds by looking at pieces of the larger puzzle. But he provides no clear or workable strategy for how such a mass of insights can be coherently organized.

We are far from the first to pursue a causal link approach. Notably, complexity theory allows different causal forces to operate along different links, and does not assume any particular organizing principle (such as equilibrium) at the outset. Max Weber had urged a social economics that would study economic phenomena, the phenomena influenced by these, and the phenomena that influenced economic

---

[2] Lawson (217) is thus harsh in his judgment of Friedman's famous argument that we can trust models that make reliable predictions even if grounded in unrealistic assumptions. We should be skeptical of such models unless we can understand how/why the assumptions are not essential to the result.

phenomena. In all cases it would not be assumed that economic phenomena would totally determine the state of others, nor would they entirely be determined by any one other phenomenon. There would always be other causal factors at work (in Swedberg 2003, 4).

Root-Bernstein (1989, 352-3) critiques the tendency to analyze science as a set of problem solutions. It is better seen as a set of well formulated questions whose investigation raises further questions. One key to tackling the big questions in science is to carefully formulate a set of sub-questions. The causal link approach does precisely this, asking how each of a broad set of phenomena affects both each other and growth itself. The causal link approach has the further advantage of making it clear what link is being addressed at any point in time. Root-Bernstein celebrates the importance of clarity in scholarly discourse.

The potential drawback of the causal link approach is that it may distract attention from the emergent properties of systems of causal links. We can join Lawson in appreciating the possibility of emergent properties in systems of causal relations. Care must be taken then to reflect on what form such emergent properties might take. This task will be engaged below and further pursued in chapter 10.

2.2 Causal Links Within and Beyond Disciplines

Emile Durkheim, one of the founders of modern sociology, noted that '... the jurist, the psychologist, the anthropologist, the economist, the statistician, the linguist, the historian – all these go about their investigations as if the various orders of facts they are studying formed so many independent worlds' (1984, 304). In the natural sciences, there is a certain logic to disciplinary divisions: chemists examine phenomena that are complex combinations of those studied by physicists, and biologists study yet more complex phenomena. The social sciences are not distinguished by level of complexity but rather by topic. The sharp disciplinary boundaries that exist today only make sense if it is imagined that the links among economic phenomena (for example) are much much stronger than the links from these to social or political or cultural phenomena. One starting assumption of this book is that the latter sort of link is potentially of huge importance for the understanding of economic growth. It is reasonable to anticipate, then, that important links will have been under-studied simply because they cross disciplinary boundaries.

While the interdisciplinarian's most useful contribution may involve the study of links across disciplinary boundaries, it would be ludicrous to study these alone. This book strives for a holistic understanding, and can hardly achieve this by ignoring links that fall within the purview of one discipline. Moreover, just because the phenomena implicated in a link fall within one discipline hardly guarantees that the theories and methods favored by that discipline are uniquely suited to its investigation (see chapter 3).

2.3 Classifying Human Science Phenomena

The task of classifying all of the phenomena of interest to human scientists might seem particularly daunting. Surely there are thousands upon thousands of such phenomena? While this is true, these phenomena can be organized hierarchically within a small number of umbrella categories. Such an endeavour can draw upon a general scientific commitment to the belief that things are made up of constituent parts.[3] The starting point for the classification in Table 2.1 is an attempt to divide the subject matter of human science into logical categories. These categories must cope with both individual and societal characteristics. At the level of individuals two categories of phenomena can be identified:

- The first is 'genetic predisposition.' As a species, humans share a gene pool that gives all a set of basic abilities, motivations, and emotions.
- While this common gene pool guarantees a certain set of characteristics that defines the species, differences in the precise genes that individuals possess, in concert with differences in environment, serve to guarantee that individuals differ from each other both physically and psychologically. This yields a second category of 'individual differences.'

All humans are necessarily part of a larger community, especially for the first few years of life. That is, one of the shared characteristics noted above is that humans are born needing the help of others. Several distinct categories of collective behaviours can be identified:

- Humans interact with the non-human environment in order to create (and distribute) food, shelter, and other items of practical utility: 'the economy.'
- Humans interact with the non-human environment to create items desired primarily for their aesthetic appeal rather than their utility: 'art.' Note that works of art, through their aesthetic appeal, may serve further purposes, such as encouraging religious belief. Such effects would be captured in causal links. Art is often viewed as a subset of 'culture'; it is treated separately here because works of art, while they contain cultural elements, are defined in terms of an aesthetic effect that transcends cultural boundaries.
- The various sub-groups of society must interact in some way: 'social structure.' There are always at least two types of sub-group, for the family is ubiquitous, albeit in different forms, and genders have never yet been treated in precisely the same way.
- Power is distributed and exercised: 'politics.'
- It is obvious that hierarchical economic, social, and political structures evolve beliefs in the correctness of those structures, or at least attempts are made by those at the top to do so. Such beliefs thus logically belong to those categories. Yet societies have a host of religious beliefs, customs, habits, and so on whose

---

[3] Krieger (1997, 31-2).

connection to these other realms is (at least potentially) tenuous: these can be termed 'culture.' Attitudes toward all categories except economy, politics, and social structure are thus part of culture. Following common usage, languages are treated here as a subset of culture. The precise definition of culture becomes clearer as the category is unpacked.

- Humans also develop knowledge of how they can best manipulate the non-human environment to suit various ends: 'science and technology.'
- The list may seem complete, but humanity must also perpetuate itself as a species, and thus 'population' must be considered. Ability to reproduce depends in turn on ability to survive. The related matter of 'health' must also, then, be considered. This deserves more attention than it receives from human scientists.
- The 'non-human environment' has been mentioned more than once above. Since it both shapes and is shaped by humanity, it deserves its own role in the classification as another category. This category (and that of genetic predisposition) would provide a link between this classification and a classification of natural science phenomena.

This list of ten logically distinct categories is also arguably exhaustive, for the ten categories subsume all human activities and characteristics. As Table 2.1 illustrates, it is straightforward to place all subsidiary phenomena within these categories. In several cases, care must be taken to establish the boundaries between categories. As noted above, 'art' can be distinguished from 'culture' by defining art as that which has an aesthetic appeal not limited to members of particular groups. These precise boundaries become clearer as the categories are further disaggregated.

Table 2.1 reflects an extensive exercise in disaggregation undertaken in Szostak (2003a). Both deduction and induction were used to develop lists of second and then third-order phenomena (Note that these titles refer only to the level of aggregation and imply no value judgment): induction in the sense of finding a place in the classification for all phenomena discussed in a wide variety of works consulted, and deduction in the sense of thinking about how phenomena could logically be disaggregated into their constituent parts. The result should be nearly exhaustive, though some phenomena may have been missed.[4] It seems a reasonable conjecture that somebody sometime will have noticed every phenomenon that affects human lives: the scholarly community can thus aspire to an exhaustive list,

---

[4] One entry has, indeed, been added to the table. Though it was noted above that culture will include attitudes toward most other categories, an entry for 'attitudes toward healing' was missing from previous versions of Table 2.1. This oversight (which was pointed out to me) was especially egregious since Wissler, in his efforts decades ago to classify phenomena, had grouped healing with religion.

at least at higher levels of aggregation.[5] Importantly, the table is inherently flexible so that new phenomena can be added if/when they are discovered. As for the organization of the table, this too is flexible: if it were found empirically, for example, that 'language' was more strongly related to phenomena in a category other than 'culture' the table could be adjusted to reflect that fact.

More often than not, there was considerable scholarly consensus on how a particular phenomenon should be disaggregated. Scholars of personality agree that there are a handful of key personality dimensions, and that these can be unpacked into traits, though they disagree about precise boundaries at both levels. Scholars of social divisions agree on most but not quite all of these. While scholars of culture celebrate the diversity of definitions of that word, few would doubt that values or stories or religion belong there. For the purposes of this book, the Table provides the best extant list of human science phenomena: while it is likely imperfect in certain respects it is a reasonably accurate account of the phenomena humans should care about.

Readers should feel no need to master this Table. Like a phone book, one need not memorize where particular entries fall but only appreciate the organizing principles at work. For the purposes of this book, it is important only to appreciate that it is possible to identify an (almost) exhaustive set of the major phenomena that characterize human societies. Table 2.1 can thus be used as a basis for further steps in our analysis.

---

[5] Sub-atomic particles are an obvious example of important phenomena only observable with advanced scientific methods. It is not clear that similarly unobservable phenomena exist in the realm of human science.

Table 2.1: The Phenomena

CATEGORIES   SECOND LEVEL PHENOMENA   THIRD LEVEL PHENOMENA

CATEGORIES	SECOND LEVEL PHENOMENA	THIRD LEVEL PHENOMENA
Genetic Predisposition	Abilities	Consciousness, subconsciousness, vocalization, perception (five senses), decision-making, toolmaking, learning, other physical attributes (locomotion, eating, etc.)
"	Motivations	Food, clothing, shelter, safety, sex, betterment, aggression, altruism, fairness, identification with group
"	Emotions	Love, anger, fear, jealousy, guilt empathy, anxiety, fatigue, humor, joy, grief, disgust, aesthetic sense, emotional display
"	Time Preference	–
Individual Differences	(Abilities): Physical Abilities	Speed, strength, endurance
"	Physical Appearance	Height, weight, symmetry
"	Energy Level	Physical, mental
"	Intelligences	Musical, spatial, mathematical, verbal, kinesthetic, interpersonal
"	(Personality): Sociability (Extro/introversion)	Talkative, assertive, adventurous, enthusiastic vs. reserved, withdrawn
"	Emotionality (Stable/moody)	Contentment, composure, vs. anxiety, self-pity
"	Conscientiousness	Thoroughness, precision, foresight, organization, perseverance vs. carelessness, disorderly, frivolous
"	Affection (Selfish/agreeable)	Sympathetic, appreciative, kind, generous, vs. cruel, quarrelsome, faultfinding
"	Intellectual Orientation (Holistic/analytical)	Openness, imagination, curiosity, sensitivity vs. closemindedness
"	Other dimensions?	Dominant/submissive, in/dependant, strong/weak, future/present oriented humor, aggression, happiness
"	Disorders?	Schizophrenia, psychoticism, ...?
"	Sexual Orientation	–
"	Schemas	View of self, others, causal relationships
"	Interpersonal Relationships	Parent/child, sibling, employee/r, romance, friendship, casual

CATEGORIES   SECOND LEVEL PHENOMENA   THIRD LEVEL PHENOMENA

CATEGORIES	SECOND LEVEL PHENOMENA	THIRD LEVEL PHENOMENA
Economy	Total Output	Price level, unemployment, individual goods and services
,,	Income Distribution	–
,,	Economic Ideology	–
	Economic Institutions	Ownership, production, exchange, trade, finance, labor relations, organizations
Art	Non-reproducible	Painting, sculpture, architecture, prose, poetry
,,	Reproducible	Theater, film, photography, music, dance
Social Structure	Gender	–
,,	Family Types, Kinship	Nuclear, extended, single parent
,,	Classes (various typologies)	Occupations (various)
,,	Ethnic/racial Divisions	–
,,	Social Ideology	–
Politics	Political Institutions	Decision-making systems, rules, Organizations
,,	Political Ideology	–
,,	Nationalism	–
,,	Public Opinion	Issues (various)
,,	Crime	Versus Persons/Property
Technology and Science	Fields (various)	Innovations (various)
,,	Recognizing the Problem	–
,,	Setting the Stage	–
,,	Act of Insight	–
,,	Critical Revision	–
,,	Diffusion/transmission	–
,,	Communication, adoption	–
Health	Nutrition	Diverse nutritional needs
,,	Disease	Viral, bacterial, environmental
Population	Fertility	Fecundity, deviation from maximum
,,	Mortality	Causes of death (various)
,,	Migration	Distance, international?, temporary?
,,	Age Distribution	–

CATEGORIES   SECOND LEVEL PHENOMENA   THIRD LEVEL PHENOMENA

CATEGORIES	SECOND LEVEL PHENOMENA	THIRD LEVEL PHENOMENA
Culture	Languages	By descent?
"	Religions	Providence, revelation, salvation, miracles, doctrine
"	Stories	Myths, fairy tales, legends, family sagas, fables, jokes
"	Expressions of culture	Rituals, dance, song, cuisine, attire, ornamentation of buildings, games
"	Values (Goals:)	Ambition, optimism, attitudes toward wealth, power, prestige, honor, recognition, love, friendship, sex, incest, marriage, time preference, physical and psychological wellbeing
"	(Means:)	Honesty, ethics, righteousness, fate, work valued intrinsically, violence, vengeance, curiosity, innovation, nature, healing
"	(Community:)	Identity, family versus community, openness to outsiders, egalitarianism, attitude to young and old, responsibility, authoritarianism, respect for individuals
"	(Everyday Norms:)	Courtesy, manners, tidiness, proxemics, cleanliness, punctuality, conversational rules, locomotion rules, tipping
Non-Human Environment	Soil	Soil Types (various)
"	Topography	Land forms (various)
"	Climate	Climate Patterns (various)
"	Flora	Species (various)
"	Fauna	Species (various)
"	Resource Availability	Various Resources
"	Water Availability	–
"	Natural Disasters	Flood, tornado, hurricane, earthquake, volcano
"	Day and Night	–
"	Transport Infrastructure	Mode (various)
"	Built Environments	Offices, houses, fences, etc.
"	Population Density	–

Source: Szostak 2004, 27-9.

2.4 The Sources of Economic Growth

Which phenomena are implicated in the study of the causes of economic growth? It is important at the outset not to be seduced by the existing literature into only paying heed to the causal connections studied in the past. Moreover, by surveying the phenomena that should be investigated we shed important light on the theories and disciplines (chapters 3 and 4) that should be included in our study.

It should be emphasized that the purpose in this chapter is to sketch plausible causal relationships. Later steps in the process will examine whether these are empirically important, and whether some are more important than others (a result that may vary according to circumstances), and also whether less obvious links emerge from scholarly analysis.[6]

2.4.1 The Nature of Economic Growth

Integration can only proceed along carefully defined causal links. Otherwise it is all too easy for scholars to talk past each other: to not realize when they are talking about the same causal relationship (or perhaps worse to not appreciate when they are talking about different links). We need thus to think at the most basic level about what economic growth is, and how this might be related to other phenomena. This simple task has rarely if ever been performed. And thus we can draw our first lesson for interdisciplinary research more generally: outline the event/process that you wish to investigate in the most careful detail possible at the outset, paying special attention to the various phenomena that might be implicated, and the variety of ways in which they might be involved.

Economic growth is defined as an increase in economic output. This can only occur in one of four ways:

1. An agent (individual, relationship or group; private or public) decides to produce more of an existing good or service at the existing market (or institutionally set) price. [And this increase in output is not matched by decreased output of another agent, which might happen either because of substitution in demand or because the new agent has taken resources they used in production]
2. An agent decides to produce more of an existing good or service at a lower price.
3. An agent decides to produce a new good or service.

---

[6] Of course, the fact that some links may only become evident after scholarly examination places limits on the strategy pursued here. We might follow previous scholars in dismissing a particular phenomenon simply because its link to economic growth was not obvious.

4. The above three types of growth are focused on the domestic market. They can each be repeated with respect to export markets.[7]

Note that in all cases growth is inherently a 'disequilibrium' process.

Each of these deserves further comment:

1. This sort of growth is what might first occur to an individual thinking about economic growth. For growth is often thought of as 'more of the same.' Yet there are obvious constraints on this sort of growth. The first occurs on the demand side. Economists assume for good reason that demand curves (usually) slope downwards: individuals are willing to pay more for the first units of a good or service that they consume than for later units. And thus agents entering a market at the existing price will find it difficult to sell additional output. But there is a complication: by increasing supply, they must also spend money – on raw materials, workers, rent, and so on. The eighteenth century economist Jean-Baptiste Say famously argued that supply creates its own demand: that any increase in output is also an increase in income, and this income can be used to buy the increased output. In the parlance of economists, the demand curve shifts to the right. But economists are doubtful that this simple relationship holds in practice. If it did, economic growth could be achieved simply by producing more stuff: central planners could simply order as much growth as they wanted (limited only by how fast they could build productive facilities), secure in the knowledge that those who earned money in production would spend it on the stuff produced. But growth is more difficult than that, and for obvious reasons. Think of food: there is only so much that an individual can consume, and thus increased output, even if accompanied by increased income, will at some point be unconsumed. The same applies to other goods and services. Note that this limit applies whether the original stimulus is on the supply or demand side: an increase in demand (say, because of increased government expenditure) might (or not) stimulate a matching increase in supply, but growth cannot proceed far without some decrease in price (and this limit is in addition to the limits in terms of ability to either borrow or inflate on government spending itself). Nor is the only problem on the demand side: economists imagine that supply curves usually slope up (suppliers raise their price as output expands) for the simple reason that the best resources will usually be used first, and thus additional agents entering a market will usually not be able to produce at the existing price.

2. Some simple supply and demand analysis thus leads us to suspect that growth will generally require some sort of 'innovation,' some discovery of a better way of doing things. This will not completely solve either the demand or supply side problems, but can shift the supply curve outward and thus allow us to move

---

[7] Sachs (2005, 52-3) speaks of four paths to growth, increased saving, trade, technology, resource discovery. Such a list inevitably privileges certain links over others.

down the demand curve. We still get 'more of the same stuff' as above, but at lower prices. Note that the act of innovation itself automatically raises the real incomes of all who buy the good or service at the reduced price. [We are talking here of real prices, of course, and will deal with the effects of inflation later] There is a potential downside, though: by reducing the cost of producing a good we may (depending on how much the quantity demanded increases as the price falls) release resources from its production. This is no problem in the first instance as growth will be recorded with respect to the good in question as long as its output increases, even if the resources used in production fall (assuming, that is, that measures of output are properly adjusted for the change in real price of the good). But these displaced resources mean that other agents have less income, and thus demand falls. Simple models may conclude that this latter effect must be outweighed by the former, but if unemployment is recognized as a possibility this need not be the case.[8]

While the word 'innovation' is most closely associated with technology, advances in technology are far from the only sorts of price-reducing innovations. Institutional changes are also important – indeed at least at some points in history were more important than technological innovation. [While our focus will be on enduring institutions here, transitory changes in governmental policies may also be important.] Note that these innovations – whether technological or institutional – may affect not just the cost of production: prices of the final good may also be reduced by decreases in the cost of obtaining raw materials, of moving materials around, or of distributing the good or service to consumers. And this raises a further sort of innovation: in networks. Since production of almost any good or service requires interactions among many agents, improvements in either the scope or strength of networks can also serve to reduce costs. Networks may be enhanced because of changes in institutions or changes in culture or due to investments in the infrastructure of transport and communication. Infrastructure investment may also have a direct influence on the cost of moving goods.

Costs may decrease also because of increased work effort. Increased work effort may in turn reflect technological innovation (as Charlie Chaplin perceptively parodied, assembly lines can determine the pace of work) or institutional innovation (supervision within the factory *may* have induced workers to work harder than in their homes). But it might instead reflect changes in cultural attitudes or in health. One might choose to describe changes in work effort, then, as a result of technological, institutional, or cultural innovation.

3. While the innovations above move us down the demand curves for particular goods and services, there is a limit to how far this process can proceed: no

---

[8] Economists often assume full employment in their models. This may be a misleading assumption in the short run. It is not clear, though, that there has been any trend upward or downward in unemployment rates over the two centuries of modern economic growth, and thus assuming away employment effects may be less harmful in the longer run.

matter how low the price, people will only want so much food or clothing, and only so many televisions or automobiles. Growth over the very long run cannot then mean just more of the same stuff but must also involve the creation of new stuff as well. But new stuff is not an unmixed blessing: we must worry about whether the new good/service is primarily a complement to or substitute for existing goods and services. If the former, production of the new good induces displacement of resources involved in the production of some existing good. As in (2) the negative effect on demand may arguably outweigh the beneficial effects on growth of the new product. [Nor is this just a measurement problem: even if the new product is priced appropriately to reflect its value in terms of that it replaces, total output may fall.] Technological innovation looms large here, but innovations in institutions and networks may also allow the provision of new goods and especially services.
4. Exporting may seem to simply duplicate the above types of growth on a wider canvass. But this in itself has important advantages. There will inevitably be a much larger set of market opportunities. And there will be much less likelihood of the appearance of a stable equilibrium with little obvious opportunity for a new venture. The potential downside is that the money earned from exports will be used to buy imports of equivalent value. Happily this should not happen. The theory of comparative advantage[9] tells us that countries should export goods/services that they are relatively good at producing, and import those they are relatively poor at producing. That is, the resources used for $X of exports should be less than the resources replaced by $X of imports. So the direct impact of trade on growth should be positive – unless governmental policies distort which goods are imported or exported. There is still a possible negative feedback through unemployment (as above).

While an uncomfortably large number of caveats have been raised in the above discussion, still more are necessary:

• The relationship between demand-side and supply-side forces is of critical importance. Growth is only sustainable if the willingness of agents (of all types) to buy goods and services expands in step with the willingness and ability of (generally other) agents to produce these. Which comes first? Causal links in both directions are possible – agents might respond to increases in demand by expanding production, and will likely devote increased income from increased production to increased consumption. One might then imagine cumulative causation: in a static world neither demand nor supply increases much, but once growth begins they reinforce each other. Obviously, though, there are limits to this reinforcement, for growth processes once underway all

---

[9] We will see in chapter 6 that this is less important than commonly assumed, but the argument made here still holds.

too often stall. One question that one might ask is whether such retrenchments generally reflect demand or supply side influences.

- The link between demand and supply likely depends on expectations. Investment decisions depend not just on demand today but on expectations of demand tomorrow. Optimistic cultural attitudes or governments that inspire confidence may thus have an important but intangible effect on growth (though we shall see that this effect is easily exaggerated).

- We must ask where investors get the funds to start their venture; they must divert resources from present consumption. This is not a problem from the perspective taken here because investment counts as output just as consumption does. That is, the effect on output is not negative in the short run when some consumption is replaced with investment. In moving from the question of what growth is to why it occurs, though, we need to inquire into the difficulties that agents may face in acquiring the necessary funds.

- Moreover if we allow ourselves to worry about the possibility of unemployment we must worry about whether the amount agents wish to invest in an economy is equivalent to the amount that agents wish to save. Total spending in an economy will be total consumption expenditure plus total investment expenditure (plus government spending plus exports). Total income must be devoted to consumption and saving (plus taxes plus imports). Keynes famously argued that unemployment would result if desired saving exceeded desired investment, though contemporary macroeconomists often assume that decreases in interest rates will solve this problem quickly by discouraging saving but encouraging investment.

- We can worry not just about the equalization of saving and investment but their level. A country in which a third of income is saved and invested will likely grow much faster than a country in which only a tenth is. And then we will naturally be curious as to why these rates differ across countries.

- It might be worried that the analysis above is too short-term in focus. In particular it might be thought that the possible negative demand-side repercussions alluded to in (2) and (3) and (4) would surely work themselves out in time (given the general observation that economies eventually return to full employment), and thus the positive effects on growth of innovation would dominate. But growth is a dynamic process, and we should not rush to assume that medium term negative impacts have no long term impact on growth prospects. Among other possible effects, it might be noted that investors generally have expectations regarding the medium term foremost in mind.

- Moreover the dynamics by which declining sectors or firms decline bear further scrutiny. Economic growth does not just mean more, but must often also mean less of some goods and services. At the level of firms, successful price-cutting (or quality improvement) by some spells disaster for others. There may be a political temptation to keep dying enterprises alive too long (alternatively, some transitional economies may have incurred unnecessarily high levels of unemployment by jettisoning these too quickly).

- Institutional change has both a dynamic and level effect. Any institutional change will create opportunities. It is entirely possible that even a bad institutional change – that is one that closes off more opportunities than it creates – may generate economic growth in the short run (if the firms it hurts die slowly). But only good institutional changes will encourage growth over the longer term.
- The economic historian Eric Jones has famously asked why growth is not ubiquitous in human history. Agents in their search for a living must always have been interested in each of the types of growth identified above. And since population has increased through human history without humanity becoming poorer (as the law of diminishing returns would suggest should happen when more people are added to a fixed amount of land), innovation must have been a common feature of human society. Yet intensive growth – growth in per capita incomes – has only rarely occurred, at least fast enough for those living at the time to recognize it. This suggests the existence of some quasi-equilibrating mechanism driving incomes toward some quasi-subsistence level. Malthus had famously suggested in the nineteenth century that humans inevitably bred faster than they could increase productivity, and thus remained near subsistence; most economic historians (but not all) suspect that this mechanism did not prevent sluggish intensive growth through much of history. Jones points instead to political barriers to innovation as the culprit. Others have suggested cultural or social barriers. Such barriers are easier to imagine, it might be noted, in a society facing little competitive pressure from trade: economic historians have long conjectured that the political fragmentation of Europe limited the ability of conservative forces to prevent innovation. The analysis above suggests that certain negative feedback mechanisms might also be at work. It also points us to explore the scope for various types of innovation in different times and places. And it invites us to explore the balance between product and process innovation: it may be that improvements in productivity only lead to enduring changes in average incomes if accompanied by the introduction of new goods and services.
- Growth depends on consumers wanting goods at the prices offered. But these wants may be 'manufactured' through advertising. This raises ethical questions of the value of growth. The fact that people have not become happier on average as real incomes have risen over the last decades may reflect the fact that they have been encouraged to want many goods and services that do not in fact contribute to human happiness. Leaving these concerns aside for the moment, advertising creates another mechanism for growth, with agents imagining new wants. This can be seen broadly as a question of cultural attitudes.

The analysis above suggests important roles for technology, institutions, investment, trade, networks, and perhaps culture. It is worthwhile to reflect here on the

various ways these interact, and then on how they might be influenced by still
other phenomena:

- We can start with networks, the element that receives the least attention from
  economists. Beyond their direct effect (above) on growth, networks can be
  crucial for investment, technology, and institutional change. Funds for investing
  are often obtained through personal networks, as are government permissions;
  big investment projects often involve cooperation among agents. While the
  traditional view of technological innovation is of the isolated genius alone in a
  laboratory, in the real world innovation almost always involves the flow of information between agents. Institutions even more obviously are rarely changed
  by one agent in isolation (even in autocracies). In none of these cases can
  networks be assumed to arise as needed: agents with good ideas often fail to
  find backing; and many efforts toward technological or institutional innovation
  fail due to lack of collaborators. Networks are a social phenomenon, and are
  generally characterized by at least the pretence of some degree of 'friendship'
  or fellow-feeling among members. As opportunistic as some networkers may
  be, networks cannot simply be conjured into existence as the need arises.
- Institutions have an obvious impact on networks, for many (parts of) networks
  are grounded in institutions: clubs, political parties, firms, business groups,
  organizations of various types. Some political institutions may also be important in determining the broader environment for networking: most obviously,
  people are wary of others in a police state. Certain institutions also influence
  the rate of technological innovation: patent laws most obviously, but firm structures, laws governing competition, universities, and a host of other institutions
  also matter. And the structure of financial institutions (among others) will
  affect investment decisions.
- Technology is more effect than cause in this analysis. One type of technology –
  communications technology – has facilitated networking, and through this
  investment and institutional innovation, especially with an international dimension. We have said little of culture, so far, but technology has had a huge
  impact here.
- Investment too appears to be influenced by these other phenomena more than it
  influences them. Of course investment in infrastructure such as roads and
  communications links can facilitate all of the other growth-inducing activities.
  Moreover it should be stressed that the impact of investment on growth will be
  mediated by other factors: most obviously the degree to which technological
  innovation is embodied in new capital goods, but also how supportive the institutional setting is.
- Where does trade fit in? Note that both technological and institutional innovations can be imported, though in both cases this process is more difficult than
  might be imagined. Institutions (and to some extent technologies) function only
  within a supportive web of cultural values and other institutions. Technologies
  (and at least some institutions) require both expertise and tacit understandings.

Investment can also be imported, and more easily than technology (which may often be embodied in part in imported capital goods) or institutions, though it raises concerns regarding financial stability, profit flows, and the power relations between investors and national governments.
- Finally, what of culture? Attitudes toward risk, work, and time (among others) will have an obvious influence on investment decisions. (And as noted above a direct influence on work effort itself.) Since technological and institutional innovation involve an 'investment' of time and energy, these cultural attitudes loom large there as well. Other cultural attitudes may be important: the attitude toward nature may have a huge impact on the rate and direction of technological innovation. The connection between culture and institutions is particularly strong because institutions almost always depend on supportive cultural attitudes: laws against littering or corruption are impossible to enforce if societal attitudes wink at these offences. [Note that we have mentioned only some of the more obvious effects of culture here; we will want to explore the effects of yet other cultural elements in later chapters.]

This variety of causal links is hard to keep track of without some organizing device. And yet more will be added below. Table 2.1 provides just the device needed, allowing us to place numerous causal links into some sort of order (Szostak 2003a performed precisely this task with respect to the study of culture).

2.4.2 Emergent Properties

While the approach here emphasizes the exploration of a variety of causal links (often with feedback effects), it is nevertheless important not to lose sight of the possibility of emergent properties of the system of causal links as a whole. Emergent properties can be defined as characteristics of a system that cannot be understood by reference to its constituent elements (phenomena and causal links) but only at the level of the system as a whole: consciousness, for example, may be an emergent property of human beings that cannot be understood by reference to the details of our biology. It might be thought that the identification of emergent properties must by nature be an inductive process: since emergent properties are defined as not being instantiated in any individual elements of the system, they cannot be deduced from the behavior of those elements. Yet if the behavior of one or more elements of a system cannot readily be understood in terms of a small number of causal links, then it makes sense to ask whether the result might instead reflect emergent properties. Needless to say, economists have rarely searched explicitly for emergent properties (and their tendency to model small sets of variables may well deter them from recognizing emergent properties in larger systems). Nevertheless two broad types of possible emergent properties have been well identified in the literature:

- The fact that business cycles and lengthy periods of unemployment are observed in developed economies has (especially since the Depression) led to the development of a whole field of macroeconomics devoted to understanding how these outcomes are generated by the interaction of (generally only economic) variables. This literature has been referred to more than once above, since growth rates at any point at time must reflect the interaction of the long-term growth process with shorter term business cycle fluctuations. However, even though economic growth theory has for the last half century been viewed within the economics discipline for both research and teaching purposes as an offshoot of macroeconomics, the two literatures have evolved quite separately and thus the links between cycles and growth (in both directions) have been barely explored. Yet it will be argued below that these links are hugely important.
- The fact that many contemporary poor economies have experienced little or no growth for decades, coupled with the observation that little or no intensive growth is the general case throughout human history, has led many to suspect that there are negative feedback effects of some sort that strongly attenuate any impulse toward growth. Such writers often speak of a 'poverty trap.' If so, then some sort of rare combination of realizations of phenomena may be necessary to get the growth process underway. 'Big push' arguments along these lines were quite popular in development economics in the 1950s and 1960s, and have recently been revived.

While the above two types of emergent properties will be taken seriously in what follows, a wider set of often implicit arguments grounded in the very structure of social science disciplines will largely be eschewed. The logic of disciplines suggests that there are relatively distinct economic, political, social, and cultural sub-systems and that the links within these are much stronger than those across these. This book would be of much less interest if this disciplinary assumption were true, for then the insights of non-economists into the process of economic growth must be trivial in comparison to the insights of economists (though even if the causal links across the phenomena studied by different disciplines were weak, scholars outside economics might still bring fresh theoretical and methodological insights; we revisit that argument in chapters 3 and 4).

While the disciplinary outlook does not necessarily imply the existence of emergent properties it does suggest that these will occur primarily within disciplinary sub-systems (since the links within are thought to be much stronger than links across). In our discussion of 'big push' approaches, we will see that non-economic arguments are common. This has not been the case for the most part in macroeconomics. Our suggestion that macroeconomic analysis needs to be more closely tied to growth analysis opens the possibility that interdisciplinary links are important for business cycles as well (as we shall indeed see below).

Outside of economics, the major argument for emergent properties that must be contended with lies in the area of cultural studies. It is often argued that cultures are monoliths, much more than the sum of their parts. I have argued elsewhere that most/all cultural analysis should proceed in terms of particular carefully identified cultural elements. I have doubted that emergent cultural properties are important. At the present moment, these are generally assumed to exist rather than carefully articulated. They are certainly not so important as to swamp the effects of individual causal links.

2.4.3 Links to Other Phenomena

It is now possible to discuss briefly how the phenomena in Table 2.1 might be causally related to economic growth. We should care not only about phenomena that might exert a powerful direct effect on growth, but also about phenomena strongly linked to the proximate causes of growth. The discussions here will be brief and focused on the first and second levels of phenomena. We will not revisit at length those phenomena already highlighted above: technology, institutions, trade, investment, networks, and culture. The purpose here is to outline the broad range of causal links that might reasonably be expected to be of major importance to an understanding of economic growth. This is necessary before more detailed theoretical and methodological discussions can be engaged in later chapters. That is, we must first establish in what directions to look for the causes of growth before actually looking. Otherwise, we are likely to look only in those directions suggested by and conducive to the use of disciplines' favored theories and methods.

2.4.3.1 Economic phenomena

Economic growth is defined as a change in total output (whether per person or per hour), and thus the first economic phenomenon, *economic output*, is central to our task. Our discussion of the four different types of growth, and especially of the importance of the development of new products, guides us to consider different components of output (*individual goods and services*). Moreover, economic growth in the past has been associated with the increased relative importance of first industry and then services. It has also been associated with a declining importance of basic goods, and increases first in goods of convenience and then goods serving purposes of lifestyle and self-actualization. These shifts must necessarily cause shifts in the relative performance of industries and firms. They must also, despite occurring across centuries, be a source of uncertainty.

What of *unemployment* and the *price level*? Economic growth is likely both a cause and consequence of business cycles. On the one hand, the structural changes associated with growth are likely the main generator of business cycles in the modern world: an economy that was not changing should be able to operate smoothly. Once generated, though, business cycles can be expected to influence growth. High levels of inflation may, for example, discourage investment. High levels of unemployment must mean that output is less than it might be in the short run: since part of today's output is devoted to investment in capital, the economy's future potential may be lowered as well.

Income distribution influences levels of investment and consumption in a society. Those with high incomes tend to save/invest a greater proportion of their income. Shifting income from poor to rich may thus encourage investment. However, it will decrease the size of the domestic market for mass-produced goods and services. These conflicting influences will need to be disentangled later.

Economic activity depends on *economic institutions* of various sorts. We will obviously wish to identify whether certain types of institution are most conducive to economic growth. The difficulties faced by the countries of the former Soviet Union in recent decades highlight the likely importance of institutions. Since institutional innovation involves the negotiation between different social groups, and reflects power balances, countries with more equal income distributions may be better able to achieve consensus on superior institutions.

Finally, the shape of institutions, as well as policies affecting unemployment and inflation, are shaped in part by *economic ideology*. This must appear then to have at least subsidiary importance. Notably, institutions and ideology are the subject of analysis across the social sciences.

2.4.3.2 Science

It has often been thought that technology is simply applied science. It is now widely recognized that technology and science have a reciprocal relationship: technological innovation (especially in the past) can occur far from the scientific frontier, and often scientists are guided by a desire to explain why a particular technology works (or sometimes why it does not work as well as expected). The field of solid state physics was almost nonexistent before the invention of the transistor. Still, for the purposes of this book natural science serves largely as an input into technological innovation – though we should not lose sight of the important fact that science is to some extent endogenous to the process of technological innovation.

An interesting parallel at least potentially exists in the relationship between social science (and some elements of the humanities, as we shall see) and institutional innovation. Social science can, and often does, identify theoretically superior institutions (and policies). To be sure, the selection environment for institutions is quite different from that for technology: for new technology whether it works well is of primary importance, while for new institutions whether they suit the interests of the powerful may dominate. Still, societal negotiations regarding institutions regularly employ arguments about institutional effectiveness. While social science can thus at least potentially influence institutional choice, in turn social science should be guided to explore why certain institutions work or do not.

2.4.3.3 Art

Art can be defined as artifacts or services produced primarily for their aesthetic value rather than their utility. Such goods are included in standard measures of economic output. Yet they comprise only a very small fraction of total output. It is thus reasonable to imagine that the causal link from art to economic output is of quite secondary importance. And thus the humanities (which we shall see in chapter 4 are largely interested in the arts broadly defined) will play a much lesser role in our investigations than the social sciences.

A couple of important caveats are in order nevertheless. Foremost, the distinction between items of utility and items of aesthetic value is fuzzy in practice. The vast majority of consumer goods (and capital goods to a lesser extent) blend the two. We could each shelter and dress and feed ourselves much less expensively if we cared not for the appearance of our house or clothes or dishes. Aesthetics matter in services too: restaurants charge for ambience and the appearance of dishes, while haircuts do much more than keep the hair from our eyes. In the absence of humanity's shared aesthetic sensibility, then, humans might have much more constrained material desires. Since growth involves the interaction of demand and supply, much less of it might have occurred in human history in the absence of this aesthetic impulse. Certainly growth would have been channeled in quite different – much more utilitarian, in the common meaning of that word – directions. Since our concern in this book is with why growth occurs faster in some times and places than others, this common aesthetic impulse is only of background interest. In practice, though, art interacts with culture, and thus some societies strive to repress aesthetic interests while others celebrate these. And such cultural influences will certainly affect the direction and possibly the pace of growth.

Growth of the third type above often relies on aesthetic sensibilities. Annual style changes in automobiles are famously often much more about appearance than performance. And thus we must take a broad view of technological innovation: a new car design (or skilful advertising) that attracts consumer interest is as useful for economic growth as an improvement in handling (leaving aside for the moment the possibility that market prices fail to capture the social value of improvements in safety or fuel efficiency). Again, though, we must worry that consumers are sometimes/often induced to buy goods that do not in fact increase their utility. During the Great Depression several authors suggested that the way out lay through greater efforts at stylistic innovation and advertising. We will suggest later that these can drive growth, but only to a limited extent in the absence of technological innovation that enhances more than the appearance of a product.

The second key caveat involves the relationship between art and technology. If goods are valued for both utility and aesthetics, then technological innovation will pursue both ends. Think in this respect of gothic churches or modern suspension bridges. The technology developed for aesthetic reasons could also serve utilitarian ends.

With respect to institutions, it is notable that political regimes always employ art: most famously in the former Soviet Union and fascist Germany. It is not clear, though, that these efforts are important relative to more direct effects at legitimation.

2.4.3.4 Politics

Economic institutions are generally forged within political institutions and may reflect political ideology. More directly governments pursue a range of policies that at least potentially have a direct impact on productivity and growth. These two types of causal influence are so obvious as to require no further discussion here.

2.4.3.5 Social Structure

It is often observed that certain ethnic minorities play a disproportionate role in investment and/or innovation and/or trade in various countries. It is also often observed that antagonism between classes/occupational groups can interfere with work effort. These divisions may both reflect and influence institutions. Women play a more active role in the economy in some countries than others. This affects output directly, but also population growth rates. Last but not least the type of family that one possesses may have important impacts on one's incentives and cultural attitudes.

2.4.3.6 Health

Each of us can appreciate how our own work effort suffers when we are sick or hungry, and should then be able to appreciate the potential impact on aggregate output in other times and places where undernourishment and debilitating disease are/were more common than in the developed world today. While the obvious effect here is directly on the second type of growth above, it is worthwhile to speculate on the possible effects on technological and institutional innovation, and on investment. All of these endeavors require the expenditure of effort, generally by many agents in concert. Innovation generally requires the expenditure of concerted effort over a long period of time, and may thus be particularly unlikely when life expectancy is low. Likewise investment may be less likely in an environment of low life expectancy, because agents have less time to recoup their investment.

Health outcomes can be affected in turn by technological innovation (agricultural technology, transport of foodstuffs to provide a balanced diet, medical technology, and so on), institutional innovation (public health measures, food buffer stocks, and so on), and investment (in hospitals, granaries, and roads).

Networks can have a negative effect in terms of disease transmission, but positive effects in lowering the cost of trade in food and enhancing the transmission of knowledge about agriculture, transport, and medicine.

2.4.3.7 Geography (Non-human Environment)

Some soils/climates are more productive than others. Some countries have more resources than others. Some countries are healthier than others. Some poor countries have good market access to rich countries. For a variety of reasons, then, we might imagine a potential link between geography and growth.

2.4.3.8 Genetic Predisposition

Economic growth is a human-driven process, and is thus entirely dependant upon basic human psychology. Most obviously, if humans did not have an acquisitive drive – for food and clothing and shelter and more – then economic growth would be very unlikely. The 'more' deserves emphasis, for humanity might well have been content with the satisfaction of basic human needs, and thus found the economic growth of the last couple of centuries in rich countries entirely unnecessary.

A variety of other genetic drives are essential to the causal links identified above: our desire and ability to forge complicated relationships is essential to networking, only our aesthetic sensibility can explain the role of art in human societies, our innate curiosity is at least one source of technological and other sorts of innovation, and so on. The very obviousness of these causal links creates a risk that they will be under-appreciated: that we will fail to trace the role of art back to our aesthetic taste or ignore the role of human curiosity in generating innovation. Thus, while the role of genetic predisposition will generally be indirect in our analysis – that is it operates through other phenomena in generating economic growth – it is also ubiquitous, and we should constantly ask ourselves if our results are consistent with our understanding of basic human psychology.

2.4.3.9 Individual Differences

The guiding question of this book can be phrased as 'Why does growth occur faster in some times and places than others?' If it is accepted that 'people are people,' that the genetic differences between groups of humans is swamped by the genetic diversity within, then individual differences can only explain cross-society differentials in growth if either:

- There are significant non-genetic causes of individual differences. The obvious suspect is culture: human personalities are generally assumed to be shaped jointly by genes and culture (nature and nurture). But we should also recall our analysis of health above: undernourished or sick people will be weaker, less energetic, smaller, and perhaps less intelligent than otherwise. Economic, political, social, and technological circumstances may also affect individual personalities and schemas. AND/OR
- Institutions affect how individuals are sorted into economic roles: are the most creative placed in research laboratories, for example?

2.4.3.10 Looking Ahead

We have identified a wide range of important causal relationships. These will be addressed in later chapters as follows (with numerous cross-references):

- Chapter 6 will deal in turn with investment, trade, technology, and geography. Chapter 7 addresses institutions. Chapter 8 tackles culture, social structure, and health/population. In each case, their effect on growth is evaluated, but also the various other phenomena that influence them. Concerns with income distribution are discussed with social structure. Science is addressed primarily as a contributor to technology. Questions of psychology (and art) are addressed as appropriate throughout.
- Chapter 9 addresses two important topics that have received little attention in the literature. The first is this: how does the rise and fall of sectors and firms relate to economic growth? The second is networks: how do these shape the various proximate causes of growth?
- Chapter 10 focuses on emergent properties. It first deals with whether there is a 'poverty trap': some forces that prevent poor countries from growing. It then turns to the relationship between business cycles (unemployment and inflation) and growth. This is the most suitable juncture at which to investigate the relationship between the demand side and supply side in generating growth.
- Chapter 11 asks what role government should play in the process of economic growth. It is in this context that questions of political and economic ideology are most directly confronted. Transport infrastructure and education are discussed in some detail.

2.5 The Importance of Precise Definitions of Phenomena

Rothstein (1998, 145) notes that some political scientists define 'institution' so broadly as to include culture and indeed everything that influences individual behavior. He draws on the work of economic sociologist Amatai Etzioni to say that if a concept means everything then it means nothing. Institutional explanations are only valid if they can be distinguished from non-institutional explanations. Greif (2006) makes a similar point regarding culture.

A profound example of the limitations inherent in vague terminology is McMichael (2000). His book is largely organized around two vague terms, defined in the glossary as follows (though vague terms abound in his book):

- Development project: An organized strategy of national economic growth, including an international system of alliances and assistance established within the competitive and militarized terms of the Cold War (351).
- Globalization project: An emerging vision of the world and its resources as a globally organized and managed free-trade/free enterprise economy pursued by a largely unaccountable political and economic elite (354).

The book largely attempts to fit postwar history under the umbrellas of these two terms, rather than emphasize the numerous caveats that could be applied (though the author applauds attempts to resist both projects). The result is a book that, despite its title, provides relatively little insight into the causes of growth: various institutions are described in turn but little attempt is made to discuss how these may have influenced growth. Admittedly, the book's aim is to provide an introductory non-theoretical overview to students, but it hardly seems that unnecessarily gross oversimplification of the complexity of the world, coupled with a complete sidestepping of the key causal questions, serves this purpose well.[10]

McMichael's definitions contain more than a hint of conspiracy theory: the development and globalization projects have apparently been conceived by somebody. In noting that the development project failed to lift all countries out of poverty, McMichael favorably cites an argument that the development project only 'sought' to integrate the top 10 to 40 percent of the population in Third World countries into the international market economy. Who was behind this malevolent plan, or what their possible motivations might have been, are not discussed. Real development is unlikely to be encouraged by such tilting at windmills. There are forces for evil in the world (or at least forces whose selfish

---

[10] Even economic terminology that can be defined precisely is not so treated by McMichael. The key insight of the theory of comparative advantage – that it is a country's relative rather than absolute advantage (it benefits from trade even if better or worse at the production of everything) that determines benefits from trade – is notably absent from his definition of the term (349). This suggests that the problem is indeed carelessness regarding terminology rather than the inherent complexity of his subject matter.

interests align poorly with economic growth for many), but these must be carefully identified rather than assumed.

Thelen (2002) discusses how the political science of business-labor relations had for decades been organized around the concept of 'democratic corporatism' that seemed to characterize certain northern European countries: all-encompassing unions and sympathetic governments were seen to sustain a highly successful social democratic variant of capitalism. In the 1980s, as economic shocks forced renegotiation of the very form of these institutions, political scientists were forced to look beyond this concept to appreciate the individual causal links involved. In particular, they came to appreciate the need to examine the interests and actions of employers (and how these coordinate their efforts): 'to bring capital back in' (372). This argument for 'bringing X back in' is not unusual in academic discourse, and is always symbolic of the sad tendency to ignore key causal links for decades.[11] Vagueness in terminology encourages scholars in a mistaken belief that they are not leaving out important considerations.

Campbell (1998, 377) notes that many scholars in many disciplines have investigated the impact of 'ideas' – both cultural and intellectual/academic –on public policy making. The two main problems have been lack of clarity about what is meant by 'ideas' and lack of empirical evidence, 'a problem that stems in part from the poor conceptualization of ideas and their effects in the first place.' In the end, though, Campbell proposes a simple two-by-two typology, depending on whether ideas are cognitive or normative, and background or foreground. The first distinction is captured in the list of phenomena above by the distinction between values and schemas (Table 2.1 also proceeds to identify important subclasses of each). The background/foreground distinction is a concern for causal analysis: when studying how public opinion and institutions are shaped by culture and schemas we would want to distinguish conscious acts from behaviors that are either subconscious or taken for granted by actors.

These various examples from diverse fields of human science all serve to make the same point: that sound scholarly analysis depends upon the careful (and shared) definition of the phenomena studied and the causal links among these. An exhaustive list of phenomena such as that in Table 2.1 provides the necessary shared set of definitions. Notably, each phenomenon is tightly defined not only in terms of subsidiary phenomena but also by being distinguished from other phenomena: we know precisely what it is and what it is not. This book will organize diverse disciplinary insights in terms of causal links among phenomena in that table (see especially chapters 6 through 11), and will thus avoid the semantic confusion that unfortunately afflicts much human science analysis.

---

[11] Lane and Ersson (1997, 7) ask – as one of their three main questions – what are the basic types of political-economic systems? Analysis would proceed much more effectively in terms of particular economic and political institutions.

3 The Most Relevant Theories and Methods

Philosophy of science is a highly contested field these days. Yet there is considerable consensus on what is no longer accepted. The falsificationism associated with Karl Popper and the Vienna Circle is almost universally discredited. It is now appreciated that no scientific method can give unquestioned falsification (and certainly not proof) of any hypothesis. A host of subsidiary assumptions are always necessary for the application of any method. Inconvenient results can always be attributed to these. Judgment must always be exercised in the interpretation of any empirical result. As a result, philosophers of science now doubt that there is any one best way of doing science. These facts are unknown or ignored by many practicing economists (and other social scientists) who continue to believe that there is one best way to perform economic analysis, and indeed argue that only statistical analysis can falsify (and for some even prove) theories.

This chapter will look first at theories and then at methods. In each case, the full range of theory types or methods is surveyed, and those with particular relevance for the study of economic growth are identified. Since no theory or method is perfect, the key strengths and weaknesses of each are outlined. This sets the stage for the evaluation of disciplinary insights in later steps. Yet the analysis in this chapter should also be of direct relevance to interdisciplinary researchers in guiding them to the careful use of theories and methods of particular value to their research program.

There is no need here for a lengthy discussion of the general advantages of theoretical and methodological plurality (such as is provided in Szostak 2004). The discussion of the strengths and weaknesses of different theories and methods should suffice.[1] Two brief points might nevertheless be made here. With respect to theories, it has long been appreciated by methodologists in many fields that theories should be tested against alternatives. In practice, though, theories are generally tested against no alternative – in large part because few scholars feel comfortable with multiple theories, but also because such tests are easier to design. Even a bad theory, which would fare poorly if tested against a theory with considerable explanatory power, may seem to explain much if tested against nothing. With respect to methods, we shall see (and this was shown in great detail in Szostak 2004) that each method is better at investigating some theories than others. In testing one theory against another, then, the use of only one method will generally bias the test in favor of one of the theories.[2] In sum, not only will theoretical and methodological plurality open up a wider range of investigation but it will allow us to better distinguish among competing explanations.

---

[1] Physicists use different theories (Newtonian, quantum, others) to cope with different circumstances of distance, mass, and time. Economists are prone to applying the same theory widely.

[2] For many economists, 'theory' is synonymous with 'model.' The approach taken here recognizes instead that valuable theoretical insights may not lend themselves readily to mathematical formulation.

R. Szostak, *The Causes of Economic Growth*,
DOI: 10.1007/978-3-540-92282-7_3, © Springer-Verlag Berlin Heidelberg 2009

Kitcher (1993) noted that the private incentives of scholars might differ from what is socially optimal: science advances best when competing approaches are contrasted, but the individual scientist may be tempted to follow the same approach used by others. Kitcher hoped that the search for glory would encourage many scholars to follow the path(s) less traveled in the hope of making a breakthrough. It could be, though, that scholars will be discouraged from such a strategy by the difficulty of publishing work that does not reflect the application of the dominant theory and method in their discipline. Interdisciplinarity – both its practice and an appreciation of its ideals – increases the likelihood that individual scholars will address problems with the full range of relevant theories and methods. In terms of Kitcher's argument, it should thus enhance the rate of advance in our understanding of economic growth.[3]

3.1 Theories

As in chapter 2, the obvious first question here is whether it is possible to classify and then survey the full range of scholarly theory. Given that new theories are created almost daily, this may seem an even more daunting prospect than the classification of phenomena in chapter 2. Yet it is quite possible to develop a typology of 'theory types' and then discuss the advantages in general of each type. One can then survey the actual theories used in the study of economic growth, and ask whether the full range of appropriate theory types has been engaged.

The discussion here focuses upon 'scientific theory': theories intended to explain how some aspect of the world works. These must first be distinguished from a variety of 'philosophical theories' regarding ethical, epistemological, and metaphysical questions. This distinction is similar to Bunge's distinction between perceptional knowledge (of things perceivable) and ideational knowledge (of things imagined) (see Strahler 1992, 221). Philosophical theories have played a small but important role in this book: ethical theories were invoked in the introductory chapter in deciding whether growth was good, and epistemological (philosophy of science) theory was invoked at the start of this chapter to justify the very pursuit of theoretical and methodological plurality. The bulk of the book nevertheless addresses insights embedded within scientific theories.

3.1.1 Classifying Theory Types

Szostak (2004) developed a simple five-dimensional typology of theory types through recourse to one of the simplest classificatory devices: asking the 5W

---

[3] I thank Judith Simon for bringing Kitcher's argument to my attention.

questions: who, what, where, when, and why. In the context of theory these yield the following precise questions (and in each case a mere handful of possible answers):

1. *Who is the agent?* There are two important distinctions here: non-intentional (including volcanoes or institutions) versus intentional agency (of beings that can act on purpose), each of which can take the form of individual, group, or relationship agency.
2. *What does the agent do?* There are three broad answers, which map imperfectly onto the six types of agency: passive (re-)action, active action, changes in attitude.
3. *Why does the agent do this?* With non-intentional agents, action can only be understood in terms of their inherent nature. With intentional agents, scholars can explore the five distinct types of decision-making: rational, intuitive, process (virtue) oriented, rule-based, and tradition-based. For groups and relationships, scholars can also ask how individual preferences are aggregated.
4. *Where does the causal process occur?* The concern here is with the generalizability of the theory: there is a continuum between nomothetic (generalizable) and idiographic (situation- or causal-link-specific) theory.[4]
5. *When does the causal process occur?* There are five broad time-paths that a causal process might follow: return to the original equilibrium, movement to a new equilibrium, change in a particular direction, cyclical, or stochastic/uncertain.

While there are still many different types of theory, the list is finite. Moreover, the typology highlights the types of questions each theory (best) engages, and thus also their weaknesses with respect to other questions. It would not be expected that each type of theory would have direct applicability to each causal link (though they might illustrate closely connected links). The typology of theory thus complements the list of phenomena in allowing the human science enterprise to be seen as the application of a finite number of theory types to a finite set of causal links. The result is still messy but at least potentially allows a coherent understanding of the complexity of human societies (though of course human understanding of any link is likely to be imperfect).

Since complex social problems such as the pursuit of economic growth involve multiple types of agency, decision-making, and so on, the typology suggests that any one theory will give incomplete guidance. That is, different types of theory will illuminate different aspects of the broader question of the causes of economic growth. Familiarity with the typology would guide both analysts and students to recognize the limitations of a particular theory for a particular question, and to identify other theories with compensating strengths. At present theoretical choices are often constrained by disciplinary preferences. The use of the typology is thus

---

[4] These terms are highly contested. Strahler (1992, 225) defines nomothetic as timeless understanding as in laws of physics and chemistry and idiographic as time-bound knowledge: generalizations that apply to only particular times.

consistent with postmodern concerns that multiple perspectives be heard. Yet whereas postmodernists are often skeptical of the ability of different communities – either scholarly communities or societal groupings – to converse with each other, the typology suggests that it is quite feasible to understand the strengths and weaknesses of different perspectives and at least strive toward some consensus on the importance of different theoretical arguments for particular questions. Note in this regard that much of the apparent inconsistency within human science results from a lack of clarity in exposition: scholars are often talking about different causal links when they appear to disagree, or are misunderstanding the key elements of another's theory.

Table 3.1: Typology of Selected Theories

Theory	Who? Agency	What? Action	Why? Decision-making	When? Time Path	Where? Generalizability
Most Natural Science	Nonintentional various types	Passive	Inherent	Various	Various
Evolutionary Biology	Nonintentional individuals	Active	Inherent	Not the same equilibrium	Nomothetic
Evolutionary Human Science	Intentional individual (group)	Active	Various	Not the same (any) equilibrium	Nomothetic
Complexity (including Chaos)Theory	Various	Active and passive	Not strictly rational	Varies by version	Generally nomothetic (supports idiographic)
Action Theory	Intentional individual (relationship)	Action (attitude)	Various; often rational	Various	Generally idiographic
Systems theory; Functionalist	Various	Action and attitude	Various; emphasize constraints	New equilibrium	Generally nomothetic
Psychoanalytic Theory	Intentional individual	Attitudes	Intuition; others possible	Various	Implicit nomothetic
Symbolic Interactionism	Intentional relationships	Attitudes	Various	Stochastic	Idiographic (some nomothetic)
Rational Choice	Individual	Action	Rational	Usually equilibrium	Nomothetic
Phenomenology	Relationships (individuals)	Attitudes (actions)	Various	Various	Various

Source: Szostak, 2004, 94.

Table 3.1 places several key grand theories within the typology. That is, the second through sixth columns indicate which answer each theory provides to the five questions listed above. The reader need not be familiar with all – indeed any – of the theories listed in the first column in order to appreciate that different theories are best suited to different types of question. For example, it would be folly to expect a theory geared toward group agency to be the key to understanding an instance of individual agency. Placing existing theories within the typology also highlights the fact that many human science theories are ambiguous about their answers to some questions. Action theory, for example, gives firm answers to 'Who?' and 'What?,' but not 'Where?,' while systems theory answers 'Where?' but not 'Who?' This highlights a weakness in these theories, and also helps those who wish to draw upon any of these theories to appreciate the key differences both across theories and within (as action theorists debate 'Where?,' for example). More generally, the typology highlights the simple fact that scholars should be looking for a *mix* of theories rather than one all-encompassing theory.[5]

The question of generalizability deserves special attention. Economics, and to some extent other social sciences, emphasizes broad generalizations. Historical research tends to stress the uniqueness of each event and historical process. Philosophers of social science have only rarely grappled with the question of to what extent social scientists can proffer generalizations that hold across time and place. Hodgson (2003) has suggested that certain theories – evolutionary, complexity, systems theory – may apply to all human societies. Likewise theories of human behavior can be universal. Most economic and sociological theory applies at best to modern societies. However, some theories may apply only within a particular institutional setting. This insight is of great importance to our project, for in integrating nomothetic and idiographic research we will often suggest that nomothetic theories are more limited in scope than their authors imagine, but also that idiographic analysis lends itself to greater generalization than its authors imagine.

3.1.2 Theory Types and Economic Growth

What theory types are plausibly necessary to the understanding of the causes of economic growth? While we can only know the value of any theory by testing it against evidence from the real world, we can usefully reflect at this point upon promising avenues for theoretical investigation. Note that in doing so we diverge from the general disciplinary practice of starting with a theory and applying it. Rather we start from our understanding (so far) of the phenomena involved in

---

[5] The typology not only facilitates the identification of the key characteristics of any one theory, but also provides a precise (though lengthy) definition of 'scientific theory' itself. See Szostak (2004, ch. 3).

economic growth and ask what theories are likely to be useful. We need not at this point worry about being exhaustive and outlining each investigation for which a particular theory type might prove valuable:

Agents: Intentional individuals are the locus of many growth-related decisions: technological innovations necessarily emerge first in one mind, and some individual usually has the final say on investment decisions. Relationships are also important: Trading involves relationships among intentional individuals, and institutions also often reflect interactions among a variety of agents. Ethnic groups are often observed to achieve quite diverse economic results within the same economic circumstances: group dynamics are thus potentially worthy of investigation. Non-intentional agents – both institutions and resources – are obviously important, and we might imagine at this stage that these could exert influences individually, or by interacting in relationships or groups.

Actions: We clearly care about many 'active actions': particular innovations or investments. Institutions, it is thought, provide constraints and incentives: passive reaction to these might often be important. Attitudes toward work, leisure, risk, and so on might well influence growth rates.

Decision-making Processes: Casual empiricism suggests that institutions evolve gradually, but often improve over time. This suggests that rationality likely plays some role, but also that tradition does. Scholars of scientific discovery have long appreciated that a mix of reason and intuition is involved: this insight also applies to technological innovation. If attitudes do affect growth outcomes, then key decisions must reflect to some degree concerns regarding virtue/process. Finally, in a world awash in information, who can doubt that economic agents sometimes follow simple decision-making rules rather than attempt rational calculations?[6] Economic theory itself recognizes that rational calculation is impossible in the face of uncertainty: yet decisions regarding both investment and innovation are inevitably embedded in uncertainty.

Interdisciplinarity supports the idea of multiple types of decision-making in many ways. Sociologists, as we shall see in chapter 4, have stressed a variety of non-rational forms of decision-making. The idea of 'habit' – that is of individuals following rules – had been central in the work of early sociologists such as Weber and Durkheim, but has been less important in economics (though Veblen a century ago and Nelson and Winter more recently have stressed it). The concept of emergent rationality associated with evolutionary game theory suggests that individuals follow rules reflecting past experiences of successful adaptation (Nee, 1998, 10). More generally, brain imaging shows that different parts of the brain are activated at different times, and make decisions in different ways (Cohen 2005).

At the levels of groups and relationships, the mechanisms by which individual choices are combined may well vary across situation as well.

---

[6] The five types of decision-making identified here bear a strong similarity, but were developed independently of Weber's typology of goal-rational, value-rational, traditional, and intuitive behaviors.

Generalizability: Each institutional and technological innovation is necessarily unique, and thus idiographic elements will be important in understanding any particular innovation. Yet we can and should aspire to identifying commonalities across these innovations.

Timepath: Economic growth occurred in the West much more rapidly in the nineteenth century than ever before, and more rapidly in the first postwar decades than before or since. In both the nineteenth and twentieth centuries multiple periods of a decade or so in length in which growth was relatively slow (by the standards of those centuries) or negative can be discerned. The growth experience of other regions of the world is even more diverse. These diverse experiences suggest that theories with cyclical or stochastic elements – allowing growth rates to both rise and fall – should be important (with the type of theory preferred depending on how regular these fluctuations are thought to be). The fact that growth rates are at least potentially much higher than a mere two centuries ago (or alternatively common prognostications that growth will soon decline) suggests that theories positing dynamic change in one direction may also have a role to play. The fluctuations observed in modern growth performance may be perturbations (needing to be explained) about some underlying trend, and thus theories of equilibrium growth rates may have some role to play as well.[7]

Reflections on this analysis: It should not be surprising, given the complexity of the process of economic growth, that every type of theory imaginable might have a role to play in our understanding of that process. Nor should this result frighten us into arbitrarily constraining the set of theories to examine. We might well find that some theory types yield very little insight, but it would be poor interdisciplinary scholarly practice to assume this result at the outset. While the fortunes of individual theory types remain to be evaluated in the steps below, one general result from the analysis above seems destined to remain robust: *No one type of theory on its own can provide a complete understanding of the process of economic growth.* This result will only surprise those whose disciplinary perspective (see chapter 4) guides them to believe otherwise.

3.1.3 Theories of Economic Growth

With the typology in mind, it is useful to survey the theories applied in various disciplines to the study of economic growth. We can place each of these theories within the typology, and identify missing theoretical elements if necessary.

---

[7] Snooks (42-3) notes that empirical work by Barro and others finds no trend in growth rates, but rather these fluctuate a lot. We need to understand why both innovation and investment fluctuate. In a similar vein, Temin (1997) notes that new growth theory cannot explain the decline in growth rates in the 1970s, except as a return to a normal growth trajectory.

3.1.3.1 Economics

Rational Choice

Though particular assumptions are occasionally relaxed, these theories involve *individuals acting rationally*; results are generally highly *generalizable* and *equilibrium*. In the context of growth theories, equilibrium is usually defined as a 'steady-state growth rate.' Rational choice theory is appealing because the rational act provides its own explanation: one only needs to understand the nature of the choices facing an individual and their goals in order to understand their decision. An appeal to norms or rules requires another level of explanation.

Rational choice theory can be applied widely.[8] Special note might be made of 'the new institutionalism' which assumes that decisions about institutional change are largely rational, and thus generally predicts that institutions evolve toward an optimal form. This new institutionalism has largely but not entirely squeezed out of the profession an old institutionalism that posited a less benign evolutionary process (see below).

The most obvious difficulty in relying exclusively on rational choice theory is that individuals often seem to act non-rationally. Rational choice theorists have often proffered an evolutionary response to this critique. It is suggested that rational behavior will dominate markets since rational actors will out-compete those guided by whim or arbitrary decision rules. But many markets – even hyper-competitive financial markets – do not seem to behave as rational choice theory predicts. Fehr and Tyran (2005) review and ultimately dismiss five common arguments that irrationality does not matter in practice: that irrational biases cancel out (but these often lean in a certain direction), that people learn through time to behave rationally (but we observe consistently irrational behavior through time), that irrational agents will be chased from markets (but this certainly is not the case in labor and consumption markets, and apparently not in financial markets), and that rational agents will determine prices despite the existence of some irrational agents (this becomes two arguments, an empirical one involving simulations that provide mixed results, and a theoretical one that need not hold if many agents act in a particular irrational fashion). The outcome, they argue, generally depends on whether irrational and rational behaviors are complements or substitutes: if it pays rational actors to mimic (in part) the behavior of irrational actors then irrational behavior is magnified (as when managers take into account the fact that workers lower their real wage demands in the face of inflation).

---

[8] Ruttan (2000, 15) argues that economic imperialists often score early victories in applying rational choice theory to other disciplines, but then retreat in the face of non-rational behavior. If so, this reflects the simple fact that there are five complementary types of decision-making.

If instead rational agents counteract irrational acts, rational outcomes may be achieved. Fehr and Tyran have run experiments that generate these two results.

Loasby (1999, 1) notes that rational decisions require that individuals be able to compare the likely outcomes of the different choices they face; in the face of uncertainty this sort of calculation is impossible. Yet uncertainty pervades decisions of all sorts. North (2005, 23-4) concurs: 'The tendency of economists to carry over the rationality assumption in undiluted form to more complex issues involving uncertainty has been a roadblock to improving our understanding of the human landscape.' Agents can sometimes reduce uncertainty by gaining knowledge or changing institutions or beliefs; all of these are path dependent processes (this term is defined below) and thus outcomes that mimic rational decisions are far from guaranteed (North, 17-21).

Uncertainty is the most noted but hardly the only barrier to rational decision-making. The key principles of Loasby's book are the following: economic theory must cope with mental representations [schemas, in the terminology of Szostak 2004; see Table 2.1] rather than assume that agents know reality (10); these are necessarily imperfect (11); schemas are maintained even in the face of conflicting information (11-2); and since decisions require closure people tend to ignore conflicting insights (12). In other words, human psychology guides agents to think that they know more about a situation than they do, and pretend to rational decision-making (even when this is not possible)[9] when actually guided by unrecognized decision rules. Though Loasby does not stress this, agents may also rely on intuition or tradition or virtues while pretending to rationality.

A variety of other limits to rationality can be noted:

- In interacting with others, we necessarily do not know their motives. If others think I am behaving strategically they will react quite differently than I might anticipate.
- Rational behavior is often attributed to groups without any effort to show how these manage to behave rationally.
- There is clear evidence that people do not rationally discount the future: the near future is discounted much more heavily than the distant future.
- Individuals are often (tautologically) assumed to maximize subject to beliefs that are assumed rather than shown. Whitford (2002) notes that rational choice theory assumes that individuals carry a set of beliefs and desires from one context to another. Even most critiques of rational choice accept this assumption. But Whitford argues that desires are shaped by context, and thus the beliefs an agent exhibits may be shaped by the situation they find themselves in. In particular, they may decide that they do not want goals that seem hard to achieve (like getting an A in a course).

---

[9] Fevre (2003) doubts that economic rationality is as pervasive as theory implies. Capitalists follow one management fad after another, but believe in rational choice theory nevertheless. He notes that if people believe an institution is the result of rational choice they will support it.

Though rational individuals might pursue a range of goals, economic applications of rational choice theory tend to assume the pursuit only of selfish goals. That is, the possibility of altruism is assumed away. If individuals are observed to behave 'altruistically' this behavior is attributed to some self-regarding motive (we are selected to take pleasure from helping kin; we know strategically that others are more likely to help us if we help them). There is now a great deal of experimental evidence across a wide range of societies that shows that most people are other-regarding: they suffer costs in altruistic behavior in situations when no plausible benefit to self occurs. One notable result of these experiments is that there is cultural variation in results but virtually no variation by gender or age within groups: this suggests that group-level processes can have important economic effects. Of course, altruism is not the only drive and thus people will often also act in a self-regarding manner, perhaps especially when the stakes are high. But the point to stress here is that they do not always do so. Economists assume away altruism not just for theoretical reasons: Putting even reciprocity (or a preference for equality) much less altruism in utility functions renders them mathematically intractable beyond groups of two or three. Mathematical modeling is much easier if agents are assumed to be selfish.

Game Theory

Game theory focuses on strategic interactions within *relationships*. Individuals seek strategies that achieve the best outcomes (which are usually defined in terms of selfish material goals, but can include more altruistic goals) given how others will react. Game theory seeks to identify stable *equilibria* in which each individual behaves as others predict, and thus no agent has an incentive to change their strategy. Notably, game theory often generates multiple possible equilibria, and thus one must appeal to insights beyond game theory in order to understand why a particular equilibrium might be achieved in a particular situation. Stable equilibria are often only possible with non-realistic ancillary assumptions (Manski 2000, 126). Counter-intuitively, game theory can produce *non-equilibrium* outcomes if the game being played affects phenomena other than those that are the focus of the game (say if a seemingly stable trading relationship succeeds in making the agents rich, and this changes their attitudes toward trade).[10] On the whole, though, '...the tools of game theory turn out to be poorly suited to analyzing conjunctures or exploring slow-moving macroprocesses' (Pierson and Skocpol 2002, 705)

Likewise, especially in the form of evolutionary game theory, at least one type of non-rational decision-making can be invoked, for there is a decided benefit to following *tradition* in that agents then start with a good idea of how others will behave (except when circumstances change such that many others abandon

---

[10] Greif (2006, 183), though celebrating the insights of game theory, nevertheless urges the development of a more dynamic framework of analysis.

tradition). Tradition may be crucial in explaining how one of many possible equilibria is achieved. Game theorists occasionally invoke *intuition*, but generally only to explain how agents would feel their way toward rational outcomes.

Models quickly become indeterminate as the number of actors is increased. Game theorists naturally focus on 'coherent strategic actors operating in well-bounded contexts where choices are clearly identifiable and payoffs relatively transparent'; they generally avoid 'broader social aggregates' or treat these as coherent actors (ignoring questions of how consensus is achieved, or how some agents are encouraged to act on behalf of others), and they ignore the fact that new actors and preferences emerge during a historical process (Pierson and Skocpol 2002, 716-7). Since growth often involves group decisions or the entry of new players or very complex and changing decision situations, game theory may not always provide appropriate guidance.

General Equilibrium

General equilibrium theory argues that markets will integrate individual actions in such a way as to generate stable equilibria. In doing so, it explores how behaviors along one causal link interact with behaviors along others. In practice, while it is possible to show mathematically that general equilibrium exists – that is, that there is a set of prices for all goods that equate demand and supply – it has proven more challenging to establish that such equilibria are stable. And of course an equilibrium is meaningless if the system does not tend toward it and stay there once it is reached. Yet in practice most economists are untroubled by the inability to identify stable equilibria mathematically. They argue that the general stability observed in market economies is evidence that stable equilibria are in fact generated. Of course, one might point to the Great Depression (or even the 1970s) or the generally-greater fluctuations observed in poorer countries as evidence that the system is not inevitably stable. Chapter 10 will explore some alternative explanations of general-but-not-inevitable stability. More generally it cannot be stressed too much that economic growth itself is always disequilibrating: new innovations or investments or trade relationships inevitably move economies away from previous equilibria (if such existed). The question of (if and) how quickly economies move toward equilibria in a world where they are constantly shocked away from it is thus of great importance for the study of economic growth.

Growth Theory

The challenge for economists theorizing about growth has always been to somehow escape the straightjacket of general equilibrium theory. Growth must involve either a movement between equilibria or a dynamic process. Early theorists focused formally on investment and discussed how increases in the ratio of capital to labor would generate growth. Such theories generally maintained the idea of an eventual equilibrium in which the rate of investment would just equal the rate at which the capital stock depreciated. Notably, growth itself was thus characterized as a disequilibrium process tending toward an eventual equilibrium. These early theories seemed unsatisfactory for two main reasons. First technological innovation and education occurred 'outside the model': theorists dealt with them only as sources of exogenous increases in productivity. Second, the prediction that growth rates would fall through time (toward zero if not for exogenous innovations) seemed inappropriate. A second generation of 'endogenous growth models' tried to bring education and/or technology in, and also to generate the possibility of continued growth. Debate between these two theories has often been driven by whether the theorist wants to encourage investment or research.

Both types of theory have tended to assume that economies tend toward some sort of steady state (an equilibrium growth rate). This assumption is generally necessary for mathematical tractability. The earlier growth models predict that growth rates would fall toward the steady state while many endogenous models predict the reverse; in the real world growth rates fluctuate. Both types of theory try to comprehend growth with a handful of variables, and tend to assume away the interactions among these variables that exist in the real world (for example investment and innovation are treated as independent even though we know these interact). They thus ignore phenomena we know to be important like crime, efficiency, and government regulations. Most importantly neither really tells us much about why some countries grow faster than others. The simple nature of these models suggests that fairly simple policies to increase investment or research can change long run growth rates, but in practice it is much more difficult to generate acceleration in growth rates.

Neoclassical (Solow) Growth Theory. The neoclassical growth theory rests on the simple idea of diminishing returns: if we add capital to a fixed population, the return to capital falls as the capital/labor ratio rises. The logic is simple: a worker with one hammer is much more productive than a worker without, but the second hammer adds little. Presumably, the worker first receives the most useful tool, then a less useful tool, and so on. If we assume that saving is a constant proportion of output, and that saving always equals investment (that is, we ignore for the moment both foreign trade and the possibility of unemployment) then investment is a decreasing function of the size of the capital stock (since additional units of capital add less to output). Depreciation is, however, a constant function of the capital stock. Thus there is a long run equilibrium where investment just equals depreciation, and then growth stops. Growth rates will fall toward zero. Technology can enter exogenously and shift both the investment and output functions up but otherwise does not change the result: the equilibrium is still where investment just equals depreciation (but with better technology a higher output is generated). Note, though, that the level of investment at any point in time does not affect the steady state level of output which is determined by the equilibrium capital stock; it affects only how fast we get there. Thus, despite being outside the model exogenous shocks such as technology or better education are the only means of increasing long run output.

In response to endogenous growth theories, there have been attempts to update the Solow model by including human capital and research investment, and dropping the assumption of diminishing returns to aggregate investment. These often fit the data just as well as endogenous growth models – but neither has proven empirically powerful.

If all countries were in equilibrium, the theory predicts that those with the higher rate of investment would also have higher levels of per capita output. If countries are not in equilibrium, this correlation need not hold. Empirically, investment levels are indeed positively correlated with per capita income, though perhaps because those with higher incomes save more.

The Solow model may have encouraged too much emphasis on savings and investment. If so, this is ironic given that in the long run these do not matter in the model. Indeed Nick Crafts worries that the Solow model can discourage interest in investment for precisely that reason. Solow himself argues that technology is clearly important in his theory despite being exogenous (and worries about the simplifications of assuming it is completely endogenous; see below).

Growth Accounting Problems. The Solow model inspired an interest in 'growth accounting' whereby economists sought to estimate the importance of different sources of growth. Economists were surprised that investment accounted for only about a third of growth. The various exogenous variables such as technology and education mattered more. Over time, the very idea of growth accounting came to be critiqued. It assumed that the various proximate causes did not interact with each other, but this is not true. Investment is often undertaken in order to utilize new technology, for example. Growth accounting also assumed away feedback effects from growth itself. Yet the level of investment likely reflects whether agents expect the economy to grow. Some variables, like human capital, are very hard to measure. Different results are achieved with different variables and functional form. Most importantly, growth accounting cannot answer the deeper question of why proximate causes themselves differ across countries. Still, the growth accounting exercises were important in steering the attention of some economists toward issues of technology and education.

Endogenous Growth Theory. Endogenous growth theories attempt to understand technological innovation as an economic activity (a minority focus instead on education). Innovation is treated as the outcome of purposeful research efforts, and thus seen as a result of economic incentives. Innovation can thus be modeled as the result of a handful of economic variables. Moreover, innovation can be seen to escape the diminishing returns problems faced by investment in physical assets (above). Whereas a machine can be used by only one worker at a time, an idea can potentially be used by all. Some early versions of endogenous growth theory indeed suggested there are 'increasing returns' to innovation: since ideas can be combined the return to innovation increases through time.[11] Economists have generally shied away from the idea of increasing returns because existence theorems for general equilibrium require decreasing or constant returns. And the idea that growth rates should increase through time seemed no more plausible than the idea that they should decrease.

There is a (manageable) conflict in these theories between emphasizing both the economic incentives for innovation and the fact that innovations are used by many agents. Firms investing in research try to limit the access of others to their innovations so that they can profit from their investment. They must succeed enough to think investment in research worthwhile, but not so well that their ideas do not 'spillover' into the wider economy.

Convergence. The Solow model predicts that poor countries should grow faster than rich countries. They are poor because they have little capital, and thus will have a higher return to investment than rich countries. We should in fact expect capital to flow from rich to poor countries as a result (but do not always see this empirically; see chapter 6). Convergence is not inevitable within endogenous growth theory: indeed increasing returns might drive divergence. Human capital seems to flow toward rich rather than poor countries, likely because the highly educated earn more when able to interact with lots of other highly educated people. Nevertheless endogenous growth theory suggests that convergence might be driven by technology transfer.

The empirical results on convergence are mixed. One does not find convergence if every country in the world is put into a growth regression. But one does find convergence within Europe over the last decades and last century. And several countries in Asia have also grown faster than richer countries in Europe and North America. The negative results in overall regressions are mainly due to the poor economic performance of many poor African countries, especially since the 1970s. If countries are weighted by population, then the rapid growth of China and India in recent decades does generate worldwide convergence. Convergence is also found if one excludes from the sample countries that lack the 'social capability' to absorb foreign capital and/or technology. The danger of course is that one then excludes tautologically those countries that have grown the least.

Countries catching up have tended to import both capital and technology from richer countries. Arguably, technology transfer has been much more important. The empirical work on convergence has largely been driven by a desire to discriminate among the different theories of economic growth; it has not succeeded, in part because the predictions of these theories are too vague. The literature has, though, encouraged a belief that poor countries can and should catch up to rich (we return to this issue in chapter 10).

---

[11] Solow has criticized endogenous growth theory: each model has a different assumption that generates exponential growth in productivity, but little justification is provided for these.

Insights of Endogenous Growth Theory. Economic theorists largely ignored growth for decades until the development of endogenous growth theories in the 1980s. Yet even economists recognize that these theories provided little actual insight into economic growth: they were important rather for suggesting that growth could again be studied using the favored methods of the profession. Joseph Stiglitz complains that he and others were talking about the ideas in endogenous growth theory decades earlier (in Snowdon 2002, 405). Nick Crafts, when asked what can be learned from endogenous growth theory (in Snowdon, 272-3) replies that it encourages exploration at the microeconomic level of how firms innovate, and it reminds us that there are important spillovers in technological innovation. Yet, as Crafts appreciates, these insights had been known for decades.[12] Brad De Long suggests that the main insight of endogenous growth theory is (from his own research with Summers) that there is a huge difference between the social and private rates of return to certain types of investment in equipment [presumably those embodying new technology]. Alan Blinder notes that when he tries to explain endogenous growth theory to non-economists, he finds himself saying that technology and knowledge matter; they respond incredulously that surely we already knew that (Snowdon 242). Barry Eichengreen argues that endogenous growth theory is just a retooled version of older growth theory, but that it [re-]raises questions that economic historians have thought about for years (Snowdon, 305).[13]

> Once the theoretical possibilities [of the Solow model] had been exhausted ... interest in this totally unrealistic growth model rapidly declined. It could tell us next to nothing about the real world. Only with the passage of a further decade or so and the attempt to introduce technological change as an endogenous variable into the neoclassical growth model did this field once more appear to offer further research possibilities. Yet, a decade on, the so-called 'new' growth theory has still to come to grips with real dynamic processes, or to offer insights that have not been known to development economists and historical economists for generations (Snooks 1998, xiii).

Gylfason (1999, 29) celebrates endogenous growth theory for 'allowing economic variables to matter.' He surely exaggerates: while the previous theories of the 1960s had recognized the importance of exogenous variables such as technology and demography as he claims, they had also emphasized within the model the importance of saving and investment, as well as productive use of resources. It is exactly these variables that he congratulates endogenous growth theory for embracing. Yet Gylfason in his excess likely touches on something: economists

---

[12] Temin (1997, 146) is even more pessimistic: 'New growth theory therefore has legitimated more detailed attention to intangible factors in economic growth, and it has provided a new vocabulary to use. But the historical narratives do not seem markedly different from those done before the introduction of new growth theories.'

[13] Walt Rostow in the 1960s had urged the profession to acknowledge the possibility of increasing returns to some types of investment, but the profession ignored this advice until models with increasing returns were generated in the 1980s (Freeman and Louca 2001, 5). Richard Nelson, in the foreword to that volume, notes more generally a divergence in the 1960s between a mainstream pursuit of formal growth theory and a minority seeking qualitative understanding of technology and institutions.

were likely to see   and reject – the appreciation of exogenous influences in previous models rather than their endogenous elements. If so the effect is surely ironic, for the logic of endogenous growth models has again guided economists to look outward for the influences of culture and institutions.

Solow (2005, 6) treats endogenous growth theories as adaptations of his models. He celebrates the increased emphasis on technology and human capital, and thus norms and institutions. He argues that the first endogenous growth models were implausible and thus misleading in policy terms, but these he feels have largely been supplanted. Solow is skeptical that putting technology in the model in a simplistic fashion advances understanding: the important thing is to recognize that technological innovation is important. We will find out more about, say, the size of spillovers through research at the level of firms than in aggregate models.

Endogenous growth theory may also have encouraged interest in trade given the possible role for technology transfer. And the emphasis on research and development may have encouraged an interest in imperfect competition (that is, an appreciation that different firms have different information) in studies of growth (but imperfect competition had already become a trendy subject of research elsewhere in the discipline). Still, it must seem that our understanding of growth would have advanced faster if these various concerns had been addressed due to a concern with explaining economic growth rather than with fine-tuning theories that themselves provide limited insight into growth.

3.1.3.2 Economic History

In addition to the above, economic historians often employ:

Evolutionary Theory[14]

Only non-intentional agents evolve, and thus evolutionary theory implies a greater appreciation of *non-intentional agency* than do the theories favored by economists. That is, one would hardly care about institutional evolution unless one imagined that institutions exerted important influences on behavior. Evolutionary theories involve three key elements:

- Some sources of mutation
- Some selection environment which determines which mutations survive
- Some imperfect transmission mechanism between generations

In biological evolution, mutations are commonly assumed to be random. In institutional, technological, cultural, or artistic evolution, mutations may be imagined

---

[14] Solow (1998, 74) notes that evolutionary theory is used less than one might expect in economics, and speculates that this is because there is no clear transmission mechanism.

to reflect varying degrees of purposive behavior on the part of *intentional agents*. Institutions might be posited to improve through time due to *rational* efforts to do so, or because selection favors beneficial mutations that might result from various forms of *non-rational* (or just uninformed) decision-making. Alternatively, it might be doubted that institutions necessarily improve through time.

Evolutionary theory can potentially explain the evolution of individual non-intentional agents, or of systems of these (*relationships or groups*), where other members of the system serve as selection environment for each member in turn. Likewise mutations could be imagined to emerge from intentional individuals, relationships, or groups. Note that a variety of non-evolutionary theories can be invoked to explain why certain mutations occur.

Mutations can involve both *actions* and *attitudes*. The former will be more important in technological evolution, and the latter in institutional and cultural evolution. As noted above, varying degrees of purposive behavior can be imagined: thus action may be *passive* or *active*.

Evolutionary theory is itself highly *generalizable*, but if mutations are allowed to be somewhat random, and the selection environment is not assumed to determine a particular outcome, then any evolutionary process must also contain *idiographic* elements.

Economic historians have often emphasized the path-dependence of evolutionary processes. Institutional mutations today and/or their selection are influenced by pre-existing institutions. Thus countries facing similar economic circumstances may exhibit quite different institutions, simply because of different histories of institutional development. Nor can one of these countries costlessly borrow the institutions of the other. Path dependency thus stresses a *stochastic* time path. A similar argument applies to technology: this will differ across countries if these have inherited differences in tacit knowledge (understandings of workers that are difficult or impossible to write down), labor relations, skills, or institutions. Thus we can see qualitatively different outputs across countries, which may be an important source of trade flows. (Note that firm and country reputations are also path dependent). Note that one path dependent process may serve as the selection environment for another: different institutions may support different technologies. There are three conditions that encourage path dependence: inter-relatedness across technologies and/or institutions so that the feasibility of changing one depends on the state of the others, irreversibilities such that it is not costless to reverse a decision once made; and increasing returns such that the benefits of a particular institution or technology increase more than proportionally with the number of users (as the value of a telephone increases as others use telephones). Path dependence is most likely to be set in motion whenever there is uncertainty about optimal outcomes – as is always the case by definition with respect to any sort of innovation. Note that alternative paths of innovation may never be explored, and thus we may never know that a superior outcome was possible.

Alternatively, it might be conjectured that selection pressure toward the 'best' institution is so strong as to ensure that the end result of an evolutionary process will be the same no matter what course it takes. One would then imagine a time path of *dynamic change in a particular direction (followed by achievement of a stable equilibrium)*. Such a time path requires that institutions evolve faster than the environment, or alternatively that the nature of the 'best institution' is impervious to changes in environment. Note also that if selection operates to choose the best outcome, then the result of evolutionary processes will be what fully-informed and rational agents would have wished (assuming for the moment that their personal interests coincide with society's): as noted above, such an argument can at times be employed to justify the use of rational choice theory in instances where individuals are clearly irrational and/or poorly informed.

Indeed, this simplified form of evolutionary theory has often been appealed to in economics to justify non-evolutionary theories. For example, economists theorize that firms maximize profits. Faced with empirical evidence that firm managers do not always do so, economists respond that in an evolutionary process the firms that survive will be those that behave as if they maximized profits. It must be recalled, though, that evolution is a messy process, and at any point in time will be characterized by 'erroneous' mutations that will eventually be weeded out. The casual use of evolutionary theory by economists requires some very strong assumptions: that the optimal mutation is always present, that selection for this is strong, and that the selection environment has been stable long enough for the optimal mutation to have been selected. Path dependence requires only the relaxation of any one of these assumptions.[15]

There has been a huge debate about whether inefficient outcomes (and thus path dependence) are possible. This has often missed the point. Efficiency has often been defined so narrowly as to be meaningless: of course agents will move to an optimal outcome if this can be identified and the benefits of switching exceed the costs. But the facts remain that optimal outcomes are often not known, and that the costs of switching trajectories can be significant.

Freeman and Louca (2001, 123) stress that evolution occurs not just with respect to economic and political institutions, but also in science, technology, and culture.[16] Each of these five evolutionary processes is characterized by distinct selection environments [and one might add distinct sources of mutation and transmission mechanisms]. While each process is important to economic growth, and must be understood in its own right (129), 'it is their interdependence and

---

[15] Loasby (1999, ch. 2) traces the long history of economist use of evolutionary theory. He argues that this theory has been bastardized in order to fudge the issue of uncertainty. But real evolutionary theory does not allow us to be sanguine that optimal choices are made, and forces us to ask how real firms make decisions under uncertainty. (He notes that marginal analysis assumes that firms make decisions on only one margin at a time, but this is not true).

[16] Richerson and Boyd (2005) celebrate the role evolutionary cultural analysis might play in unifying the social sciences (245-6). Evolutionary theory can support both generalizations and path dependent arguments (247-8), encourages the treatment of both individuals and social aggregates as causal actors (246-7), and can embrace both functional and symbolic arguments (249). Evolutionary processes can generate both good and bad outcomes (249-50).

interaction that provides major insight' (124). They stress that causal priority should not be assigned to any one of these, but that each influences the others.[17]

Evolution and altruism. It was noted above that there is much empirical evidence that people behave altruistically. Yet it has been difficult to see how altruism could have been selected for: altruistic individuals should be less fit than self-regarding individuals. I am aware of three possible arguments:

- Game theory suggests that reciprocity – treating others as they treat you – is the best strategy in many games. If reciprocity were previously selected for, then altruistic individuals might find their kindnesses returned.
- Richerson and Boyd (2005) note that culture emerged early in human evolution, and that small communities would have encouraged various forms of cooperation culturally. Genes and culture might then have co-evolved to favor altruism.
- It has long been noted that groups characterized by altruism should dominate other groups (many economic activities require cooperation, but perhaps warfare is especially important here for it requires a huge willingness to sacrifice for one's group). I have elsewhere criticized applications of 'group-selection' theories for glossing over the critical question of how altruism could first become established in a group. Bowles and Gintis (forthcoming) suggest that individuals might self-select into groups (this is, notably, a type of gene/culture co-evolution if the self-selection occurs in terms of attitudes). They still invoke chance to get the process started, but once a handful of altruists exist they can coalesce into a group that will dominate others.

3.1.3.3 History

(Non-economic) historians have for the most part striven to be non-theoretical in outlook. They have feared that explicit involvement in theoretical debates would encourage biased reporting of history. They have instead tried to let historical facts speak for themselves. When historians have used human science theory explicitly they have borrowed eclectically from a minority of the theories on offer, such as psychoanalysis or Marxian theory (Burke 2005). In striving to be atheoretical, historians have been necessarily *idiographic* in orientation. They have

---

[17] Hodgson (1999, ch. 4) traces the rise and fall and rise of evolutionary theorizing in economics and other social sciences. Evolutionary theory suffered in the early postwar period because it had been associated with wartime racism. Later, he notes that economists often assume evolution toward some optimal outcome, but that this sort of outcome reflects either poorly specified evolutionary mechanisms or the use of discredited versions of evolutionary theory. He criticizes economists for using evolutionary argument to justify neoclassical theory, and then forgetting evolution. They also stress endogenous sources of mutation, when exogenous sources of change are also important (143). He argues that entirely endogenous processes cannot produce novelty.

implicitly accepted the idea of path dependence, for historical accounts almost inevitably explain the course of history in terms of unique actors and events.

Historians often applaud the idea of comparative history but only rarely perform this. The atheoretical approach is one important barrier to comparison: if each historian strives for a unique account without reference to more generalizable theories, it can be very difficult to ascertain what is similar or different across accounts of different times and places. An even greater problem arises at the level of phenomena, for non-theoretical historians need take no great care in defining which phenomena provide the basis of their analysis.[18] Comparative historical analysis might otherwise provide a useful complement to the more theory-driven efforts of other scholars, particularly in identifying idiographic elements.[19]

3.1.3.4 Sociology

Sociology is characterized by much greater theoretical diversity than is economics. I have shown elsewhere (2003a) that this diversity can and should be made intelligible by recourse to a typology such as that outlined above. As we shall see in the next chapter, sociology tends to focus on groups and relationships, attitude formation, non-rational decision-making, and idiographic and non-equilibrium processes to a much greater extent than economics. For present purposes, we can focus on a handful of theories that possess the most obvious implications for understanding economic growth. The integrative process is open-ended and one purpose of this book is to provide a framework where other scholars can more readily identify how still other theories might add to our understanding.

Systems theory

Talcott Parsons sought to explain social stability in terms of mutually supportive systems: economic, cultural, political, and so on. It was thus clearly an *equilibrium* theory, though Parsons and others struggled at times to explain how such systems might change through time. In terms of the typology above, the theory can be critiqued for vagueness with respect to agency, action, and decision-making process. In terms of the classification of phenomena in chapter 2 it can be critiqued for emphasizing links within categories rather than across categories. Nevertheless, it can usefully remind us that institutions, culture, and other phenomena do not operate in a vacuum but rather interact with each other in a manner that generates

---

[18] Jones (2006) cites Rodney Stark to the effect that historians are not trained to distinguish concepts from instances. Moreover historians seldom work with clearly defined systems of concepts.

[19] Thus Greif (2006, 190-1), though hesitant to appeal to 'ad hoc' historical elements in understanding institutional change, recognizes that game theory generates multiple equilibria, and thus the determination of a particular equilibrium must depend on particular historical circumstances.

a fair degree of social stability. Since economic growth is an inherently de-stabilizing process, it must necessarily overcome whatever stabilizing mechanisms a society has in place.

World Systems Theory

Though originally developed within sociology, world systems theory has always been interdisciplinary in orientation, and has been pursued also in political science and anthropology. Though its subject matter is primarily economic, it has been shunned for the most part by economists and economic historians.[20] The theory borrows from Marx the idea that capitalists exploit labor in a relentless pursuit of profit. It builds on Lenin's theory of imperialism to stress the international dynamic. It is argued that there is an international division of labor in which poor countries (the periphery) export raw materials and labor intensive goods, while importing goods (from the core) that embody high skills and advanced technology. While the exploitation of workers within developed countries themselves may be quantitatively more important than the exploitation of workers in poor countries, it is argued that the latter has been qualitatively *essential* in lessening tensions between capitalists and workers within developed countries. The workers in rich countries are given social policies financed by the exploitation of poor countries (Eades 2005, 29-30). The fragmentation of the world into numerous competing states is also important in preventing any one state from disciplining its capitalist class. Nations can only be understood within a global context, and classes are also global in nature (but limited in effectiveness by nationalism).

World systems theory argues that the behavior of capitalists from core countries (aided by their governments) serves to maintain the peripheral status of the periphery. It is thus an *equilibrium* theory. Capitalists act to ensure that these countries continue to export only raw materials and labor-intensive manufactures. The precise motives and mechanisms by which capitalists exert this influence is not carefully specified. And the empirical evidence is weak: Shannon (1992, 176) though supportive of the theory appreciates that the historical evidence in its favor is selective and controversial.

One obvious empirical challenge is that some countries, especially in East Asia, have moved from peripheral to core status in recent decades. A category of semi-periphery has been created for countries that are in between core and periphery (these are argued to produce the goods of industries in decline in the core), but this does not fully capture East Asian experience. Some world systems theorists have moved away from a strict categorization to speak of a continuum. But if countries can move smoothly from peripheral to core status, the value of the entire theory is called into question.

---

[20] Note that we are organizing our discussion in terms of the disciplines in which a theory is most common. If we were organizing theories by subject matter, this would be an 'economic' theory.

The theory has also been criticized for stressing economic causation over political. Some theorists have responded by paying more attention to political mechanisms (and even more recently to cultural arguments). It is appreciated by many that core country governments are not fully controlled by capitalists – some degree of autonomy is necessary for legitimacy – but then it is not obvious why these governments will necessarily work against the interests of the periphery.[21] Notably, Immanuel Wallerstein – the scholar most closely associated with the theory – has dismissed these criticisms as semantic on the grounds that the economic and political mechanisms are so intertwined that it makes no sense to ask which is most important (Shannon 157). It was argued in step 2, however, that we need to understand every causal link within a system of links. To pretend that world systems theory can only be evaluated at some holistic level is to invite facile evaluation: the continued poverty of some (but far from all) poor countries is taken as evidence for the theory as a whole, even though many other possible explanations exist. The fact that some profits are earned in the periphery is taken as evidence that core capitalists rely on these.[22] The particular causal links need to be carefully specified, and evidence provided for each.

World systems theory can be applauded for emphasizing the international dimension to economic growth. Sociology in particular had previously tended to treat each society as autonomous. And the theory can also be applauded for reacting to modernization theory (below), which had presumed that all states would develop toward Western capitalist democracy. The main empirical conclusion of the theory – that peripheral status is (semi-) permanent – rests on several arguments that deserve to be addressed separately when questions of trade and investment are engaged later: Do core countries use their power in trade negotiations to limit growth in the periphery?; Are profit rates for multinationals higher when these invest in less developed countries?; Do multinationals depress wages in poor countries? Does openness to trade hurt or help economic performance? More generally the role of governance in economic growth deserves serious attention: if governance is found to matter, what circumstances give rise to good or bad governments? In addition to exploring particular causal arguments implicated (at least implicitly) by the world systems approach, we will also engage the broader question of whether a 'poverty trap' is an emergent property of the growth process in chapter 10.

---

[21] Developed countries have been able to provide workers with high incomes and many freedoms. Many world systems theorists argued that workers are more harshly exploited in poor countries, and this necessarily militates against democratization (Shannon 1992). Exploitation is not carefully defined or measured, and democratization has lately blossomed in poor countries.

[22] Early versions of world systems theory emphasized the quantitative importance of these. But trade between poor and rich countries is small relative to the size of rich country economies. The 'qualitative' importance of these flows is generally assumed.

Sociology of Knowledge

The field of sociology of knowledge has in recent decades moved away from extreme views that scientific and technological understandings (*attitudes*) were entirely 'constructed' socially. It is now appreciated that these understandings are shaped both by how well they fit with reality and by the socio-cultural influences acting upon scientists and innovators. There is still some tendency to stress the latter rather than the former.

The field is influenced by the broader theory of the social construction of reality. Just as the belief systems of Trobriand Islanders served to make sense of their world and gave meaning to their actions, modern Westerners imagine 'an ineluctable set of physical and social laws' which may seem equally bizarre to future historians. They see anti-trust law as reinforcing nature's laws of competition, but both laws are cultural inventions. More generally societies with quite different institutions [that work] can be expected to imagine that their institutions are the natural way economic life should be organized (Dobbin 2001, 402). This approach should encourage skepticism of all widely held beliefs in what follows.

Modernization theory

Popular in the early postwar period, this theory posited a reciprocal relationship between economic growth and democratization, and suggested that all countries would modernize.[23] Though long out of vogue, Lane and Ersson (1997, 8) say that the theory is again of interest. Larrain (1998) speaks of three types: sociological, psychological, and economic. All are characterized by a stress on the inevitable movement of poor countries toward the economic, political, and cultural attributes of rich countries. They can all be conceived as theories of *change in a particular direction,* though there was a common tendency to imagine that there was some sort of final *equilibrium* to the modernization process. Modernization theories stressed the direction of change: sociologists (following Parsons) emphasized the breakdown of tradition, increased division of labor, and increased importance of merit; psychologists (following McClelland) emphasized achievement motivation; and economists (following Rostow) stressed the putting in place of institutions and infrastructure that would allow economic growth. All were a bit vague in describing the agents, actions, and decision-making processes driving modernization (though the psychological version arguably stressed individuals, attitudes, and perhaps rationality – but McClelland also argued that individuals could be educated to value achievement and thus invokes passive reaction to non-intentional individual agency). The word 'entrepreneurship' is often invoked in modernization theory,

---

[23] McMichael (2000, xvi) suggests that sociological texts on development are usually grounded in theory: dependency versus world systems versus modernization; liberal versus Marxist; structuralism versus neo-liberalism; and so on.

not because of careful causal analysis, but as an 'abstract definition, the embodiment of many variables,' and perhaps tautologically as the source of the various changes associated with modernization (Larrain 99). All types of modernization theory assumed *generalizability*.

3.1.3.5 Political Science

Irrationality

'Political scientists have long been sensitive to the irrational and arational aspects of political life: the workings of socialization and ideology within mass belief systems' (Goodin and Klingemann 1998, 18). Political scientists are not always careful to define what sort of *non-rational decision-making* they envisage. They often stress how beliefs about what is good and important guide behaviors. That is, ideas matter. There is much work on how schemas or conceptual models are formed and passed on. Goodin and Klingemann (1998, 19) see this as a recurring theme in political science: 'the internal mental life of political actors, meanings and beliefs and intentions and values – all these are now central to political analysis across the board' (Goodin and Klingemann 1998, 22).

Dependency theory

Dependency theory was an important precursor of world systems theory (discussed above). Like the latter it argued that rich country governments and corporations acted to limit development in poor countries in order to ensure cheap supplies of raw materials. Dependency theorists thus discouraged participation in world trade. The success of export-oriented East Asian economies discouraged dependency analysis. Interest in this theory declined rapidly as it came to be thought that inward-looking policies not only precipitated the crises of the 1970s but failed miserably when attempted in response to these (Geddes 2002, 348)
    Larrain (1998, 114) distinguishes two types of dependency theory: highly generalizable theories of inevitable underdevelopment, and historical analyses which tend to stress class conflict and see development as a possible outcome. Larrain's first type is *equilibrium* and *generalizable* and tends to stress *non-intentional agency*. The second type is *non-generalizable, stochastic*, and tends to stress *group agency* (and power relations between groups). But the first type also has important elements of group agency: it is often argued that elites in poor countries serve the interests of rich country capitalists rather than of poor country workers. Both types of theory stress the 'exploitative' relationships between rich countries and poor countries. Larrain is critical of the first type for often leaving

the mechanisms by which this occurs vague, and compares them to modernization theory in this respect (130). The second type is diverse, though it tends to emphasize the actions of classes and states.

Dependency theory had borrowed from theories of worsening terms of trade associated with Raul Prebisch. Faced with sluggish economic growth especially in Latin America, these theories hypothesized that poor countries would not benefit from international trade as much as rich countries (due either to the fact that technological innovation would reduce the relative value of raw materials, or because rich countries protected local sources of raw materials), and urged states in poor countries to restrict trade in order to encourage domestic industrialization. [We shall see in chapter 6 that there has been no trend in terms of trade.] The technological determinism can be treated as above as *non-intentional agency*. Unlike later dependency theories, these earlier theories tended to assume that states would act in the interest of their population.

3.1.3.6 Psychological Theories

Psychology plays an important but subsidiary role in our investigation. It is important nevertheless that the theories we use should not depend (too much) on *individual human* behaviors that do not in fact reflect how humans behave. If they do, we must evaluate to what extent the insights of such theories are unrealistic.

Evolutionary psychology [24]

Various human characteristics – abilities, emotions, even motivations and attitudes – were likely selected for during the millennia in which humans operated as hunter-gatherers. These need not be ideally suited to modern life. Note that this theory violates a common ('tabula rasa' or blank slate) assumption of much cultural theory – that human societies might choose any consistent set of cultural elements: it argues instead that our genetic predisposition constrains the possible set of cultural attitudes. Likewise, humans may be predisposed toward certain types of institution or technology, and guided to abhor others.

Humans may act to overcome genetic predispositions that serve them poorly. For example, it is likely that anger and aggression were more valuable to hunters than to postal clerks. Various human institutions designed to curb displays of anger and aggression might be unnecessary if humans had evolved differently. Economic institutions, such as those that govern long distance trade, would have been easier to fashion if humans were less disposed to such behaviors.

---

[24] I confess to personally liking evolutionary psychology and thus giving it greater attention here than many psychologists might.

Evolutionary psychology concurs with many other strands of psychological analysis in suggesting that humans are not strictly rational, but rather rely on an amalgam of the *five types of decision-making*.

Situational Perspective

This stresses that preferences are context-dependent. The individual utility function (even if one assumed rationality and self-regard) would thus be enormously complex for an agent's goals would change with each situation. This perspective is useful in reminding us that people – even with similar basic outlooks – may behave quite differently in poor countries from rich.

3.1.3.7 Complexity Theory

Newell (2001) argued that interdisciplinary analysis was best suited to questions characterized by complexity. Simple questions might be handled by one discipline, but the sort of (especially non-linear) causal relationships imagined by complexity theory would be handled poorly within disciplines. Economic growth must certainly qualify as a complex process, both as the term 'complex' is used in common parlance and as it is defined within complexity theories. Economic growth involves the interaction of numerous phenomena. Along at least some causal links it is at least plausible that small differences in the realization of one phenomenon yield huge differences in the realization of another.

While economists tend to assume equilibrating mechanisms, complexity theory argues that positive feedbacks such that a system continues to *move in a particular direction* are common. Asset markets, including foreign exchange markets, often exhibit positive feedback, for example: investors take rising prices as a good sign and push them even higher. Likewise investment by one actor sends a positive signal to others about the future, and encourages further investment. Such behaviors reflect at least two of the non-rational forms of decision-making listed above: agents to some extent *do what they see others doing*, but not exclusively; they also develop *rules of thumb* as to how to interpret the behaviors of others. Since expectations must depend on our observations of others, non-rational decision-making will likely be of importance in any forward-looking behavior.

Complexity theory emphasizes the iterative nature of systems of causal links (Colander 2000, 3). If one does not leap to a conclusion that the system necessarily equilibrates – an assumption common not just in economics[25] but in sociology and elsewhere when societal stability rather than conflict is stressed – then one is

---

[25] Bowles and Gintis (forthcoming) observe that in economics it is acceptable to show only that an equilibrium is locally stable whereas in biology one must show that a particular equilibrium is a plausible outcome of system dynamics.

guided to study each causal link in turn, but also emergent properties of the system as a whole. That is, one strives to identify the iterative processes rather than structural relationships (Colander, 3). Needless to say, one must keep a close eye on the feedback effects that operate within a system of causal links: as general equilibrium analysis illustrates in economics, partial analyses of one or a few links can give misleading insights by failing to take into account feedbacks along other links (Baumol 2000, 19). Still, one can recognize such feedbacks without presuming equilibrium outcomes. Indeed Colander suggests that we are never in equilibrium. Ignorance alone ensures that there are both mistakes and unexploited profit opportunities.

Colander (2000) urges economics textbooks to innovate in three ways in order to incorporate the main insights of complexity theory (though he would prefer a complexity-based text)[26]:

- Stress the value of induction as well as deduction. This will be done in our discussion of methods below.[27]
- Emphasize sequential decision-making. We have discussed above the five types of decision-making. But it is worth stressing that individuals do not foresee the full results of their decisions, and thus one decision sets the stage for others. This is important in understanding both institutional and technological change, for both are characterized by a series of small path-dependent steps.
- Stress path dependence and multiple equilibria [that the system may tend toward but never achieve.]. It will indeed be argued in this book that historical processes are often path dependent, and thus many outcomes were possible. This is particularly important with respect to institutions, for it limits the ability of one country to borrow institutions from another.

Colander (2000b) boldly predicts that complexity theory is the wave of the future. He stresses that while complexity theory can be applied broadly its implications are *less generalizable* than those of rational choice theory: 'Equilibrium may sometimes occur, or it may not. Complex systems are always evolving and expanding with new complex patterns emerging, making all patterns of complex systems potentially temporary.'

---

[26] Ramaswamy (2000) warns that unless complexity theory yields teachable formal models it will, like development economics, be viewed as heterodoxy by mainstream economists. See chapter 4 for a discussion of the fate of development economics. Colander argues that complexity theory can be formalized and should thus not be viewed as heterodox. Arthur (2000) celebrates the fact that while complex models cannot be solved analytically computer simulations allow them to be simulated. [Given the path dependence of complex systems, however, one must be skeptical of the results of such simulations.]

[27] Colander (14) compares modern econometrics to Mondrian: it is too orderly and linear. He urges statistical analysis that is capable of coping with multiple equilibria [notably a prediction of game theory as well] and seeks broad patterns. More generally Colander notes that informal understanding can precede formal understanding – Adam Smith did not formalize his arguments about the workings of markets – but modern economics insists on immediate formalization.

One problem with complex systems is that no hypothesis can be falsified because some other circumstance can be blamed for a particular outcome (Loasby, 1999, 2-7). This is a challenge faced by all theories of course, but is arguably of greater import here because of the number of causal forces studied in concert. And Colander has suggested that complexity should guide us away from the traditional approach of supposedly testing models against data, and instead search for patterns. These observations suggest that the empirical basis for any insights emanating from complexity theory need to be carefully evaluated. They also reinforce the focus of this book on the careful analysis of individual causal links.

3.1.3.8 Marxian Approaches

Marxian analysis begins from an ontological premise of the dialectical: All things are interrelated and interdependent. The relations between things are more important than the things themselves. The whole is always greater than the sum of its parts (holism). This assumption goes against the basic analytical approach of conventional science (including neoclassical economics) that focuses on the parts themselves. Moreover, all things are always in flux, always changing, always moving. Nothing is ever the same. History is a moving stage.[28]

Change is also conceived as evolutionary. But the Marxian approach uses a particular sort of evolutionary theory that involves *change in a particular direction.* Evolution is assumed to be progressive from simple to complex. However, progress is not necessarily cumulative in any simple linear fashion, nor is the particular historical path pre-determined, nor is any specific time frame predictable. Only the general trend and outcome are eventually inevitable. For Marx, then, the transition from feudalism to capitalism had been inevitable (at least for Europe), and a later transition to socialism was also inevitable.

Despite the ontological holism, the Marxian approach embraced an epistemological approach of dialectical materialism. This holds that the relationships among and between material phenomena are regular and law-like. Generalizations about these relationships are discoverable through an empirical process, that is, a scientific method. However, the holistic perspective guides us to look at these in the context of other relationships. Thus, the Marxian approach contains a set of interacting causal arguments.

Marx in some passages emphasized technological determinism and in others stressed the importance of class struggle. The first is a form of *non-intentional*

---

[28] Change is driven by the tensions, the internal oppositions within all things. Marx agreed with Hegel that the dynamic of the unity of opposites characterizes all phenomena. From the atomic coherence of negative and positive charges to the societal complementarity of the class struggle, conflict at one level evolves into a higher systemic unity which involves a new set of oppositions. The counter philosophical position (Aristotle) believes that oppositions and conflict are unnatural and destructive. The market model of neoclassical economics takes this approach. Supply/demand equilibria are harmonious relationships. See Miller (2008).

individual causation, while the latter reflects *intentional group agency*. The first invokes inevitability and thus *passive reaction* to technological innovations. The second argument also at times assumed inevitability but at other times Marx (and especially later Marxists) stressed *active action*. Marx spoke at times of class consciousness, and thus did not neglect attitudes – though note that if class conflict is assumed to be inevitable then these attitudes play no distinct causal role.

When Marx assumed the inevitability of historical processes, his theory predicted the move to a new (socialist) *equilibrium*. When he (or his followers) allowed for historical contingency, then his theory became *stochastic*. At such times, his theory thus also allowed for *intentional individual or relationship agency* (but he did not discuss at length their decision-making processes, though later Marxists could). While Marx is generally perceived as a generalist, he did at one point caution that the historical process he outlined applied only to Europe (Larrain 1998, 35).

While Marx differs along many dimensions from classical political economy, Larrain at least would stress his emphasis on class. Szostak (2004) noted that with respect to group and relationship agency one would have to worry about how individual preferences were aggregated: democratically, through negotiation, by the exercise of authority. Marx of course stresses power relationships. But the exercise of power is stressed between classes, and thus it is not always clear how decisions are made within classes.

As with other theories, we can examine the particular causal links stressed within Marxian theory while remaining agnostic about the possibility of some inevitability in the course of human history.

3.1.3.9 Classical Theories of Imperialism

As with the classical Marxism from which most of these theories derived, most writers saw imperialism as a prelude to the inevitable collapse of capitalism, and can thus be characterized as describing the movement to a new socialist *equilibrium*. But some authors (especially later) stressed that socialist revolution was not inevitable and thus described a *stochastic process*.

Theories of imperialism stressed the role of large corporations. These supported imperialist policies in pursuit of raw materials and/or markets (different authors stressed different motives). These theories thus stressed *individual intentional agency* more than did classical Marxism (though Marx also talked about the relentless pursuit of profit by individual capitalists). Note that the corporation is legally an individual, though one might still wonder how exactly corporations reach decisions: writers in the Marxian tradition would stress the exercise of power within the corporation.

With respect to *generalizability*, early authors tended to argue that the colonized would develop in similar directions as the colonizers, but later authors tended to doubt this.

3.1.3.10 Women in Development

Social science theory often focuses on the activities of men. Under the broad banner of 'women in development' four broad approaches can be identified:

- Female labor market behavior is analyzed to see in what ways it differs from male behavior.
- Female economic agency (including reproductive agency) is examined and its implications for both women and growth outlined.
- Power differentials and how these can be overcome are examined.
- The above approaches are integrated, and it is appreciated that different women have different interests.

Each approach was inspired by feminist scholarship; but each has arguably neglected the worldviews of women in poor countries. This lacuna has been gradually closed in the last decades as feminist scholarship has striven to be more inclusive. Nevertheless, care should be taken in what follows to ensure that insights are applicable to both genders and to both rich and poor.

3.1.3.11 What Theory Types are Missing?

At the most general level, the range of theories surveyed above has engaged every type of agent (except perhaps non-intentional relationships, though political institutionalism might do so), action, decision-making process, and time path (though cyclical time paths have rarely been addressed).[29] Most theories have been quite nomothetic, but some have had idiographic elements. Yet since these theories have had quite different foci, it remains quite possible that only a subset of relevant theory types have been applied to particular causal links.

3.2 Methods

Methods span disciplinary boundaries to a much greater degree than theories. Nevertheless, each discipline tends to emphasize only a subset of possible methods. We will not survey methods by discipline as we did with theories. Rather we will discuss several methods in turn, noting in each case their strengths and weaknesses for the study of growth. As with theories, it is useful to begin with a general classification of methods and their strengths and weaknesses derived from Szostak (2004), and a discussion of the value of integrating across methods.

---

[29] We will engage one sort of cyclical theory, 'long wave theory' when discussing technology in chapter 6.

3.2.1 Strengths and Weaknesses of the Dozen Scholarly Methods

Philosophers have long debated whether there is a 'best' scholarly method. For much of the last couple of centuries, experimentation was viewed as at least the best and perhaps the only scientific method. Biologists, though, only rarely have recourse to experiments, and thus have urged instead careful observation of the world (and the physical traces left by past life forms) and careful attempts at classification. Economists in recent decades have pursued mathematical modeling and statistical analysis to the exclusion of almost all other types of analysis. Historians have stressed the careful evaluation of particular 'cases' employing a variety of methods to this end. Humanists in turn have instead emphasized textual analysis and/or the application of intuition. Given these differing perspectives on appropriate method, it should hardly be surprising if it turned out that multiple methods should be applied within the scholarly enterprise.

This book – and interdisciplinary scholarship more generally – is grounded in an appreciation of the value of multiple methods, and a concern that academic over-specialization limits the willingness of scholars to appreciate evidence from diverse methods. 'What distinguishes good from bad in learned discourse … is not the adoption of a particular methodology, but the earnest and intelligent attempt to contribute to a conversation … Not all regression analyses are more persuasive than all moral arguments; not all controlled experiments are more persuasive than all introspections' (McCloskey 1998, 162,177). As McCloskey stresses this does not mean that 'anything goes' but rather that we strive to evaluate all sorts of argument and evidence in an open-minded fashion. We would obviously benefit in such an exercise from an appreciation of the (compensating) strengths and weaknesses of different methods. Yet open-minded discourse also requires a change in attitude in most disciplines, where at present editors and referees strongly favor some methods over others.

How many scholarly methods are there? There is no obvious way to answer this question deductively by identifying some logical typology of 'types of method.' It is possible, however, to inductively identify some dozen methods used in the scholarly enterprise:

- Experiments (including natural or quasi-experiments)
- Surveys
- Interviews
- Mathematical models (and simulations), including game theoretic models
- Statistical analysis (often, but far from always, associated with models) -including secondary [that is, collected by others] data analysis
- Ethnographic/observational analysis ('Participant Observation,' in which the investigator interacts with those under observation, is most common, but discreet observation is also possible).
- Experience/ intuition [some would treat this as an important subset of observational analysis, since we are in effect 'observing' ourselves here]

- Textual (content, discourse) analysis
- Classification (including evolutionary analysis)
- Mapmaking (both representational and conceptual)
- Hermeneutics/semiotics (the study of symbols and their meaning)
- Physical traces (as in archaeology, and including DNA analysis)
- Some would treat 'evaluation' of programs as distinct, though it can be seen as a combination of some of the above methods. Similar arguments can be made with respect to demography, case study, feminism,[30] and perhaps also hermeneutics.

Having inductively identified these dozen methods, it is then possible to ask the Who, What, Where, When, and Why questions of these. This allows one to see if there are methods well suited to the investigation of each type of theory. In asking these questions, some subsidiary questions emerge:

- How many agents can a method investigate?
- Does the method identify any/all of the criteria for specifying a causal relationship? These are: that the cause and effect are correlated, that the cause occurs before the effect (at least this is the general case), that intermediate causal factors be identified, and that alternative explanations of correlation be excluded.
- Does the method allow scope for induction (or is it entirely deductive)?
- Does the method allow movements through time to be tracked?
- Does the method allow movements through space to be tracked?

Table 3.2 shows how ten of the above methods answer these five as well as the original five questions. The subsidiary questions are listed right after the question that they build upon. Thus the first row indicates which type(s) of agent a particular method can investigate, while the second captures how many agents that method can investigate.

Table 3.2 establishes that there is no 'one' scientific method, but rather a dozen such methods with different strengths and weaknesses. In trying to comprehend the full complexity of human life we can usefully have recourse to each (while remaining cognizant of each method's limitations). These methods, notably, are not just of use within the scholarly enterprise, but can usefully be applied in public policy, and even in everyday life. Table 3.2 shows that there are methods appropriate to the investigation of each type of theory. In some cases, methods are very well suited, as experiments are to the investigation of the passive reactions of non-intentional agents. In other cases, even the best method may be more problematic. Table 3.2 can guide scholars as to which methods to employ in a particular inquiry. In all cases, there are multiple methods that can potentially shed light on a particular question. A proposition that is supported by investigation using multiple methods should be trusted more than a proposition supported by

---

[30] Hall and Hall (1996) note that the feminist critique entails no unique method but rather concerns about why particular questions are asked and problems addressed, and respect for the subjects (people) being studied. Feminists have tended to favor qualitative research.

only one. The use of multiple methods is especially important when different theory types are compared. Scholarly understanding advances by comparing theoretical explanations, and seeing which is most important along a particular link (but not necessarily dismissing the losing theory as completely unimportant). If only one method is used in such a test, the results will generally be biased toward whichever theory that method is particularly suited to investigating. This result is particularly noteworthy, for disciplines tend to choose a mutually supportive set of theory and method (and phenomena), and can be blissfully unaware of or hostile to contradictory evidence produced using other methods. Such close-mindedness is not conducive to enhancing our understanding of the complex world we inhabit.

What methods are likely valuable in the study of economic growth? Since technological innovations, institutions, and cultural values are necessarily unique, we need some sorts of idiographic investigation (but with efforts to generalize). The analysis above suggests also that we need qualitative analysis to clarify the causal processes suggested by statistical analysis. 'There are certain qualitative features of the growth process such as technological change, political change, and migration which are pretty hard to understand in a purely abstract framework' (Ben Bernanke, in Snowdon 2002, 200). Yet this hardly means that the mathematical modeling and statistical analysis favored by economists should be eschewed. We shall see that some very important insights have emerged from the application of these methods. Since we found earlier in this chapter that every sort of theory type might be relevant to the study of economic growth, and have noted that different methods are suited to different theory types, we should be open to the use of each of the dozen methods in our exploration of economic growth.

3.2.2 Triangulation Across Methods, Maintaining Standards

Those who favor methodological pluralism borrow the word 'triangulation' from surveyors. Different methods look at the same issue from different angles. Ideally, the use of different methods allows us to triangulate upon the best feasible understanding of an issue. Since each method has its biases, use of only one method will generally not do so. In political science, 'there has been a growing effort to blend research methods and use their respective strengths to triangulate on the evidence' (Katznelson and Miller, 2002, 17). Though they do not make the point, this healthy outcome may reflect the discipline's lack of consensus on method. It also reflects a recognition of the complexity of their subject matter: 'Questions about an important topic like civic engagement and democracy can rarely be adequately addressed with just one type of data or one technique of empirical analysis' (Pierson and Skocpol 2002, 718). Denzin and others have argued that triangulation is much more common in sociology than in economics. Encouraging triangulation in economics will thus open it toward other social sciences.

Table 3.2 Typology of Strengths and Limitations of Methods

Criteria	Classification	Experiment	Interview	Intuition/ Experience	Mathematical Modelling
Type of Agent	All	All; but group only in natural experiment	Intentional individuals; relationship indirect	Intentional individuals; others indirect	All
Number Investigated	All	Few	Few	One	All
Type of Causation	Action (evolutionary)	Passive, Action	Attitude;acts indirectly	Attitude	All
Criteria for identifying a causal relationship	Aids each, but limited	Potentially all four	Might provide insight on each	Some insight on correlation, temporality	All; limited with respect to intermediate, alternatives
Decision-making Process	Indirect insight	No	Some insight; biased	Yes; may mislead	Some insight
Induction?	Little	Some	If open	Yes; bias	Little
Generalizability	Both	Both	Idiographic	Idiographic	Both
Spatiality	Some	Constrained	From memory	From memory	Difficult to model
Time Path	No insight	Little insight	Little insight	Little insight	Emphasize equilibrium
Temporality	Some	Constrained	From memory	From memory	Simplifies

Stanley (2001) urges economists to pursue meta-analysis – where the empirical analyses of 'all' relevant studies are combined – but only to combine regression analyses. He notes that meta-analysis is 'the' method in other sciences (notably medicine) where it has often served to overcome heated debates by identifying the sources and relative importance of conflicting results.[31] All relevant studies should be included, a relevant metric for comparison developed (that is, a particular dependent variable must be identified), and moderator variables (independent variables) selected to explain cross-study differences. While judgment must still be exercised regarding inclusion, this is less the case than in standard literature reviews. Yet notably when he discusses problems with survey articles the first bias addressed is the tendency to exclude studies on methodological grounds (he notes that 'all studies have potential problems'). Combining results obtained using different methods would, it seems, provide an even more powerful antidote to bias.[32]

---

[31] Meta-analysis in medicine may only set the stage for focused experimentation. Chapter 11 will embrace the idea that the results of integrative research should be subject to further testing.

[32] Lipsey (2001) notes that the insistence on modeling in economics discourages the careful accretion of empirical knowledge. Especially when exploring novel problems, informal movement between theory and fact should be pursued (184). Elegant error is preferred to messy truth, as

Criteria	Participant Observation	Physical Traces	Statistical Analysis	Surveys	Textual Analysis
Type of Agent	Intentional individual; Relational, groups?	All; groups and relationship indirect	All; groups and relationship indirect	Intentional individuals; groups indirect	Intentional individuals; others indirect
Number	Few; One group	Few	Many/all	Many	One/few
Type of Causation	Action (attitude)	Passive, Action	Action, Attitude	Attitude; Acts indirect	Attitude, Action
Criteria for identifying a causal relationship	All, but rarely done	Some insight to all four	Correlation and temporality well	Some insight on correlation	Some insight on all
Decision-making Process	All	No	No	Little	Some insight; Biased
Induction?	Much	Much	Some	Very little	Much
Generalizability	Idiographic; nomothetic from many studies	Idiographic; nomothetic from many studies	Both	Both	Idiographic; nomothetic from many studies
Spatiality	Very good; Some limits	Possibly infer	Limited	Rarely	Possible
Time Path	Some insight	Some insight	Emphasize equilibrium	Little insight	Some insight
Temporality	Good up to months	Possibly infer	Static, can be frequent	Longitudinal somewhat	Possible

Source: Szostak, 2004, 138-9. Note: The 'criteria' reflect the ten questions from the text above.

The major barrier in practice to the use by scholars of multiple methods is a concern with 'standards.' Most scholars are intimately familiar with only one or two methods, and fear that scholarship using other methods is less careful and thus less reliable. Geddes (2002, 366) suggests the following [laudable] standards of argumentation in mainstream political science, and argues that these can be met by both quantitative and qualitative research:

- Arguments will be tested using observations chosen in ways that do not bias the results.
- Measurements and classifications of key concepts will be explicit.
- The author's argument will be confronted with rival arguments from the literature.
- Some means will be found for holding constant other factors known to affect the relationship of interest.

---

when the realism of Keynesian models is rejected in favor of assumptions of prices clearing flawlessly and perfect competition (188-9). Likewise, theoretical tractability is preferred to empirical relevance (190-1). While he does not address economic growth directly, his message seems to apply particularly forcefully to its study.

Some practitioners of case studies argue that they must bend the first and last rule, and also the second. Geddes argues that unbiased case selection is possible, as is concrete definitions of terms. The approach of this book is very much in line with Geddes. While the use of multiple methods is urged, sloppy or inappropriate use of any method is abhorred. Disciplinary purists fear alternative methods as a dilution of standards. This book is based on the premise that all methods can be applied carefully, and that the best evidence for any line of argument is that it is supported by the careful application of multiple methods.

In the previous section it was noted that Table 3.2 guides us as to which methods are most useful for a particular question. With respect to standards, it can be noted that familiarity with the potential weaknesses of each method assists us in deciding when a method is being poorly or inappropriately applied.

3.2.3 The Rule Critique

Rule (1997) argued that all disciplines in human science are guilty of emphasizing the testing of theory rather than the explanation of real-world processes. To be sure, scholarly understanding should be theorized. But a scholar focused on explanation may borrow from many theories or develop new ones, whereas a scholar focused on showing that a particular theory is right or wrong will not. Importantly, the theory-oriented scholar will ignore empirical observations that are not covered by the theory, while the explanation-oriented scholar at least potentially will contemplate all relevant empirical observations. Rule worried that theory-oriented research is forgotten when the theory goes out of vogue, whereas explanation-oriented research can be developed cumulatively through time. This has been a greater problem outside economics than within, for rational choice theory has dominated the discipline for the last century (macroeconomic theories have of course shown a greater tendency to rise and fall). But the tendency to overlook relevant empirical information has arguably affected economics as much as any discipline (see for example Szostak 2005b).

For present purposes, the obvious implication of Rule's analysis is that we should ensure that inductive methods play some role in our research agenda. Deductive methods will ignore much that may be important. But the Rule critique also supports the broader enterprise of this book in important ways. It provides another argument for theoretical and methodological plurality. And it indirectly provides an important justification for the causal-link approach: a cumulative explanation-driven research process is only feasible if inter-related causal arguments are clearly identified, and insights are organized in such a manner that successive researchers can build on previous efforts.

3.2.4 Mathematical Models

Modelers would claim two important benefits of modeling.[33] First, models clarify theoretical arguments. 'Critics of mathematical models often recoil at their simplicity, yet simple models are an effective prosthesis for a mind that is poor at following intricate quantitative causal pathways – tools to help us think a little more clearly about complex problems. Without such models we would be forced to rely entirely upon verbal arguments and intuitions whose logical consistency is difficult to check' (Richerson and Boyd 2005, 240). Second, mathematical models set the stage for statistical analysis.[34] This author has argued strenuously for clarity of theoretical exposition above, but doubts that this can only be achieved in mathematical form. Indeed, mathematical models themselves need to be justified in words. As for statistical testing, the fact is that many/most models are never really tested.[35] Some models contain so many unobservable variables that they could not be tested. In such cases modelers sometimes argue that the model itself establishes the plausibility of a set of causal arguments. But there exists a model that embodies any mutually compatible set of hypotheses; the fact that one creates the model does not really tell us anything we did not know (Szostak 1999).

Against these potential advantages, some key disadvantages must be counted:

- Assumptions and causal arguments are often made simply to achieve mathematical tractability. Rationality is often assumed in both economics and economic history in order to make the mathematics tractable (Freeman and Louca 2001, 21-2). Snooks (1998, ch.10) notes that the idea of steady states enters both old and new growth models purely to generate mathematical tractability. Solow (2005, 6) notes that most/all new and old growth models assume that an increase in one or more variables can raise the trend rate of growth. The results flowing from any such linearity assumption needs much more justification than they usually get.
- Models are often applauded even when the results are driven by questionable assumptions. 'A "crucial" assumption is one on which the conclusions do depend sensitively, and it is important that crucial assumptions be reasonably

---

[33] The strengths and weaknesses of each of the dozen methods is surveyed at length in Szostak (2004, ch.4).

[34] Cameron and Morton (2002, 795) bemoan the fact that much statistical analysis does not derive estimating equations directly from models, but at best uses models as suggestive devices as to what variables might be important [in which case we do not need formal models], but then appreciate that there is much debate about how exactly models should relate to empirical work (such as how to think of the error term).

[35] Modelers are often guilty of ignoring standards of evidence, and merely providing a couple of real world anecdotes to establish plausibility. Yet models are not themselves evidence but formalized arguments. Those outside the community of modelers find them unpersuasive without evidence (Geddes 2002, 368). Dogan (1998, 109) worries that too many political scientists develop untestable models or apply complex statistical analysis to limited data.

realistic. When the results of a model seem to flow specifically from a special crucial assumption, then if the assumption is dubious, the results are suspect' (Solow 1956, 65). Cameron and Morton (2002) criticize those who attack the unrealistic assumptions of models; at least these assumptions are in the open whereas the assumptions of less formal research are often unappreciated even by the investigator (794) But modelers often forget their assumptions too. Importantly, then, this is an argument for clarity, not for a particular method.

- Models necessarily oversimplify.[36] 'Mathematical models are, as we have said, deliberately shorn of all the rich detail that makes people themselves so interesting. Foolish indeed are the mathematical modelers who confuse their abstractions with reality. But when used properly, mathematics schools our intuition in ways that no other technique can' (Richerson and Boyd 2005, 255). Simplification can be a valuable step in scholarly understanding, but the insights gained need to be placed in a realistic context.
- Models have little inductive potential. Solow (1998, 74-5) notes that economists should first look at reality and ask what is happening, but that model-builders often omit this step. In the study of growth, arguably what is most needed is more understanding of how the process unfolds in the real world.

The excellent survey paper by Acemoglu, Johnson, and Robinson (2005) provides some interesting insight into methodological attitudes toward the use of models in the study of economic growth. The authors are disturbed that while endogenous growth theory brought technology in, it left institutions outside of the analysis. They seek 'a unified framework' (389), which apparently for them means incorporating all key elements in one model. While their paper provides a laudable mix of formal modeling and case study analysis they conclude that 'the framework we outlined was largely verbal rather than mathematical, and thus, by its very nature, not fully specified' (463). I would suggest that we are more likely to appreciate the role of institutions in economic growth by embracing multiple theories (rather than insisting on only one) and looking at both quantitative and qualitative evidence (the latter may benefit little from formal modeling). It is not at all clear that a mathematical specification would usefully clarify the general role of institutions in growth. Empirically, their chief concern is that scholars 'lack the comparative static results that would allow us to explain why equilibrium economic institutions differ' (389). It seems that this goal drives them to downplay the possibility of path dependence, and instead seek a simple explanation in terms primarily of income distribution (see chapter 9). They argue further that it is because of their emphasis on comparative static results that economists stress the proximate causes of economic growth. At least indirectly, then, the emphasis on modeling has prevented economists from looking at the more interesting questions regarding the forces acting upon the proximate causes.

---

[36] 'Like John Maynard Keynes, I maintain that the flux of reality is too complex to be represented by a set of simultaneous equations' (Snooks 1998, 3).

3.2.5 Statistical Analysis

Statistical analysis is the dominant method in economics, and is increasingly popular in sociology and political science. A set of highly sophisticated techniques have been developed for coping with different types of data and estimating equations. The results of statistical analyses will often be cited in later chapters. Ideally such results are easily interpreted and value free. In practice, though, statistical analysis of the process of economic growth has proven problematic.

Aghion and Durlauf in the preface to their *Handbook of Economic Growth* (2005), note that 'One theme of [the empirical section] of this Handbook is that there exist limits to what may be learned about the structural elements of the growth process from formal statistical models' (xiii). Solow (2005, 6) in the first chapter is deeply suspicious of cross-country regressions given the huge differences in institutional structures between developed and developing countries (with the latter often having to be excluded from the data set); 'This is something that needs to be straightened out; and detailed analysis of institutions is probably a better method than cross-country regressions.'[37] 'The translation of any 'institutional' question into the language of an aggregative model is always tricky. The concepts and quantities that appear in an economic model need not be capable of expressing what a knowledgeable observer would like to say about institutional differences' (Solow 2005, 7).

Durlauf, Johnson, and Temple (2005) survey the literature on statistical analyses of economic growth. While guardedly optimistic about the future, they note that growth econometrics has been plagued by several serious problems. First, there are many more possible explanatory variables (they provide a seven page table of different variables that have been used) than countries, and thus it is difficult to conclude which are the most important. Moreover, regression analysis must assume the accuracy of the model generating the estimating equations, but there are several competing models of growth. The endogenous growth models involve important non-linearities, and the best method for estimating non-linear equations is still a subject of much dispute. Regression analysis tends to make the unrealistic assumption that all countries grow in the same way toward the same steady state; methods for dealing with the possibility of different steady states are in their infancy (and will face the problem of limited data points). More generally they note that growth models originally designed for developed countries are applied to less developed countries without any attempt to model the characteristics of poor countries – such as structural change as workers leave agriculture (647). For these and other reasons, growth econometrics has not achieved the 'standards of evidence routinely applied in other fields of economics' (558). The results of econometric analyses, even when different studies concur (and

---

[37] Elster (1993) warned of the limitations of cross-country regressions given that individual countries are complex and idiosyncratic. He urged the study of mechanisms – 'particular and partial causal links' – through a variety of methods and theories.

disagreement on most major issues is common) must thus be treated with caution. This is especially true for the consideration of long-run questions, for good data from before World War Two is available for only a few countries. The authors note that there is still a huge unexplained residual (which they argue cannot simply be assumed to represent differences in total factor productivity) in estimations of the causes of growth (607). The authors stress that statistical results cannot be taken as given but require the exercise of judgment as to their importance, reliability, and implications (582). This point – long championed by McCloskey – deserves emphasis, for it implies that the oft-heard argument that statistical analysis is more objective than other methods is at least exaggerated.

Laudably, the authors at many points thus urge that statistical analysis be complemented by other empirical methods. 'One implication of these limits [in statistical analysis] is that narrative and historical approaches have a lasting role to play in empirical growth analysis' (561). Case studies are advocated at many points. In particular case studies are necessary to identify the causal relationships that might underpin observed empirical correlations (646). Statistical evidence alone cannot distinguish among theories or causal factors. Case studies of why some countries are able to 'climb the ladder' of technological complexity faster than others will be especially valuable, as will those in the area of political economy [largely what we would call institutions] more generally because of the difficulty of measuring key variables (648). Moreover statistical analyses naturally stress variables that can be quantified, and are thus unbalanced in their treatment of the possible causes of growth (650).

Temple (1999) worries that parameters likely differ across countries. We will have much cause in this book to see that the assumption of common parameters across different countries is untenable. At best, then, regression results can be seen as a guide. Temple also worries that outliers dominate results. That is, a couple of countries with very fast or very slow growth affect the results disproportionately. Often, results are not robust to small changes in functional form: coefficients on many variables vary considerably depending on what other variables are included (and theory cannot tell us which to include).

Data limitations deserve special attention. Maddison is the only purveyor of data for many countries before the mid-twentieth century. While he draws on the work of others he also often makes heroic assumptions (such as assuming [2001, 248] that GDP in Austria, Denmark, Finland, and Sweden grew by 17 percent annually from 1500-1820). Likewise the Summers-Heston Penn data set dominates the study of post-1950 economic growth, but much guesswork was involved there, especially for the poorest countries. Economic historians have often been guilty of ignoring the fragility of estimates while running regressions (and the use of interpolation in generating data sets defies the assumptions of independence between data points required for statistical analysis), and macroeconomists will be even less accustomed to worrying about the possibility that the data is only a very rough estimate. Even in modern developed countries we have poor data on productivity in services, and hours worked; and there is huge debate about say, the effect of information technology on productivity in transport.

These problems in the statistical analysis of growth are superimposed on the general limitations of statistical analysis as a method:

- Notably even in the simple case of competitive market interactions, one cannot statistically distinguish supply curves from demand curves (since one only observes their intersection) without making simplifying assumptions. Manski (2000, 125 and elsewhere) urges economists to start by making only plausible assumptions, even at the cost of only being able to identify broad ranges of parameter values, and then identify which assumptions are necessary to narrow the range of estimates.

- The variety of econometric techniques available means that economists can often reach different conclusions from the same data. Slight differences in data set can also yield different results. Different statistical packages often produce different results. There has been much concern over the years that economists play with their data too much: choosing data series and tools that generate significant results. This situation might not be problematic if the profession paid greater attention to replication, and if it was able to achieve consensus in areas of disagreement over time (recall the discussion of meta-analysis above). In practice the pretence that statistical analysis is more scientific or solid in practice than other methods is clearly exaggerated.[38]

- The approach of this book, guided by the experience of Szostak (2003b), is predicated on an expectation that important causal relationships exist between almost any pair of phenomena. Yet a standard assumption in most statistical analysis is that there is no connection among explanatory variables but rather that they independently generate effects on the dependent variable. If causal relationships exist but are assumed away, the result is multicollinearity. Analysts can test for the degree of multicollinearity, but these tests in turn presume certain types of interaction. Care must thus be taken in interpreting the results of multiple regressions. The use of more flexible functional forms should be encouraged. And also one should look for other types of evidence that can convey a more nuanced understanding of the particular causal relationships at work.

- Regressions at best establish correlation, not causality. 'The key insight in the literature of twentieth century econometrics was the discovery of the conditional nature of economic knowledge. The justification for interpreting an empirical association causally hinges on the assumptions required to identify

---

[38] Amazingly Heckman (2000, 86) argues that 'Few empiricists now embrace the Cowles research program advanced by Haavelmo that remains the credo of most structural econometricians and is implicitly advocated in most econometrics textbooks.' Popperian falsificationism [now disdained by philosophers] underpins the old idea that models should be developed first, then tested, but in practice models are built up from data. Yet textbooks highlight the problems in testing models on the data that generated them (87). Empirical results are reported as if they had followed official practice (89).

the causal parameters from the data' (Heckman 2000, 47). Philosophers had long argued that the same data could justify multiple theories. Econometricians have developed different approaches to identification but each is problematic. Judgment must be exercised throughout the estimation process, and especially in interpreting correlation as causation.

- As Heckman has argued, estimation of simultaneous equation models has been frustrating in economics because stable causal relationships are only rarely found. Cameron and Morton (2002) recommend clarifying the precise causal relationships involved in theory, and further elaborating models. This in some ways fits well with the approach of this book, for stable causal relationships when they exist will likely hold only if a wide variety of other variables are held constant. The recommendation also seems to accord with the critique of Lawson (1999) that the economy is inherently an open system (that is, its phenomena are causally related to other phenomena), and thus that any statistical analysis must exclude important linkages and is thus inevitably mis-specified.[39]
- Regressions generally but not always have limited inductive potential. VAR regressions do not need a theoretical structure (but need to assume that parameters do not change). They are thus potentially inductive. Likewise, Geddes (2002, 365) applauds the inductive potential of throwing a wide range of variables into regressions and seeing what patterns emerge. She argues that Barro and Acemoglu, Johnson, and Robinson in studying the causes of democracy follow this strategy. Once empirical regularities are established, theories can be developed to deal with them. Yet data limitations will always limit the range of variables included. While inductive analysis is possible, most statistical analysis is deductive rather than inductive.

3.2.6 Case Studies

In discussing models and statistical analysis, most attention was focused on their weaknesses. This was because their applicability to the study of economic growth is widely appreciated. As we turn now toward methods that have been less commonly employed in the study of economic growth it is useful to reflect a bit more on the advantages. We begin by addressing the case study approach in general, and note that advocates of this approach can be found across disciplines.

'For many people, statistical research on growth seems rather cruder and less informative than historical case studies. Certainly it is important to remember that

---

[39] Lawson argues that the purpose of science is to uncover causal mechanisms, not the regularities that these might generate. He thus worries not just about openness, but also whether the variables we observe accurately represent the phenomena that are causally related (see Szostak 2004, ch. 2). And he notes that we do not really understand underlying causal mechanisms if we cannot explain why observed correlations differ across time and space.

growth regressions will never offer a complete account of the growth process, and that historical analyses must have an important complementary role' (Temple 1999, 119-20). Temple, an economist, later bemoans the lack of dialogue between history and empirical research (149).

The economist Rodrik (2003) encouraged and summarizes a series of country studies. Unfortunately little attempt at comparison is made. The case study approach allows the identification of causal forces that act over a long time frame (such as an argument that the seeds of Indonesia's post-1997 problems were planted during its previous success). They serve to identify sudden transitions between good and bad performance. They also identify idiographic elements (Mauritius benefited from special treatment of key exports, but also wise politicians as in Botswana). The editor stresses institutions, and downplays trade openness and geography, but the case studies could be read differently (since many of the success stories were countries that were open). The volume thus serves both to signal the advantages of the case study approach and also the need for careful comparison across cases.

The economic historian Greif (2006, 20-1) argues for theoretically informed case studies of particular institutions in order to inform our general understanding of institutions. He urges scholars to blend induction and deduction (ch.11).[40] Since game theory generates multiple equilibria, deduction alone cannot explain observed reality. Since some variables are unobservable, induction alone will miss much that is important. [We will critique Greif's argument that culture is unobservable in chapter 9, but can still accept the general point].

Political scientists Lane and Ersson (1997, 240) argue that case studies are 'necessary to unravel the complex links between the state and the market.' Vartiainen (1999) pursues comparative case studies. She argues (203) that it is not possible to generalize as much as economists wish given the diversity of institutions and paths to development.

The sociologist Ragin (2000, 33) argues that one advantage of case study analysis is that it shows how causal factors interact, rather than assuming independence. It is also possible to appreciate that several different combinations of causal factors may generate the same result.

Beyond the general advantages of methodological flexibility, we must appreciate that technological and institutional innovations are necessarily unique. Some elements of these cannot be quantified. We can only appreciate the essence of the process of technological or institutional innovation through qualitative analysis.

Case studies naturally have their problems too. Most obviously they can be idiosyncratic. Scholarly understanding only comes from the comparison of diverse cases. This is only possible if phenomena and causal relationships are carefully defined. Historians often fail to do so, and scholars in all disciplines are less

---

[40] Snooks (1998, 71) reports that a battle between induction and deduction in late nineteenth century economics was won by the latter, in part because it is easier to train deductivists. Snooks suggests that good inductivists require 25 years after graduate school before they hit their stride.

careful than they might be. Even when careful definitions are provided, comparison often faces the challenge (noted above with respect to statistical analysis) that there are more possible explanatory variables than cases.

Case studies cannot fully cope with the complexity of the growth process. Different scholars emphasize different elements. Woo-Cummings (1999, Preface) notes that different authors find different lessons in East Asian experience: some see markets at work and some see state direction. After the 1997 crisis, many scholars who had previously emphasized the positives now stressed the negatives. One problem with all of this literature is that it fails to recognize the many differences among East Asian countries. Along with careful definitions of phenomena and causal relationships, two other characteristics of good case study research are suggested by the literature on East Asia: respect for the diversity of historical experience (while nevertheless seeking generalization when possible), and open-minded non-ideological discourse. These characteristics are often missing.

3.2.6.1 Surveys and Interviews

In our discussion of theory, we suggested that understanding how people form attitudes might be very important. Economists have tended to be very skeptical of asking people what they think and why. When Alan Blinder co-authored a book in 1998 called *Asking About Prices*, the first half had to be devoted to justifying why it made sense to ask people how they set prices. Economists tend to assume that individuals act rationally, and thus that they need not be asked why they believe/act as they do. When asked, though, individuals mocked ideas cherished by economists, such as that they adjusted their prices in response to changes in the size of inventories. Some economists would respond that these people are misleading themselves, and actually do behave in accord with rational choice theory (and if they do not will lose in competition with those who do behave rationally). If, though, it can be established that people sometimes behave non-rationally – and the uncertainty surrounding many decisions guarantees this result – then there seems little choice but to ask people how exactly they develop beliefs about how to behave.

That being said, surveys and interviews have their limitations. Interviews especially are costly to administer, and thus dangers of biased sampling arise. Answers in both interviews and surveys depend on how questions are phrased and the order in which questions are asked. Individuals faced with multiple choice questions often wish to provide further detail; if open-ended answers are allowed, it may be difficult to interpret these or draw comparisons across individuals. Most seriously, individuals may lie to themselves and/or to others about why they do what they do, and what exactly they believe. Beliefs that are socially criticized (such as racist beliefs in Western society) or are embarrassing will be under-represented.

Sadly, individuals find it much easier to answer 'how?' questions than 'why?' questions. When asked why they did something, they will often respond with a description of how they did it. They may not have reflected previously on why they acted as they did. Or they may not wish to admit their motives. We will find in chapter 7 that survey results on institutional quality are often included in cross-country growth regressions. This is done for the most part due to the limited availability of alternative sources of data. It is noteworthy that survey results are accepted with little question in this instance while rejected out of hand elsewhere in the economics discipline.

3.2.6.2 Observation

Observation has been used even less than interviews or surveys in the growth literature. The exception is in science studies, where teams of scientists are often observed over time. This method has been less commonly applied to industrial research, in part due to difficulties in gaining access. Studying people on the floor of stock exchanges might establish how they interpret events.

Though discreet observation is possible, it is rarely employed. Both for ethical reasons and to allow freedom of observation, researchers generally make their presence known to those they study (though at times they are less than completely candid about their purpose). Informal (sometimes formal) interviews almost always form a part of participant observation processes: individuals are regularly asked why they did what they did. A key danger is that individuals will behave differently when being observed; this may not be possible if individuals are observed over a very long time period.

Observation may be the most inductive of all methods. Agents may often behave or think in ways totally unanticipated by the researcher. Or they may interact with others in important ways that had not previously been appreciated. We will discuss network analysis in chapter 9; networks are often studied through observation for this reason.

3.2.6.3 Experiments

Experiments have become increasingly common in political science, and have added insights in diverse area such as public opinion formation, voting behavior, and committee work. Experiments are also employed in economics, generally to study some of the more basic elements of microeconomic theory (that is, the theory of markets) or game theory. When experimental results differ from the predictions of theory, economists commonly reject the results rather than the theory.

Experimenters can now observe not only how individuals act but also their brain activity as they act. This allows some insight into why people act as they do. Experiments using brain imaging show that seemingly irrational behavior – such as rejecting offers in one-time ultimatum games (that is, giving up a present benefit with no chance of a future reward) – are associated with emotional rather than cognitive brain activity. Cohen (2005) notes that this sort of behavior is consistent with evolutionary selection: when humans interacted in small groups, it was then advantageous to punish others when these acted unfairly. Emotionally we act as if we anticipate future interactions with the same people even when cognitively we know this to be unlikely. In general, different parts of the brain are activated at different times, and make decisions in different ways.

One value of experiments is that one need not have a complete model of all the other variables that might influence a causal link, for the experiment can control for all. On the other hand, if one has ideas about what these might be, variations in other variables can be integrated into experimental design (Green and Gerber 2002, 810-11).

Experiments are better suited to the study of non-intentional agents. With intentional agents the question arises of whether agents behave the same in a laboratory. When intentional interactions are studied, does the artificially-formed group behave as real relationships or groups? Various adjustments in experimental design can mimic reality. In the end, though, experimental results need to be complemented by some method(s) that study people in real-world settings.

Experiments are very reliable – the same experiment can be repeated many times. But reliability is only possible because experiments are generally very simple: only a small number of variables are allowed to change within any one experiment. Experiments can thus identify certain causal mechanisms. Green and Gerber (2002) advocated linked experiments that address different elements in a causal chain. Nevertheless, experiments need to be supplemented by other methods when complex interactions are to be studied.

3.2.6.4 Textual Analysis

Many literary theorists claim that texts are inherently ambiguous: contradictory messages can always be identified. Yet most scholars would agree that central messages can usefully be identified. Nevertheless, the analyst should look for contradictions, and use these to clarify the thought process at work. As with interviews, the reader must be wary that the author has ulterior motives that may guide them to (consciously or not) shade the truth. The reader should ask what basis the author has for the claims they make. The act of reading is also subjective, and thus the reader needs to interrogate their own biases. This book will take the point of view that both sorts of biases can be mitigated enough that the central message of a text can generally be appreciated.

Language itself is ambiguous, and thus any one text must be placed in context: its words have meaning only within a particular conversation. While literary theorists often analyze texts only in the context of other texts, it is also useful to place texts in the context of understandings gained from other methods.

4 Relevant Disciplines and Disciplinary Perspectives

This chapter first identifies the key disciplines (and interdisciplinary fields) that must be engaged in this project. It then summarizes the disciplinary perspective of each. As will be argued below, disciplinary insights can only be understood and evaluated within the context of the 'disciplinary perspective' from which they emerge. The interdisciplinarian must strive to convince their audience that they understand both the insights and the relevant perspectives (Repko 2008). This chapter naturally draws upon chapters 2 and 3 since disciplinary perspective is grounded in and largely comprises the mutually compatible set of phenomena, theories, and methods that is chosen by the discipline. But disciplinary perspective is more than this, and attention must thus also be paid to ideological, ethical, and epistemological dimensions. In turn chapter 4 sets the stage for the evaluation of disciplinary insights in later chapters.

4.1 Which Disciplines Should be Engaged?

Which disciplines need to be engaged in this study? The previous chapters have indicated that the causes of economic growth likely include institutional, technological, cultural, social, and geographical elements. We can thus imagine that the various social science disciplines – economics, sociology, anthropology, political science, and geography – will need to be included in our purview. We must familiarize ourselves with the perspectives of each of these disciplines. We will also want to identify insights relevant to economic growth from each. We will not need to survey any of these disciplines in its entirety in this respect, but only those subfields of particular interest: the sociology of knowledge but not (for the most part) the sociology of religion. In doing so, we should, as ever, be careful of not being seduced by existing scholarship: we should ask ourselves not only what insights sociologists have generated but also what insights might have been generated by their unique perspective if they had paid more attention to growth.

Technology is studied not only in various disciplines but in the major interdisciplinary field of 'science and technology studies:' since technology and science is the only major category of phenomena discussed in chapter 2 that is not the primary focus of a discipline, this field might be thought to represent a missing discipline. Culture too is the focus of an interdisciplinary endeavor(s) termed 'cultural studies.' Marxian analysis also crosses disciplinary boundaries. Linguistics is not likely to play a central role in our discussions, though one can imagine that there are some economic advantages to a society in speaking one of the world's major trading languages (but perhaps disadvantages as well). Psychology may usefully guide us to understand why humans behave as they do in various

DOI: 10.1007/978-3-540-92282-7_4, © Springer-Verlag Berlin Heidelberg 2009

situations. It has been suggested that 'art' – the primary subject matter of the humanities – plays some role, though likely a secondary one, in the process of economic growth. Nevertheless, methods of textual analysis originating in the humanities are clearly important. Since both the processes of technological and institutional change have idiographic elements, they can only be fully appreciated through historical analysis; the discipline of history is thus at least potentially of great importance. Since the field of economic history combines economic and historical analysis, it will be treated as a distinct discipline in what follows.

We will thus largely limit our attention to the social sciences (including applied social sciences such as in business schools) and (less so) humanities in this work. It should be noted, though, that insights from the natural sciences and engineering contribute to our understanding of both past and future trajectories of technological innovation. Likewise, the health sciences inform our understanding of human capabilities in diverse circumstances. For example, if it is true that the tropics are less conducive to economic growth in part because of their effects on human health, then epidemiologists may have much to contribute to development policy in tropical regions (Snowdon 2002, 103 citing Sachs). We will in what follows rely for the most part on the use made by human scientists (social scientists and humanists) of understandings from beyond human science, but can appreciate the desirability of future interdisciplinary researchers in this area taking a closer look at the literature in natural science, engineering, and health science.

4.2 The Nature of Disciplinary Perspective

What strengths and weaknesses does each 'discipline' bring to the study of economic growth? This question involves an analysis of 'disciplinary perspective.' Interdisciplinarians have stressed that every academic community shares a set of attitudes that guides their collective research, but have struggled to define the key elements of 'disciplinary perspective.' I have argued elsewhere (2003b) that the theoretical and methodological preferences of a discipline and its choices of phenomena to study (and thus others to ignore) are key elements of disciplinary perspective. We thus inevitably combat some of the most central biases in diverse disciplinary perspectives simply by integrating across phenomena, theory, and method. But we do not necessarily capture all such biases in this manner. In particular, we should note that each community of scholars has some (largely unspoken) 'rules of the game' that determine what type of research is valued/accepted within that community. These rules determine the career success of members of the community, and thus encourage them to use the 'right' theory and method in order to analyze the 'right' set of phenomena. The rules also encourage adherence to other elements of disciplinary perspective.

Disciplines also differ in terms of ethical outlook. These differences can usefully be summarized in terms of the five broad types of ethical analysis identified in Szostak (2004, 2005a). Economists are predominantly consequentialist in outlook: institutions or attitudes are viewed positively if they yield good outcomes. Anthropologists tend naturally to value tradition. Sociologists and especially political scientists are much more likely to judge with respect to virtues: is an outcome fair or just? Marxians are broadly deontological in the sense of evaluating outcomes in terms of a firm idea of how the world should work. Humanists often appeal to intuition: good outcomes are those that feel good. As with any element of disciplinary perspective it is too easy to exaggerate such differences. Counterexamples abound in each case. And each discipline claims, albeit to different degrees, to perform value-free research. Yet the implications for our present topic can nevertheless be profound. Since economists view growth as a good outcome, they will support almost any growth-inducing practice (unless these obviously work against some other outcome they value such as freedom). Other social scientists will be tempted to argue against growth-enhancing policies that seem unfair or unjust or accord poorly with their sense of how the world should work. Yet we shall see that institutions thought to be fair and just are more likely to work, and thus can well imagine that a concern with fairness and justice might at times point toward superior strategies in both consequential and virtue terms. We will also see that there are good reasons to be cautious in changing societal institutions, and thus a respect for tradition can also usefully complement consequential analysis.

Disciplines also differ ideologically. These differences should not be exaggerated: we must embrace the idea of disciplinary perspective without needlessly stereotyping members of academic communities. Economists tend to think that markets work well in most situations and thus tend to be more suspicious *on average* of government intervention in the economy than other human scientists. But some economists are very interventionist while many political scientists argue that power is usually abused. Few academics are able to evaluate the case for markets versus governments dispassionately. Interdisciplinarians likely tend (as academic rebels) on average to be politically liberal or radical. The particular interdisciplinarian writing this book blends fiscal conservatism with social activism, and thus tries to rationally evaluate what works best in any situation. He also uses all five types of ethical analysis, not merely the consequentialism that the last statement might imply.

There are also epistemological differences. Economists tend on average to be unreconstructed positivists, believing that their theory and method allow objective analysis of the nature of the world. Other social scientists, and especially humanists, are much more skeptical of the possibility of accurate or unbiased perceptions of reality. Some even doubt the very existence of a unique external reality to be analyzed. These epistemological differences affect the sort of argumentation provided. Some scholars are dedicated to arguing 'from the evidence' while others feel free to argue from the societal goals they have decided to pursue. Both tend to downplay the biases that afflict their work.

4.3 Does Disciplinary Perspective Really Matter?

Two key objections can be briefly dealt with in turn: that disciplines do not matter, and that perspectives do not matter. Dogan (1998 and elsewhere) argues that interdisciplinary integration occurs at the level of sub-disciplines rather than disciplines. And we have appreciated above that we need not embrace all of political science and sociology, nor even economics itself, but rather just those insights and theories and methods relevant to the causes of economic growth. Should we then examine sub-disciplinary rather than disciplinary perspectives? To be sure sub-disciplines often communicate less with each other than they do with cognate sub-disciplines in other disciplines. And they may thus absorb some of the outlook of these others. In the case of economic growth, it is likely true that the attitudes of economists have been seriously engaged by those examining economic questions in other disciplines, though not always favorably. It will be useful as we proceed in this chapter to note when sub-disciplines may differ significantly from the rest of their disciplines in terms of perspective. In such cases it will be particularly important to ask how the broader discipline might have approached issues of economic growth. Yet the case for studying perspective primarily at the level of disciplines (or institutionalized interdisciplinary fields) is still strong for very practical reasons. Students gain their PhDs in programs managed by disciplines, and scholars are hired, granted tenure, and promoted by disciplines. These simple institutional facts of life provide a powerful incentive (often absorbed subconsciously) to behave in accordance with the expectations of those who will determine whether you have an academic career and how successful it is (Szostak 2002, 110). While sub-disciplines may (consciously or not) emphasize ways in which they differ from the rest of their discipline, they necessarily define themselves in relation to that discipline, and can only differ from it in some ways rather than all or the sub-disciplinarians would never be hired.

Does perspective matter? It is useful to stress at this point the importance of scholarly judgment. Members of most of the disciplines to be analyzed below believe that they pursue some objective path to truth. They would bridle at the very argument that their investigations are shaped by anything but the unbiased pursuit of truth. But scholarship is never perfect: there is no complete proof or even falsification of any argument (see chapter 3). This insight is now well accepted among philosophers of science, but can still astound scholars elsewhere (especially, perhaps, in economics). As McCloskey has noted on many occasions, even the statistical analyses favored by economists require the exercise of judgment as to whether the results are important (a step that economists often skip, she notes). Once it is appreciated that scholars cannot follow any simple formulaic path to enhanced understanding but must rather exercise fallible human judgment at every step of analysis, then the possibility that scholars are guided by disciplinary perspective – as well as more general human failings – must be admitted.

4.4 Disciplinary Perspectives of Relevant Disciplines

The negatives rather than the positives are emphasized below. While this might be thought to reflect an intellectual pessimism, it reflects rather the intent in the steps that follow to respect the output of each community unless there is a good reason for skepticism. In all cases a general discussion of disciplinary perspective is followed by an analysis of how this might affect the study of economic growth in particular.

4.4.1 Economics

4.4.1.1 Theory and Method

Economics is characterized much more than any other social science by theoretical and methodological agreement. The vast bulk of theorizing in the discipline involves some variant of rational choice theory. Mathematical modeling and/or statistical testing dominate the literature: almost all articles in economics journals today contain some formulae. The advantages of such a situation are obvious: conversation among economists is greatly facilitated by a shared theory and method. And an important element of the rules of the game is made transparent: *express your thoughts mathematically*. Yet the disadvantages of the situation are equally obvious: any insight that reflects an alternative theory or is best justified by recourse to an alternative method will have difficulty gaining a hearing. Note that many/most economists would worry little about this potential drawback, simply because they assume the superiority of their favored theory and method.

Of course, economists can point to exceptions: some papers that relax one or more of the assumptions of rational choice theory, and some efforts to employ experiments and even surveys in economic analysis. Yet those who try to publish experimental or survey results in general economics journals must always justify in detail their methodological choice, just as those relaxing a rational choice assumption must justify that decision. And thus these papers are subject to referee critiques of their basic theory and method, whereas papers pursuing the approved theory and method (which as we saw in chapter 3 are also imperfect) are not. Disciplinary perspectives are never ironclad, and thus the existence of a few exceptions should not surprise us. The fact remains that there are overwhelming incentives toward the use of one theory and one method.

Special note should be made here of methodological individualism. With the partial exception of game theory, economists rely almost exclusively on individual-level analysis. Macroeconomists even struggle to explain business cycles in terms of autonomous individual decisions. Other social scientists, as we shall see, have been much more open to group and relationship agency. In recent decades, these other disciplines have embraced methodological individualism to some degree. We can and will celebrate this opening to theoretical flexibility (if only rarely to integration of these different approaches). Still, we may have most to learn from these other disciplines when they engage group or relationship agency, for they are then most likely to generate insights distinct from those of economists.

Ideas foreign to the theoretical and methodological predispositions of the profession are generally ignored.[1] Several times I have heard stories of someone trying to explain an idea to an economic theorist and being told that they could/ would only understand the idea in the form of a mathematical model. Yet some insights are not easily modeled formally. And thus economics often simplifies insights. The dense argumentation of Keynes was soon turned into a simple mathematical model by Hicks and Meade. Marxian ideas were ignored unless they were squeezed into familiar form. Herbert Simon eventually won the Nobel Prize but his idea of bounded rationality was only accepted once it was formalized as a transaction cost. This book will make absolutely no attempt to translate the insights of other disciplines into formal models. Indeed the author firmly believes that ideas should be clearly stated in words foremost, and will thus translate formal models into words instead.[2]

Manski (2004) notes that several developments in economic theory (including endogenous growth theory itself) encourage economists to take a broader look at social interactions. Economists need to understand how expectations, preferences, and knowledge are generated. [In other words, economists need to care about attitudes.] But they are hampered by the imprecise definitions of terms such as social capital (see chapter 8). More fundamentally they are limited by 'the data that economists commonly bring to bear to study social interactions' (117): these allow economists to measure certain outcomes but not to identify how these might be generated by various processes of interaction. [Recall the discussion of the criteria for identifying a causal relationship in chapter 3.] Manski thus urges both experiments and 'careful elicitation of persons' subjective perceptions of the interactions in which they participate.' He later critiques the emphasis on formal models and equilibrium outcomes: 'it has become clear that many processes of substantive interest are too complex to be analyzed directly' (120). Manski notes that economists are trained to study what people do, not what they say, and thus economists

---

[1] The case study method is often unintentionally important when – as during the Great Depression, stagflation of the 1970s, or more recent efforts to curb pollution – it is felt that existing theory gives limited policy advice. But the effect is transitory unless the insights can soon be expressed within accepted theory and method.

[2] 'Economics is sick. Economics has increasingly become an intellectual game played for its own sake and not for its practical consequences for understanding the economic world. Economists have converted the subject into a sort of social mathematics in which analytical rigor is everything and practical relevance is nothing' (Blaug 1997, 3).

worry that surveys do not elicit careful or honest answers (131). He has found however that survey results do provide good predictions of consumer behavior.

Economists can with some justice claim to be more empirically oriented than (most) other human scientists. Statistical testing is common, and does indeed often lead to adjustments to economic models. Yet empirical observations that do not fit within the accepted theory and/or method are too readily ignored. Szostak (2005b) provides one important example. Hodgson (1999) notes that there was empirical evidence in the 1930s that firms did not maximize profits. However, theoretical arguments that only profit-maximizing firms would survive (an optimizing sort of evolutionary theory), in concert with a methodological argument that models with misguided assumptions could be used if they made good predictions, combined to keep the idea of profit maximization at the core of microeconomic theory. Note that economists in this case judged theories and models to be 'good' if they predicted profit maximization, because economists wished to assume this result in other theories and models, not because of evidence that firms in fact behaved that way. Only once ideas of firm routines and bounded rationality and information asymmetries could be formally modeled did (some) economists begin to consider the possibility that firm behavior might deviate considerably from simple profit maximization. 'We may open the pages of any leading mainstream economics journal to confirm the modern predilection is for the exploration of the characteristics of a model rather than the characteristics of reality' (Hodgson 1999, 3).

Interdisciplinarity naturally suffers in such an environment. Economists cite other social scientists much less than these cite economists, and textbooks in economics make little attempt to situate economics within a broader discourse (Gasper 2004). Psychological analysis was used early in the century by writers such as Keynes and Irving Fisher, but was replaced by optimizing behavior as mathematization proceeded postwar. Economists are belatedly working on the challenges of modeling more complex psychological behavior (Thaler 2000). But should the insights of other disciplines simply be ignored until they are dressed up to fit the methodological preferences of economists? This book is premised on the belief that this should not be the case.[3] Moreover, it joins Lawson (1999, 107) in worrying that even as economists strive to add psychological complexity to their models they constrain individuals to be predictable. Economists are thus more open to the idea of fixed routines than to other forms of decision-making (100-1). Psychological insights (as those from any other discipline) should be appreciated whether they are easily modeled or not.

There have long been minority traditions in economics: Marxians, post-Keynesians, Austrian economics, feminist economics, and so on. These have often

---

[3] Bunge (1998) suggests from a philosophy of science perspective various ways in which economics could become more scientific: eschew over-simplistic philosophies such as falsificationism, recognize the biases that affect scholarship, embrace psychological insights, appreciate but do not exaggerate the value of mathematics, operationalize theoretical concepts, emphasize dynamic disequilibria, recognize both individual and societal causation, and pursue interdisciplinarity. All of these are addressed in this book.

pursued the ideal of a separate single alternative to the mainstream. Each heterodox group can be seen as deviating from one or more of the theoretical (and/or
methodological) assumptions of neoclassical economics. From the perspective of
this book, then, economics would benefit from a variety of heterodox approaches.
Interestingly, these 'heterodox' groups have recently moved toward the embrace
of pluralism (with the formation of groups such as the Association for Heterodox
Economics and the International Confederation of Associations for Pluralism in
Economics). This move toward pluralism shares (though not self-consciously) the
values of interdisciplinarity: critical evaluation, and seeking a common ground
that takes the best from all approaches (Szostak 2008b). We will not survey
heterodox approaches in detail here but will reference them later as appropriate.

4.4.1.2 Closed Versus Open Systems

Lawson (1997) argues that the theory and methods of economics reflect a
mistaken belief in 'covering laws': that economics like physics can identify law-
like regularities between variables. He argues that covering laws are only possible
in closed systems, where extraneous variables cannot interfere with the relationship in question. The economy, he argues, is an open system, for the economic
variables that economists analyze are clearly causally related to a host of non-
economic phenomena. While this latter point is clearly true, one can argue that
the difference between economics and physics is one of degree rather than kind.
Physicists too must specify the circumstances under which particular causal relationships will hold (Lawson, 27, appreciates that there are indeed few law-like
relationships in physics, and these only hold when much else is held constant).[4]
Economists face a tougher challenge here – as noted elsewhere, they like other
social scientists are generally guilty of not carefully specifying the range of applicability of their theory. And given the role of human intentionality,[5] economists
can only at best suggest behavioral regularities (people will usually buy less
when prices rise) rather than laws. Though Lawson (1997) rejected mathematical
modeling, Lawson (2003) has recognized the value of this in at least situations ap-
proximating a closed system.

Lawson at various points lauds theory types neglected by economists which he
argues are more suitable to open systems: idiographic analysis (40), non-rational
decision-making (106), stochastic as opposed to equilibrium analysis (102), and
active as opposed to the passive (reactive) agency often assumed in economic

---

[4] Physicists use experiments while economists stress statistical analysis. Physicists would struggle
to identify precise relationships if they relied on statistical analysis of real-world occurrences, for
other variables would inevitably intervene.

[5] It is not, as Lawson suggests, that intentional behavior is stochastic. Potentially, we can seek to
understand the internal causes just as the external causes of human behavior. But the complex
interaction of these – with personality and schemas determining how an individual understands a
situation – makes it much harder to understand or predict intentional behavior.

models (78). We could hardly understand the course of institutional or technological innovation in terms of passive agents.[6] More generally, Lawson argues
that all theories must of necessity leave something out, and thus a full understanding of complex reality comes only from multiple theories.

Lawson urges us to be wary of theories that rest on unrealistic assumptions.
These may seem to explain occurrences in the real world, but are unlikely to
be robust to quite different circumstances. We will not review here the extensive
literature regarding Friedman's famous (and often exaggerated) claim that the
realism of assumptions is unimportant if the model provides good predictions.
The argument here – that we cannot be confident of the predictions unless we
understand the process that generates them – would be accepted by the majority of
economic methodologists. This does not mean that models with unrealistic assumptions are valueless, just that care must be taken in applying them. The careful
evaluation of assumptions will be a key component of interdisciplinary analysis
below.

4.4.1.3 Ideology

Economists are often accused of ideological bias. While the average economist
may indeed be politically more conservative than the average sociologist, a blunt
ideological argument misses more than it captures. The models of economists alert
them to how well the market can achieve socially desirable results under the right
circumstances. Those same models can be used to show that selfishly rational
politicians and bureaucrats will introduce policies that do not serve the public
interest. Of course economists' models also define various situations in which
markets do not work well: when there is monopoly power, when there are external
(that is, non-priced) costs such as pollution, and when there are external benefits
(such as when I benefit from my neighbor hiring a security service).[7] Given that
neither governments nor markets are perfect, scholars should look situation by
situation at which is less bad. Economists are prone to emphasizing governmental
failure over market failure, and many other social scientists are prone to the opposite bias. The interdisciplinarian is in the happy position of integrating across these
countervailing biases, but should be careful of assuming that (as opposed to investigating whether) any result from any discipline reflects such a bias.

---

[6] Heterodox economists generally critique economics on one or more of these grounds. They are
also much more likely to reject methodological individualism in order to emphasize classes or
other social groups. In chapter 3, we treated rational choice theory as emphasizing active action,
but noted that the assumption of rationality allows economists to assume that the individual
merely reacts to the choice set they face.

[7] Hodgson (1999, 31-2), despite his powerful critique of economics, doubts that it is accurate to
claim a pro-market bias as many exceptions can be found. He does, though, appreciate that
economic theory simplifies markets and thus under-appreciates the roles markets play: Lange
would not have thought planners could mimic markets otherwise.

4.4.1.4 Disciplinary Perspective and Economic Growth

While the question of how disciplinary perspective affects the study of economic growth can only be addressed fully after the insights of economists have been evaluated in later steps, some fairly obvious implications can be identified at this point. Foremost, the theoretical and methodological predilections of the discipline have caused economic growth to be studied much less than an outsider might have imagined. Indeed, despite its obvious importance, economic growth has received limited attention from economists over the last century relative to (less important) questions of business cycles or competitive market behavior. This has occurred precisely because economists had nice mathematical models in the latter cases but not the former. There was a flurry of activity in the 1950s and 1960s associated with the 'neoclassical' growth models of Solow and Swan, but growth almost disappeared from the main economics journals in the 1970s – partly because the stagflation of the 1970s refocused attention on fluctuations, and partly because research within the neoclassical tradition ran out of steam. [In the eighteenth and nineteenth centuries, classical economists such as Adam Smith emphasized economic growth in their non-mathematical formulations.] Within the last two decades, a sizeable minority of economic theorists have engaged questions of economic growth, following the development of endogenous growth models in the 1980s (and also the availability of new data sets), though it is widely appreciated that the insights embodied in these models had been known for decades (see chapter 3). The interdisciplinarian should naturally wonder what insights have been missed because they do not fit these theoretical and methodological predilections.

Rodrik (2006, 976) celebrates the fact that the World Bank has belatedly recognized that 'government failures that affect accumulation or productivity change are much more costly, and hence more deserving of policy attention, than distortions that simply affect static resource allocation.' Why would the World Bank for so long have stressed static efficiency over growth (even though its mandate is growth)? The obvious answer is that economists had a well-developed body of theory that suggested very particular policies for achieving efficiency, and relatively little to say about growth.

The curricula of economics departments reflect this situation. Courses devoted to economic growth are rare. Economic growth has generally been covered explicitly only as one topic in senior-level courses on macroeconomics (that is, theories of business cycles). In the last few years textbooks have finally appeared that are suitable to an introductory course on growth. These inevitably emphasize elements such as rates of investment that can be most easily captured mathematically.

Baumol (2000, 11-3) argues that it is just a historical accident that growth theory is associated with macroeconomics. The insights that growth theory provides guide us to pay more attention to the essentially microeconomic issue of how to stimulate technological innovation [though the link between cycles and growth is important and will be addressed in chapter 10.]. Endogenous growth models themselves cannot answer that question. Of particular importance for our present purpose, Baumol (14) notes that growth models are ahistorical and thus tell us little about why particular countries succeed or fail. The obvious solution to this problem is to complement these models with detailed case study analyses of particular times and places. We will also find that care must be taken with the empirical insights Baumol celebrates: these too tend to be much more time-and-place specific than is generally appreciated in the economics literature.

Institutions were an important component of economic analysis through most of the eighteenth and nineteenth centuries, but in the methodological battle of the late nineteenth century abstraction won out over contextual analysis (Swedberg and Granovetter 2001, 4), and an understanding of economic processes as being embedded in larger evolutionary processes (Outhwaite 2000, 49).[8] Economics in pursuing formal models of wide generalizability detached itself from the study of institutions. It is not easy to reintroduce institutions into economic analysis.[9] Economists have – inspired by the work of economic historians – devoted renewed attention to institutions in recent years. But there has been an understandable tendency to assume that institutions are a result of rational decision-making and thus (though this does not necessarily follow) that observed institutions are likely the optimal solution to some economic challenge. The interdisciplinarian should worry that institutions will be both under-appreciated and over-simplified.

Economists can take justifiable pride in the clarity of their terminology. As economists step gingerly toward the integration of social and cultural variables into their understanding of growth, however, terminological confusion reigns. Economists varyingly argue that countries need 'social capital', 'social capability', or 'social infrastructure', but these terms are vaguely defined (Jones in Snowdon 2002, 360). One of the purposes of this book is to identify key social and cultural influences more carefully.

What of ideology? I have argued elsewhere (2005b) that economists have exaggerated the importance of money over real variables in their analysis of the causes of the Great Depression. This in turn arguably reflects a bias toward imagining that markets will function well if properly managed and thus that economic calamities must be due to government mismanagement. Interestingly, economic historians have joined economists in their exclusive focus on monetary explanations of the Great Depression, though they emphasize other factors in their explanations of all other periods of economic history. Eichengreen, an economic historian who has argued that the Great Depression should be attributed to the operation of the Gold Standard, provides a quite different explanation of the post-war boom: 'The fundamental factor underlying the "golden age" was the backlog of technology that, owing to the Depression of the 1930s and Second World War,

---

[8] Hodgson (2003) notes that the losers in this methodological battle such as the German Historical School had stressed an accumulation of facts and failed to show how theories could be grounded in these facts. He recommends a balance between specificity and generalization.

[9] Jones (2002, 40) attributes incautious lending in East Asia before the crisis of 1997 to the fact that the economists working for Western financial institutions had never been taught about institutions, and thus did not appreciate the weakness of financial regulation.

hadn't been commercialized and fully exploited, especially in Europe' (in Snowdon 2002, 311). But then maybe the Depression (and perhaps also the stagflation of the 1970s which puzzles Eichengreen and others) was in part due to a limited supply of technological innovations? Actually, this is too simplistic: the problem was too little new product innovation coupled with an abundance of labor-saving process innovation (Szostak 1995). Is this an isolated example? Arguably, the recent focus of economists and the IMF on balanced budgets and monetary policy without concern for the effects on public spending on real things like schools reflects a similar bias.

4.4.1.5 Development Economics

Economic growth was naturally of interest to two connected subfields of economics: economic history (which examines the historical development of economies) and economic development (which focuses on postwar less developed economies). Both of these fields have dwindled in importance (in terms of relative numbers of economics professors) over the last decades. Both have attempted a balancing act between responding to the methodological expectations of the wider profession and trying to respect the complexity of the growth processes they studied.[10] Paul Krugman – one of the more open-minded of modern economists, I might note, wonders 'Why did development economics fade away ... the leading development economists failed to turn their intuitive insights into clear-cut models that could serve as the core of an enduring discipline' (1995, 23-4).[11] Economic history differs enough from the rest of economics as to be treated as a separate discipline below. Economic development is similar enough to economic history that its insights and perspective can be subsumed under that of economic history for our purposes. It would have been desirable if these two subfields were more strongly linked in practice: development advice and research should be informed by understanding how present-day developed countries achieved their success, while economic history research could usefully be informed by questions of modern policy relevance in less developed countries.[12]

---

[10] 'The first post-World War II generation of development economists attached considerable importance, at least at the rhetorical level, to the role of cultural endowment, social structure, and political organization in the process of economic development. But professional opinion did not deal kindly to the reputation of development economists who made a serious effort to incorporate knowledge from other social science disciplines to development theory or to the analysis of the development process ... Their work typically received favorable reviews – and then was promptly ignored' (Ruttan 2000, 3)

[11] To be sure the decline of development economics also reflected the poor quality of much of the early policy advice. Among other things, development economics proffered highly generalized advice; it is increasingly appreciated that different countries require different advice.

[12] Chang (2002, 9) bemoans the existence of only a few works that explicitly attempt to draw lessons from history for developing economies. More generally, he regrets the fact that neoclassical theory has squeezed a long tradition of historical sensitivity out of economics.

4.4.2 Economic History

Economic history is treated here as a separate discipline for multiple reasons.[13] It is logically an interdisciplinary field, combining economic and historical approaches. While in practice the vast majority of economic historians reside in economics departments, an important minority in both North America and especially some European countries are housed in history departments. A few distinct economic history departments still survive outside of North America, though most have disappeared over the last decades. More important than its institutional distinctness, economic history can be distinguished from economics by theory and method. To be sure, the cliometric revolution which began in the 1960s stressed both the application of neoclassical economic theory and the use of mathematical models and statistical tests. In North America, and to a lesser extent elsewhere, cliometrics squeezed out an older tradition of descriptive economic history. One unfortunate side effect was the serious diminution of the interdisciplinary nature of the field as historians abandoned economic history and moved instead into social history (and other social science historians found less cause to interact with economic historians). Happily, as the cliometric revolution has consolidated itself, the field of economic history has come to appreciate both the value of alternative theories (such as evolutionary theory) and the value of a case study approach to the examination of technological and institutional change. While the majority of articles in economic history journals may still bear a strong resemblance to those in economics journals (albeit hopefully with a greater attention to historical detail), a significant minority are quite different in approach. This is of great importance, for it is these case study analyses that generate the greatest insights of economic historians into the causes of growth (see Szostak 2006).

Having argued for the distinctiveness of economic history, it can still be maintained that it is not distinct enough. This is hardly surprising, given that the vast majority of economic historians reside in economics departments. They must convince these departments to hire them, give them tenure and promotions, and offer their courses.[14] Less obviously, but also importantly, economic historians being human will likely prefer it if those they work closely with every day see some value in their work. So while the avenues to theoretical and methodological flexibility are much greater in economic history, the pull of the mainstream is still strong. Most economic historians thus do at least some 'mainstream' research, especially early in their careers.

---

[13] Swedberg (2000) also treats economic history as a separate discipline from economics.

[14] Economic historians have dwindled in numbers in many countries as retirees have not been replaced. Eichengreen (in Snowdon, 1998, 304-5) believes this practice is most common outside the top departments because there 'method dominates substance.' Yet ironically by aping the method of other economists economic historians have reduced their ability to claim that they add something unique.

The cliometric revolution can be hailed in many respects. It promoted analytical clarity among economic historians: almost all work in the field now asks one or more fairly precise questions and strives to answer these (albeit with the almost inevitable side effect of pretending to more precise answers than one can provide). Yet in stressing mathematical modeling it discouraged the pursuit of insights best expressed in some other way. It also encouraged economic historians to quantify that which can be quantified (though this practice is inevitably associated with the temptation to put precise numbers on variables for which the data is simply too weak). Cliometrics can also be applauded for encouraging greater efforts at generalization, though most work in the field still stresses particular times and places and is not as explicitly comparative as it might be (the pursuit of generalizable theory may nevertheless have dissuaded economic historians somewhat from careful attention to historical detail and the pursuit of the idiosyncratic).

Economic historians have studied both institutions and technological innovation in much greater detail than have economists: it would scarcely have been possible to make sense of the grand sweep of economic history otherwise.[15] More generally, the attempt to understand particular events and processes has guided economic historians to engage exogenous causal factors such as culture or politics. Economic history benefits not only from a broader topical focus but also a broader temporal focus. Economists for the most part study only the last few decades and thus miss insights into the longer run aspects of economic growth. And an emphasis on only a few decades dissuades economists from an appreciation of the discontinuities in economic growth itself and also in the processes of technological and institutional innovation. Yet in stressing quantification economic history itself discouraged research on periods with limited data availability (Jones 2002) and thus limited our understanding of very long run economic growth.[16]

In sum, we can applaud economic history for its openness to a broader range of theories, methods, and phenomena, and also for examining a wider range of historical experience. We should nevertheless be wary of a strong preference within the field for mathematical modeling and quantification even when these approaches are ill-suited to the question at hand. And we should also be aware that efforts at generalization have proceeded less far than they might.

---

[15] 'Within our profession it is economic historians who have most carefully examined the role of institutions' (Charles Jones, growth theorist, in Snowdon 2002, 346). 'Economic historians know more about the mechanisms of growth than either macro theorists or macroeconometricians' (Ken Hoover, macroeconomist, in Snowdon, 339). Vartiainen (1999, 201-2) is horrified by the limited attention economists have paid to institutions – since markets depend on supportive institutions, but appreciates that economic historians have emphasized institutions.

[16] Freeman and Louca (2001, 5) argue that cliometrics attempted to linearize history. I myself have often thought cliometrics tended to smooth away the turning points in history: the Industrial Revolution, Great Depression, major innovations, all masked by seemingly smooth GDP series (often created by interpolating). Freeman and Louca note that an evolutionary perspective points instead toward the appreciation of random mutations. More controversially, they suggest (13) that economic history pursued only 'ideologically safe' topics. I myself have identified a potential ideological bias in approaches to the Great Depression (see above).

4.4.3 History

Historians were jolted from complacency in the early postwar years and forced to recognize that history as written was far from identical to either history as it occurred or history as it was recorded at the time. Historians necessarily bring some 'frame of reference' to historical analysis with which they order their account. It was widely suggested by leading historians in the 1960s and 1970s that the best 'frame of reference' was social science theory. However, if historians became involved in social science debates, they would become partisan and likely to bias their historical accounts. The best path, then, was to be minimally aware of social science theory and certainly never seek to contribute to theoretical debates. McDonald (1996) fears that this misplaced concern with bias is the major reason that historians do not engage theory more forcefully.

A quite different approach is arguably preferable. Historians should clearly outline the theoretical perspective they pursue. Historians can then help to identify the range of applicability of theory, detail the time path of a causal relationship itself, and identify realizations of other phenomena that are important or necessary or sufficient for a causal mechanism to operate. These latter tasks will be especially important when the theory itself is poorly specified. As Reuschmeyer (2003, 328) recognizes, far too many of the so-called theories employed by historians fail to specify 'what is referred to, by whom, and under what conditions.'

To be sure, this approach may tempt some historians to bias historical accounts toward a particular theoretical position. However, such biases would become more explicit: at present historians often do not disclose their guiding theories. The important question is whether the historical enterprise as a whole is biased: if different historians are explicit about the different theories they apply, the community of historians will be much better placed to transcend bias than if theory is only implicit. And an explicitly comparative approach provides further opportunities for competing visions to be compared and contrasted. Finally, recall that scholars (and scholarly communities) are often guilty of choosing phenomena, data, and method that will support their favored theory: interdisciplinarians have long celebrated the fact that openness to the widest range of phenomena, data, and method provides a powerful antidote to theoretical bias.

As hinted above, historians are not as explicitly comparative as they might be. While the idea of comparative research is generally applauded, there are concerns that few historians are familiar enough with multiple cases to be able to perform comparative research well (almost all of those interviewed by Pallares-Burke, 2003, betray both sentiments). Comparative research is hampered by the fact that historians only rarely make explicit causal arguments or even carefully define the phenomena of study.[17] Comparisons are only feasible if different historians are clear about what they are studying. Terminological confusion provides a further

---

[17] The philosopher Dilthey had criticized Hegel and others for oversimplifying historical processes but still maintained that history was an important means of understanding causal links.

barrier: historians speak of 'guilds' in China, for example, but these were not independent of government and could thus not serve the bargaining role on behalf of merchants and artisans as they did in Europe.

Specialization of historians by time and place has a further negative impact: the very long run is only rarely studied (Jones 2002). The increasing interest in 'world history' or 'global history' may change this. It may also encourage a greater focus on comparison and even explicit theorization.

For our purposes the limited amount of explicit analysis and explicit comparison means that historical research has not generated the generalizations that it might have. Historians often identify important idiographic results. But even these may not be obvious to social scientists because historians will not have related their findings to the prediction of any theory, or indeed have even made an explicit causal argument.

4.4.4 Business History

Before the 1960s, business history was for the most part an isolated subdiscipline producing works of great detail but with little theoretical content. The work of Alfred Chandler was important in introducing a theoretical orientation to the field (and also in encouraging a comparative approach – he would in various works compare firms, industries, and countries). Chandler argued that technological developments had encouraged/generated the development of the modern multidivisional corporation, and discussed how the institutional character of that corporation solved various problems associated with the generation and application of modern technology. Business historians in the Chandlerian tradition implied that the modern corporation was the efficiency-maximizing endpoint of a lengthy process of economic development. European business historians were somewhat more likely to be suspicious, given the continued importance of large family firms on the Continent. As the information technology revolution opened up an enlarged role for small firms and for networks between firms, business historians everywhere increasingly studied these aspects of the business environment. Piore and Sabel's *The Second Industrial Divide* was an important work here. Chandler himself in his most recent books on the electrical and chemical industries has stressed the symbiotic relationship between small and large firms in both sectors. At the same time, the Chandlerian approach was criticized for ignoring the institutional and social environment in which firms operate: the modern corporation was arguably shaped less by technology than by decisions made by the American government that favored the corporate form over alternatives. There has thus been an increased focus on institutional differences across countries, and a retreat from the previous tendency to assume that outcomes observed in the Anglo-Saxon world were optimal. As the theoretical and empirical range has expanded in business history, the field has become more interdisciplinary: political science has encouraged an emphasis on the struggle for power among businesses (though Chandler and others stress that big firms still only emerge if suited to the technology), and evolutionary economics, economic theory (game theory and asymmetric information in particular), sociology, corporate finance, and corporate governance have all been drawn upon by business historians. This eclecticism has likely been encouraged by the tendency of business schools to emphasize (relative to social sciences) real world relevance over theoretical unity. There has also been a greater attention to technological history, and recognition that the Chandlerian approach may be better suited to the Second Industrial Revolution of the late nineteenth century than to any other period. While internalist histories of particular firms are still common, there is an increased effort to place firm behavior in a broader context. Comparative studies have always been urged but only rarely performed, though there are signs that this is changing. Business historians are still somewhat more likely to stress the causes of different types of business organization rather than the effects; this limits the insights they have to offer into the causes of economic growth (See Amatori and Jones 2003).

4.4.5 Cultural Studies

This term denotes several rather than one unified community. '[T]he scholarly study of cultures and cultural processes has been radically affected by trends in sociology, philosophy, linguistics, and elsewhere, and cultural studies as a discipline, if such it is, stands today as a fragmented and contested domain' (Throsby 2001, 154). The common characteristic is a belief that culture is important. Such a belief carries an inherent danger: that the importance of culture will be assumed rather than stressed. The first use of the term 'cultural studies' was by the Birmingham School, and for them the term denoted a political project. They argued that the best way to achieve political progress was to encourage cultural progress, for progressive cultural ideas would eventually be instantiated politically. Such a program was especially popular with the large group of leftist intellectuals disenchanted by the declining fortunes of socialism in various countries. Lacking a clear goal in political activism, they could embrace a project that promised an alternative path to societal change. With not just scholarly identity but their very purpose in life associated with a belief that culture matters, the bias toward finding precisely that effect might be particularly strong.

Nevertheless, such a bias (and recall that all disciplines can be expected to exaggerate the importance of 'their' phenomena) should be investigated rather than assumed by the interdisciplinarian. Here a much graver, though not insurmountable, problem arises. Culture is defined in literally thousands of distinct ways in the literature. Writers are notoriously careless in clarifying what is meant by the term in a particular study. Yet my own experience reading extensively in the literature is that one can usually identify which subset of the phenomena identified in Table 2.1 (note that some non-cultural phenomena are often subsumed under culture by scholars) are important to a particular study (Szostak 2003b). The interdisciplinarian must then evaluate the evidence phenomenon by phenomenon.

Ironically, then, the practice of cultural studies, whereby definitions of concepts and statements of causal arguments are much less clear than they might be, makes it hard for the importance of culture to be appreciated outside the field. Interdisciplinarians have two important tasks here. They must first seek to identify important cultural arguments. And they must second urge scholars of culture toward much greater clarity.

4.4.6 Development Studies

Larrain (1998) treats this as an interdisciplinary field, though he stresses sociological elements. He notes that it has flipped from extremes of modernization theory to extremes of dependency theory and back again. There are many theories which straddle many disciplines. Since there is no unified body of 'development studies,' we can evaluate the insights of these various theories in terms of their disciplines of origin.

4.4.7 Political Science

Political science is concerned with the exercise of power within societies. Since the state is the most powerful organ in modern societies, it is not surprising that states have been the main focus of political science. Similarities to the exercise of power in other contexts, such as in the family or the marketplace, may thus have been neglected.

'Characterized by a wide variety of questions, methods, and borrowings from other disciplines, [Political Science] is distinct from the crisp methodological individualism that marks postwar neoclassical economics or analytical philosophy. It is also less permissive and open than, say, the fields of English literature or anthropology in recent decades' (Katznelson and Miller, 2002, 3). The discipline has focused primarily on the study of liberal political regimes, and increasingly of democracy itself – especially in the study of American institutions, but also in political theory (which stresses social contracts), comparative politics (which compares liberal regimes with others) and even international relations (which often asks how liberal regimes can survive in an anarchic world). It until recently left questions of social bias and race to sociologists, but each of these areas is now important. It has concerned itself with how institutions can be constructed to limit the abuse of political power. European political scientists have tended to a unitary conception of the state whereas American political scientists have stressed particular institutions. Political science early distinguished itself from shorter-term policy analysis. It has focused primarily on the interactions between the state and civil society – thus public opinion, voting, legislative behavior, and interest representation have been important. Though the relative emphases have changed through time, political scientists have always recognized that the state is a combination of institutions, norms, and power relations; naturally scholars differ in how these interact (Katznelson and Miller 2002, 3-17).

Lasswell famously defined politics as decisions about 'who gets what, when and how,' but contemporary theorists doubt that distributional issues dominate either the motives for or results of exercises of power (see Goodin and Klingemann 1998, 8). Nevertheless, political scientists are guided to a suspicion that power is exercised primarily in the interests of some rather than all. Still, while some political scientists are as likely as economists to stress the selfish motives of political actors, most stress a mix of selfish and altruistic motives in policy making.

Our efforts at integration in this book will be greatly aided by a contemporary celebration of integration within political science itself. Both the behavioral revolution of the 1950s and 1960s, and the more recent 'rational choice' revolution, had involved bitter exchanges between those who argued on the one hand that all analysis should start from an examination of individual intentions, and those who conversely argued for the longstanding emphasis on the effects of institutions and the overall 'structure' of society. It is now widely accepted in the discipline that individuals both influence and are influenced by institutions (Goodin and Klingemann 1998, 11). The term 'new institutionalism' is often used to describe this consensus. This result reflects in part the spread of economic analysis to the discipline. We may as interdisciplinarians have most to learn from political scientists that do not exclusively embrace the methodological individualism or stress on selfish motives of economists.[18]

Methodologically this integrative impulse is reflected in the recognition of both generalizability and complexity. This in turn allows a place for both large-scale statistical analyses and careful case studies (Goodin and Klingemann 1998, 12). Testing formal models statistically was rare in political science as late as 1995, but not now (Cameron and Morton 2002). 'Political science – indeed social science as a whole – benefits from the coexistence and competition of varied approaches to theory and research. And it benefits even more from dialogue that crosses distinct traditions.' (Pierson and Skocpol 2002, 719). Historical analysis has an extensive pedigree in the discipline, and the insight of historical institutionalism that particular historical circumstances shape institutions which then have enduring effects (that is, path dependence) is now well accepted in the discipline. Historical study also stresses the mutual interdependence of various institutions and cultural elements.

---

[18] More generally political science has been characterized by much more rapid change in theory than in economics. 'But only a handful of theories formulated before World War II are still alive.' (Dogan 1998, 108).

Nevertheless, Pierson and Skocpol (2002, 717) warn of the dangers of both a single-theory-driven agenda and a single-method-driven agenda in political science. They are skeptical also that understanding of the big picture will emerge from careful analysis of small questions. They argue that their field of historical institutionalism is protected from these temptations by its focus on big questions. Our experience above with theories of economic growth in economics should lead us to expect that interest in big questions is no certain antidote to these biases.

There are three main empirical approaches in political science: rational choice modeling, behavioralist surveys, and historical institutionalism (Pierson and Skocpol 2002, 693). The last has many varieties. But all varieties address big questions (of interest beyond political science), take time (history) seriously, and look at the combined effects of institutions and processes (695-6). They are concerned with contingent processes and thus do not model general processes. They generally embrace path dependence: institutions, schemas, and 'patterns of mobilization' are each likely self-reinforcing (700) This provides an antidote to functionalist assumptions that observed institutions must serve the purpose they were designed for. Also common are threshold effects which allow slow processes to have sudden effects (703). Political scientists focusing on the present may identify trigger mechanisms but not deeper causes; historical institutionalism stresses the deeper causes. However, historical institutionalism is criticized for relying on a small number of cases, and choosing atypical cases (where an interesting result has occurred) while ignoring other cases (713). Potentially at least, historical institutionalists can both compare across cases with different results and rigorously examine mechanisms within a particular case; most importantly individual studies are often built upon cumulatively (714-5).

4.4.7.1 Institutionalism

Rothstein (1998, 135) argues that political science is basically about the causes and effects of political institutions. But he notes that the standard subfields of the discipline are not organized logically about the study of institutions. In particular, comparative politics often involves the study of any aspect of some other country's politics. [As in economics] political science in the early postwar period emphasized theories of behavioralism or structuralism in which the precise shape of institutions was ignored: political institutions were assumed to reflect some needs of the wider society. This began to change in the 1980s not just in political economy but also in international relations, comparative politics, and even Marxian analysis. This was in part a reaction to the 'failure' of behavioralism or structuralism (or Marxian analysis) to generate workable hypotheses. But Rothstein also suggests that it reflects an appreciation that the world was not relentlessly converging, and that differences in institutions might explain rather than just reflect differences in political mobilization and class solidarity [that is, that there was path dependence]. Historical institutionalism emerged as an approach to understanding how particular institutions (of the state) shaped historical processes (Rothstein, 135-42). [19]

The field of political economy[20] focuses on two central questions: how do institutions evolve, and how do they affect the performance of economic and political systems? (Alt and Alesina 1998, 645). The field thus overlaps with political institutionalism: indeed they are hard to distinguish definitionally. The difference lies in theoretical orientation: rational choice is stressed in political economy, and institutions are seen as the equilibrium outcome of some social game. Nevertheless Alt and Alesina note that 'the actual evolution of institutions looks nothing like the aggregate purposive implementation or even decentralized natural selection of efficient forms' (645). As in economics, the interdisciplinarian must worry that the optimality of observed institutions will be assumed rather than shown.

4.4.7.2 Other Fields

One important characteristic of modern disciplines is their fragmentation into sub-disciplines. Interdisciplinary analysis is facilitated by the simple fact that for any question – even a big question like the causes of economic growth – the interdisciplinarian need only address in detail a minority of fields within any discipline. In political science our emphasis will be on the study of institutions. We can largely ignore the field of political behavior: why do people vote, and bother to become informed?; how do networks influence political preferences?, what is the role of the media? To be sure such questions may be important as we try to understand why some countries achieve superior institutions to others, but we can hope that the literature on institutions itself will address such a question and draw on the literature on political behavior.

Comparative politics is a major field. Incredibly, however, this has no substantive focus, beyond the emphasis on comparison. Some have thus suggested that it should not be a separate field of study. Teaching and research in the field is often organized around the study of some other country with little explicit comparison. More usefully the field also performs a variety of explicit comparisons, and investigates best practices for comparative analysis. But comparative research characterizes both other subfields and other disciplines too. In the last decades,

---

[19] Rothstein (142) provides examples: constitutions of Sweden, Britain, US, influenced distribution of tax burdens more than organizational strength of classes; relative power of courts versus legislature influenced different strategies of British versus American unions; administrative capacities of government are crucial for path of social and labor market policy.

[20] Robotham (2005) defines an alternative form of political economy in terms of an emphasis on who controls the mode of production (and how: what are the relations of production?) in contrast to the emphasis of others on exchange. The labor theory of value and exploitation are stressed [it seems that exploitation is not carefully defined]. The early emergence of private property in Europe, in contrast with various sorts of communal property right in Asia and Africa, is seen as crucial to European advances in production.

comparative politics has sacrificed global scope in favor of more detailed analysis of institutions in a few countries (this reflects an increased appreciation of the value of small focused comparisons). Naturally there has been much interest in what forms of democracy less developed countries should choose (Dalton 1998). There has been a blossoming of studies of democratization, but due to the complexity of the process and the vague terminology often used little in the way of theoretical generalization or consensus has occurred.

The field of international relations can largely be ignored. Of course, a country's economic prospects may be affected by its place within international alliances. But the field understandably has focused on how to achieve peace rather than economic growth.

The field of political theory (political philosophy) takes as its starting point the ideal that political actors at least some of the time pursue social ideals. While we shall see (and other fields of political science show) that this is often not the case, we should not abandon the identification and pursuit of ideal political forms. The concerns of political philosophy are largely beyond the scope of our present investigation, but we should not lose sight of the goal of creating polities that provide the maximum amount of justice, fairness, and self-actualization. We might even be willing to sacrifice some economic growth toward the achievement of such goals. Happily we will find below that just and fair and participatory governments support growth. While political philosophy is overwhelmingly liberal in orientation, there is some debate about whether the ideal form of government varies culturally, a possibility that should not be forgotten (nor assumed).

The subfield of public policy analysis is associated more with the interdisciplinary field of policy analysis than with political science: all major journals are interdisciplinary. The emphasis on practical insight separates the field from the more theoretical interests of the rest of the discipline. While most research has been done in the American context alone, the subfield of comparative policy has investigated how policy outcomes vary across polities (with the general result that economic variables are more powerful than political variables, though this may reflect specification problems). The field addresses several interesting questions: how policy 'problems' are identified, how those who lose legislative battles try to delay or pervert implementation in bureaucracies (especially in federal systems), more generally how bureaucrats behave, and how program evaluations seem rarely to lead to program discontinuation (though radically changed programs may be falsely counted as continuations). These insights fall on the border of our inquiry, and thus will only be addressed tangentially. We might, though, make special note here of a longstanding debate in the field regarding the proper balance between expert advice and mass political participation. This debate has obvious implications for how advice regarding economic growth should be communicated and to whom. A second point worthy of note is that different types of policies (such as distributive or not) appear to be dealt with through quite different political processes. This insight should give us pause in attributing quite different policies to a single characteristic of the political environment (see chapter 11).

4.4.7.3 Political Science and Economic Growth

While we can learn much from the general literature on institutions, we are naturally also interested in what political scientists have had to say about 'economic development.' In the early postwar period, this literature focused primarily on two competing grand theories: dependency theory and modernization theory (see chapter 3). In more recent decades, this debate has given way to a more pragmatic and focused (on particular causal links) approach which can be termed state-society analysis (Kohli 2002, 84-5). Much of the discourse focuses on particular problems, but a shared terminology and approach allows ready integration across problem areas. The five key questions investigated have been: why do revolutions occur?; why has political stability been so difficult for most less developed countries to achieve?; why has there lately been a pronounced movement from authoritarian to democratic governance?; why do some states encourage economic growth?; and why do some states actively alleviate poverty? (91-2). The key defining characteristic is to see the state and other social phenomena as causally linked in both directions (and thus to eschew social or economic determinism, and also to embrace the possibility of path dependent processes). While some analysis occurs in terms of these broad categories (and others prefer to speak of elites and classes or masses), much occurs at a disaggregated level: leaders, parties, regimes, and bureaucracies; and economic and non-economic groups, upper and lower strata, organized and mobilized forces, and civil society (88). While some of the latter terms are very vague, we can applaud these efforts at disaggregation and analysis of multiple causal links. Kohli urges further disaggregation of some phenomena (such as moving beyond the democracy/authoritarian distinction to looking at different types of each), inclusion of political variables in analyses that at present stress bureaucracy, and a greater emphasis on comparative analysis (85).

Geddes (2002, 345) notes that early postwar scholars interested in developing countries necessarily immersed themselves in particular countries because there was a dearth of published information. Comparative research was rarely pursued in such an environment, and thus scholars did not have rigorous reality checks on their analyses. But students are now trained to apply both theory and comparison. 'Area specialists are gradually assimilating into the mainstream of political science' (346). There is thus a relatively small body of generalizable theorization of political influences on development.

'Because students of developing countries have always focused as much on economic development as on more narrowly political outcomes, ideas current among economists have always influenced us' (Geddes 2002, 346). The fact that development economics was less technical than other fields of economics made it more accessible to other social scientists. Especially given the openness of political science to outside influences, we can imagine that the influence of the disciplinary perspective of economics may have been important. Such influences will likely loom larger in how economic development is conceptualized than how political influences are theorized. But we cannot assume this result.

4.4.8 Sociology

'The term "sociology" really makes little sense today' due to fragmentation (Dogan and Pahre 1990, 106). While this judgment is a bit harsh, it is true that the broad discipline of sociology contains the most diverse body of subfields in social science, and it is not always easy to identify what they have in common. Szostak (2003b) identified four distinct subject areas: the study of population, the study of crime, the study of social divisions, and the study of culture. Each of these has obvious implications for the study of economic growth. Nevertheless only a minority of sociologists has directly confronted issues of economic growth.

Until the last decade or two, sociology was united around an emphasis on the causal importance of social aggregates. Individuals were seen primarily as being affected by culture or social structure rather than affecting these.[21] Methodological individualism was largely eschewed, but has since become more important in the discipline due to the rise of rational choice theory in particular. Not surprisingly, this transition was characterized by conflict. There is now a widespread though far from universal sense in the discipline that causation runs in both directions (though the primary emphasis is still on causation from society to individuals). Granovetter (2002) notes that sociologists have reacted against the oversocialized (people constrained by culture) views of the mid-twentieth century, but should not go to the other extreme of ignoring such constraints: scholars should look at how norms and self-interest interact. Sociology is thus closer to integrating the insights of societal causation and methodological individualism than any other discipline. However, the two research approaches still tend to be largely distinct.

The emphasis on societal aggregates encouraged the popularity of systems approaches and functional/structural arguments. It was assumed that each element of the system served some purpose. If one element changed, all had to change.[22] Yet functionalist explanations to be convincing should describe not only the role an element plays but how it emerged: it is tautological to argue that it emerged because it had a purpose. Systems must be analyzed link by link; otherwise any observation of stability can be taken as evidence of the existence of a particular system. Systems analysis tended to assume a regularity and even predictability to system behavior that many later theorists rejected.[23] Giddens and others have thus urged the integration of the functionalist stress on structure with an emphasis on agency. We could hope that such a project would embrace all types of agency.

---

[21] But while this approach has dominated, many analyses, from Tocqueville and Weber to today, have emphasized 'rational action bounded by institutions.' (Nee, 4) Rather than debate individualism versus holism, 'a more constructive approach is to model the reciprocal interaction between purposive action and social structure' (Nee, 1998, 5).

[22] Interestingly, the very idea of endogenous growth theory echoes the macrosociology of Parsons, the idea that there are relatively isolated subsystems of phenomena.

[23] Foucault moved to post-structuralism because of a 'loss of confidence in underlying structures and a stress on the unpredictable interplay of multifarious relations' (Outhwaite 2000, 59).

Sociology can be contrasted to economics in several important respects (in addition to its non-reliance on methodological individualism). Sociologists are much more likely than economists to engage both non-rational and non-selfish motives. This follows from the tendency to see individuals as influenced by culture and social structure. Individuals wish to belong and to be respected, and will thus do or say things that go against narrow self-interest. The emphasis on social structure leads to a further difference: while economists will often speak of a 'representative agent', sociologists are conscious that each individual performs a unique role in society (due to occupation, gender, family situation, ethnic and religious affiliation, and so on). Attitudes and behaviors are conditioned by the roles we play. Sociologists are thus also more likely to stress power relations than economists.

While economists are content with a progressive account of history in which economic development is viewed as a powerful force for good, sociologists and cultural theorists are much more likely to recoil at the argument that any society is somehow better than any other (e.g. McMichael 2000, xv). Nor will they be soothed by arguments that economic success need not imply any individual or cultural superiority. They are naturally suspicious of arguments that certain cultural attributes encourage economic growth, or at least prone to emphasizing the positive effects that these attributes can have in other realms.

While economics can be criticized for its narrowness, sociology can be bewildering in its use of a wide range of concepts. Ruttan (2000) bemoans the tendency of research communities to coordinate around vague themes like modernization and dependency. Manski (2000) attributes this to the lack of formal mathematical analysis in sociology. I myself would instead point to the need to rely on well-formulated theories rather than poorly-defined concepts in social scientific analysis. While Manski is right that verbal argumentation *can* be less precise than mathematical, it need not be so. It is, quite simply, poor scholarly procedure to organize scholarly conversations around vague terms like community or culture. Scholars need instead to develop both careful theoretical arguments and careful definitions of phenomena. Interdisciplinarians should urge sociologists toward clarity at the same time that they urge economists toward theoretical and methodological flexibility.

4.4.8.1 Economic Sociology

Though the earliest sociologists – Durkheim, Simmel and especially Weber (who was an economist by training and appointment) – often treated economic subjects, through much of the twentieth century economic topics were only rarely touched by sociologists (an 'old economic sociology' was broadly respectful of economic theory, and treated peripheral subjects like economics and religion). Talcott Parsons even at one point remarked that sociology was about how people choose goals, and economics about how they achieve these, though he wrote a book on economic sociology later in his career. Fortunately for our purposes in the 1980s several sociologists began to perform research on economic issues (partly as a response to earlier incursions by economists into sociology) (Swedberg and Granovetter 2001, 6).[24] Still, 'few sociologists have attempted to provide [economic sociology] with a solid theoretical underpinning;' Instead there are diverse studies of different elements of the economy (Guillen 2003, 505). However, economic sociology is grounded in two concepts: social construction and embeddedness. Both of these concepts emphasize the interaction between culture and economy. The field is political in approach, and thus concerned with power, influence, and legitimacy. It thinks agents are not just guided by efficiency concerns, but seek stability and reduced uncertainty (Guillen, 506). In recent years, economic sociologists have increasingly stressed institutions (Swedberg 2005).

Swedberg and Granovetter (2001) identify several distinct types of economic sociology:

- The application of rational choice theory in sociology (which we, like they, can treat as economic analysis, even if done by sociologists).
- Economic imperialism (overlapping with the above, an attempt to explain family life and other sociological issues using economic theory).
- New institutional economics (again a borrowing of theory and method from economics).
- Game theory (ditto).
- Behavioral economics (a new field dominated by psychologists and economists which attempts to move past the simplifying psychological assumptions of economic theory; we discuss psychology below).
- Law and economics (an important area in which economic theory is used to suggest how laws should be drafted and applied to achieve efficient outcomes; this will only be of tangential interest to us).
- The new economic sociology (which the authors practice, and which assumes that economic problems can be better analyzed by taking social considerations into account).

It is clearly this last broad approach that most concerns us here.

4.4.8.2 Sociology and Economic Growth

Parsons had developed 'modernization theory' to explain how less developed countries would feel challenged to develop and would respond by adopting Western culture and institutions. Modernization was identified with the increased

---

[24] Fevre (2003) suggests that sociology emerged as economic behavior came to play a larger role in people's lives; the classical sociologists struggled to re-assert a role for culture and ethics. Fevre is critical of contemporary economic sociology for focusing on how culture might enhance economic productivity rather than attacking economic rationality itself. While Fevre is correct to argue that a value such as trust should not be seen as just a means to an economic end, he goes too far in neglecting how growth-enhancing rational decisions can increase human welfare.

specialization of both individual roles and institutions. When economic development proceeded more slowly than some had hoped, more pessimistic accounts, such as dependency theory, became popular. The success of several East Asian economies induced a more careful comparative focus on the (primarily institutional) sources of success or failure (such as Evans 1995).[25] Here too historical developments have influenced both the direction of inquiry and the conclusions drawn [as has occurred in other disciplines]. Japanese and German institutions were hailed when these economies outperformed Anglo-Saxon rivals, but criticized as Japan and Germany experienced difficulties. The new economic sociology strives for more careful and specific analyses. It moves away not only from the under-socialized agent of economics but the oversocialized agent in Parsons.

In doing so, economic sociology can build upon a long tradition of institutional analysis in sociology. 'Since its founding sociology has been closely associated with the study of social institutions and the comparative analysis of institutional change … Unlike the early sociological institutionalism pioneered by Talcott Parsons (1937), however, the new institutionalism seeks to explain institutions rather than simply assume their existence' (Nee 1998, 1) Indeed, sociology departments, especially in the United States, were formed in large part in the early twentieth century around the institutionalism that had been squeezed out of economics departments (Manski 2000, 121). Economic sociologists follow the earlier sociological tradition in placing much greater emphasis on non-rational decision-making in the development of institutions. They are also much more willing to explore how particular cultural values shape institutions: 'a theory of institutions should address the question of how differences in cultural beliefs give rise to different institutional structures' (Nee, 8). The interdisciplinarian should be wary, of course, that non-rationality and the importance of culture may at times be exaggerated.

4.4.9 Geography

Economic growth occurs spatially. Innovation and investment both cluster regionally and nationally, with regional and national leadership changing but infrequently. Countries in temperate climates fare much better economically than tropical or desert climates. A geographical approach to understanding growth is thus advisable. In recent years economists have developed a 'new economic geography' for exactly these reasons. Geographers have complained that the new economic geography raises issues that they found fruitless decades ago: why clusters occur, and why regional income differences persist. Moreover, they reject the highly formal approach in favor of an appreciation of differences across locality.

---

[25] Modernization theory was criticized for ignoring social conflict, ignoring sudden changes, not appreciating internal differences across countries, assuming nevertheless that the problems of less developed countries were internal, and assuming that growth was good (Shannon 1992).

Landes (1998) notes that many geography departments have been shut down. Geography has had more trouble than other social science disciplines in defining a unique place within social science. It has developed methods of mapping various sorts of human and natural activity. It can perhaps better be identified in terms of these mapping methods than in terms of theory or phenomena. It has been much less successful in developing a set of generalizable theoretical insights. Geographers tend to assume that 'space matters' but nevertheless space is often under-theorized in their research, and this is often thus indistinguishable from the work of sociologists or historians. We should be open to the methodological insights of geographers, and the theoretical insights that flow from the application of these. But we should be wary of simply assuming that space matters.

4.4.10 Anthropology

Carrier (2005, 2) states that 'anthropologists tend to want to see people's lives in the round.' That is, they try to see how economic behaviors are interconnected with other aspects of individual and collective life, such as religious belief. They are particularly interested in what people say/believe and what they do: how practices shape beliefs and vice versa. Anthropologists often find that what people do is different from what they say (pension fund managers claim to evaluate investment firms carefully, but rarely fire underperformers). Anthropologists care about the meanings attached to economic and other activities. Methodologically, participant observation dominates almost completely, and anthropologists are suspicious of experimental results because they believe that people should be observed in a natural setting. Interviews, mapping, and textual analysis can be important complements to participant observation. This methodological preference, coupled with the desire to see people's lives 'in the round' guides anthropologists away from generalization. It is an idiographic discipline, and generally argues that the particularities of any situation overwhelm any generalizations. Markets are placed in their cultural and institutional context. The discipline is held together not by shared theoretical generalizations but a shared belief that certain phenomena – like kinship systems – are important across societies. The theoretical generalizations of Karl Polanyi, dependency theory, world systems theory and a variety of political economy approaches did influence anthropological research, but these influences have waned in the most recent decades.

Comparative anthropology was pursued widely in the 1960s and 1970s, but this impulse faded away. There is, though, evidence of a renewed effort toward comparison. Eades (2005) argues that while generalizations are important to only a minority of anthropologists they will become increasingly important as anthropologists study modern developed societies, and as they appreciate that societies should be studied within a global context. Anthropologists interested in comparison recognize that this is only possible if phenomena are carefully defined and hypotheses carefully specified. Since there has been little theorization in the past, comparative anthropologists may embrace overly simplistic theories.

The idiographic bias of anthropology can severely limit its contribution to the present project. Applbaum's (2005) review of the literature on the anthropology of markets indicates (implicitly) that anthropologists have focused on showing how quite different market institutions are observed in different cultural settings. But there is little or no comparative research of the sort that might illuminate the question of whether markets function better in some circumstances than others. We will review the survey of work on economic development in Lewis (2005) below, but can note here that Lewis provides no example of generalizable insights to be incorporated in our later analysis. The papers in Cohen and Dannhaeuser (2002) tend to address fairly focused issues: how the supply of wood carvings evolved over time in a traditional community (the least productive were not shaken out because they had a low opportunity cost); how local control of tourism might have economic and environmental benefits; how farmer assessment of risk can be subject to moral suasion (in this case by priests with an agenda); how the word 'participation' is abused by aid agencies and governments such that locals do not bother providing input; how a lack of economic opportunity can encourage religious and political extremism; and how different actors will worry about different risks and costs (governments about legal risks, teachers about social risks).

Despite their holistic interest, anthropologists have tended to emphasize cultural aspects of the societies they study. They have thus been attracted to the suggestion of cultural studies that culture shapes politics and economic relations (Robotham 2005). And anthropologists have tended to emphasize links from culture to economy rather than the reverse, even though it is clear that some elements of culture respond quickly to economic changes. Anthropologists have, though, tended to follow Karl Polanyi in arguing that economic transactions are less embedded than they once were. They thus disagree with new economic sociologists in this respect. Nevertheless the work of anthropologists can usefully identify cultural and social influences on growth. As with other communities care must be taken that these links are not exaggerated.

Anthropologists celebrate diversity, and are thus suspicious of a universal ethics. They are especially opposed to the western emphasis on self-interest. They argue that capitalism disrupts local cultures by replacing gift exchange with market exchange, and substituting exchange value for use value. The uniqueness of communities is limited when everything has a price. This ethical outlook not only supports the general suspicion of change but guides anthropologists away from seeking to enhance the performance of markets.

4.4.10.1 Economic Anthropology

The field of economic anthropology has always been more theoretical than the broader discipline, but has rarely addressed issues of economic growth directly.

Economic anthropology long emphasized non-exchange relationships such as gift-giving. Another important activity was developing taxonomies of types of economy: pastoral, horticultural, agricultural. These taxonomies shed some limited light on the path of economic growth in early societies. The boundaries between economic anthropology and economics have become fuzzy as the former has studied modern societies and the latter has seen heterodox developments.

4.4.10.2 Anthropology and Economic Growth

Anthropologists have long had an ambiguous relationship with development, for development 'threatens and challenges many of the assumptions which anthropologists have traditionally held dear, about the value of the traditional, the local and the autonomous' (Lewis 2005, 483). Three broad and overlapping attitudes can be detected. Some anthropologists are hostile to the very idea of development, or at least the motives of development policy-makers. 'Some anthropologists select the ideas, processes and institutions of development as their field of study, but such work has tended to be highly suspicious, if not frankly critical, in its approach' (Lewis 2005, 476). Anthropologists worry about the effects of development on local cultures and social relations, but they may celebrate the ways in which local groups react to and shape these pressures. Anthropologists have examined why certain development projects fail much more than why others succeed: they have usefully exposed the necessity of local knowledge – especially of culture and social structure (gender roles and extended families in particular) in development planning. A small number of studies have looked at aid agencies or states, and documented how bureaucratic structures can interfere with development, but these 'made no claim to offer answers or solutions to the still disappointing results being obtained by those in search of development' (478). Anthropologists are often uncomfortable with the very idea of development for defining poor countries as places that should be acted upon by rich countries; they favor instead local initiative. When some anthropologists do study how development can be pursued, other anthropologists respond that the core purpose of anthropology is the description and analysis of societies as little tainted by development as possible (478).

A second approach involves working within development organizations, and often reflects the existence of job opportunities rather than zeal toward the project.[26] But this sort of work was also encouraged by a desire to show how anthropology could be relevant to policy, an interest in power relations (encouraged by dependency theory), and postmodern encouragement of a more reflective approach to fieldwork (479-80). The anthropologist Geertz famously looked at

---

[26] Anthropologists do not run development projects as some did in the 1960s but rather serve an advisory role regarding cultural communication and the causes and effects of cultural change. They are often called in when a project is failing (Cohen and Dannhaeuser 2002).

how agricultural technology was shaped by the interaction of culture and economic pressures in Indonesia. Lewis (484) recognizes and seems to support calls for anthropologists to move from being critics after the fact to supporting the development of better policies for economic growth.

Third, many anthropologists combine their field work with grassroots activism (Lewis 2005, 472). This activism generally focuses on issues of 'cultural survival' in the face of development, and often aims to frustrate development plans (482). Ironically, activism is often opposed by cultural relativists as outsider interference in local cultures (482-3). A more balanced interest in growth and culture might be encouraged. Participant observation can identify ways in which economic activity in general and development projects in particular are affected by power relations, and thus point toward more equitable strategies (481). Likewise anthropologists can expose the mistaken assumptions of foreign experts regarding local culture. And anthropologists can show how local knowledge can be harnessed to improve productivity.

Cohen and Dannhaeuser (2002) also recognize that some anthropologists work in the development field while others critique the very idea of development. There is thus no reliable mid-level anthropological theory of development. While appreciating that anthropologists have tended to stress the effects of development on culture, they emphasize that in the 1960s there was anthropological research on how values might be encouraged to change in ways that enhance growth and collective wellbeing (and thus how values and institutions influence growth). Anthropologists at that time also searched for non-Western models of economic growth (and thus implicitly accept the idea that growth occurs in different ways in different places). Recent research stresses globalization and the environment, but a reorientation toward growth might be possible. They argue that the key lessons from anthropological research on development are the need to see local communities as active and calculating agents, to realize that these communities are non-homogenous, and to appreciate that the poorest often do not benefit from growth.

This book might encourage more anthropologists to perform research on the causes of economic growth. It will highlight the widespread scholarly appreciation of local knowledge. It will also detail the key mechanisms involved in growth; anthropologists can then ponder how to best set growth in motion. How can investment, trade, innovation, and institutional change be pursued while minimizing cultural and social disruption? More controversially, what changes in culture and social structure would encourage growth, and what other effects would these changes have? These questions are well-suited to the detailed analyses of culture and social structure performed by anthropologists, but would require anthropologists to transcend a suspicion of cultural change of any sort. Anthropologists can also usefully continue to study the internal workings of aid agencies, but should be less reticent about suggesting ways in which these might be improved.

4.4.11 Marxian Approaches

Marxian analysis can be applauded for trying to bring in those many elements ignored by neoclassical economists: institutions, the state, ideology (Miller 2008). Marx stressed how property rights conditioned the course of economic change long before mainstream economists worried about such things.

But Marx, while at times appreciating multiple lines of causation, tended to emphasize the causal links from technology to economics through class struggle to politics. For Marx, technology (the means of production), in concert with institutions (the social means of production) determined class relations. As technology evolved, class tension was inevitable. But the centrality of class struggle to history is perhaps the distinguishing feature of Marxian approaches ('The history of all hitherto existing society is the history of class struggle'; Marx and Engels 1968, 79). While Marxians increasingly appreciate other social cleavages such as gender they do not join other scholars in wondering if class is less important in modern consumer society than at the time of Marx.

Later Marxians, though, and especially in the last decades, have stressed the causal importance of culture and politics. In classical Marxian analysis, political institutions were assumed to have no independent causal function, but rather to mirror the basic economic structure of society (Rothstein 1998, 141). But in the 1980s Marxian scholars came to see institutions as important. Marx also argued that in capitalism market exchange – in pursuit of profit rather than satisfaction of human needs – became so dominant that social relations came to be viewed as economic transactions. Later Marxians are more willing to see an autonomous role for culture. Marxian analysis, like any other school of thought, should neither be completely accepted nor rejected. There is as in other communities of scholars a danger that certain causal arguments are assumed rather than established.

The French 'regulation' approach, while bearing some similarities to North American institutional and evolutionary thinking (it stresses institutions, interdisciplinarity, path dependence, and complex systemic interactions) was also strongly influenced by Marx. The technical and social division of labor is associated with a complementary pattern of production and consumption, and these are reinforced in turn by an (emergent) 'mode of regulation' – norms and institutions – that governs five key economic attributes: wage relations, enterprise form, the financial system, the state, and international trade and finance. Institutions exert their main influence on growth by affecting the surplus extracted by capitalists. Crises result from falling profits. Institutions are changed to generate another age of rising profits. This is not done purposefully but rather each change in technology calls forth complementary changes in culture and institutions. The regulation approach guides us to not neglect the role of institutions in channeling class conflict, and more generally to appreciate that the institutional structure has to change as the economy develops (some suggest that postwar labor peace involved workers giving up power for income). Yet the approach is criticized for oversimplification and naïve functionalism. We can appreciate each of the causal links identified by regulation theorists without assuming successive stable systems of regulation.

4.4.12 Science and Technology Studies

Given the importance of technological innovation to our project, it would be anticipated that the interdisciplinary field of science and technology studies (STS) would be of great importance. Szostak (2003b) noted that 'technology and science' was the only main category of phenomena not taken as the major subject matter of at least one discipline. While we will draw upon the insights of the field, there are several characteristics of the field that limit its role:

- It stresses science much more than technology.
- It has traditionally taken a skeptical stance, arguing that scientific theories are accepted for socio-cultural reasons rather than because they seem to fit reality. This argument is sometimes extended to technology. It must seem, though, that at least technology must actually 'work' in order to be accepted. The cultural arguments put forward by STS scholars should not be ignored, but must be treated with caution. Happily, the field seems to be moving toward a compromise that recognizes that both science and technology are influenced both by culture and by how well theories and technologies actually work.
- When technology is studied, the approach tends to be idiographic.
- The causes of innovation are stressed more than the effects (which are often assumed to be negative). This may be changing.[27]

The integrative approach taken in this book is consonant with that advocated in various spheres of science studies, especially environmental studies. It is increasingly recognized that complex scientific issues such as global warming or biodiversity require integration of diverse insights. Gallopin et al (2001, 223) even define a complex system as one for which there is 'the need to use two or more irreducible perspectives or descriptions in order to characterize the system.' (a view in accord with Newell's, 2001, definition of interdisciplinarity in terms of analysis of complex systems). They encourage researchers to 'include all important factors, even those that are not quantifiable;' yet confidently assert that, 'Ours is most certainly not a call for the relaxation of scientific rigor; on the contrary, we believe that [the study of complex problems] should be the more rigorous by being better informed about the inter-linked and complex nature of reality' (227-8).

---

[27] Before the 1940s there was little work in the field, with exceptions such as Lewis Mumford. The pendulum then swung sharply toward technological determinism (among historians, economists, and philosophers). Then technology became a social construct for many years. It is now generally recognized that technology is both cause and effect.

4.4.13 Psychology

Psychology will only indirectly be a subject of our investigations. It will be drawn upon to refine our understanding any time that the theories of other disciplines make assumptions about human behavior. Psychologists stress certain elements of human psychology that are at odds with the theorizing of economists and other social scientists: the human brain is only loosely unified such that different 'modules' perform different tasks in a loosely coordinated way (whereas social scientists tend to think of some unified program); we are driven by subconscious desires (whereas economists at least tend to emphasize conscious decisions), we develop schemas or maps of reality that guide our behavior (again economists tend to assume that we have accurate perceptions of the world),[28] and we mimic others (economists assume we are independent beings). All of these characteristics interfere with the exercise of rationality.

Social scientists and especially economists have been wary of grounding explanations in unobservable characteristics of the human mind. Psychologists to be sure must often infer the nature of the mind from observations of behavior. This limits their ability to objectively evaluate theoretical propositions. But careful experimentation has generated several results that seem robust to a variety of laboratory conditions. And new diagnostic tools increasingly allow psychologists to observe brain activity.

Psychological experiments have generally been performed on college students in the developed world. This creates a danger that results thought to be universal are in fact culture-specific. Increasingly, experiments are performed cross-culturally. This practice should allow psychologists over time to distinguish psychological from cultural effects.[29]

It is useful to identify the psychological elements thought to be of most importance for economic activity, but that are generally neglected in economic theory. Goodwin, Nelson, Ackerman, and Weisskopf (2005, ch. 2) have attempted to incorporate a more nuanced psychological understanding into an economics text:

- Individuals do not just follow external incentives such as financial or legal rewards and punishments, but respond to intrinsic motivations such as a desire to be honest, or a sense of loyalty to some group or organization.
- Individuals are in general partially motivated by self-interest and partially by altruism. The latter is important, for the level of trust essential to a modern economy might be unachievable if all were entirely self-interested.

---

[28] The sociologist Anthony Giddens has argued that it is not enough to understand how people perceive their situation, but that we must also evaluate the accuracy of these perceptions. After all, one role for perception is to mask reality (Outhwaite 2000, 58).

[29] Ortiz (2005) notes that some anthropologists have drawn upon the ideas of the psychologists Kahneman and Tversky to examine how individuals frame decisions. Efforts to encourage new crops or technologies will be more successful if one understands how particular peasants frame complex decisions: which dimensions they think of first, and so on.

- Individual behavior may reflect habit, choice or constraints. With respect to the latter, the authors appreciate that individuals do not always actively decide to act, but often passively react.
- Individuals are not faultlessly rational in decision-making. The authors are cautious here. Note that they have in the above bullets recognized the possibility of being guided by habit (which opens the door to decision-making according to tradition or rules) or intrinsic motivations (such as intuition or virtues). Cohen (2005) notes that the pre-fontal cortex can over-ride emotional responses, and thus people can be trained to behave rationally – but this ability is not expressed equally across individuals or societies for personal and cultural reasons.
- Attitudes toward time – how willing one is to sacrifice today for tomorrow – differ across individuals. Some attitudes may be irrational.[30]

The authors thus implicitly endorse the 'what' and 'why' elements of the typology of theory outlined in chapter 3,[31] but also guide us to think carefully about altruism and attitudes toward time.

Behavioral economics, an interdisciplinary field between psychology and economics, investigates a similar set of five deviations from the common assumptions of economic theory:

- As above they recognize the importance of altruism. They stress that in some situations this is an important element in incentives.
- As above they stress that attitudes toward discounting are inconsistent across time. People are impatient in the short run, but patient in the longer run. Individuals thus save less than they wish they had for retirement, and will often purchase illiquid assets in part to remove the temptation to spend. Governments can then enhance savings rates and lifetime utility by making property rights in illiquid assets secure, but also by compulsory retirement funds.
- As above, deviations from rationality are posited. Individuals do not calculate probabilities well, but instead use faulty heuristics. They exaggerate the importance of small samples. They also 'anchor' estimates to a particular value and deviate less than they should from this. These various biases are particularly important in financial markets, and provide an explanation of why these are more volatile than economic theory predicts.
- Similar to the above mention of habit, behavioral economists stress a 'status quo bias': individuals dislike losses much more than they value gains. (They

---

[30] The authors do not note that people do not discount the future as economic theory often presumes. Importantly I distinguish today from a week from now, but do not distinguish a year from now from a year and a week from now to the same degree, yet economic theory predicts a constant discount rate. Cohen, 2005 explains this result in terms of the fact that the limbic system is activated when reward is imminent, and pushes us to emphasize the future.

[31] With respect to 'what' it is clear that attitudes are important for the authors. Later they also address the 'who' question, noting that it is a mistake to focus only on individual actors, and mentioning relationships and a couple of types of groups.

thus take sunk – unrecoverable – costs into consideration when making decisions, even though economic theory suggests they should not).
- It is also stressed that individuals do not maximize utility, for this would be
  computationally complex. Rather they follow certain rules of thumb for searching and deciding, and seek outcomes that are 'good enough'.

Note that behavioral economists are careful to speak of non-rational rather than
irrational behavior. While people will sometimes act on impulse they even then
tend to have some reason for their actions. Some economists such as Thaler (2000)
thus hold out hope that a more realistic underpinning for economic theory needs
not to be too messy: people may deviate from rationality in predictable ways in
certain circumstances. The idea of a status quo bias is an example. Behavioral
economics has in recent years moved from a fringe activity to become widely used
in certain fields such as labor economics and development economics.

4.4.14 Philosophy

Philosophy has little to say about the causes of economic growth, but much to say
about how we might investigate the causes of economic growth. Philosophy of
science and ethics were both drawn upon in the introductory chapter in order to
motivate this study. Philosophy of science was again used to motivate chapter 3.

4.4.15 The Other Humanities

Art is likely the least important of the categories in Table 2.1 for our present
inquiry. We will however often have recourse to textual analysis in what follows.
Our remarks about literary/art studies can be brief. We will accept the argument
that texts are ambiguous, but doubt that these are so ambiguous that central
meanings cannot usually be identified. Literary scholarship all too often celebrates
ambiguity to a degree where the hope of enhanced scholarly understanding
evaporates.[32] As with other disciplines, literary scholars have also been guilty of
exaggerating the importance of texts, even while denying their core messages.[33]

---

[32] Nor is this problem limited to the humanities: 'scholars inspired by the literary turn in some of
the social sciences [have] a philosophical concern about causal explanation as a worthy end of
scholarship' (Kohli 2002, 89).

[33] The 'cultural turn' across the social sciences and humanities encouraged the 'hegemony of
literary criticism as the chief epistemology of these disciplines, requiring the textualisation of
the practices and phenomena of everyday life for analytical purposes' (Kockel 1992, 1). This
'ontologisation' of text has since been criticized by others who stress the importance of studying
lived experience.

5 An Interdisciplinary Literature Survey

5.1 The Literature Survey Performed, with Advice for its Extension

Repko (2008) makes several important points regarding interdisciplinary literature searches. He notes that the task is harder than disciplinary literature searches for several reasons. First, there is simply more ground to be covered. Second, library catalogues are organized along disciplinary lines, and different terminology is used in different disciplines. Interdisciplinarians must thus master the terminology used in each discipline of interest. Note that interdisciplinarians may fail to appreciate that a particular discipline is relevant to a particular problem if they search works in that discipline using the terminology of another. To be sure, books may be classified with respect to multiple subjects, and some of these subjects span disciplines, but this only partially alleviates the problem. Third, and less obviously, while disciplinary specialists will readily understand and place in context most works in their discipline (or at least subdiscipline), the interdisciplinarian must place the insights of a particular discipline within the context of its disciplinary perspective, and this will mean reading not only about insights relevant to a particular question but more generally regarding the discipline's theories, methods, and subject matter, among other disciplinary elements. It also means that careful attention must be paid to the disciplinary identity of authors.

Repko urges us to identify the following information regarding each discipline: its perspective, insights, concepts, theory, data, assumptions, and method. Chapter 3 has already addressed questions of theory and method. Chapters 6 through 11 will deal with relevant disciplinary insights. Assumptions are not treated separately but critiqued along with other elements of theory. Data is likewise analyzed with method. Repko stresses the importance of mastering a discipline's overall perspective. This is one of the more challenging tasks facing the interdisciplinarian. This challenge was addressed in chapter 4. The author benefited enormously in this task from his previous exposure to these various disciplines. Repko urges authors to provide in-text evidence of mastery of disciplinary perspectives; this is one purpose of the exposition in step 4. If errors are found there, their effect can be traced through later steps.

Of the disciplinary elements listed by Repko, the one that receives the least explicit attention in this book is 'concepts.' For reasons discussed in the introductory chapter, we focus in this book on jargon-free theoretical statements and generally eschew concepts (but occasionally clarify the meaning of these). I have argued elsewhere (especially 2004, ch. 2) that useful scholarly concepts lend themselves to precise definitions in terms of phenomena, theories, or methods. Scholarly concepts that do not lend themselves to precise definition are problematic.

R. Szostak, *The Causes of Economic Growth*,
DOI: 10.1007/978-3-540-92282-7_5, © Springer-Verlag Berlin Heidelberg 2009

We will return to this issue when we discuss culture and especially 'social capital' in chapter 8, for vague definitions of these terms do much to hamper the accretion of scholarly understanding. When the concepts used by a discipline do lend themselves to a (fairly) precise interpretation, we can discuss the relevant phenomena, theories, or methods in plain English without (much) loss of understanding. I should note that many interdisciplinarians would suspect that I underestimate the problem of ambiguity of language here. My response is that I am not at all unaware of the fact that many social scientists and humanists are too careless in their terminology. But disciplinary insights that reflect cumulative scholarship within any discipline (that is that emerge from a significant body of detailed argument and evidence) must generally reflect a fair degree of consensus regarding terminology. This consensus can then be expressed plainly as the relevant insight is outlined.

Repko recommends the use of a variety of guides to disciplines: dictionaries, encyclopedias, handbooks, and databases. I will follow Repko's advice and generally not cite encyclopedias in what follows, but note here that I consulted several. The *International Encyclopedia of Economic Sociology*, edited by Jens Beckert and Milan Zafirowski (Routledge 2006) was particularly useful. I also quite like (and contributed to) the *Oxford Encyclopedia of Economic History* edited by Joel Mokyr. Several handbooks, most obviously the two-volume *Handbook of Economic Growth* edited by Aghion and Durlauf (which while focused on the economics literature nevertheless made some interesting comments regarding the wider literature) were consulted, and are cited many times in what follows.

After encyclopedias and handbooks, Repko suggests looking at books before articles as books generally provide more context for the insights provided. Repko notes, though, that much can often be accomplished using just the insights drawn from fairly general sources. Given the broad scope of this work, I have necessarily relied heavily on fairly general works, but have delved more deeply when the subject matter required this. As emphasized in chapter 2, this book chooses breadth over depth: it seeks to identify all relevant causal links, and thus necessarily cannot treat each one in the same detail as a monograph devoted to one of these could. It cannot be stressed too much that scholars following up on particular aspects of this work will want to revisit the literature survey.

The author would point to a couple of particular weaknesses in his approach. First, minority points of view within disciplines (especially outside economics) have not received the attention they deserve because of the approach taken in the literature survey. Such minority points of view are of obvious relevance to the interdisciplinarian in evaluating disciplinary insights (and also in clarifying disciplinary perspective). Second, a glance at the references will show that books were relied on more than journal articles to a greater extent than Repko would advise. Survey articles were consulted, but more focused articles only rarely. As Repko notes, the article literature in a discipline may differ from its book literature. It is difficult to know how large or in what direction such a bias may have been in this case.

Repko urges careful attention to the disciplinary source of insights so that these can be evaluated against the appropriate disciplinary perspectives. This has been the general strategy of this work (though some works of tangential interest have been less carefully analyzed in this manner). Authors are often identified by discipline in what follows. It would, though, be tedious to do so for every author cited, and thus such identification is omitted when it is (hopefully) clear in context which discipline (or interdisciplinary field) a particular insight comes from. The fact that the disciplinary source of insights is not always explicitly listed should in no way be taken as a sign that each insight was not evaluated in the context of the discipline that generated it.

Repko reminds us that a discipline may have important insights despite producing little relevant research. We should thus not dismiss a discipline from consideration just because it has not devoted a great deal of attention to the issue at hand. Indeed even when it has said nothing directly about an issue it may nevertheless provide insight by addressing related or similar issues (or phenomena at higher or lower levels of aggregation; the classification of phenomena from chapter 2 can be useful here). This advice is particularly important for this work. Disciplines outside economics and economic history rarely address 'economic growth' directly (though some address the related topic of 'development'), and thus this work would not have been possible if a wider net had not been cast. Various disciplines study the key proximate causes of growth identified by economists, and even more scholars address the various causal links identified in chapter 2.

Dogan (1998, 97 and elsewhere) stresses that interdisciplinarity (which he thinks is a misnomer) involves work across subfields of disciplines rather than disciplines as a whole. This will certainly be true of the study of economic growth, for only certain fields within several disciplines concern themselves directly with issues related to growth such as institutional or technological change. This simple fact makes the literature survey manageable. It is still useful to consult general works in each relevant discipline:

- To identify relevant subfields
- To reflect on disciplinary perspective.

It is not necessary, though, to survey every subfield of the discipline. Only those addressing issues of direct relevance to the study of growth need be investigated. The obvious danger is that other subfields may have something useful to say; this again is a possible avenue for extension of the literature survey strategy pursued in this work.

Note in the latter regard that the subfields of other disciplines focused upon economic activities may be somewhat atypical of their disciplines. They will almost inevitably interact with economists, and thus make some sort of accommodation to the dominant theory and method of that discipline. They may, for example, emphasize methodological individualism or statistical analysis more than other fields in their discipline. They may also borrow economic terminology: in such cases care must be taken that subtle changes in definition do not affect insights. The same is somewhat true in reverse of economists interested in questions of growth: these are somewhat more interested than their colleagues in political and cultural phenomena, and somewhat more open to other theories and methods. Yet economists have proven less likely than other social scientists to borrow theories and methods. Still, one central insight of interdisciplinary scholarship is that even unusual disciplinarians are affected by their disciplinary perspective. Economic sociologists may borrow much from economists but will still in many ways approach questions in the manner of sociologists. Nevertheless, as noted in chapter 4, one further purpose of engaging disciplinary perspective is to be able to ask how 'mainstream' sociologists might approach economic questions.

It should be clear by now that the author is an unusual and very interdisciplinary sort of economist and economic historian. Nevertheless I am an economist and have long read and taught the economics and economic history literature on economic growth. I teach courses in both Canadian and European Economic History, and stress economic growth, institutional change, and technological innovation in both of these. I have created a second-year course in Economics called 'Technology, Institutions, and Economic Growth' which while increasingly interdisciplinary has tended naturally to stress the economics literature. It was thus much easier for me to achieve some depth of coverage in economics and economic history than in other disciplines. I have been very interdisciplinary in my research, and have thus read widely in especially political science and sociology and history in the past, but not as deeply as in economics and economic history. I have focused my efforts while writing this book on these other disciplines (and have perhaps mastered the political science, sociological, and historical literatures better than the anthropological, cultural studies, and science studies literatures), but would confess that I likely still understand the literature in economics and economic history better. Still, if the book in places reads as a constructive critique of the economic literature, this reflects not my expertise as much as the present state of the literature on economic growth where certain central questions are studied almost exclusively by economists and economic historians.

In addition to searching by discipline and sub-discipline, general subject searches of library catalogues were performed for a handful of key terms:

- Economic growth
- Technology
- Institutions
- Economic Development.

Researchers interested in a particular link are urged to perform link-specific subject searches. Care must be taken in so doing that the terminology of different disciplines is adequately reflected in the search terms: it can not be stressed too much that the same or similar phenomenon or process may be called quite different things in different disciplines. While library shelves are organized by discipline, there have been efforts to make subject headings interdisciplinary, though with mixed results. Information scientists have compiled thesauri that can help immeasurably in suggesting alternate search terms. Yet even thesauri are generally constructed on a disciplinary basis.

One useful strategy is to keep track of the subject headings of works found to be useful, and later search under these headings. Note though that any book is classified under at most a handful of subject headings, and thus that relevant books that relate economic growth to other topics not searched for may be missed. Another strategy once one has identified some very useful works is to trace either works cited in these (for recent works) or to use citation indices in order to identify recent works that cite the work found useful. The obvious danger is that citations of a work are much more likely within its own discipline, and thus interdisciplinary connections will be under-represented. Moreover, citation trails will tend to under-represent minority discourses within any discipline. A further difficulty is the uneven treatment provided by existing citation indices: these generally survey articles rather than books, and capture some fields better than others.

5.2 A Tangential Diatribe

I cannot conclude this chapter without a diatribe against existing systems of library classification. These all serve interdisciplinary scholarship miserably. I will inevitably have missed much of value in this work simply because relevant analyses were for some reason classified in a place I did not think to look. I have long advocated a universal classification system that would be grounded in classifications by phenomena and causal links rather than disciplines. In such a classification, a researcher could simply search for works on, say, the link between attitudes toward hard work and economic growth. I have also argued that works could easily be coded by the theory and method applied. If this were done, the researcher could then quickly identify works on this link which had employed statistical analysis, textual analysis, ethnographic analysis, and so on. Such a classification system would not erase the value of survey works but would greatly facilitate their performance. And such a classification is obviously feasible.

Szostak (2008a) provides a philosophical rationale for such a classification. Szostak (2007b) provides an overview of arguments for both the feasibility and desirability of such a classification system. The classifications of phenomena, theory types (see also Szostak and Gnoli 2008), and methods discussed in chapters 2 and 3 could be used as a basis for this classification system. The Integrative Level Classification project sponsored by the Italian chapter of the International Society for Knowledge Organization (www.iskoi.org/ilc) is the most promising attempt to develop just such a classification. Their website also contains the Leon Manifesto, issued after the 2007 conference of ISKO-Spain (the conference theme was interdisciplinarity), which calls for this sort of classification.

6 The Causes of Economic Growth: Investment, Trade, Technology, Geography

We will quickly become awash in confusion if we simply reproduce by discipline all of the theoretical insights relevant to economic growth. As we saw in chapter 2, a number of distinct causal links can be identified. We will thus organize our discussion around causal links here. The potential drawback of this approach is that many theories address multiple links. Yet we can only hope to compare and contrast the implications of different theories – which will often address overlapping sets of causal links – if we examine each theory link by link. In practice it is straightforward to do so (see Szostak 2003b). We will address interactions across links as appropriate (and will address emergent properties in chapter 10).

Some scholars would see the sheer number of causal links as a drawback. They want a simpler understanding of the growth process.[1] As we have seen, economists emphasize (in their models, but not necessarily their regressions) a small number of variables. Kohli voices a similar predilection from political science: 'a good explanation of why some developing countries have industrialized more rapidly than others must take account of multiple factors but without sacrificing parsimony'(380). While recognizing the importance of such factors as education, entrepreneurship, and work effort, he argues that these all reflect state initiatives, and thus we should focus on what types of government encourage growth. If, though, governments have much of their effect through intermediate variables, then we can only understand the role of government by looking at the particular causal links both from government to education and from education to growth. Kohli implicitly assumes that the same type of government excels along each link. This need not be the case. Nor need all intermediate variables depend equally on government. Thus we must eschew the siren song of oversimplification.

De Long wonders if growth processes may be largely stochastic (in Snowdon 291-2): he suggests that there are many positive and negative feedback loops and thus Ghana might well have ended up like Korea. Easterly (2002, ch. 10) likewise emphasizes the role that unpredictable complementarities (and disasters or forces beyond the control of a single nation) play in economic growth, and thus the stochastic nature of growth outcomes. He notes that our inability to explain differences in growth performance (though we praise the policies of lucky countries after the fact, and look for mistakes when the success ends) invites such analysis. Such a hypothesis is best evaluated link by link: if many links appear to be highly stochastic then the outcome may indeed be stochastic. Note, though, that very small differences in growth rates can have huge effects if sustained over a long time. And thus we may mistakenly leap to the conclusion that Korea's success relative to Ghana was due to good luck rather than seemingly smallish differences.

---

[1] Bernstein (2004, 4) appeals to a popular audience by stressing four necessary conditions: property rights, advanced capital markets, scientific rationalism, and improvements in transport.

R. Szostak, *The Causes of Economic Growth*,
DOI: 10.1007/978-3-540-92282-7_6, © Springer-Verlag Berlin Heidelberg 2009

A more promising supposition is that causal links are not so much stochastic as influenced by a wide array of realizations of other phenomena. They will appear stochastic if we do not understand how they are shaped by other phenomena. Thus Rodrik (2003, 10) suggests that different causal links are more important at different times and places. Economic modeling increasingly reflects this diversity of experience. Rather than develop an infinite variety of models, we will seek here to identify the key external influences that may affect each individual causal link.

This chapter (and the next two) addresses in concert two of the steps in the interdisciplinary process outlined in Szostak (2002): 'evaluation of insights' and 'comparing and contrasting' insights. In practice, these steps interact more than most. Moreover, for presentational purposes they are best combined. Szostak (2002, 112) identified five useful strategies for evaluating disciplinary insights:

- Identify omitted phenomena.
- Refer to flaws in the general theory type and method used.
- Refer to disciplinary perspective.
- Refer to a list of common scholarly errors and biases.
- Compare the insights of different disciplines. Note that if disciplines with quite different perspectives generate similar insights, we can have greater confidence than if only one discipline generates that insight.[2]

Szostak (2002, 114) suggests three strategies for overcoming differences in insight between disciplines:

- Ask if the apparent difference is merely semantic.
- Ask what changes in assumptions are necessary to achieve common ground.
- See if the different theories have different ranges of applicability.

In this chapter, then, we will both evaluate individual insights and compare the insights generated by multiple disciplines. We will in so doing suggest how these diverse insights might be integrated.

6.1 A First Lesson from Economic History

Europe in the eighteenth and nineteenth centuries provides a wonderful laboratory for the study of economic growth: first Britain achieved rapid economic growth from 1820, then France, Germany, and Belgium from mid-century, and then several other countries later in the century. Can one identify common factors in these various growth success stories? Much of the research on this question drew on the bold theoretical claims of either Rostow or Gerschenkron. Rostow (1960) had argued that growth involved progress through a series of stages, and in the

---

[2] In evaluating, we can also keep in mind a question from Rule (1997): would someone outside a research community find these results interesting?

first of these various necessary conditions for future growth were put in place. Gerschenkron (1962) argued that different generations of industrializers would need different pre-conditions: for example France and Germany needed more developed financial institutions than had Britain because the optimal scale of industrial establishments had grown; later industrializers would need the state to play a major role in fostering heavy industry (which he saw as a leading sector). Neither of these hypotheses withstood detailed empirical examination very well. Given the number of different European states that experienced growth during the long nineteenth century, exceptions could always be found to any posited 'necessary factor.' Even the examples drawn upon by Rostow and Gerschenkron were shown to be exaggerated: the big investment banks were less important to German industry and the state to Russian industry than Gerschenkron had presumed. Rostow suggested that advances in agricultural productivity were a necessary precursor to industrialization, but Russia managed to industrialize despite a backward agricultural sector. It seems then that there are multiple paths to economic growth.

The same concern has been voiced, albeit using quite different theories, by dependency and world-systems theorists in sociology and other social sciences. These scholars also argued that growth occurred (or not) quite differently in different places. Yet the growth accounting exercises of economists tended to assume that there was some common experience of economic growth across time and place. Since these scholars in other disciplines did not directly address the assumptions of growth accounting (to my knowledge) it remains for the interdisciplinarian to draw the connection.

That being said, there is little doubt that most/all of the factors identified by Rostow or Gerschenkron, though not necessary for growth, had a positive influence on growth. And it is possible, and even likely, that some limited set of combinations of these factors were necessary.[3] Moreover, an argument for necessity can be sustained even for individual causal factors if lower thresholds are set. German investment banks may not be essential, but some sort of banks likely is. Some transport infrastructure linking areas of economic activity is essential. And technological innovation of various sorts requires that some people be educated.

The lesson from economic history nevertheless is that we should be careful of expecting any causal link to be as powerful in one time and place as in another. That is, we need to carefully identify the conditions under which a certain causal relationship holds. This may at times force us into a more 'qualitative' analysis than economists prefer: we may only be able to identify a fairly wide range of possible effects rather than a specific parameter value. Yet notably many economists who study growth, including Rodrik (2005) and Sachs (2005), have reached a similar conclusion. We can strive to be as precise as possible, but should not sacrifice accuracy to precision.

---

[3] The method of qualitative comparative analysis can identify sets of jointly necessary variables in comparative case studies (Ragin, Berg-Schlosser, and de Meur 1998, 760). The method has not been applied in economic history.

6.2 Investment

Much of the empirical research of economists over the decades has involved estimating aggregate production functions. Output must at any point in time reflect the interaction of land/resources, labor, and capital. The contribution of each of these and the 'total factor productivity' which determines how well inputs are transformed into output (and thus captures both technology and how efficiently the economy allocates resources to their most productive use) can in principle be identified. Such research has produced interesting insights over the years. It was soon discovered that investment (that is, increases in the capital stock) was important – it seemed that about a third of the growth experienced in developed countries could be attributed to investment – but not as important as many economists had previously imagined. Economists naturally strove to identify the sources of this huge residual: what caused the other two-thirds of growth? The idea of human capital was introduced, and adjusting the labor variable for 'quality' associated with skill acquisition through education decreased the residual significantly. A large residual still remained, and this could only be explained as a result of increases in total factor productivity. In other words, only about half of economic growth in developed countries could be attributed to increases in the inputs of physical and human capital; the other half had to be explained in terms of how well these were combined. Technology was the most obvious answer, and as we have seen the development of endogenous growth models was driven by a desire to have this huge influence on growth rates brought into the model. Less obviously, but also importantly, some economists appreciated that institutional advance might be responsible for advances in the efficiency of resource allocation.

The result that investment in physical capital explained a third of economic growth had a seemingly obvious policy implication: increasing levels of investment would increase rates of economic growth.[4] Easterly (2002) describes how much of the early postwar policy advice to developing countries indeed focused on artificially inducing investment. Sadly, this insight from the results of growth accounting exercises in developed countries did not translate into growth in less developed countries.[5] In part this reflects a failure to appreciate that growth occurs differently at different times and places (above). And in part it reflects a failure to appreciate the precise causal mechanism between investment and growth.

The effect of investment on growth varies much more than growth accounting endeavors might lead one to suspect. If one looks at developing countries, or transition economies (before or during the transition) one often finds a weak or nonexistent connection between investment and growth. One reason is that investment

---

[4] Indeed the attention of economists to the role of investment in generating growth was in large part driven by its policy implications: should investment be subsidized?

[5] Dale Jorgensen has argued that much of the growth accounting residual disappears if human capital and research and development are treated as investment. This sort of analysis ignores the complementarities between different types of investment, but rather treats them as substitutes.

was often devoted to inappropriate uses: factories or machines that never produce anything, or that produce goods at uncompetitive prices, do not generate growth. Aid agencies mistakenly thought investment was both necessary and sufficient for growth in the 1960s, and calculated necessary levels of investment to achieve desired growth rates; they have now appreciated that investment is only at best necessary (Easterly, 28-9). Investment only encourages growth (potentially) if it is devoted to the production of goods and services that can be sold for more than the cost of production.

A second reason is that investment is complementary to technological innovations, and thus investment that introduces new technology encourages growth much more than investment embodying old technologies. Poor countries unable for whatever reason to use advanced technology will not be able to benefit as much from investment as rich countries (Easterly 2002). The failure to appreciate the connection between innovation and investment was also responsible for a heated debate about whether East Asian growth had been due to investment rather than innovation (and would thus inevitably falter as diminishing returns to investment set in); regressions allowing for complementarity between investment and innovation show a healthy input of the latter (Easterly 2002, 66). Lau (1996) argues that countries in the early stages of economic growth (including nineteenth century North America and the Asian tigers) grew mostly because of growth in capital stock, but advances in technology became more important later. Nevertheless he recognizes an overall complementarity between these two (and human capital): the more a country has of one the more productive the others can be. Especially in less developed countries growth strategies should be three-pronged. He calculates that 80 percent of technological progress is embodied in new capital. But this calculation too reflects excessive generalization: different technologies require investment to quite different degrees. Nevertheless, there has been a general tendency in history for rates of total factor productivity growth to be correlated with rates of increase in the capital/labor ratio, suggesting that there is some strong link between the two.

While the Solow growth model suggests that investment in poor countries can lead to rapid growth, it also suggests that the rate of return should be much higher there (and should have been much higher a century ago in developed countries too). But in fact rates of return vary little across countries or over time. The reason would seem again to be the complementarity of investment and technology: poor countries lack the ability to absorb advanced technology and thus do not provide spectacular returns to investment (Easterly, 55).

Not only are average rates of return not higher in less developed countries, but they vary considerably within those countries (Banerjee and Duflo 2005). This is important, for it defies the assumption of aggregate production functions that investment is channeled to its most productive uses. If this were so, investment would flow into the most profitable sectors until the rate of return fell to the average level in the economy. And thus the authors conclude that aggregate production functions are not a good starting point for the analysis of growth. In poor countries at least, various microeconomic problems – bad governments, credit market constraints, extended family resource-sharing – cause different agents to face quite different borrowing costs and expected returns. As well, some are much better able to insure themselves than others. If these constraints could be lifted these countries would benefit as investment was channeled to its most productive uses.

While economists have belatedly appreciated the relationship between investment and technology, the role of networks is less obvious. Yet surely one key reason why rates of return differ across projects so much in less developed countries is that some agents have access to limited networks: they may have to rely on too little capital to realize economies of scale, they may have difficulties obtaining inputs or disposing of outputs, and they may be less well treated by bureaucrats. Well developed financial institutions can compensate to some extent for deficiencies in networks, and thus less dispersion in rates of return is observed in developed countries, but there too some agents are able to achieve much better returns than others because of network opportunities.

These adjustments in our understanding of the relationship between investment and growth are entirely in accord with the strategies for interdisciplinary analysis outlined above: growth accounting regressions naturally omit many variables that condition this relationship; the structure of those regressions does not allow for independent variables to act in concert; the approach reflects a disciplinary tendency to identify supposedly enduring causal relationships without careful concern for the set of conditions in which these might hold; and the growth accounting analyses thus represent a widespread tendency in scholarship to assume greater generality for one's results than they deserve. The approach, it might be noted, also reflects the simplistic view of growth as 'more of the same stuff' critiqued in chapter 2: investors succeed by producing good quality and/or at reasonable prices. It should be stressed that appropriate caveats were often included in the original analyses, but were forgotten as these works were cited. This practice of forgetting caveats is also common across disciplines. While economists thus strove to identify *the* relationship between investment and growth, economic historians (and development economists) were driven by their interest in diverse times and places to show that no such fixed relationship exists.

Yet this conclusion too may be overdrawn. It is true that no fixed coefficient between investment and growth exists across all times and places. What, though, if the debate is framed instead in terms of necessary and sufficient conditions? Clearly, investment is not a sufficient condition for growth. But might it be necessary? Can a country grow much without investment? Institutional change may increase the efficiency of resource allocation, and openness to trade may allow gains from comparative advantage, but these benefits will be one-time (though there may then be a multiplier effect as the initial income increases are spent), and even these will generally require some investment (in port facilities, for example). While some technology is generated in the form of ideas, most new technology must be embodied in machines. Bruton (1997, 68) notes that technology may be embodied in replacement capital, and thus can be accommodated without net investment (but argues this will not work in the longer run). While growth without investment is thus possible to some extent, growth with investment is likely to be much more common and much more robust. And thus one might expect (as is indeed observed) that there is a correlation between investment and growth, but only a rough correlation (with much dispersion) because of the importance of links between investment, technology, markets, institutions, and networks.

Ironically, the simplistic approach to investment likely also reflects an excessive desire for terminological clarity. Economists generally pride themselves on more careful definition of terminology than other social sciences. The reliance on statistical testing, coupled with the discipline's focus on a constrained set of economic variables, has encouraged careful and consensual definitions of terminology. Nevertheless, terminological issues are sometimes fudged. During the 'Cambridge controversies' of the 1960s, it was argued (by those in Cambridge UK) that one simply could not define capital in an aggregate production function independently of the output it was supposed to help generate: if you stopped producing buggy whips then all those whip-making machines ceased to be of any use. But since data on capital stock could be collected, economists (and not just in the United States) continued to estimate aggregate production functions. Opinions differ on how problematic this is: for our purposes the main cost of fudging the definition of capital is that it distracted attention from the fact that investment matters only to the degree that the capital stock created is useful. A policy that maximizes total investment need not encourage growth if the wrong sorts of capital are created (think of the former Soviet Union). Theodore Schultz, the Nobel prize winning development economist, emphasized that in a world of disequilibrium growth the return to much older capital falls as it becomes outdated; differences in the rate of return across different types of capital is in fact one of the potential sources of growth. As for aggregate production functions, one might well anticipate that the contribution of investment to growth would differ across time and place depending on how useful the new capital was (which would likely vary both with institutional structure and with technological potential). Still the fact that measured capital per worker is \$150,000 in the United States, \$40,000 in Mexico, and \$6000 in India likely tells us something useful about the role of investment in growth, despite the problems in accurately measuring 'useful capital stock.'

If not for our discussion of necessity, the results of our analysis to this point may seem mostly negative in a policy sense: countries cannot reliably trigger growth by encouraging investment alone. Yet such a result is valuable in discouraging wasteful government practices. Nor should it deter policy-makers from attention to investment, but encourages a focus on investment that responds to (or generates) consumer wants, embodies superior technology, and takes advantage of strong network ties. Just as it is a mistake to focus on investment in isolation, it would be a mistake to focus on technological innovation or network building while ignoring investment. The decades of effort devoted to estimating aggregate production functions were not entirely in vain, for they identify investment rates as potentially one of a handful of key proximate causes of growth.

6.2.1 Encouraging Useful Investment

How might governments encourage useful investment? Economists have had much less to say about the causes of investment than its effects. Much economic analysis assumes implicitly the first sort of growth outlined in chapter 2. Thus investment would occur gradually to allow and be financed by increased production of the same stuff. Such a process, we might well imagine, might be prone to falling apart at any time that expectations of future aggregate growth turned sour. Of course, in real life only some investment is devoted to just more of the same. Most investment is devoted at least in part to introducing new products or processes, or to serving new markets. By encouraging innovation and trade, then, governments will also encourage investment.[6] At times, such investment may simply replace existing capital stock: if new products replace old or new methods replace old. Consumers still benefit from better or cheaper goods. More commonly new capital works alongside old in the economy, and thus capital/labor ratios rise.

Governments can also create institutions that support a healthy financial sector. This means not just making it possible for financial institutions to exist but carefully regulating them so that both borrowers and lenders can have confidence in them. Less developed countries often crack down on informal credit markets before creating an extensive formal capital market. Even very profitable investment opportunities may be missed in such a situation. Since financial institutions cannot perfectly evaluate investment opportunities, investment depends a lot on firm cash flow and net worth in any environment (Stiglitz 2000). More general laws and regulations of private businesses will thus also affect levels of investment.

Rodrik (2006, 983) provides a 'diagnostic' flow chart of potential causes of low investment in poor countries. This may reflect high costs of borrowing, which may in turn reflect limitations in financial institutions or low levels of domestic savings. The latter may have institutional roots as well: compulsory pension plans are one institution that increases savings. Even if borrowing costs are low, investment may be hindered by a lack of profitable opportunities. This may reflect limitations in infrastructure or human capital (both of which governments might address). Or it could reflect a lack of confidence in the government to respect property rights and/or to provide macroeconomic stability. Or it might reflect limited market exchange; again the government may be able to improve markets by developing market institutions.

While governments can influence investment in a variety of ways, the most direct means (at least in developed countries) is by influencing interest rates. Yet for most developed countries interest rates are treated as a policy instrument for coping with business cycles rather than for encouraging growth. As we have seen

---

[6] Keynes had recognized in his *Treatise on Money* that investment was largely determined by the rate of innovation but in the *General Theory* emphasized the marginal efficiency of capital. This reflected among other things the level of technological understanding rather than its rate of change. Fostering innovation would still encourage investment, but less so than in the *Treatise*.

elsewhere, theoretical treatments of business cycles are rarely related to theoretical treatments of growth. Economic theory would predict that lower interest rates would encourage investment which would in turn (subject to the caveats above) encourage growth. Rodrik (2005) observes (see chapter 11) that successful East Asian economies achieved rapid growth while depressing interest rates (he talks of how banks were thus driven to encourage deposits).

Care must be taken, though, in extrapolating from cases of permanently lower interest rates to cases of temporary fluctuations. Does growth suffer if interest rates are raised from a low level for a year or two? To some extent, foregone investment today may be replaced tomorrow, but this cannot be guaranteed. Moreover, since growth is a cumulative disequilibrium process, decreasing investment even temporarily by artificially raising the interest rate will likely (at least under certain conditions) permanently lower the growth trajectory. Moreover investment today encourages growth and thus more investment tomorrow.[7] If the investment embodies new technology, the process of 'learning by doing' will also be delayed, and thus the time-path of incremental improvements to the technology.

Note that interest rates are raised to limit inflationary pressures. The negative impact of higher interest rates must thus be weighed against the negative impact of inflation. While double-digit inflation increases transactions costs and causes uncertainty, there is little empirical evidence that inflation rates of around 5 percent or so are bad. There is even a theoretical argument that moderate levels of inflation can be beneficial. Economic efficiency requires that wages reflect worker productivity. But productivity increases more rapidly in some sectors than others. Workers will protest a nominal wage cut much more than a wage freeze in the face of inflation, even though both have an identical impact on their purchasing power. And thus it is easier for relative wages across sectors to adjust in order to reflect productivity in an environment of moderate inflation.

Governments hope that by adjusting interest rates (and perhaps fiscal policy) business cycle fluctuations will be lessened. And interest rate policy affects consumption expenditures as well as investment. Restricting consumption expenditure during booms and encouraging consumption expenditure in downturns might have more benign effects on growth, for investors can be confident of stable demand in future. In this light, raising and lowering interest rates may to some degree affect growth positively. Note though that investment decisions reflect particular market circumstances much more than general market circumstances. That is investors will invest in X if they foresee increased demand for X even in the face of fears about a general downturn.

More research is warranted on the relationship between interest rate policies and growth. If the relationship is strong, this may be an easy and powerful way of fostering growth in developed countries.

---

[7] Macroeconomists used to talk a lot about 'the accelerator mechanism,' the effect of growth on investment. Prasch (2000) notes that present interest in increasing returns and path dependence should re-invigorate thinking about the accelerator mechanism.

6.2.2 The Capital Goods Sector

This sector, as I found in my own research on the Industrial Revolution, has powerful incentives to innovate, for capital goods firms compete on the basis of what their machines can do for producers. Economic historian Nathan Rosenberg has also worried that the capital goods sector is still of critical importance to growth, as was the case in the [eighteenth and] nineteenth centuries, but that small countries may not be able to sustain such a sector.[8] Bruton (1997, 70-1) stresses the advantages of close connections with capital users, so that machines can be designed to serve their needs. In less developed countries, one particular advantage may be the pursuit of labor-using technology (that is technology that economizes on scarce capital by utilizing abundant labor). Moreover, capital goods firms can learn by observing their machine in use (and the adjustments that users make). Bruton stresses that while some firms in the sector are huge, this need not be the case. Institutional economists have long noted the role of the capital goods sector in promoting innovation, and thus often recommend that countries protect this sector. On the other hand most neoclassical economists are skeptical that poor countries should nurture capital goods sectors: these often produce the same goods as in developed countries; it is usually possible to use existing technology in a labor-intensive manner; and such a policy goes against comparative advantage. The costs and benefits of such a policy deserve further investigation.

6.2.3 Foreign Investment

The Solow model predicts that capital will flow from rich countries to poor. This is sometimes but not always observed in the real world. In recent years capital has flowed from poor countries into the United States, in part to finance government debt. Arguments for increasing returns – whether in endogenous growth models or the new economic geography (see below) – could explain flows from poor to rich. Then the return to capital is higher where capital is concentrated.

Despite the dramatic increase in international capital flows in recent decades, domestic levels of investment are still closely correlated with domestic levels of saving for most countries. That is, most investment in most countries is financed by local savings. One reason for this result is that the vast bulk of foreign investment flows within the capital rich high-savings developed world. The limited scope of inflows into poor countries may simply reflect the inability of those countries to absorb substantial investment flows due to poor infrastructure and/or financial systems.

---

[8] As mechanization proceeded in the eighteenth and nineteenth centuries, specialized firms emerged to build machines for industry (industrial producers had previously built their own). Over time some firms came to specialize in tools for building machines.

Scholars have long debated whether large capital flows are a good thing for poor countries. Historically, the record is mixed. The lands of new settlement in the nineteenth century – Canada, the United States, and Australia – grew rapidly while receiving massive inflows of foreign investment. Other less developed countries fared less well. The benefits of investment flows are:

- Most obviously, they increase the capital to labor ratio, and thus should raise per capita incomes.
- New technology may be transferred along with foreign investment.

The costs of foreign investment are:

- Foreign investors may – in part due to corrupt influence on poor country governments – earn a flow of profits that more than absorbs the social benefit of their investment.
- Foreign investment may increase instability in financial markets (because it may suddenly be withdrawn). This problem is greatest when financial regulation is weakest. Notably, this concern is greater for short-term capital flows than for longer-term investments.
- Fear of capital flight may limit a country's ability to manage macroeconomic policy or financial regulation as it wishes. (Alternatively, governments may be encouraged in this way to pursue macroeconomic and financial stability.)
- Foreign investment is usually good for producers of exports, but may hurt producers of import substitution goods. These results depend on the availability of local entrepreneurship.

Stiglitz (in Snowdon 2002, 396) argues that foreign direct investment is good for growth but short-term capital movements may do more harm than good. A less controversial sort of common ground between the two perspectives would argue that good governance (financial regulation, lack of corruption) will accentuate the positive effects of foreign investment while limiting the negative effects. We will reach a similar conclusion in our discussion of trade policy below.

6.2.4 Foreign Aid

There has been lots of empirical work of late on whether aid works. At the country level there is no correlation between aid received and growth experienced. But David Dollar at the World Bank has shown that when aid is spent in the right countries – those that are poor but have good governance – aid is important.[9] At present, countries with bad policies get more aid than countries with good policies,

---

[9] Africa has received very little non-military non-emergency aid, and thus its failures cannot be blamed on aid (Sachs 2005, 310).

but aid agencies (like Canada's) increasingly appreciate the role of governance. Collier and Gunning (1999) follow many studies in suggesting that aid is helpful under good political regimes but harmful under bad. Fears that aid is channeled to corruption or war can be dealt with by working through non-governmental organizations. Aid may also be used as an incentive to encourage good governance, though it is not yet clear how successful this policy is. Sachs (2005, 266-8) suggests that the existing cycle – whereby poor countries only pretend to reform when this is demanded by international agencies – can only be broken by raising aid levels, but then actually penalizing countries that do not reform.

Aid agencies have also slowly learned some important lessons over the years. Aid works best when locals are consulted about its likely effects. Irrigation schemes have in particular often foundered in the past due to a lack of local consultation. Sadly, while aid agencies all now give lip service to consultation, locals are still often faced with a limited set of choices. Aid agencies also increasingly emphasize the sort of public services that are provided by governments in developed countries: infrastructure, health, education, water, and so on. Research is another potentially important area for aid: Poor countries cannot afford research on tropical diseases or agriculture, energy systems for remote areas, fragile ecosystems, and climate forecasting (Sachs 2005, 282-3).

6.2.5 Microfinance

Microfinance helps the poorest. It provides very small loans, but these allow poor people to buy capital equipment or raw materials, and thus establish financial independence. It is largely self-financing but start-up capital is needed. There are substantial economies of scale, and thus interest rates on lending can fall with size. Expansion should thus be encouraged where leadership and institutions are in place, and lots of poor could benefit. Commercial credit, and even regular banks, can sometimes support microfinance. These often wish to charge much higher interest rates, and there is a huge debate these days regarding the pros and cons of strictly profit-oriented microfinance as commercial banks move into the field. Daley-Harris and Awibo (2006) want to see a quadrupling of the number of people served over the next decade. Microfinance requires a supportive network of banks, rating agencies, consultants, and information services for entrepreneurs. Microfinance institutions increasingly do not just lend but provide saving and other services.

It should be stressed that economists and others had under-appreciated the effect that very small loans could have on very poor people. They also had underestimated the degree to which peer pressure within small groups could ensure high rates of repayment from individuals too poor to provide collateral. They thus failed to appreciate how culture could be drawn upon to substitute for missing economic considerations.

6.2.6 Psychology and Investment

Attitudes to both time and risk will influence investment decisions. Individuals and cultures differ in how much they are willing to make sacrifices in the present in order to gain in future.[10] Note, though, that differences in savings rates also reflect differences in institutions, age distribution, and expectations of communal sharing. As for risk, poor people tend to be more averse to risk for the simple reason that bad outcomes threaten their very survival. A social safety net can encourage risk-taking behavior.

6.3 Openness to Trade

Solow (2005, 4) argues that there has been less modeling of how growth occurs in open economies than he would have expected fifty years ago. Growth models tend to focus entirely on the internal dynamics of the growth process. This is unfortunate. Static economic analysis suggests that free trade is good, for countries by pursuing their comparative advantage will be able to increase the value of their total output. They will export goods that they are relatively good at producing, and import goods that they are relatively poor at producing. This is one of the most powerful insights in all of economics. Yet it is not clear that it carries well into a dynamic context. What if productivity is advancing fastest in the goods a country imports? It will still benefit by being able to import more as the international price of these goods falls, but not as much as if its own economy was experiencing rapid productivity growth. And thus there is a theoretical possibility that a country might benefit in the long run by sacrificing some of the short-term gains from trade in order to encourage production of goods where productivity is advancing.

6.3.1 The Empirical Literature

Though theoretical analysis has been limited, there has been a great deal of empirical investigation of the link between trade policy and growth. Both cross-section and time-series analyses suggest a strong effect of openness on growth. Indeed the correlation found is generally much stronger than can be explained by static considerations of comparative advantage – which for the most part generate a one-time benefit to openness rather than sustained growth. Paul Romer and other growth theorists note that economists lack a rigorous model of why there would be

---

[10] Societies should likely discount the future less than individuals, for societies need not die, and the happiness of future generations should not be sacrificed for the present. Thus, public goods like schools might be pursued which provide a lower return than private investment.

more than a one-time effect of trade openness (Romer stresses information flows and scale effects; see below)

Recently, some economists, notably Dani Rodrik, have questioned the robustness of these empirical results. Rodrik notes that 'openness to trade' is difficult to measure in practice, and may be credited mistakenly to countries that are growing and thus experiencing increases in exports (and perhaps imports) as a result. The statistical results are also highly sensitive to the time period examined: trade openness seems associated with growth since the 1970s but not before (Easterly 230-1). This reflects the fact (stressed by Chang 2002) that most less developed countries grew faster in the 1960s while pursuing protectionist policies than after with more open policies. Still, Rodrik does not dismiss entirely the advantages of openness, but argues that any successful trade regime must be coupled with good institutions (see below) (Snowdon 2002, 187-90).[11]

The economic history literature casts even greater doubt on the advantages of openness. Kenneth O'Rourke and others have found that growth was correlated with protectionism in both the nineteenth century and interwar period, but not in the postwar period. This result accords well with the more general tendency of economic historians to stress domestic factors in explaining economic growth in the eighteenth and nineteenth centuries. It should be stressed that levels of protection in nineteenth century Europe were much lower than those observed in postwar less developed countries. Still one might wonder why protectionism would appear advantageous at some times rather than others. Crafts wonders if openness is only a good policy in later stages of development (in Snowdon 274-5). It is thus a good strategy for modern developed countries but not for countries at early stages of the development process. Or it could be that protectionism was more useful in an age of manufacturing than in a world dominated by services.

Taking a longer timeframe and treating trade more generally, recent scholarship in economic history suggests that economic growth in the centuries before the Industrial Revolution was driven primarily by trade expansion rather than technological innovation. Agricultural productivity expanded where market access was greatest. Epstein (2000) suggests that growth occurred fastest where barriers to trade were lowest.

Chang (2002) argues that the trade policies pursued by developed countries when they were developing are quite different from the policies they now urge upon developing countries. Britain protected its industry as well as agriculture well into the nineteenth century, and only embraced free trade when it was already clearly the world's most developed economy. France, Germany, Sweden, and the United States were highly protectionist until much later in the nineteenth century.

---

[11] Trade liberalization is good, but some critical caveats must be kept in mind. First, partial liberalization can cause more distortions than improvements. If there are severe internal market imperfections, trade liberalization may be detrimental. If the economy is large, it should worry about optimal tariffs. (this may have been the case for cocoa exports from West Africa). These caveats (and others) might be ignored if there was unambiguous evidence that trade liberalization systematically improves economic performance, but there is not (Rodrik 2005, 985-6).

Yet these nations all argued against tariff protection in the colonies they held and used their military strength to induce other developing nations to agree to low tariffs. Chang thus argues that present International Monetary Fund policies, though likely unintentionally, can be seen as a continuation of nineteenth century policies that denied developing countries the use of tariff protection. Chang's analysis can be critiqued on a couple of grounds. He does not entertain the possibility that the tariffs he described were intended in part to generate revenue rather than protect (though he is aware that countries at the time had limited sources of revenue; 101). Yet Chang can be excused here for it does seem clear that the tariffs were set at a level designed to discourage imports rather than raise revenue (since revenue only accrues if goods are actually imported). Still, in giving advice on trade policy to less developed countries one should take care to ensure that their fiscal capability is not unduly hampered. A more serious critique is that Chang only establishes correlation rather than causation. To be sure, the correlation shows that growth is hardly impossible in a protective environment. But it can not establish the stronger argument which Chang implies: that protectionism encouraged growth. Chang doubts that the fact that protectionist policies are observed across all of these countries can be a coincidence, but economists have no difficulty in attributing protectionist policies to self-interested politicians rewarding special interests. Most economists could read Chang and remain happily convinced that these countries would have grown even faster if not for protectionism.

Chang himself takes pains to emphasize that tariffs may not have been the most important component of these countries' industrial policies. All European countries engaged in industrial espionage (55-6). None gave protection to foreign intellectual property until late in the nineteenth century. They also variously invested in industry, provided subsidies, or supported research and development (66). Chang also appreciates that historical attempts to protect 'infant industries' during the early stages of industrial development often fail(ed). Yet he still concludes that industries would have had a hard time competing with more advanced countries without some tariff protection. Industrial espionage provided an imperfect understanding of foreign technologies, and thus years or decades were required to catch up technologically. The lower wages of relatively backward countries were not enough to overcome this gap.

This last argument deserves further attention. Arguably, poor countries might be able to overcome technological backwardness because of their lower wage rates: they can then be less productive but still competitive. This argument is potentially powerful but is generally not carefully expressed in terms of comparative advantage. Comparative advantage supplanted in the nineteenth century the misguided theory of absolute advantage: that countries only exported goods that they were better at producing in some absolute sense. David Ricardo showed that countries would still benefit from trade even if in some absolute sense they were better (or worse) at producing everything. Arguments about the advantages of low wages are often implicitly couched in absolute advantage terms. But low wages characterize the entire economy. And comparative advantage appreciates what absolute advantage neglects: that the country cannot export everything (for it would have no imports to spend its export earnings on – ignoring the alternative of capital imports for the moment). The country will export those goods in which it has a comparative advantage, and those will be goods for which its advantage in terms of wages is counteracted to the least extent by international differences in productivity. Low wages then provide no benefit to those industries suffering the greatest productivity disadvantage. And thus low wages will often not allow countries to successfully close a technology gap: comparative advantage will guide them to export goods where they have less of a technological disadvantage.

6.3.2 An Alternative to Comparative Advantage

I have long puzzled over the connection between trade and growth, but from a different angle. If trade is indeed driven by comparative advantage, then why should an increase in trade signal superior economic performance – it can only mean that the country is increasingly different from others (leaving aside for the moment changes in trade barriers). Why should being different be such a good thing? If we move away from explaining trade flows in terms of comparative advantage this question disappears. If trade is not driven by comparative advantage but rather by qualitative differences in goods (so that countries effectively export goods that cannot be produced elsewhere), then an innovative economy will have more qualitatively different goods to export. We can celebrate Japan's export prowess because this reflected a reputation for reliable and innovative automobiles and electronic products. In turn the failures of planned economies reflected the fact that they produced few goods attractive to foreign markets for quality reasons.

Comparative advantage, while attractive theoretically, is simply not the main force driving trade. The weak force, comparative advantage, is stressed by economic theory, but the stronger force of absolute differences in technology and organization is not.[12] An appreciation of such absolute differences explains why exports are a sign of economic prowess. It also explains the Leontief Paradox: the fact that most trade in the world occurs between rich countries, whereas comparative advantage suggests that trade should occur between countries that are quite different. Rich countries export and import qualitatively different goods, embodying different technologies (or organizational capabilities), from each other. Countries may both import and export automobiles, for example, but different models of automobile have different characteristics. So a country's share of world trade is a function of its qualitative/technological advantages in particular goods. When

---

[12] Economists are often guilty of applying the results of well-developed static theories such as comparative advantage while ignoring dynamic causal linkages. The World Bank has belatedly recognized that 'the conventional package of reforms was too obsessed with deadweight-loss triangles and reaping the efficiency gains from eliminating them, and did not pay enough attention to stimulating the dynamic forces that lie behind the growth process' (Rodrik 2006, 976).

technology is examined later, we will see that it does flow across borders but not instantaneously, and moreover that certain forms of tacit knowledge (that is, understandings that are hard to put in words) flow very slowly; it is thus possible for firms and countries to maintain a technological edge in a particular product line for many years. When institutions are discussed we will see that institutions, including organizational forms, develop slowly through time, and thus that it can be hard for one society to copy the organization of production observed in another.[13]

Seen in this light, any correlation between trade and growth might reflect reverse causation (as Albert Fishlow famously contended), or both might reflect successful technological innovation. That is, even if a correlation were to be found statistically, it should not necessarily be interpreted as indicating that openness to trade caused growth. A country with goods to export to the world is likely to be more interested in trade. A country that is technologically innovative will both grow faster and trade more than a country that is not (other things equal).

Romer (1994) has argued that the most powerful evidence that technology differences are important for trade flows is that human capital flows to where it is already abundant.[14] Comparative advantage would suggest that the return to human capital should be highest where it is less abundant. However, if some countries have better technology, and this is human-capital intensive, flows in the observed direction should be observed. There are alternative explanations of human capital flows, however: if there are increasing returns (so that human capital is most valuable when it interacts with other human capital) or agglomerative economies (such that economic efficiency is enhanced when activity concentrates geographically), these would also generate flows in the observed direction. Both of these possibilities are addressed later in this chapter. But this should not dissuade us from confidence that qualitative differences drive trade flows. It could be that the most powerful evidence is in fact casual empiricism: we know as consumers that different firms and countries export goods that are perceived to be qualitatively different.

This alternative theoretical approach suggests that empirical research of the link between openness and growth has been misguided. There may not be a strong causal link from openness to growth even when a correlation is observed. But there may be: the alternative theory guides us to look even more closely at the possibility that technology is transferred along with trade. To be sure, this cannot happen instantaneously, or absolute technological advantages could not exist. But it could happen slowly over time: the innovating country may use the technology for a while before the technology migrates to a country with more suitable resources

---

[13] The business historians Hall and Soskice (2001) stress that different institutions generate different abilities to handle risk, innovation and cross-sectoral competition (and thus globalization need not lead to institutional convergence). They note that economists rarely examine institutions as a source of comparative advantage.

[14] Harrigan (1997) notes that many have tested theories of comparative advantage, but he was the first to look empirically at differences in technology as a source of trade flows. This is due in large part to the difficulty of measuring technology – others have looked at how rates of innovation influence trade flows.

(this sort of technology transfer has indeed long been posited within 'product cycle' theory). Most importantly this alternative theory suggests that the idea of 'dynamic comparative advantage' needs to be taken seriously – and perhaps renamed 'dynamic absolute advantage' – for countries will grow faster if they are able to achieve some technological advantage in a range of goods.

6.3.3 Trade and Institutions

Social scientists, as we shall see, worry a great deal about the quality of institutions. That is, they recognize that countries differ a great deal in how well they manage/enforce institutions that may look quite similar on paper. In the realm of trade, however, analysis tends to proceed with respect to a dichotomy between openness and managed trade. There is usually an implicit or explicit assumption that countries cannot manage trade very well. Kohli (2004), a political scientist, argues that the key difference in developmental prospects is between countries that can manage/enforce *any* institutions well, and countries that can manage/ enforce *no* economic institutions well. He argues, for example, that South Korea effectively managed several years of import substitution as well as decades of export promotion (that is, the government was not 'captured' by private industries and encouraged them to improve productivity under both regimes). On the other hand, Nigeria failed miserably with respect to both types of policies (both were perverted to reward friends of the government, and productivity advance was not encouraged) (2004, 376). Kohli appreciates that export promotion may be a superior policy – though he speculates that import substitution may be useful at very early stages of development. But he argues that nevertheless the choice of policy is less important than the skill and dedication and integrity with which it is implemented. Rodrik (2006, 978), an economist, broadly concurs: 'Trade liberalization would not work if fiscal institutions were not in place to make up for lost trade revenue, capital markets did not allocate finance to expanding sectors, customs officials were not competent and honest enough, labor-market institutions did not work properly to reduce transitional unemployment, and so on.'

Economists in criticizing managed trade have recourse to two types of arguments: pointing to the failures of managed trade in many less developed countries, and arguing that successful East Asian economies managed trade less extensively than is generally imagined. Kohli would suggest alternative explanations in both cases. Most less developed countries lacked the ability or will to manage trade effectively. East Asian governments were focused on making their firms internationally effective and thus naturally did not ignore market signals while managing trade. Kohli's analysis may provide a more powerful argument for freer trade among countries with limited institutional capability, for freer trade may be easier to manage. But it raises the possibility that effective governments might usefully deviate in significant ways from free trade.

There may be a feedback effect from trade to institutions. Rodrik (2003) argues that trade and good institutions are mutually reinforcing empirically. It could be that companies that trade put pressure on their countries to develop institutions that enhance the country's ability to trade. There is some support from economic historians for the conjecture that trading companies were a force for institutional improvement in at least European economic history.

6.3.4 Trade and Resources

Should poor countries worry if they find themselves exporting agricultural goods or natural resources while importing manufactured goods? The analysis above suggests a potential problem if productivity is advancing fastest in manufactures.[15] Yet staple theory – developed by Canadian economic historians to understand economic growth in lands of new settlement, but since extended more generally (Altman 2002) – suggests that there may well be advantages to such exports, especially in early stages of development. Staple theory suggests linkages from the exported good. Backward linkages are those necessary to bring the good to market: transport infrastructure and the tools needed to farm or mine are the best examples. Forward linkages involve the processing of the good for export. The final demand linkage captures the local market created as workers earn money in the export sector. Exports may thus stimulate local industry in these three ways. The key insight of staple theory is that goods differ hugely in their linkage effects. Thus the benefit that a country receives from these sorts of exports depends on what goods it exports. If these exports generate useful transport (or other) infrastructure for the wider economy or create a skilled and well-paid labor force (including in processing), then economic growth may be stimulated profoundly.

6.3.5 Costs and Benefits of Openness

The analysis above suggests that a much more nuanced approach to trade may be valuable: it appears that openness may at times have much greater impacts on growth than comparative advantage can explain, and at other times have a negative impact. With respect to the former, economists have for the most part emphasized information flows. Imported goods (especially imported capital goods) carry with them technological information: they encourage local innovators to adopt foreign technology and give them ideas on how to do so. More generally, trade flows are accompanied by people flows: domestic entrepreneurs travel abroad, and

---

[15] Exporting agricultural goods while importing manufactures will shift income from profits to rents, and thus likely reduce investment.

foreign entrepreneurs visit the local economy. In this way, ideas about not just technology but institutions can be communicated. [Note though that foreign direct investment may be a more powerful conduit for information flows, and may be encouraged by tariffs that force the foreign firm to produce locally.] In this way, growth of the fourth type encourages growth of the second and third types.

In chapter 2 we speculated on the direct advantages of growth of the fourth type. Some African countries still have over 80 percent of their population in agriculture. The average for less developed countries is over 50 percent. There may be a limited internal market and little incentive to invest in such countries, and thus access to foreign markets may be of particular importance.

In addition to technology transfer and market access, openness to trade may have the following positive effects:

- Competitive pressure on local firms to compete with imported goods
- Better institutions (see above)
- Export orientation limits the ability of governments to do stupid things; mistakes are recognized faster than if firms only serve a protected local market.

On the negative side several arguments have been put forward:

- As discussed above, the idea that technologically backward countries cannot compete in product lines where technological innovation is rapid.
- Static theories of comparative advantage assume full employment. If, though, unemployment is allowed, then the effect of allowing imports of goods that are difficult to produce locally may release resources that are not absorbed by the export of goods that the country is relatively good at producing (though the increased income resulting from trade should increase demand for domestic goods). On the other hand, though, managed trade may result in the export of capital-intensive goods and exacerbate unemployment difficulties. In practice, trade expansion seems to have had little effect, positive or negative, on unemployment rates in poor countries. But this empirical regularity may reflect conflicting causal mechanisms.
- The effects on income distribution need likewise to be considered. While trade openness should largely benefit unskilled workers in less developed countries to the extent that comparative advantage drives trade flows (as those countries should have a comparative advantage in exporting goods produced with such labor), objections can be expected from poor country capitalists and rich country unskilled labor. In some cases, political stability may be threatened by changes in trade policy. And liberalization must be politically sustainable, or agents will fear a reversal (Rodrik 2005, 985-6).
- Some have worried that the terms of trade (the volume of exports needed to purchase a given quantity of imports) will necessarily move against less developed country exports (but there has been no trend in either direction postwar, though there had been 1870-1940). This tendency might be exacerbated by the fact that trade is most liberalized in manufactures.

Most economists will not readily accept a suggestion that openness to trade is not necessarily a good thing (even this author finds it difficult). Though this reaction is in large part driven by the rhetorical power of comparative advantage theory, we have seen that economists have proven willing to accept arguments that the dynamic gains swamp the static comparative advantage gains. The general confidence of economists in market exchange rather than government directive may be at play here. But if arguments for huge dynamic advantages are allowed, then arguments for dynamic disadvantages cannot simply be ignored. Given the limited degree of theorization of dynamic effects, heavy weight must be placed on the empirical evidence. The statistical analysis, though indicative of a large positive effect at times, is not conclusive. Moreover, any correlation need not imply causation in a particular direction. The historical evidence points in the direction of protectionism being beneficial, but again correlation need not imply causation. Case study analysis is tricky here: it is much easier to identify the many many failed infant industries – those that received protection from government but failed to grow up – than to observe industries that grew behind tariff protection and establish that they could only have done so if protected. In the first case observation alone is enough; in the second a counterfactual needs to be carefully tested.

The idea of dynamic comparative advantage is still viewed with suspicion by economists. It is much more popular in other disciplines.[16] States with 'transformative aspirations' thus pursue leading sectors, and wish to shed lagging sectors (Evans 10). As with the analyses of economists, though, care must be taken in assuming that observed interferences with trade flows were beneficial.

While both theoretical and empirical analyses are thus more muddled than we might like on the grand question of openness, some narrower questions seem much clearer. These important insights can be thought of as 'common ground' in the debate between advocates of openness and advocates of trade barriers:

- Countries must ensure that firms face clear incentives to enhance productivity.
- Countries with incompetent and/or corrupt bureaucracies should be particularly wary of managed trade.
- The inflow of information about technology and institutions should be encouraged, and trade in goods is one way of doing so.
- If governments intervene, policies other than tariffs such as support for research may be of greatest importance.
- The results of empirical analysis might be improved if we looked beyond aggregate measures of openness to ask what sectors are protected and why? Protection only makes sense if there is good reason to expect rapid productivity advance. Trade policy should also not hinder exports that might encourage economic growth.

---

[16] 'Sociologists and historians have long postulated such connections between social and institutional endowments and subsequent positions in the international division of labor ... In a world of constructed comparative advantage social and political institutions – the state among them – shape international specialization' (Evans 1995, 9).

6.4 Technology

6.4.1 Interdisciplinarity and Technology

The existence of the interdisciplinary field of science and technology studies sends a powerful signal that interdisciplinarity is especially important in the study of technology. Meeus and Hage (2006) edit an interdisciplinary handbook precisely because of a feeling that management specialists, economists, sociologists, historians, political scientists and others need to integrate their efforts. They despair of the narrowness of much previous research. They note that political scientists tend to stress government policies, management scholars look at firm behavior, economists and sociologists emphasize industry-level analysis, and STS scholars stress scientific innovation (but that very few scholars in any discipline have until recently looked at behavior in research laboratories); they urge a co-evolutionary perspective in which the interactions among different levels of analysis are appreciated (2006, 4).

6.4.2 Technology as a Cause of Growth

As was noted above in our discussion of investment, growth accounting suggests that increases in productivity have been far more important than increases in capital stock in generating growth, at least in the modern Western world. The same result is found in more recent cross-country growth regressions: differences in productivity growth rates explain more than half the difference in economic growth rates across countries. This result is widely assumed today by economists, but was viewed as a surprise when the first generation of production function estimates found that investment could explain only a third or so of economic growth. Over the decades, it was found that adjustments to the labor variable to reflect higher levels of educational attainment proved able to explain a further fraction of the growth experience. After all plausible adjustments to functional form had been made, a sizeable residual remained, which was generally thought to primarily reflect technological advance (but also advances in economic efficiency due to institutional improvement). Moreover, as noted above, the return on investment itself depends critically on whether new machines embody new technology. In addition to its direct effect on productivity technological innovation may enhance both the amount and quality of investment (Grossman and Helpman 1994).

We have seen above that one must be careful in interpreting the results of these growth accounting regressions. And this is especially the case with the residual:

any errors in the estimation will inevitably be reflected in the residual. And thus thoughtful economists look elsewhere for corroboration. 'Perhaps the most convincing direct evidence in favor of viewing industrial innovation as the engine of growth comes from the work of economic historians ... As yet no empirical study proves that technology has been the engine of modern-day growth' But the thought exercise of what the world would be like without electricity, steel, or computers suggests this is so (Grossman and Helpman 1994).

While it is now well accepted that innovation is the engine of modern economic growth, the links between innovation and growth in the shorter run are harder to establish. Both electrification and computers took decades to show up clearly in productivity statistics. One problem may be the failure to distinguish product and process innovation (see below): product innovation is largely missed by productivity measures. Another is that the effects of an innovation depend on both diffusion and improvement, both of which take time. Moreover, it should be emphasized again that technology affects not just productivity but investment. The development of new products likely also stimulates consumption, and we shall see below that innovation likely also affects levels of (un)employment.

6.4.3 The Course of Technological Innovation (Endogeneity)

While endogenous growth theory can be applauded for both re-invigorating the interest of economists in economic growth and re-focusing attention on innovation, it carries the obvious danger that economists will actually believe that innovation is entirely endogenous.

> In the New [endogenous] Growth Theory, the entire learning process, and the conditions on which its success and development depend, are represented by inserting two variables into its equations: (a) investment in research and development, and (b) investment in tangible capital (together with some observations about increasing returns and learning by doing). The actual 'progress of technology' remains an unopened black box (Rosenberg 2000, 81).

Technological innovation is both exogenous and endogenous. Innovators respond to economic incentives. But they are constrained in doing so by the state of existing technological and scientific understanding. And they are influenced as they operate by a host of institutional, cultural, and political phenomena as well. Attempts to encourage innovation while ignoring these non-economic influences are likely to be misguided and perhaps ineffectual.

Predicting economic growth or providing policy advice relevant to (especially technological aspects of) economic growth without reference to the state of knowledge is particularly misguided. 'The obvious notion that economies are limited in what they can do by their useful knowledge bears some emphasizing simply because so many scholars believe that if incentives and demand are right, somehow technology will follow automatically' (Mokyr 2002, 16). Solow (1994) also critiques the endogeneity assumption on this ground: 'For one thing there is probably an irreducibly exogenous element in the research and development process, at least exogenous to the economy. Fields of research open up and close down unexpectedly, in economics as well as in science and technology' (51-2).[17]

Many firms reduced their research expenditures in the 1970s due to a feeling that there were fewer technological opportunities. An endogenous growth theorist might mistakenly attribute the growth slowdown in the 1970s to such decisions. It might be more accurate to attribute both (in part) to the fact that the technological trajectories that had fuelled postwar innovation and growth had been largely exhausted, and new trajectories such as biotechnology had not yet emerged.

There are also unforeseen results of innovation. Marconi never imagined commercial radio. Innovators cannot predict either their likely success at innovation or the likely impact of their innovations. There is thus no constant relationship between research expenditure and results. The uncertainty that inherently plagues innovative activity is a problem for economic models, for rational decision-making is impossible in the face of uncertainty (chapter 3). In the face of this uncertainty, we should be careful of assuming that innovators respond in some simple fashion to economic incentives. Indeed we have seen in chapter 3 that various non-rational decision-making strategies may come into play in the face of uncertainty. One such strategy involves 'doing what others do' and thus we must expect that cultural beliefs may play an important role in determining what are perceived to be promising avenues of research.

Nelson and Winter (1982) argued that while economic and other factors influenced innovation, there are also natural trajectories of innovation. A generation of neo-Schumpeterian scholars followed them. Authors showed how innovations in aircraft or microelectronic technology followed a logical and somewhat predictable trajectory. But the sociologist Donald McKenzie in 1990 warned us not to be too sure of the naturalness of trajectories. Such trajectories exist only if scientists and engineers believe these are fruitful directions for research. Such beliefs become even more important when we study how different technological trajectories interact. In addition to appreciating how innovations depend on previous innovations, then, we must also appreciate how culture, politics, and other phenomena influence what innovators perceive to be viable avenues of investigation.

Now that much innovation is institutionalized in industrial research laboratories, economic motives may play a greater role than in the past.[18] But note both

---

[17] One powerful piece of evidence for the argument that there are 'technological trajectories' is the common experience of simultaneous innovation in history. Bell and Gray invented telephones within days of each other in 1876. Of course, simultaneous innovation may also reflect supportive changes in culture or politics.

[18] Rosenberg (2000) argues that science and technology have become much more endogenous over the twentieth century due to the rise of industrial research labs and increased university/industry collaboration; scientists may still be driven by curiosity but decisions about how many of which type to employ are not (and even the best scientists want fame). But Rosenberg stretches the concept of endogeneity to include the idea that successful innovations encourage

that independent innovators are still important, and also that there are organizational challenges in ensuring that employees of industrial research laboratories act in accord with the wishes of their supervisors (see below). As well, different firms pursue different research strategies, guided by their unique organizational capabilities and perceptions of opportunities. If innovation were truly endogenous to economic incentives, we might expect much less diversity across firms.

Endogenous growth theory not only abstracts away from the range of causal influences on the rate of innovation but may support a mistaken impression that technological innovation occurs *quickly*. Empirical work often assumes that changes in economic incentives result in fairly immediate changes in the rate of innovation. Scholars of technological innovation have identified several characteristics of the innovative process that are neglected by endogenous growth theory:

- A particular innovative process can be broken into stages. First, the problem to be solved must be appreciated. Then, the relevant pieces of information (which of course cannot be known beforehand) must be brought together. An act of insight is then possible. But this must be followed by a period of critical revision during which the idea is made practicable. These steps each take time, and all except the act of insight generally involve multiple people and organizations. It could be that curiosity plays a big role in early steps, and financial incentives are more important in later steps.
- The development of a technically feasible innovation sets the stage for a further set of steps in which the innovation is scaled up for use, incubated, demonstrated, promoted, and transmitted. Again these steps take time and generally involve multiple agents.
- Innovative processes do not happen in isolation but interact. Technological evolution differs from biological evolution in this way, for biological species only rarely cross-breed. The cross-fertilization of ideas increases the uncertainty associated with innovation, for the value of a particular innovation often depends on other innovations of which the innovator may be entirely unaware.
- The success of an innovative effort is far from a simple function of the resources devoted to it. Some directions of research will be more successful than others, but the best path cannot be flawlessly predicted in advance. Radical innovations in particular involve the integration of understandings from diverse fields that nobody had previously thought to put together.
- Evolutionary processes are inherently wasteful. Most mutations (innovative ideas, in this case) fail.
- We can think of technological innovation as a branching process where certain decisions constrain choice for a while until another decision point is reached. There is thus path dependence: the research trajectory of today reflects a series of past decisions. Scholars differ on how important this is in the long run: if

---

more research along those lines. He recognizes (66) that the return to research depends on the state of technological knowledge, and especially whether there have recently been major new innovations (see below).

one technology is much superior to alternatives there may be a variety of paths that lead to its discovery.

- Learning by doing (where innovations are developed relatively unintentionally in the course of production) is clearly important (though it has been difficult to measure) but cannot be the major source of innovation. It cannot proceed far without requiring changes in capital.
- Some innovations result from chance, when a technique works better or worse than expected.
- We can also stress the importance of history. As was stressed decades ago by the economic historian Abbot Payson Usher, innovation is of necessity a 'historical' event. Indeed he saw a/the special role for economic history in the explanation of the emergence of (technological and institutional) novelty. Innovation cannot be predicted in advance, but can be explained after in terms of the information that was combined in the mind of the innovator and the innovator's various incentives to innovate. Particular innovations, that is, must be explained in terms of an analytical historical narrative.[19] But Usher warned against the tendency of historians to tell a tightly-bound story: any innovation was not necessarily the end of a story but might lead to others. Usher thus reacted against the 'genius' explanation of innovation that attributed advance to isolated geniuses: not only was this inconsistent with the historical record of collaboration in innovation but it left the scholar with nothing to explain. Usher also objected to the explanation of innovation uniquely with respect to the demand for innovations: necessity is ubiquitous but only some human needs or desires are rewarded with successful innovation. He thus would have objected to treating innovation entirely as a response to economic incentives.

Historians of technology, as we have seen in chapter 4, explain particular innovations with reference to a mixture of technological, economic, and socio-cultural influences. This large body of scholarly research should not be ignored when discussing the sources of technological innovation. Yet it can be hard to draw generalizations from innovation-specific historical work. The role of technological trajectories is perhaps easier to comprehend than the diverse influences that institutions and culture may play. One point to stress is that the various causal factors – technological trajectories, economic incentives, cultural and political influences – are of different relative importance at different stages of the innovative process. Economic incentives may loom largest in the later stages, but then their effectiveness will depend on whether earlier stages have been prosecuted (and prosecuted successfully) for other reasons.

---

[19] See the 'classic review' by George Grantham of Usher's *History of Mechanical Innovation* on www.eh.net.

6.4.4 Clustering, General Purpose Technologies

Two characteristics of the history of innovation are treated here. First, some innovations are more important than others. Certain innovations, generally styled 'General Purpose Technologies (GPTs),' – examples are steam engines, electrification, and computers – are so important both economically and technologically that they spawn a series of follow-up innovations. Second, some historical periods see more innovations than others. This clustering seems often to extend beyond the confines of any one GPT. For both these reasons, there is much greater innovative potential at some times than others.[20]

General purpose technologies can be defined imperfectly in terms of both their pervasive use and their pervasive instigation of a series of incremental innovations. (Economists often also stress the steady improvement of the GPT itself). GPTs often encourage an initial drop in productivity as workers and managers learn the new technology, but later yield major productivity advances. (Thus the acceleration in productivity growth observed in the 1920s and 1990s is attributed in large part to electrification and information technology, both GPTs). It should nevertheless be appreciated that the balance between product and process innovation may vary by GPT. GPTs are also associated with creative destruction: new firms and sectors arise at the expense of old. In the twentieth century GPTs have increased the skill premium and thus worsened income distributions, but this may not be a general outcome (Jovanovic and Rousseau 2005).

Lipsey, Carlaw, and Bekar (2006) discuss the causes and effects of GPTs in some depth. History is not characterized by the steady development of technology, but by the occasional occurrence of major innovations: these in turn generate opportunities for a series of comparatively minor improvements to these technologies. Thus, for technological reasons alone, some periods are more conducive to innovation than others. The terminology used to distinguish major from minor innovations is still vague, but the general point is nevertheless clear: the steam engine, the internal combustion engine, and the electric generator all ushered in periods of refinement and application. Nor are major innovations limited to power generation: new processes of iron manufacture or textile manufacture or the late nineteenth century refinements in the theory of organic chemistry all likewise ushered in periods of intensive technological innovation. While we can make some generalizations about GPTs, each GPT's effect on economy and society are dominated by path dependence associated with unique [idiographic] characteristics of the GPT. Note though that GPTs tend to have effects across a range of sectors.

Bruland and Mowery (2004) bemoan the tendency of historians to identify eras in terms of a handful of key technologies. They instead stress the changing nature

---

[20] 'These observations add up to an essentially Schumpeterian view of long-term development. Major economic expansion periods appear driven by the widespread diffusion of a host of interrelated innovations – a technology cluster – leading to new products, markets, industries, and infrastructures' (Grubler 1997, 28).

of economic activity. But they then define the first Industrial Revolution in terms of craft-oriented trial and error, the second in terms of industrial research labs, and the recent third Industrial Revolution as more diffuse but characterized by a large role for the state and for new firms. Still, their analysis is important in stressing that GPTs are not the only reason for clustering, and that a variety of cultural and institutional factors may play a role as well.

Perez (2002), drawing on decades of work with Chris Freeman and others, argues that technological revolutions occur every half century or so; that these provide high but risky returns in the early stages and thus encourage financial exuberance (and inevitable bubbles); that these not only lead to the rise of new industries but the revitalization of some old industries; that these encourage and require developments in infrastructure, industrial organization, management, and other institutions (education, intellectual property, corporate governance, international trade); that these other changes have important effects on the direction and rate of technological innovation (thus technological determinism is avoided); that these other changes occur slowly and thus the full benefits of the revolution occur with a long time lag (and also because of continued improvements in the technology itself); that structural unemployment is common in the early stages; that a recession/ depression is likely a couple of decades in; that some countries and regions are better able or willing to adjust and thus there are changes in economic and technological leadership. The approach is intended to organize our understanding of the rich diversity of history rather than place it in a straightjacket. Still, most scholars (including this one) are skeptical that this approach assumes a much greater regularity in historical experience than seems to be the case. As with other 'systems' theories, one can appreciate the individual causal linkages without accepting the prediction of regular cycles. Though the Perez ideas are controversial, the link between technological and institutional change (and particularly that new technology often requires new institutions) is widely appreciated and has been the subject of much research (Fagerberg 2005; also regulation theory). If institutional innovation is required in order to benefit fully from new technology (especially GPTs), then countries better able and willing to undertake these institutional changes may assume technological leadership.

I will not rehash the whole literature on Long Waves (sometimes called Kondratiev cycles), as it has fallen out of favor – but note in this regard the remark by Mandel in the 1970s that this literature tends itself to Long Waves that peak during economic downturns.[21] As noted in chapter 10 there are medium term economic fluctuations, and thus the idea of Long Waves – regular cycles in economic activity of about a half century in length – is empirically plausible. But whether these fluctuations are 'regular' or reflect the confluence of diverse causal

---

[21] The interdisciplinarian may well have recourse to past works in a discipline but this complicates the task enormously; at least within disciplines evaluation is aided by historical sensibility. Indeed one of the sources of scholarly bias identified by Szostak 2004 lies in the time path of evolution of disciplinary thinking.

mechanisms is an open empirical question. Much but not all of the literature on Long Waves stresses technological cycles (others stress movements in profits or inventories or trade). The literature on GPTs itself implies that irregularity in the time path of innovation might underpin unevenness in growth experience over time. But is there a feedback such that GPTs themselves are more likely at different points in the cycle? Empirically, it is not clear that innovations cluster during particular types of economic performance (statistical analysis needs to be complemented by careful case study analysis here, given the problems with data on innovation). Theoretically it can be argued that radical innovation is most likely when firms are struggling during a downturn (a point of view consistent with Nelson and Winter's (1982) view of firms clinging to routines until shocked into change); alternatively innovation of all types may be more likely when firms have high profits. Research expenditure certainly does not increase during downturns, but risk-taking might. There is also less risk that radical innovations will suffer from improvements to existing technology during a downturn.

6.4.5 Research and Growth

Will the rate of technological innovation observed in the recent past continue in the future? Optimists suggest that the possibilities for innovation are still expanding. While it is exceedingly rare for species to cross-breed, technological innovation often combines diverse elements. Gilfillan (1935) defined innovation as a new combination of existing ideas. This suggests that possibilities for combination increase through time as we generate new ideas. Pessimists fear that we may be approaching the limits of human understanding. They note that the rate of innovation has not expanded anywhere near as fast as the level of investment in research in recent decades. There are ten times as many researchers today in the United States as a half century ago (Weil 2006). If the ratio of innovation to research expenditure has been falling, it may not be possible for the level of investment in research to continue to rise at the same rate in future. The discussion of the preceding sections leads us to be wary of predicting trends on the basis of the last couple of decades. The size of the research establishment and the return to investment in research is likely to fluctuate through time. Nevertheless, policymakers can usefully reflect on the implications of rising or falling returns to investment in research.

Endogenous growth models suggest that spillovers are very large (that is, technology is used by many who did not develop it), and thus the social return to innovation – and likely to investment in technology-embodying equipment – is much higher than the private return (some estimates have placed the social return as high as 75 percent). If so, an increase in research expenditure would have a noticeable effect on growth (though this might take time). It might then be worthwhile for governments to encourage more research (see below). Note that this result continues to hold even if it is thought that returns to investment in research might be falling. However, our discussion above leads us to expect that returns will differ dramatically across research projects.

At the local level, there are likely complementarities between research and skilled labor and capital (and between one skilled worker and others). Highly trained workers tend to flow to high technology areas (unless the technology can flow to them). Given these complementarities it may be necessary to kick-start the process in poor countries: the return to investment in physical or human capital or technology will be low until some critical threshold is reached.

6.4.6 Product Versus Process Innovation

Meeus and Hage (2006, 4) find that their very efforts to define 'innovation' require the specification of the distinction between product and process innovation. Product innovations create new or at least qualitatively new products (the automobile, airplane, or compact disc). Process innovations instead generate improvements in the way existing products are made. Damanpour and Aravind (2006) note that the distinction has been found important by many scholars in explanations of business cycles, product cycles, firm-level management, production, employment, imitation and the appropriability of innovation. Yet endogenous growth theory rarely heeds this important distinction.[22] Solow (1994) worried that new growth theory focused only on product innovation (with decreased costs seen as product innovation in intermediate goods) and that this would bias future theorizing. Ironically, empirical work often uses productivity as a proxy for innovation, and this captures process innovation much more than product innovation (and also includes non-technological developments in economic efficiency).

Szostak (1995) stressed the quite different nature and effects of the two types of innovation. Economic growth in the long run requires both (for they respectively generate the second and third types of growth identified in chapter 2). If the past centuries had consisted only of process innovation, we would have trouble spending our incomes only on goods available in 1800. Yet we can afford the range of new products introduced over the centuries only because of the income increases associated with process innovation. Fortunately most major innovations yield streams of both product and process innovation. During the interwar period, there was a huge amount of process innovation and almost no product innovation (at least in the decade after 1925). Much of interwar unemployment can be attributed to this technological imbalance, for the medium term effect of product innovation is generally to increase investment, consumption, and employment, while the medium term effect of process innovation is generally the reverse (see chapter 10).

---

[22] Aghion and Howitt (1998, ch. 12) are one of the few cases in which this distinction is included in models. They were attempting to place limits on the increasing returns associated with innovation. They argued (implausibly) that spillovers only occur within product lines.

Researchers may at times be guided to pursue one or the other type of innovation. In the late 1920s there was arguably more potential for process innovation, due to the time-path by which the technological potential of the GPTs of the Second Industrial Revolution (electrification, chemicals, internal combustion) was discovered. It may also be that industrial research laboratories at the time were biased toward process innovation (Szostak 1995). Given that process and product innovation likely differ in important ways in both their causes and effects, academic research that ignores this distinction is likely to provide misleading results.

6.4.7 Technology Transmission

Technology transmission generally refers to the movement of technology between countries; diffusion is used for transmission within one country. The two processes are similar in many respects. A simple but important insight is that the technology must first be moved and then adopted. These are interdependent steps but face different challenges. The first step involves the communication of the new technology. The second involves a decision to adopt the new technology. The first depends primarily on transport and communications, but also on institutions. International patent laws have an important effect on the willingness of companies to communicate ideas to others. Much of the international communication of technology occurs within multinational firms. The second depends on whether the receiving firm/country thinks the technology superior; this depends on how suitable the technology is economically (including whether it can be improved to make it more suitable), but also on cultural attitudes toward foreign ideas. Note that since the selection environment for (innovation and) diffusion includes institutions and culture, the economically superior option is not necessarily chosen.

Keller (2004) surveys a wide range of empirical work by economists which suggests that imports of technology are responsible for as much as 90 percent of productivity growth in most countries (and 60 percent even for the United States). Both regressions and case studies (he recommends the use of both) suggest that technology transfer is encouraged by trade flows (though the effect of exports in encouraging technology imports is found only in case studies) and foreign investment, as well as the availability of local technological capability.

Advances in transport and communication technologies have not surprisingly enhanced the rate at which technology diffuses. It took 5000 years for agriculture to reach Britain, 2000 years for metal tools, and only 250 for iron-making technology (Diamond 1997). We should be careful not to neglect the 'transport' component: while modern communications technologies allow ideas to be transmitted instantaneously throughout the world, the movement of people and/or machines is generally required for successful technology transmission.

The fact that technology diffusion generally requires personal interaction reflects what literary scholars would call a signifier/signified problem: blueprints and instructions represent imperfectly a particular technology.[23] This raises the possibility that scholars of technology might learn from literary scholars and philosophers about sources of ambiguity and what types of information tend to get lost in written texts. Unfortunately most literary analysis focuses on establishing yet more examples of ambiguity rather than clarifying which types of information are most poorly communicated and why. But literary scholars and philosophers might potentially contribute to the literature on technology transmission by analyzing technical materials.

If institutions matter, then poor countries may be tempted to encourage the inflow of technology. They may encourage multinationals, guarantee patent protection,[24] or even subsidize the import of technology. Various empirical studies suggest that foreign direct investment is associated with technology transfer (Easterly 2002, 185-6). Note that poor countries may at times be guilty of subsidizing the import of technologies ill-suited to local conditions. If we assume that trade is governed by comparative advantage, and that technology flows freely to its best use, then it would make no sense for countries to try to attract technology. If these assumptions are relaxed, then a technology policy becomes theoretically advantageous. As with trade policy above, this will only be true in practice if governments can properly administer such a policy.

Hall (2004) reprises the work of the sociologist Rogers on whether a country will adopt a new technology: in addition to five individual-level factors (the relative advantage of the innovation, its compatibility with existing technology, its complexity, its ease of testing, and observability), the likelihood of diffusion is also affected by four social considerations: whether decisions are made by individuals, groups, or the state, the internal communication channels involved, norms and networks, and the actions of change agents. Economists stress individual evaluation of costs and benefits, though they increasingly appreciate network effects and will speak of the importance of industrial structure. Sociologists encourage a greater appreciation of relationships and group processes. Hall also notes that the economic historian Nathan Rosenberg has stressed that both new and old technologies evolve during diffusion (due to a feedback effect), and these changes can have an important effect on the rate of diffusion. Moreover, since multiple technologies are diffusing at the same time, rates of diffusion will depend on whether these are complementary. These insights from economic history point to the importance of case study research in understanding diffusion/transmission, and suggest that there may be important elements of path dependence in the process.

---

[23] Metcalfe (2006) distinguishes the knowledge that exists in our minds from the information that we write down. The former is generally greater than the latter. Moreover the same information is interpreted in different ways by different people (this is why one can usually not adopt new technology without doing one's own research). Innovation occurs first in our minds and then needs to be codified. He suggests that if all of us had identical knowledge there would be no innovation.

[24] Not protecting intellectual property rights helps poor countries at first but likely limits the willingness of companies to export higher tech industries to those countries.

For modern poor countries, the greatest concern with respect to suitability is that modern technologies are developed in rich countries possessing lots of capital but high wages; they may not be well suited to countries with little capital but abundant labor.[25] Some scholars suggest that new technologies are often superior across a wide range of factor prices (see our alternative to comparative advantage above). Some modern technologies have traveled well: vaccines and antibiotics are used worldwide, and mobile phones have spread in countries that never developed extensive wired networks. Even if the technology is not immediately suitable it may often be possible to adapt technologies so that they use more labor and less capital. The skills required to adopt a technology are quite similar to the skills required to improve it: Fagerberg (2005) notes that countries that catch up must both innovate and imitate. In sum it becomes largely an empirical question as to how serious the problem of inappropriate technology is with respect to particular technologies.[26] It may be that foreign aid to subsidize research, especially in the areas of tropical medicine and agriculture, would have a very high social rate of return.

While poor countries may face difficulties in adopting the latest technology, they may also have advantages. In the case of mobile phones, entrepreneurs (or the state) in poor countries do not have to worry about competing with extensive wired networks. Those who have invested in old technologies will often try to use their political influence to delay the advent of competing technologies. Countries that can leapfrog over a generation or two of technologies may find themselves able to adopt the latest technologies more quickly than rich countries (Easterly 187-8). This will be especially the case if they have some local advantages with respect to the new technology. Japan and Italy had little coal but much hydroelectric power potential, and quickly adopted electrification in the nineteenth century.

A related problem involves infrastructure. New technologies may require a wide range of raw materials, and thus only be suited to countries with good transport networks. This problem is not new; Szostak (1991a) discussed how transport improvements in eighteenth century England facilitated the adoption of new technologies. Availability of skilled labor, repair facilities, and managerial capabilities may also be problematic.[27] If the new technology is expensive, its adoption may depend on the sophistication of local financial institutions.

Agricultural technology faces greater barriers in transmission, especially across climatic zones. Most agriculture research has focused on the crops and soils of

---

[25] Innovation does not have to be high tech. South Africans invented a rolling barrel for carrying water. Clay ovens are much more energy efficient than open fires. Small turbines can power small villages missed by limited national grids.

[26] Some empirical results suggest that one third to one half of lower productivity in less developed countries may be due to the fact that low-skilled workers are utilized where high-skilled would be more appropriate; these countries may alternatively use older technology requiring fewer skills (Gancia and Ziliboti 2005, 140).

[27] Banerjee and Duflo (2005) note that different firms in poor countries use quite different technologies. The problem is thus not social capability in an aggregate sense but spreading this widely in the economy.

temperate climes, and the resulting technology is often of limited use in warmer or wetter climates. Technologies for processing agricultural goods are sometimes easier to adapt to different crops.

Economic history suggests that cultural attitudes have been important in technology transmission. Europe appears to have been more open to foreign ideas than were Asian civilizations for most of the last millennium, and borrowed and improved many Asian technologies: wind and water wheels, stirrups, and gunpowder among them. Culture also matters in terms of whether local markets exist for goods and services produced with new technologies. The business historians Sabel and Zeitlin (1997, 12-3) note that entrepreneurs in the nineteenth century were well aware of technologies and institutions employed elsewhere, but decided that these were ill-suited to local demand or labor conditions. For example Europeans worried that mass produced goods would fare poorly in fragmented and design-conscious markets. They happily adopted mass production of intermediate goods.

David Jeremy has in many works perhaps studied technology transfer more than any other scholar. He argues that technology transfer has economic, cultural, and technological components, and that no one model deals adequately with all cases. Communication reflects economic and political motives, while adoption depends on capital formation, market size, factor prices, financial institutions, entrepreneurship, and the role of the state. Culture has a large impact on diffusion, with opinion leaders being important. Technical considerations, including the rate of improvement in technology, the availability of local machine-making firms, bottlenecks in related activities (such as supplying necessary inputs), and local technical knowledge also matter.

6.4.8 Links to Technological Innovation

6.4.8.1 Economy → Technology

We have critiqued endogenous growth theory for arguing that technological innovation is entirely endogenous to economic influences. But we could hardly deny that such influences are important. The role of such economic variables as investment in research, market size, wage levels, and financial institutions has been touched on above. The focus here will be on how innovation is best encouraged at the level of firms and industries. While economists have long worried about the connection between industrial structure and innovation, they have had much less to say about what goes on within firms. That literature has tended to be dominated by sociologists (of organization) and business scholars.

What is the relationship between industrial structure and innovation? Competition among firms should encourage innovation. But competitive industries provide lesser opportunities for profit, and thus firms may have less ability to finance innovation (retained earnings are an important source of finance given the uncertainty surrounding research). On the other hand, monopolies are profitable even without innovation and thus incentives to innovate may be slight (Bell Labs is a counterexample of an innovative monopoly; its research was in part motivated by a desire to maintain its monopoly). Economists have long suspected that oligopoly – where a handful of firms compete – may thus be best: firms then have both a competitive motive and profits to invest in research. But this result is not inevitable. Numerous empirical studies establish that oligopoly is correlated with higher levels of research expenditure.[28] It is harder to establish that oligopolies are more innovative given the difficulties of measuring innovation. There is some evidence that the optimal industrial structure for innovation varies by place, time, and sector.

Meeus and Hage (2006, 5) describe the results of research by management scholars at the firm level: these have emphasized the value of division of labor within the research endeavor, decentralized decision-making, and risk-taking strategies. More recently, economists and network analysts have looked at various economic variables, and STS scholars have performed observational analyses of laboratories. Damanpour and Aravind (2006) later in the volume suggest that results at the firm level are mixed, in part as studies have generally failed to distinguish product from process innovation. They speak of ambiguous results regarding firm size and degree of competition, but argue that large firms are much more likely to produce process innovations, but only slightly more likely to produce product innovations. There is little effect of profits on either type of innovation. Diversified firms are more likely to do product innovation and less likely to do process innovation [this may be because they employ diverse processes]. Separation of ownership and control may decrease innovation of both types. Competition is expected to reduce product innovation more than process (due to the possibility of reverse-engineering by competitors) but no effect has been found empirically. Indeed both competition and concentration have been found to have positive effects on both types of innovation [which may reflect the importance of oligopoly]. There is no evidence for the hypothesis that firms shift toward process innovation as industries mature. No effect is consistently found for either technological opportunity or appropriability. There is some evidence that expanding demand encourages innovation. The authors suggest that many of the weak results may reflect the fact that industries will differ in innovative behavior, but most studies lump together diverse industries; likewise firms differ in the technical capabilities inherited from the past. The authors do not make the point but it seems that case studies could usefully supplement statistical analysis here.

---

[28] It could be that the latter generates the former: only a few firms are able to maintain such a research enterprise. When a new technology emerges there are often many firms that pursue it. As technologies mature, only a few firms survive (think of the early automobile industry). That is, only the handful of firms that was able to innovate successfully remains in the industry.

Hage and Meeus (2006) argue that the sociological/management theory of innovation is simple: radical innovation in particular requires a diversity of perspectives, integration of these, and a high-risk strategy by group leaders (without one of these, incremental innovation is more likely). The necessary degree of diversity is increasingly found by looking outside one organization through networks of collaboration, both formal and informal. With respect to integration [a theme that resonates with the approach of this book], they argue that it is important not just to get the right people together but to have shared goals and strategies (549). The problem, here, of course, is that these shared goals and strategies may limit the very creativity required for radical innovation. The authors refer to the hybrid car, where perhaps the path forward seemed clear. The integrative process outlined in this book is designed to encourage integration without constraining creativity. It stresses not goals and strategies but a shared *process* which is flexible enough that researchers can pursue any idea while still readily communicating to others how their research fits together.

Lam (2005) discusses three distinct strategies of scholarly research on innovation at the firm level that should be integrated. A structural approach asks how firm structure affects the propensity to innovate. The cognitive foundations approach shows that different structures generate different types of learning and thus different innovations. The third literature examines processes of organizational change. Within the first tradition, informal relationships are increasingly appreciated along with formal (this change has been inspired by network analysis). The best structure is contingent upon such factors as scale, technology and environment; more fluid structures are superior when there is lots of change.

The second tradition relies on cognitive psychology. It talks about mental models [schemas]. If actors in an organization share mental models they interact more readily but may have blind spots [this argument again has parallels with our discussion of the value of interdisciplinarity]. It is theorized that organizations do have common mental models. If so, interaction with other organizations is critical in overcoming inertia. Institutions shape how firms innovate: long-term employment encourages incremental innovation along the same lines, while new firm entry encourages radical innovation.

Theories of organizational change are of three types. Some stress slow evolution. Some add 'punctuated equilibria' such that there may be brief periods of rapid change. Some further add the idea that firms have some ability to purposely change as the environment changes. Our understanding is limited by the limited contact between scholars of innovation and scholars of organization.

An interdisciplinary approach guides us to pay special attention to the emerging field of 'management of complex systems.' Businesses, especially but not exclusively in their research endeavors, need to cope with complex systems of interaction. Since complex systems are inherently unpredictable, firms should frequently monitor and reassess their goals and strategies. They should embrace change. And they should not only experiment but appreciate that they learn most from failed experiments. Of course, firms must also make money in the short term, and must thus combine these 'complexity' behaviors with hard-headed focus on short term goals as well.

While research at the level of firms has been scattered and statistical analysis largely inconclusive, a handful of key insights can still be noted:

- Large firms need to combat the conservative effect of bureaucracy. Fagerberg (2005) appreciates that firm routines can stifle innovation, and thus encourages novel thinking throughout the firm. Small firms thus continue to play an important role in (especially radical) innovation. Even when big companies develop breakthroughs like the transistor it is often small companies that successfully commercialize them.

- In facing up to the conflict between encouraging creativity and maintaining managerial control, firms face a set of decisions. These include how to allocate funding, how to choose projects, how much freedom to give researchers, how to connect research to production and marketing arms, whether to be bold or reactive, who should be the champion within the firm for new technologies, and should there be spillovers across products. All of these decisions involve uncertainty.

- Successful innovation requires good communication both within and outside firms. Hierarchy limits this.

- The importance of outside links has only recently been emphasized. Firms increasingly network with other firms doing complementary sorts of research. Note that firms need to have in-house research capability in order to utilize externally-generated technology.

- There is a tradeoff between cost of innovation and time to innovate. Competition may push firms to innovate faster.

- Times of major change in technology in a sector are generally associated with changes in industrial leadership internationally. Product cycle theory predicts such changes, but new trade theory does not. Leadership internationally sometimes reflects resources (only rarely natural; more often labor or capital) or institutions or market size, or may simply reflect the development of superior technology. Different forces operate at the level of nations, regions, and firms.

- Financial institutions generally lack the ability to evaluate the risk and uncertainty associated with high technology. Thus retained profits become a particularly important source of financing.

- Recall that evolutionary processes are wasteful; most mutations fail. The danger of big research programs is that firms will not recognize mistakes and will become locked in.

- Loasby (1999, 136) and Mokyr (2000) both make the point that division of labor allows an increase in the total knowledge base but presents challenges in terms of putting the pieces together. By definition, one cannot know whether another possesses useful information until one asks.

- A couple of chapters in the *Handbook of Innovation* stress that innovation occurs in different ways in different sectors, due to differences in technology, institutions, and networks. Policies should be tailored to different sectors. In particular, service innovation is likely quite different. But we have not identified specific policies for services. Fagerberg (2005, 17) suggests that there is lots of research on how different regimes in different industries lead to different results for innovation.

6.4.8.2 Non-human Environment → Technology

Economic historians have long debated the role of natural resources in economic growth. Many of the countries to experience rapid economic growth in the eighteenth and early nineteenth centuries had abundant coal (the main energy source of the time).[29] But not quite all. Japan and Switzerland are two countries that have succeeded despite resource limitations. Resource-rich countries such as Spain and Russia were very slow to develop. At times, resource deficiencies have arguably encouraged growth: it has been suggested that Britain switched to coal (which arguably had greater technological potential) in part because of the rising price of wood. But of course not all countries respond successfully to resource scarcity either. In the modern era, resource abundance (with the exception of oil) is negatively correlated with growth in poor countries. Resource exports may cause exchange rates to rise and make it difficult for other sectors to export. Resource revenue may encourage governmental corruption. And fluctuations in resource revenue may cause governments to incur debts. As noted above, staple theory argues that the economic benefits of resources vary significantly by resource.

As for transport, we need to appreciate the importance of large networks to facilitate the flow of information. This may have mattered more in the past (Szostak 1991a) but note that many poor countries still have very limited transport infrastructure. Both topography and climate affect the cost of building roads and railways or maintaining waterways.

6.4.8.3 Genetic Predisposition → Technology

Technological innovation is almost but not quite unheard of in the animal kingdom. So the rate of technological innovation we observe among humans is firmly rooted in a set of physical and mental characteristics of the species. Physically, humans have the capability to make tools. Mentally, humans are ambitious,[30] curious, imaginative, and can adjust schemas to include items of novelty. These

---

[29] Earlier in time, Diamond argues that only some regions were well suited to agriculture: he thus provides an environmental explanation of the rise of Euro-Asian civilizations.

[30] Adam Smith told a parable of a poor man's son who regretted his life at the end: Smith recognized self-deceit (including foolish ambition) as part of the view of self, and appreciated that this might encourage growth.

mental characteristics may seem as obvious as the physical, but models of rational innovation can all too readily exclude any role for curiosity or imagination. And firm managers who ignore the importance of curiosity and imagination are likely to discourage innovation among their employees.

North (2005, 26) follows Giovanni Dosi in identifying several characteristics of learning in an evolutionary environment. Individuals change their system of mental schemas incrementally, and may have difficulty with new information that fits poorly with previous schemas (or this may encourage a radical change in schemas). Individuals follow heuristics (decision rules) in pursuing new information. The value of new information depends on the context in which it is placed. People learn through pattern recognition more than abstract logical reasoning. Clarence Ayres argued that youth dominates innovation because conceptual preoccupations do not limit their ability to form new combinations. Societies that limit the role of the young may thus see less innovation. Cultures provide commonalities in the patterns people recognize and thus shared cultural understandings may encourage communication within research groups (27). Interdisciplinary scholarship suggests, though, that creative tension emerges when understandings are not shared.

6.4.8.4 Individual differences → Technology

As noted above, innovation depends not just on rational calculation but ambition (desire for fame or self-efficacy), creativity, and imagination.[31] Altruism is also important: most innovators are driven by a desire to make the world better in some way, and many are willing to eschew any personal benefit (as when Jonas Salk refused to patent his polio vaccine). A slight degree of excess optimism may also be important, given the number of failures that tend to precede innovative success.[32] Indeed, the course of innovation may have been much slower historically if innovators had a more accurate perception of their likely chances of success. Ability to focus, self-discipline, flexibility, openness to experiment, risk-taking, and being both cooperative and competitive are other characteristics that likely encourage innovation. While (almost) all humans possess these characteristics to some degree, individuals differ a great deal in their levels of curiosity, altruism, and optimism. Some at least of these characteristics are influenced by culture, and thus we can anticipate societal differences. Societies may also differ in their ability to channel the most curious toward technological innovation. The stress level in a society may also be important: Excessive preoccupation of any kind – financial, religious, professional – is inimical to the free play of the imagination.

---

[31] Snooks (1998) argues that innovators do not rationally calculate but follow hunches, guided by self-confidence. They are more often supported by friends who believe in them than financial institutions. Despite disliking evolutionary arguments, he speaks of selection across innovations.

[32] Excess optimism may be important for investment as well. Keynes spoke of how 'animal spirits' animated investment decisions; Hirschman likewise noted that many businessmen would not have started a new firm if they had known how difficult this would be (Swedberg 2000, 23).

Creativity in general has three components: expertise, thinking skills, and motivation. Education affects all three. Firm structure may have its greatest impact on the last. Creative people look for new connections and challenge existing assumptions. Creative people tend to be risk-takers, nonconformists, persistent, and flexible.[33] They respond to failure by trying a different approach. They function best in environments that are flexible and where they interact with diverse people. Success should be rewarded but failure not punished.

6.4.8.5 Social Structure → Technology

Societies with limited social mobility will tend not to channel those best suited to innovation toward innovative careers. On the other hand, minority groups discriminated against in other realms are often observed historically to play a disproportionate role in innovation. The innovative potential of women has not been fully harnessed in any human society: this has likely led to biases in the sorts of technologies produced.

6.4.8.6 Science → Technology

A simplistic view of the relationship between science and technology would treat technology as applied science. It would thus follow that technological advances are always preceded by scientific understanding. Economic historians and historians of technology have long disagreed with this simplistic story. The earliest human technologies were developed before anything like science existed (though humans have always had some understandings – not always accurate – of how the world works). Technologies have often been developed through a process of trial-and-error experimentation without a full understanding of why they work. Nineteenth century developments in steelmaking largely preceded (and encouraged) scientific understanding of the chemical composition of steel. Rosenberg (2002) recounts how developments in transistors and lasers led to massive growth in scientific research in solid state and fiber optics. Technological advance not only suggests questions for scientists to pursue but provides them with instruments to use in their studies. Often the best (albeit indirect) evidence of the correctness of scientific knowledge is that technology grounded in this works. It is thus best to see technology and science as existing in a reciprocal relationship.

The link from science to technology has undoubtedly strengthened in the last centuries. Mokyr (2002) tries to move past the science/technology debate by

---

[33] Business scholar Chris Agyris had famously posited 'theories of action': the schemas that guide behavior may be quite different than the schemas we consciously use to explain our behavior. When our behavior fails to achieve our goals, we should strive to revise this consciously. We should further engage in deep introspection that may allow us to adjust our subconscious schemas (which include goals, strategies, and views of oneself and others).

broadening his concept of 'epistemic knowledge' to include folk wisdom, engineering, classification, and recognition of patterns and regularities. While it is possible for a society to have innovations whose basic science is misunderstood, it is unlikely to have an extended series of such discoveries (though a brief reinforcing cycle in technology is possible). The rapid technological innovation of the nineteenth century was only possible because of advances in scientific understanding and scientific method (but the eighteenth was largely characterized by technology without a scientific base). This relationship intensified with industrial research labs and research universities in the Second Industrial Revolution.

Meeus and Hage (2006) suggest that not only is science becoming more important but that firms are finding basic research increasingly risky [uncertain] and are thus shifting the onus back toward universities. Later in that book it is remarked that even mundane goods like mattresses use new materials generated by basic scientific research. There has been very little empirical research on how science influences modern technology, in part because there is no good measure of the importance of a scientific advance.

6.4.8.7 Politics →Technology

The economic historian Joel Mokyr has argued that if there were no barriers to change there would be chaos because of all the new ideas. Mokyr has also argued that every major innovation is an act of rebellion against conventional wisdom and vested interests.[34] Various forms of resistance have to be overcome before a technology can be applied. Resistance can be motivated by economic interest, ideology, or lack of strategic complementarity. Resistance is likely to be lesser in smaller countries and city states because they will reasonably fear that competing states will use the technology against them. Economic historians have thus long suspected that political fragmentation in Europe encouraged innovation.

All innovations hurt someone. Governments may always be tempted to limit the damage. Modern democracies rarely limit innovation to protect jobs, though governments in the past often did so. Environmental concerns are a more likely contemporary source of technological suspicion. Product liability laws may also limit certain sorts of innovation. In general, though, modern democracies are more likely to encourage innovation than to oppose it.

If a country wishes to encourage innovation, it is far from clear how this can best be done. There is little theorization of technology policy and little empirical work. Some key questions can be identified:

- Should technology policy focus on creation or diffusion? That is, should governments devote most of their efforts to fostering innovation or to ensuring that

---

[34] Moe (2007), a political scientist, performs a handful of comparative historical exercises to show how countries that restrict innovation in order to protect vested interests have less innovation than their competitors.

innovations (including foreign innovations) are diffused? The latter strategy may be better in poor countries with limited innovative capability (but recall that some research capability is required just to borrow technology from others, and that technology imports are very important for all countries). But such a policy has problems, especially in rich countries. Encouraging diffusion may discourage innovation, for a new technology now has to compete with the widespread adoption of its predecessor. A diffusion policy may alternatively work against itself as potential adopters choose to wait for an even better technology. Support for diffusion can only be justified if there is lots of uncertainty, secrecy, or capital market failure (such that potential adopters have trouble borrowing the funds they need), and especially if there are network externalities (so that the benefits of adopting increase as others adopt as well – as with the benefits of a telephone). Diffusing information, notably in agriculture, has a long tradition of success. Government standards can increase diffusion if there are network externalities (such as standards for television broadcasts).

- If governments foster innovation, should they identify particular technologies or encourage all types of innovation? The analysis above suggests that some avenues of technological investigation have much greater economic impacts. But these are hard to predict in advance. It is not only hard to predict the direction of technological innovation (50 years ago it was thought space travel would be common by now), but also whether particular innovations will be successful in the market (and whether a technology will serve purposes unforeseen), whether new technologies will complement each other, and how/whether institutions will evolve in concert/opposition with technology. Even experts in a field generally provide poor predictions (Nye 2006). Breakthroughs often come from outsiders, and inventors often do not appreciate what they have achieved. Public efforts to encourage certain innovations (as in the space race) have often but not always been hugely expensive or ineffective given the difficulty of predicting promising paths of research (and because bureaucracies unlike markets do not quickly identify mistakes). Given the uncertainties surrounding technology many scholars suggest that it is best to encourage many innovations. However, subsidies to all types of research are often abused by firms, and thus it is not clear empirically whether the benefits exceed the costs.
- What role should scientific research play? Policy has often stressed science and basic research, in part due to misplaced faith in the linear model of technology as applied science.
- How can governments encourage technology transfer? Forcing technology transfer by limiting entry of goods embodying foreign technology may have worked at times for Japan and Brazil, but one needs a large market and social capability, and should worry about the danger of losing benefits of trade.
- What is the best balance between public and private research? As noted above private firms facing competition may be less likely to (choose and) lock in to a suboptimal research trajectory. But they are more likely to be secretive. There may also be undesirable duplication of research efforts in the private sector.

And some sorts of research (AIDS vaccines for poor countries leap to mind) that may seem unprofitable despite potentially large social benefits. Basic scientific research may often seem unprofitable, and so governments may have a special role there. Private firms benefit from public knowledge, and so the best outcomes come from a mixture of public and private.

- Which policy instruments should be used? Direct funding of research or diffusion, and subsidies to research have been treated above. We need to appreciate that various policies – trade, regulation, competition policy, government procurement, environment policy,[35] and macroeconomic policies especially – influence innovation. These policies and others – patents, regulations, and universities among them – will influence different sectors in different ways, and thus the best policy depends on which sectors one wishes to encourage (Mowery and Nelson, 1999).

6.4.8.8 Institutions → Technology

Technological innovation can only lead to sustained growth if supported institutionally. During the Industrial Revolution, patents, property rights more generally, learned societies, and universities were among the set of supportive institutions. The British government importantly refused worker pressure to forbid mechanization. Later, corporations and industrial research laboratories would matter, and also large markets, firm entry and exit, and venture capital (Mokyr 2005). Easterlin (1996, 56) also takes a 'social capacity' approach to the spread of technology. He stresses several sorts of institutions: property rights, corporations, stable polities, and market institutions. He devotes particular attention to education. He argues that institutions are under-studied because they are hard to measure.

Institutional structure within firms also matter. There is a widespread belief, for example, that new technologies such as computers do not have a big effect on growth until managers change the institutional structure so that the workforce can take advantage of them. While these institutional changes do not reflect formal research they may nevertheless have a huge impact on productivity.

Hall and Soskice (2001) note that while economists have come to appreciate the role of institutions their analysis tends to assume that the same institution enhances productivity everywhere. From a comparative business history perspective, though, different countries have different institutional structures. Across developed countries, these differences do not affect overall economic performance, but determine comparative institutional advantages of various sorts. The authors suggest that the cooperative (both between firms and between labor and management) institutional structure of Germany and Japan is more conducive to incremental innovation: workers are not frightened by these and thus often develop them, while

---

[35] Some think that environmental regulations interfere with innovation by decreasing firm choice while others stress the incentives to innovate.

firms cooperate in redeveloping supply chains. Radical innovations are more likely in a country like the United States where firm takeovers and layoffs are easier. Firms may thus benefit from doing different types of research in different countries. In turn, though, technological innovations induce changes in firm organization, and thence to relations between firms and supply chains.

There is an interdisciplinary literature that examines 'national systems of innovation.' The term is not always well defined but tends to include at least the following institutions: government policy, corporate research, education and training, and industrial structure. The economist Richard Nelson has argued that differences in national systems can largely be explained in terms of country size, industry mix, and defence procurement. But he appreciates that (cultural) attitudes toward government in general also matter. And he appreciates that there is path dependence such that institutions may differ across countries simply for historical reasons. Indeed Nelson appreciates that technology and institutions co-evolve.

The 'national systems of innovation' approach identifies several potential systemic barriers to innovation: a country may lack necessary infrastructure (including research universities), actors may have difficulty adjusting to new technological paradigms, old technologies may be 'locked-in' due to network effects such that new technologies require a societal transformation that is not forthcoming, there may be institutional and/or cultural rigidities, network links may be too weak or too strong (such that insiders do not look outside), and firms may lack technological capability. But the approach provides no theoretical guidance on how to deal with these through public policy.[36]

6.4.8.9 Culture → Technology

Historians of technology give roughly equal attention to the technological, economic, political, and socio-cultural influences on the creation, dissemination, and use of innovation (Nye 2006). Nathan Rosenberg and others have suggested that culture and other social influences are more important with respect to radical innovations: flying wings did not look like planes to pilots and were thus rejected. Incremental innovations are valued primarily on technical grounds.

The anthropologist Lemonnier (1992) argues that technological schemas are inevitably embedded in wider schemas of what a tool or structure means. For example, men may shun items associated with women, or groups may shun ideas associated with outsiders. The technology of building structures and tools serves

---

[36] Chaminade and Edquist (2006) argue that we should first identify various innovative activities – research itself, identifying markets, entrepreneurial and organizational change, networking, and support for innovation through incubators, finance, and consulting – and then identify policy aids: public research, education, standards [as for HDTV], government encouragement of entry, and so on [their list is frustratingly vague]. Notably, their approach moves away from the emphasis on emergent properties one might expect from a 'systems' approach toward a focus on particular links. We can follow their lead and stress particular causal links as well.

aesthetic as well as practical purposes, and thus technological choices cannot be fully comprehended without reference to values as well as practicality. Dobres and Hoffman (1999) argue that we need to understand how symbols are manifest in techniques, and how technology reaffirms fundamental social representations (6). They note that modern people, unlike traditional people, feel a conceptual distance from technology, but this does not mean that technology is not influenced by culture (10). '... technological actions are seamlessly interwoven into the social and material lives of cultural agents' (213).

Culture affects not only which innovations are pursued but the overall level of innovation in a society. Mokyr (1991) emphasized four key cultural attitudes. Since innovation is inherently risky, cultural attitudes toward risk are important. Since innovation requires time and effort, attitudes toward work matter. Since new technologies often have an environmental impact, attitudes toward nature matter.[37] Last but not least, culture affects the goals humans pursue. Mokyr (2005) stresses that innovation is rarely entirely motivated by economic factors. Fame and altruism are other key motivators. The Enlightenment encouraged the selfless betterment of society through innovation (1141-2). Several innovators of the time – including Berthollet, Davy, and Franklin – refused to patent their innovations. Their drive to innovate must have reflected altruism (and perhaps a desire for fame).

6.4.9 Technology and Social Structure

We have focused to this point on causal links toward technological innovation. Given the role that innovation may play in affecting income distribution, we discuss one causal link from technology here (and note a potential feedback to public support of innovation). The relationship between growth and inequality is discussed later. Technological innovation can affect income distribution in three ways. First it may increase or decrease the relative demand for skilled as opposed to unskilled labor. While this effect will depend on the nature of the technology, we noted above that twentieth century GPTs encouraged inequality by increasing the skill premium. Second, all technologies will replace old skills with new: in the short term this will mean that the demand for some skills falls sharply and for others rises sharply. Increased inequality is a likely result. Likewise, the third effect is that some sectors rise while others decline; again increased inequality [and structural unemployment] is a likely outcome. Social stability can be weakened as income distributions worsen. Societies may need to pursue various policies – increased skills training or active redistribution – in order to sustain technological innovation without risking discontent.

---

[37] Tim Ingold in the Foreword to Dobres and Hoffman (1999) notes that individuals may care more about the process of making something than the end result: invention is a 'skilled socially situated performance' (x). He stresses that goods serve both economic and artistic purposes.

6.5 Geography

6.5.1 Climate and Location

Diamond (1997) [a biologist] has explained the rise of Eurasian civilizations in terms of geographic characteristics. Eurasia is a large area with few natural barriers to the transmission of information (and since it lies in an east-west orientation unlike other continents it contained a vast area suited to the same crops). It was also well suited to agriculture. And the llama is the only non-Eurasian member of the list of major modern domesticated animals (in part because the large and diverse Eurasian landmass was hospitable; in part because animals in the New World and Australasia were hunted to extinction when humans first arrived since the animals did not fear humans). Africa alternatively had only a handful of domesticable crops north of the equator, and none south (until Europeans brought them). And Africa had few large animals, and apparently none suited to domestication.[38] Europe's environment was less fragile than the Middle East, where the cutting of trees and overgrazing led to desertification. The political unity of China can be attributed to the lack of barriers (Europe had mountains and narrow peninsulas). The New World also had few crops (corn is low in protein) and lacked large draft animals, and possessed many physical barriers to the diffusion of ideas. Diamond stresses that both Africans and people of the New World quickly adopted domesticated animals when these became available.

In the contemporary world the vast majority of rich countries are in temperate climates, while most tropical countries are poor. Tropical countries average half of world GDP per capita, while temperate countries on average attain double the world level of GDP per capita. Three characteristics of the tropics are often blamed for their poor performance. The heat saps work effort. The disease environment weakens the people (and animals). And the agricultural potential is severely limited: tropical soils yield a protein-deficient diet. Yet one might explain tropical experience in other ways: perhaps economic growth naturally spread first to countries that were geographically and culturally close to Britain. Moreover there are exceptions such as Thailand which have experienced rapid growth in recent decades. Diamond (1997) notes that Europe was an economic backwater for millennia, and that the early civilizations in the New World were tropical.

---

[38] A domesticable crop must have high yields in the wild, grow quickly, and be readily stored. A mixture of cereals and legumes is necessary for human health. A dozen plants account for 80 percent of modern agricultural output by weight: most are from Eurasia. New Guinea likewise had only low protein crops and no draft animals. As well, the Highlands were isolated from other agricultural areas. Australia had few native domesticable plants.

Landes (1998) doubts that it is a coincidence that the tropics are poor. He hypothesizes that the heat contributes to slavery and the subjugation of women such that work is done by those who cannot refuse. The rise of the New South in the United States is only possible with air conditioning. Medicine has done much to combat tropical disease but still has far to go: he suggests that there may be a very high social return to research in this area.

Many scholars are uncomfortable with geographic arguments, for they encourage pessimism and policy inaction. Note though that there may be technological solutions to the problems of the tropics – medicines, air conditioning, and new crop varieties. Collier and Gunning (1999) looked at Africa. In addition to geographical arguments (including climatic variability), they noted a lack of trust due to tribalism, limited infrastructure and public services, corruption, interference with markets, limited contract enforcement, trade restrictions (in addition to the natural barriers), and limited financial system development. As a result both investment and the average return on investment are low. They conclude that these other problems are more important than geography, and can be alleviated by policy changes under way in many countries.

Some economists have recently addressed another geographical argument. Statistically, regions that lack access to oceans are poorer than regions that have access. They are less able to engage in world trade, and thus likely absorb external information less rapidly. Being located close to rich countries is also positively correlated with economic success.[39]

6.5.2 Resources

In the nineteenth century, most but not all of the fastest growing economies were rich in resources. In the late twentieth century, however, resource abundance was negatively correlated with growth. Scholars have identified several ways in which resource abundance both helps and hurts an economy, and put forth hypotheses as to how the balance of good to bad effects might be encouraged.

The positive effects include:

- The 'resource rents' earned: that is the earnings accrued because of possession of the resource, above and beyond the wages and return to capital employed in its extraction.
- The linkage effects identified in staple theory (see above).
- Industries that rely on resource inputs may locate near the resource. This effect decreases in importance as transport costs fall.

---

[39] Durlauf, Johnson, and Temple (2005) list several variables that have been included in regressions: latitude, disease ecology, frost days, landlocked, length of coastline, arable land, rainfall (and its variance), and maximum temperature. One can see that none of these perfectly captures the causal arguments at work.

The negative effects include:

- Resource exports may push up the exchange rate, and thus limit the possibility of manufactured exports. This (plus effects on the government budget) is the so-called 'Dutch disease.'
- There may be a dynamic comparative disadvantage if productivity growth is slower in resources than in manufacturing.
- Resource rents may encourage government corruption.
- Fluctuations in resource prices may cause governments to borrow heavily when their revenues fall.
- Less concretely, the ease of resource revenues may discourage governments from actively pursuing economic growth, and/or encourage negative cultural attitudes.

How can the good effects be accentuated and the bad effects minimized? The main insight may be that there is no resource curse when good institutions and high levels of human and physical capital are in place. Countries then get the full benefits of rents and linkages without suffering as much from corruption (Lederman and Maloney 2006).

6.5.3 Country Size

There are economies of scale in the provision of both private and public goods. Moreover governments of large states can capture more of the positive externalities associated with public goods. Large countries can also act to cushion regions from exogenous shocks (or can redistribute income more generally). And big countries are less threatened by foreign aggression. On the downside, congestion costs and administrative complexities grow with country size. These costs of size cannot explain the very low median size of contemporary countries (population of 6 million). This may best be understood in terms of governance: good governance depends on social cohesion (see above), and this is more easily achieved in small states, especially in regions of the world characterized by numerous ethnic divisions. Empirically, there is no correlation between country size and economic performance, so it would seem that the governance disadvantages roughly balance the economic advantages. Fortunately for small countries trade liberalization reduces the advantages of size (Alesina, Spolaore, and Wacziarg 2005).

6.5.4 Regional Clusters

Paul Krugman (economist) and Michael Porter (business scholar) drew attention to regional clusters (such as Silicon Valley) in the 1990s. They, like economic geographers before them, have stressed agglomerative economies. That is, there are economic advantages to performing a lot of a certain type of economic activity in one location – due to reliance on shared infrastructure, labor pools, finance, and also knowledge base. The latter in particular can be self-enforcing through increasing returns: knowledgeable workers are attracted to a locality with lots of job opportunities, and the benefits of operating in that locality increase as the knowledge base expands.

An alternative approach is to use network theory. This approach does not mistakenly assume that firms are atomized entities. Silicon Valley is usually explained as reflecting concentrations of skill, venture capital, specialized suppliers, infrastructure, and knowledge spillovers from universities. But its success relative to Route 128 in Boston is best understood in terms of the dense networks between small firms as opposed to secretive and hierarchical large companies. Silicon Valley could thus adapt more quickly to changes in technology or economic conditions. Silicon Valley firms had relationships with multiple suppliers, and could thus latch on to improvements in components (whereas large companies were loyal to internally produced components) (Saxenian 1996).

The two approaches – agglomerative economies and network analysis – can be seen as complements. Neither, though, gives a convincing explanation of why clusters occur in some places rather than others. There may well be scope for a great deal of path dependence: a fairly random location decision by one or a few entrepreneurs may set the stage for a regional cluster. In the modern world, clusters of technology firms are generally in proximity to a research university. Highly skilled workers may also be more easily attracted to areas with good schools and cultural amenities.

While clusters clearly exist it is harder to establish their aggregate economic importance. How much of American GDP growth can be attributed to Silicon Valley? How much of the British Industrial Revolution can be attributed to the clustering of the cotton industry in Lancashire and the metal industry around Birmingham? (Szostak 1991a speaks of 'regional specialization' but cannot narrowly quantify its importance). Many scholars are skeptical that the aggregate importance is large. If they are wrong, and if clusters are more likely in developed countries, then clustering becomes a powerful argument for continued divergence between rich and poor countries.[40]

---

[40] Some economic historians have estimated that doubling of city sizes in the nineteenth century (in some countries) resulted in productivity increases of 5-10 percent. The effect may have been smaller later, perhaps as diseconomies set in.

6.5.5 Environment

We have skated over environmental problems in the introductory chapter but might note here that humanity could be much less wasteful in its use of resources of all types. Land use could be cut in half if humans became vegetarians. There has in any case been no global increase in land use in half a century despite population growth. If less developed countries could approach best developed country yields per acre 10 billion could be fed on half of the existing farmland. Half of the metals used in the United States are now recycled (Ausubel 1997).

Locally we see resource depletion all the time, with closed mines and fisheries. And Diamond is hardly the first to blame societal collapse on environmental degradation. Yet economists generally remain confident that price adjustments and technology solve the problem at the global level. Pessimists note that rates of resource use are expanding and that there is only so much of any resource.

Brock and Taylor (2005) support the idea of an environmental Kuznets Curve (the only strong result of the empirical literature). This suggests that environmental quality decreases in the early stages of economic development but increases thereafter. Air quality has improved in developed country cities, and emissions of many pollutants have decreased. However, pollution with less visible or geographically extensive effects, especially global problems such as climate change, have proven more difficult to alleviate. For such environmental challenges it seems that economic growth needs to be combined with democratic decision-making and often a considerable degree of international cooperation as well.

The environmental measures employed to date have cost at most 1 or 2 percent of GDP. Note that economists may assume a negative effect here: environmental control can even increase GDP if it increases employment or leads to the growth of firms specializing in environmental control. And this is as GDP is conventionally measured: if we focused instead on a measure of economic wellbeing that included environmental considerations, then environmental improvements could more generally be observed to have a positive effect.

7 The Causes of Economic Growth: Institutions

Our analysis in chapter 2 guides us to ask a series of questions. We must first address the inter-related questions of whether (and how) institutions encourage growth, and which sorts of functions it is most necessary for institutions to perform. The latter question has a more particular facet: can we identify superior institutional forms for various institutional functions? Special attention will be paid of course to the relationship between institutions and investment and technology. Since we will find evidence that institutions are indeed important, the next major question is how to encourage beneficial types of institutional change. Part of the answer here is institutional itself: certain political institutions may facilitate the adoption of certain economic institutions.

Unlike in the study of investment, we face the advantage and challenge here that many disciplines have studied institutions. Institutional analysis was rediscovered in several disciplines in the 1980s and 1990s: economics, economic history, sociology of organizations, social anthropology, and industrial relations, along with several fields in political science (Rothstein, 1998, 144). This simultaneity was not entirely coincidental but reflected conversations across disciplinary boundaries. Nevertheless we shall see that there are important differences in disciplinary approaches. We shall also find that much remains to be done. While the fact that institutions are essential to long run growth has now been amply demonstrated by both historical and statistical analyses, this research has occurred at a very general level (Rodrik 2005, 1005).

7.1 Institutions and Growth

Institutions were largely ignored by economists from the 1840s through the 1970s, but interest rebounded for a variety of reasons: in part as theoretical developments (especially in game theory) suggested that institutions mattered, and in part due to empirical interest in comparative economic performance. Most rich countries seem to possess 'good' institutions while most poor countries seem to lack these. It is now well understood that market exchange is not 'natural' but depends on a host of institutions. Different economists emphasize different causal links from institutions to economic performance: Douglass North (economic historian) has stressed the reduction in transaction costs and also uncertainty (by limiting the range of behaviors observed) that good institutions provide. Oliver Williamson has emphasized the ways in which institutions increase economic efficiency. Jack Knight, like many sociologists, emphasizes the distributional effects of institutions. Loasby (1999, 46) argues that institutions are a response to uncertainty: a means by which individuals acquire patterns of behavior from others. Happily there is no need to choose among these competing visions, for they are entirely

R. Szostak, *The Causes of Economic Growth,*
DOI: 10.1007/978-3-540-92282-7_7, © Springer-Verlag Berlin Heidelberg 2009

compatible. All except the distributional argument suggest that good institutions can lower costs of production and/or distribution, and will thus encourage growth of the second type: producing and selling goods for a lower price. Distributional arguments remind us that institutional change is not necessarily pursued with society's best interests at heart, and thus helps us to understand why superior institutions from the perspective of society are often not adopted.

Transaction costs deserve some explanation. In the most basic economic theories, exchange occurs whenever both buyer and seller benefit. In real life a host of problems arise: the potential trade must be identified, the relative benefits to buyer and seller must be haggled over, and the buyer must be assured of good quality and the seller of payment. Economists speak of 'asymmetric information' when one agent possesses information that the other does not. Exchange always involves asymmetric information, and thus mutually beneficial trades may not occur if one agent doubts the veracity of the other (and disadvantageous exchanges can occur if misleading information is believed). If the trade takes place over distance and/or time these problems grow larger. A problem of 'moral hazard' emerges if agents may fail to do what they promised. Economic historians have suggested that half of modern economies may be devoted to exchange, and that reductions in transactions costs have been an important – at times perhaps the most important – source of economic growth. Transactions costs may vary little with the size of a transaction, and tend to be easier to control when lots of similar trades are occurring: one can thus imagine a virtuous cycle in which expanded exchange encourages yet more exchange. Institutions can reduce transactions costs in many ways – sharing information, enforcing contracts, coordinating transactions that require synchronization – but these solutions are not costless.

The most important development in economic theory in recent decades has likely been the recognition that information is costly to obtain and that economic decisions are thus generally made in the context of both imperfect and asymmetric information. These simple insights overturn some of the central tenets of economic theory: market exchange need not generate efficient outcomes in the face of information imperfections; nor is a stable equilibrium guaranteed [but information problems are even more serious for government planning] (Stiglitz 2000). Nor is information like most goods. It has public good properties, since information can be shared – it can thus be difficult for agents to appropriate the returns from generating new information. And it is hard for buyers to judge the value of information in advance: if they knew what the information was they would not need to buy it. Issues of reputation (and thus culture) and incentives for honest behavior (and thus institutions such as tax laws and employment contracts) are thus of critical importance. Since knowledge is cumulative, history (and especially institutional structures in place in the past) shape present knowledge and its distribution. 'The key question is one of dynamics: how the economy adapts to new information, creates new knowledge, and how that knowledge is disseminated, absorbed, and used throughout the economy' (Stiglitz 2000). Stiglitz urges both an interdisciplinary approach and an emphasis on institutions in the study of information.

While the information literature has focused on microeconomic issues, and to a lesser extent on business cycles, information is obviously important for growth as well. Most obviously, any type of innovation involves the generation of new information. Since growth requires success in production and exchange, the informational problems identified in these spheres are important for growth as well. More generally since growth necessitates change, informational issues are widely implicated in the study of growth. A key general question, then, is how well societies manage the generation and dissemination of all types of information.

How important are institutions empirically? While economists have in recent years included many institutional measures in growth regressions, it has proven difficult to establish any relationship empirically. This outcome reflects in part the fact that economists disagree not only about the theoretical relationship between institutions and growth but also over the precise definition of 'institution' and which particular institutions might be most important.[1] Aron (2000, 100) surveys the types of indicators used by economists in regressions:

- Institutional quality (especially with respect to property rights enforcement)
- Political instability (riots, civil wars, coups)
- Characteristics of political regimes (elections, constitutions, executive powers)
- Social capital (Extent of civic activity and organizations)
- Social characteristics (income distribution, ethnic divisions, measures of historical background such as experience of colonialism).

The most obvious problem with this list is that it includes several variables (in the last two bullets) that are not properly institutional at all. Social capital and social structure (characteristics) will be discussed in chapter 8. Secondly, the list emphasizes political over economic institutions: yet the former for the most part influence economic growth only indirectly through the latter. While there may be direct effects, say on investor confidence, of political stability, this and especially more mundane questions of electoral practices or executive powers will have their primary effect through shaping the nature of economic institutions. Why not then stress economic institutions in growth equations (with perhaps other equations linking economic and political institutions)? A third problem is relevant here: it is all too easy for incompetent or corrupt governments to create the appearance but not the essence of good institutions. Just as autocrats often glory in meaningless elections, so in the economic sphere they can proclaim the protection of property while actively interfering with property rights. Economists thus stress the quality of institutions (but a very limited set of these). But of course quality is always hard

---

[1] Moreover Aron worries that growth regressions as an enterprise face serious problems of data, methodology, and identification. These are generally more severe than regression analysis elsewhere in economics. Statistically significant results are rarely tested for robustness to different specifications, data outliers, reverse causality, or bias due to omitted variables. While structural estimations involve separate equations for growth and for investment, reduced-form estimations do not. They are thus unable to capture causal links among exogenous variables and cannot distinguish different mechanisms of effects on growth (Aron 2000, 100-1).

to measure. A fourth problem also flows from the second (and is stressed by Aron): economists often combine several indicators, though each may have a quite different avenue of impact. Moreover, the various institutional variables may interact with each other, and reflect feedback effects from growth itself, but simple regressions ignore these possible effects.[2]

Aron surveys in a lengthy table (107-13) the main institutional indicators used. Many are based on surveys (all measures of institutional quality are, as are most measures of social capital). Aron worries (114) that such surveys may reflect endogeneity: businesspeople and others will think well of a country that is growing. There is also a problem of hysteresis: judgments of institutional quality may be slow to change when institutional quality does. Aron also worries that such evaluations are ordinal, but regressions assume cardinality (that a score of 4 is twice as good as a score of 2): there are techniques for transforming one to the other, but these are often not used.

Still, Aron concludes (128) that it is quality of institutions rather than the more objective measures of instability or social capital or institutional characteristics that matters in regressions. She notes that variables like political stability may have an indirect effect, but that the precise mechanism by which this occurs needs to be identified. However, given her concerns with cross-effects and feedback effects, along with other problems, she feels that even these results should be treated with caution.

While some of the problems identified by Aron can be alleviated through more careful definitions and theoretical specifications, others cannot. Institutions (and perhaps growth more generally) are not particularly well-suited to statistical analysis. Institutions are inherently unique. With respect to property rights protection – likely one of the simplest institutional functions – one might want to evaluate this in terms of the various elements of property rights: right to possession, right to use, right to sell, and so on. Different countries may excel in different respects. Moreover, they may differ along other dimensions: the courts may be fair but the police incompetent in one country, while rights may be enforced without much recourse to courts in another. Such complexities call for comparative case studies, and suggest that efforts to describe a type of institution in terms of one numerical indicator are likely to be fraught with difficulty. Such a measure must necessarily conflate diverse characteristics of an institution. This does not mean that such regressions should not be performed, but that they need to be supplemented by other forms of research.

It is noteworthy that economists embrace the results of survey research in these regressions while elsewhere disparaging surveys. Economists generally worry that survey respondents have little incentive to respond truthfully and may in any case

---

[2] One likely result of cross-effects is that one variable may be credited with a causal influence more properly credited to another variable with which it is correlated. Indeed, Lal (1998) cites Sala-i-Martin to the effect that different regressions show different policy variables matter, but disagree on which (because these are strongly correlated). As for feedbacks, the danger is that an observed correlation will be wrongly perceived as an effect on growth rather than of growth.

have limited understanding of both their own motives and how the world works. The recourse to surveys in this context seems to reflect the absence of any other way of developing a quantitative measure of institutional quality.

Economic historians have performed a great deal of case study analysis. They have in particular detailed the importance of property rights in a variety of historical settings, and shown how a variety of peculiar-seeming institutions such as merchant guilds may have served to enhance efficiency in societies unable to support modern institutions. Yet Ogilvie (2007) argues that economists and economic historians have focused on often-clever efficiency explanations of observed institutions while downplaying their distributional role. She suggests that while guilds and serfdom and communal village management of fields may (or not) have had some good efficiency characteristics, they are more readily understood as bestowing economic advantages on the politically powerful. Economists sometimes argue theoretically that distributional issues can be ignored: competing interests should all agree to the institution that maximizes the size of the economic 'pie' and then fight over how the pie is shared. But in practice competing interests cannot agree on what is the best institution nor even what sort of 'pie' they want. Nor can the powerful make credible commitments to not steal what others produce under efficiency-enhancing incentives. So in practice distributional and efficiency/ growth aspects are decided jointly, and we should be careful of suspecting that only one of these considerations has been at work. As we shall see below, political scientists and sociologists are even more likely to stress the distributional role of institutions.

Economists and even economic historians have tended to emphasize effects on efficiency more than growth in their study of institutions. Increased economic efficiency should increase incomes, but may only have a one-time effect on economic growth. Of the proximate causes of sustained growth, enhanced trade is the most obvious implication of institutional improvement. Much of what has been said in this section has referred to the role of institutions in fostering exchange. We have discussed previously the role of institutions in technological innovation. We turn our attention next to investment and infrastructure. Education will be discussed later.

7.1.1 Institutions and Investment

Potential investors will want to be confident that their property is secure and that the contracts they enter into can be enforced. They may also need to engage with formal financial institutions. It is thus theoretically plausible that institutions will have an important impact on investment. In addition to works looking at growth itself, there have been some papers that have found a positive effect of institutions on investment (Acemoglu, Johnson, and Robinson 2001). North has suggested that institutions affect both the level of investment and its impact. Bad institutions may encourage only small scale and short term investment, or divert funds from their most productive use. Aron (128) suggests that institutional qual- ity affects the quantity of investment much more than the efficiency of investment. But only a minority of scholars uses structural estimations that can disentangle these two effects, and thus this conclusion is tentative.

7.1.2 Institutions and Infrastructure

My own research as an economic historian on the Industrial Revolution focused on the role of transport infrastructure: I showed that Britain had developed by far the best systems of both road and water transport in the world in the decades pre- ceding the Industrial Revolution and detailed many ways in which this transport system encouraged both the institution of the factory and technological innovation (Szostak 1991a). Let me reprise one important line of argument. Once a national network of all-weather roads were in place a national network of road carriers soon emerged (as is well documented). And then industrialists were able to sell goods by sample or by catalogue, rather than leading trains of packhorses around to markets and fairs as before. But they then faced a problem: consumers buying from a catalogue or from a salesman's sample tend to want an identical good (whereas variety in form is advantageous when selling face-to-face in a market). Isolated workers in their own cottages could scarcely create such a homogenous output. And thus industrialists were given a very powerful incentive both to gather workers in factories under supervision, and to mechanize production.

These transport developments were in turn due to a seemingly peculiar set of institutions: turnpike trusts and canal and river improvement companies created by individual Acts of Parliament. In these Acts a group of local landowners and merchants (generally all the men of substance in a community) were granted three critical rights: to charge tolls, to borrow money to finance construction and main- tenance, and to exercise the power of eminent domain (that is, force landowners to sell at the market price) over the land needed for the road or waterway. These trusts and companies were, notably, some of the very earliest corporations, and paved the way for widespread acceptance of the corporate form.

When I first presented this research to audiences of economists, I would start by talking about the effects of transport improvements, but would immediately be questioned about the origins of these improvements. These questions, I came to realize, reflected a belief that the infrastructure necessary to economic growth would be called forth by the economy itself. But this was not and is not so: broadly similar economic circumstances in other countries did not translate into better roads and waterways simply because an appropriate institutional structure did not exist. Britain had a Parliament that could pass turnpike trust acts, and was both able and willing to bestow important rights upon these trusts. Merchants and landowners might despair of miserable roads elsewhere in the world but had no feasible means to change this situation.

For present purposes, two key insights can be drawn from this research. First, Oliver Williamson was wrong in arguing that the factory emerged because it was inherently more efficient than dispersed production in the home. Rather, the factory only became more efficient because of the transport improvements. In an environment in which an entrepreneur could not be at all confident of receiving supplies in a reliable or timely manner, a factory owner would need to incur huge inventory costs in order to keep the factory running; workers in their own homes simply performed other tasks if supplies did not arrive. Indeed, I showed (1989) that the transport improvements shifted the balance toward factories with respect to at least a dozen of the thirteen criteria Williamson himself had used to compare the efficiency of different organizational forms.[3] We should be careful then of assuming that institutions which seem to fit well the modern world would always have served well. And thus we are reminded that our institutions have emerged from a lengthy (and likely path dependent) historical process during which circumstances were often quite different. Our institutions may well still contain elements best suited to the past, and may need to change again in future.

Second, the transport institutions themselves are a powerful example of how quite unique institutions can serve economic growth. No economist ignorant of the course of the Industrial Revolution if transported back to the England of 1680 would have advocated this particular institution. (Nor indeed did those pursuing transport improvements imagine they would generate an Industrial Revolution.) They might have urged government expenditure on roads and waterways. This would be the path followed by most nineteenth century nations (but not the United States, which inherited these institutions like others from Britain, and would develop its road and waterway network in much the same way, albeit with a greater role for government subsidy; Szostak 1991b). In Continental Europe, the goal of catching up to Britain focused governmental attention on transport infrastructure, but the political realities of the Continent prohibited the extension of the power of eminent domain to non-governmental bodies. In the eighteenth century, though, governments lacked the money and administrative capability: the French government lavished funds on a few main roads emanating from Paris, and built many monumental bridges in the process, but failed to provide an economically useful road network. Some economists see the turnpike trust as a sign that private enterprise can perform tasks widely performed by governments. And it can hardly be denied that if governments lack the financial or administrative capacity a private

---

[3] I also at that time (and in a Reply in the 1992 issue of that journal) addressed the alternative argument, made by SRH Jones, that the factory was a response to technological developments. The first factories of the Industrial Revolution date from the 1750s and used the same technology used in cottages (the upsurge in technological innovation is generally dated to the 1770s). Once factories existed, innovators hooked machines together and attached these to a power source. (It would have made little sense to develop large powered machinery when production occurred in the home.) Once this technology was developed, factories were even more advantageous.

toll road or canal will be preferable to no transport improvement. Still, it is important to appreciate that all of the turnpike trusts and most of the waterway companies in Britain were never expected to turn a profit: social pressure encouraged all men of wealth to subscribe for the benefit of all. They were thus a quasi-public enterprise. It was their de-centralized nature which was critical. At a time when the British government had a limited local presence, these trusts were able to identify the most useful routes. And while individual turnpikes were only a few kilometers long, they soon formed a network that linked every town in England and Wales with roads capable of supporting wheeled traffic year-round (horses can pull eight times as much in a wagon as they can carry on their backs). Again, our fictional time-traveling economist, accustomed to national transport authorities, might well have urged some national direction of transport infrastructure. This was not feasible at the time. Likewise in less developed countries today we should embrace peculiar-looking institutions that manage to serve a useful purpose (micro-credit banks based on communal pressure leap to mind). Even in the area of transport, local groups allowed to charge tolls might be able to link isolated villages to the outside world long before impoverished governments are able to do so.

7.2 Which Functions?

Table 2.1 lists institutions governing ownership, exchange, finance, labor relations, and production (safety, pollution, standards); and also organizations (firms, unions, bureaucracies, associations, NGOs, etc.). All of these have fairly obvious implications for growth. We worried above that economists have not clarified which institutions are most important for growth and why. However, Clague (1997) argues that we know much more about which institutional needs are most important than about how good institutions are developed: he suggests competitive markets, property rights, macroeconomic stability, efficient provision of public goods, and perhaps democracy as the most important institutions. He thus includes a political institution (we will discuss democracy below), and assumes an answer to the question of the relationship between cycles and growth (chapter 9), while ignoring labor relations, production, and organizations. We will instead look in turn at each of the major types of institution listed in Table 2.1.

7.2.1 Ownership (Property Rights)

Cross-sectional statistical analyses (looking across a wide range of postwar countries) find that the existence of property rights and the rule of law are positively correlated with economic growth (Greif, 2006, 6). Wendell Gordon argued in the 1960s that in the absence of political and legal security agents will pursue large profits on small shipments, and thus incentives toward mass production and productivity advance are severely weakened. The connection between security of ownership and investment is almost universally accepted: agents will be wary of investing, especially in visible structures, if they fear arbitrary confiscation.

7.2.2 Exchange

'Every advanced economy has discovered that markets require extensive regulation to minimize abuse of market power, internalize externalities, deal with information asymmetries, establish product and safety standards, and so on. ... Finally market outcomes need to be legitimized through social protection, social insurance, and democratic governance most broadly' (Rodrik 2005, 1006). That is, beyond the basics of contract enforcement, complex economies require a host of institutions to govern market exchange. A glance through regulations governing stock markets gives some idea of the complexity involved. While the institutions created by developed countries over the last decades should not be viewed as prerequisites to begin growth, something like them should be seen as necessary for catching up.

Perhaps the single greatest symptom of the role institutions play in exchange is the decline in economic output experienced as Eastern European economies transitioned from command to market economies in the 1990s. While a variety of causal forces were at work, one of the key difficulties was that firms needed to identify and negotiate with new trading partners, and this took time.

7.2.3 Finance

Levine (2005) surveys many works – both at the country level and the firm level – and concludes that financial markets and financial intermediation have an important impact on economic growth. Nor do financial institutions arise inevitably as economic development proceeds. While in the 1970s it was thought that financial development flowed naturally from economic growth, there is now much empirical evidence in economic history that suggests that financial development precedes growth. Financial institutions must be created through the efforts of both public and private bodies.

Financial institutions have their most obvious effect on investment. But financial institutions first emerged to serve the needs of trade rather than production, and still play a critical role in financing trade. Financial institutions are also important in generating macroeconomic stability by limiting the number and scope of banking and exchange panics; macroeconomic stability in turn likely encourages growth (chapter 10).

7.2.4 Production

It is interesting that institutions governing production and labor relations have received much less attention than institutions governing ownership and trade. There is a literature on the factory (see above) that discusses how and why gathering workers together increased productivity. The business history literature has discussed the advantages of large corporations (and more recently small firms). But this literature often stresses innovation more than production.

We can identify a handful of major sources of productive inefficiency, and suggest the sort of institutions that might deal with these:

- Most obviously some economic activities are unproductive: they distribute resources from one agent to another without adding to total output. Some redistribution may be worthwhile (see below). But theft and rent-seeking (lobbying governments for personal favors) are almost always not socially beneficial. Criminal laws and transparent governance are among the institutions intended to discourage unproductive activities.
- Some sectors/firms are more productive than others. Institutions that subsidize weak sectors/firms or discourage resource movement between sectors will prevent the economy from allocating its resources in the most productive manner.
- Unemployment means that labor resources are idle. Various institutions – training programs, relocation programs, employment policies, fiscal policy – have an effect (not always desirable) on unemployment rates.
- There can be little doubt that institutions that encourage work effort can have an important impact on economic growth. Parry (2005, 143-4) argues that work effort is determined by more than culture. The type of labor relationship (such as short versus long term) will also matter, as will financial incentives and possibilities for coercion.

7.3 Which Institutions?

Political scientists identify four key elements of institutions: these respectively develop rules, apply these, adjudicate disputes regarding them, and enforce them. A particular institution may excel at some of these while performing others poorly or not at all. Given this complexity, and the recognition that each institution works in concert with other institutions, care should be taken in assuming that any institution is best in all times and places. Moreover, economic history establishes (see the discussion of infrastructure above) that the best institution changes as economic (and other) conditions change. Indeed, Nick Crafts has suggested (in Snowdon 2002) that this is one of the two major insights of economic history (the other involves creative destruction; chapter 9). Sabel and Zeitlin (1997) likewise argue that the main lesson of modern business history is that technology and institutions are in flux. The ideal institution depends on a host of factors that are changing all of the time. Even in the nineteenth century it was already true that the ideal institution was not possible to identify – though agents struggled with much success to identify better institutions.

As Solow (2005, 7) has argued, the easy part in scholarly analysis of institutions is appreciating that institutions such as property rights matter. The hard part is identifying the best institutional forms to achieve various goals. Rodrik (2005) stresses that quite different institutions can support economic growth. This point is now widely appreciated (he provides several citations on 1007-8). Even such basics as property rights and markets can be supported in quite different ways. 'Reformers have substantial room for creatively packaging these principles into institutional designs that are sensitive to local constraints and take advantage of local opportunities' (973). He thus urges a 'search and discovery' approach to institutional reform, in which attempts to achieve general goals (such as property rights or macroeconomic stability) that suit a particular country are tried and carefully evaluated (989). 'An immediate implication is that growth strategies require considerable local knowledge' (996).[4]

Dobbin (2001, 401), a sociologist, argues that the idea that evolutionary pressures generate the most efficient institutions is belied by the observation that quite different institutions seem to serve modern economies well. 'It may be that there are institutional prerequisites for economic growth, but that they are much broader than we think they are.' Dobbin goes on to argue that the shape of the polity (federalism, centralization, and so on) tends to be copied in economic institutions: the French state emphasized central direction of economic activity while the weak American federal government stressed arbitrating among competing interests.

What institutions should we recommend to poor or transitional economies? Rodrik (2003, 14) stresses that we should identify the key institutional constraints at a particular time and place, and fix those first. Bolivia had good macroeconomic policies but lacked rule of law and thus fared poorly. They should thus work on institutions that support the rule of law. He notes that policymakers should focus on the possible: this may mean politically feasible but weird 'transitional' institutions (as in China) in early stages of development (12-3). Likewise, ad hoc reforms may work better than a comprehensive overhaul of the institutional system (15). Eventually, though, sophisticated institutions are necessary.

It is important not to focus exclusively on the benefits of institutions. Aron (129-30) speculates on the cost of good institutions: some authors worry that poor countries cannot afford good institutions, while Posner and others argue that some simple rules governing property rights can be inexpensively introduced. This again

---

[4] 'We know that that growth happens when investors feel secure, but we have no idea what specific institutional blueprints will make them feel more secure in a particular context' (Rodrik 2006, 979). He notes that China achieved massive levels of investment in the 1990s with very peculiar institutions, while Russia achieved much less despite borrowing standard Western institutional forms.

suggests that poor countries should envision a process of institutional evolution rather than the sudden importation of complex institutions from other countries. It is worth noting that the institutions now urged upon less developed countries were not generally in place in developed countries when they were at similar levels of development (Clague 1997). Corruption was common in Europe and North America in the nineteenth centuries, and bureaucracies were often slow and incompetent (with hiring done through nepotism rather than merit). Limited liability corporations were not allowed in many European countries until the 1870s. Chang (2002, 133) urges us not therefore to denigrate the importance of such institutions (which indeed may be more important now than then) but rather to appreciate both that they take time to develop and require a certain minimal level of government capability to pay for and manage.

It is important to appreciate that a range of institutions can serve each of the functions outlined in the preceding section. The danger is thinking that an infinite range of institutions can do so. Such a belief can lead one to imagine that institutions have no distinct causal role: some appropriate institution can be expected to pop up to serve each function. In practice, though, while there may be many possible forms of good institutions, there are also many possible institutions that do not serve these functions well. And thus we need to carefully distinguish good institutions from bad – keeping in mind that our answer to this question will change through time as circumstances change.

How much do we know about the range of institutions that can successfully achieve one of the institutional functions identified above? 'In short our knowledge base for institutional design is often much weaker than people changing government in settings such as the former Soviet Union would desire' (Peters, 1998, 216). We do not, that is, have a very good idea of how to distinguish potential institutional improvements from institutional mistakes. As with investment above we must be careful of going overboard in celebrating diversity of experience. There may well be common elements running through apparently diverse institutional forms. These will only be uncovered through detailed comparative analysis.

7.3.1 Property Rights

Economists tend to think exclusively in terms of private property rights. As Rodrik (2005) notes, though, these could be private, public (as in China, for example) or cooperative. While governments are the best enforcers of property rights, economic historians have identified various historical episodes in which individuals collectively established property rights. The greatest danger to property rights is often government expropriation, and thus constraints on governmental abuse of power can be critical, but these constraints come in various forms. Some sort of registry of property is also very important, and the ability of property owners to borrow and invest may be severely limited if they cannot prove ownership.

Given the importance of technological innovation in economic growth, special attention should be paid to property rights over ideas. The United States in the mid-nineteenth century developed a patent system with low fees (one tenth the French level), no restriction that a device had to be working already, and enforcement by courts. The United Kingdom, which had had the latter two characteristics for a century (though courts could not often enforce their decrees), soon matched the low fees, and other European countries followed the American example. Since patents created property rights we saw then and now a market for the sale (or license) of these: small firms sold out to larger firms with the resources to commercialize. While regional licenses were possible, national licenses were most common.

Surveys find that patents are important for two-thirds of pharmaceutical firms and a third of chemical firms. They are also important for automobiles and office equipment. Chemicals and simple mechanical products are easy to reverse engineer and thus depend heavily on patent protection. Other industries rely instead on secrecy plus the difficulty of figuring out how a certain product was produced. Small advances in electronics are protected through tacit knowledge. It is difficult to patent process innovations, and these are hard to copy anyway. Secrecy is used to limit the spread of process innovation. But firms are often observed to eschew secrecy in order to impress customers, attract scientists and engineers, and to guide suppliers. Discussions of patent policy should reflect the differing needs of different sectors and firms.

Patents have always involved a public policy tradeoff. On the one hand they encourage certain sorts of innovation by providing a financial reward.[5] On the other hand they slow diffusion by prohibiting others from using an innovation (unless licensed) for several years. In recent years, several scholars, including the economists Richard Nelson and Joseph Stiglitz, have suggested that patents should be made much less important. They are guided in part by the recognition that many technologies are hard to copy even in the absence of patents. Contemporary concerns regarding patents often reflect one of two developments. The first involves the increased importance of industrial research laboratories. These, by patenting a stream of small product improvements through time may effectively maintain patent protection on a product line for decades (see Nye 2006). The second involves the global impact of patents. Recent trade agreements have included international recognition of patents; companies in rich countries have worried that producers in poor countries were ignoring their patents. Such agreements limit international technology transfer. Stiglitz has suggested that patents be replaced with government-financed prizes for useful innovations: these prizes would maintain financial incentives for innovation without limiting diffusion.

---

[5] They may at times encourage 'too-fast' research. If firms are working in the same area, patents exaggerate the reward for developing a feasible product first.

7.3.2 Financial Institutions

Financial institutions serve five major roles:

- Facilitate financial transactions.
- Mobilize funding for large projects.
- Transfer savings across space and time (and individuals).
- Facilitate risk-sharing.
- Transmit price signals.

Rodrik (2005) notes that there is a range of appropriate financial institutions to perform these functions. Different institutions may perform different functions, and the best institution for a particular function may change through time (for example, the advantage of specialized mortgage lenders has disappeared in recent decades in developed countries). Particular institutions may also fulfill multiple roles. Economists generally applaud currency stability (which depends in turn on both governmental and central bank credibility): this will aid the transmission of price signals but also facilitate financial transactions, and less directly the other three bullets as well. Given these different functions, we should be wary of any one aggregate measure of financial development. Economic historians have often wondered if English and French banks in the nineteenth century performed the second function as well as German banks (though recent research suggests that the importance of this causal link has been exaggerated). They may have been superior with respect to other functions.

Complex modern economies rely upon a variety of financial institutions to provide a variety of financial instruments; each of these in turn requires a complex system of regulation. Even the richest countries are far from immune to the occasional financial scandal or panic, but the system depends on a general confidence in the fairness and competence of regulation of banks, stock markets, and other institutions. Poorer countries may have difficulty providing the same level of regulation, and may thus from time to time lose the confidence of foreign investors.

7.3.3 Labor Markets and Work Effort

What institutional structures best encourage work effort? When we discussed financial institutions, we could begin from a sound theoretical understanding of the functions of financial institutions. Here we must start with some basic questions about how to motivate workers. Until these are answered more concretely, a wide range of different approaches to organizing production will seem potentially valid. A likely starting hypothesis is that different approaches are best suited to different sorts of enterprise and perhaps different cultural and political environments.

The sociology of work has confronted this issue most directly. It has noted that workers respond not just to financial incentives but to values of fairness and respect. Workers allowed some control over the pace and details of their work are observed to work harder. Workers who believe that they are treated unfairly work less hard.

Control versus discretion: American industry has for the most part been organized on a hierarchical basis. Recent research on within-firm networks suggests that informal contacts are as important as those formalized in organizational charts (see chapter 9). Nevertheless the American top-down approach can usefully be contrasted with the Japanese emphasis on team-based production. The team-based approach has been experimented with in American industry with mixed results; some thus suggest that it works better in less individualistic cultures. However, teamwork has functioned well in more innovative sectors like computer software.

Workers in poor countries may face pressure from peers not to work hard. This may reflect a belief that some workers will be fired if labor productivity increases. The challenge for management is to ensure workers that if they all are more productive they can all earn more. This may require better managers, better technology, and better education.

Extrinsic versus intrinsic motivation: Frey (1997) argues that extrinsic motives (that is, rewards bestowed by others) crowd out intrinsic motives (our internal sense of accomplishment) for three reasons: a feeling of loss of control, loss of esteem because of a sense that our intrinsic motives were underappreciated, and loss of ability to express good motives. A child paid to do chores she used to perform voluntarily may thus respond by working less hard. Crowding out is most likely [intrinsic motives highest when] employer and employee are personally related (most likely in a small firm or group); the task is interesting, employees have a role in decision-making; and when punishments are used rather than rewards. Frey notes that economists emphasize extrinsic and psychologists stress intrinsic motives. He argues that economists must become interdisciplinary in order to appreciate intrinsic motives.[6]

Many empirical studies show that paying workers on the basis of performance (rather than just a straight wage) increases effort and output. Yet such schemes are fairly rare. In addition to the arguments above regarding intrinsic motivation, such schemes face several practical challenges. Such schemes are risky for workers, as their incomes may fluctuate. There are also managerial fears that workers would ignore tasks not rewarded; performance pay may be poorly suited to situations where workers perform many tasks, some of which are not easily measured. In such situations, concerns regarding fairness are also critical.[7] On the other hand,

---

[6] McCloskey (2006) notes that two thirds of American workers, and similar proportions in other developed countries (only half in Britain), like their jobs (137). She appreciates the importance of valuing what one produces, but notes that peasant labor was pretty monotonous (ch. 45).

[7] Likewise, promotion systems may encourage effort, but may also encourage risky behavior by losers, and raise concerns regarding fairness, and thus most firms rely on seniority.

profit-sharing seems to have a much larger effect than it should (given the small role profits play in total income), perhaps due to peer pressure and a feeling of belonging (that is, to intrinsic motives).

Efficiency wage and x-efficiency arguments: Do higher wages increase productivity? This argument has long been made by heterodox economists in terms of 'x-efficiency'. It has in recent decades been made also by neoclassical economists in terms of 'efficiency wages'. The argument in both cases is that workers work harder if paid more. It may thus be possible for firms to benefit from increasing wages.

Altman (2001) reviews and extends the literature on x-efficiency: He notes that we need not appeal to managerial irrationality in order to explain sub-optimal wages (from the perspective of firms) for managers may prefer subservience to efficiency. Firms can survive if low wages match low productivity. Minimum wage laws may in such a situation force firms to increase productivity. Upward wage pressure may force firms to explore new technologies (and take other risks) as well. Since increased x-efficiency means increased work effort it need not benefit workers, but can support better wages and working conditions.[8] In addition to sloth by workers, x-inefficiency may result from conflict with managers or managerial sloth. X-efficiency may be a source of divergence between countries if high wage countries are forced to innovate and otherwise enhance productivity. Likewise labor market discrimination may encourage low productivity among disadvantaged groups.[9] George Stigler has argued that one cannot speak of x-inefficiency if one properly accounts for the social costs associated with increasing productivity, but Altman argues that a wage shock can lead to utility-enhancing improvements in productivity.

Much empirical research in the last decades has focused on the effect of minimum wage laws. This research has found little negative effect on employment, and perhaps even some positive effect. One does not have to appeal to efficiency wages to explain such a result; imperfections in labor markets can do so. But the result nevertheless flies in the face of standard supply and demand analysis. If agreement cannot be achieved on the value of minimum wage laws, it is hardly surprising that there is little consensus on more complex questions regarding wage incentives.

Long-term employment versus turnover: Japanese firms were long hailed for the worker loyalty that came with the tradition of lifetime employment. As the Japanese economy ceased to outperform, and as some firms in Japan reluctantly laid off workers, the applause died down. European governments in turn are often castigated for employment policies that force firms to pay out high severance

---

[8] With some modern technologies, even the slightest error leads to disaster. Production thus can only occur with highly skilled workers. These will be paid a premium relative to similar workers in other industries.

[9] Insider-outsider theories of labor market discrimination would also suggest that other workers will work less hard if forced to work with the discriminated group.

packages. These policies are routinely blamed for stubbornly high unemployment rates in some European economies. As with Japan, there is little scholarly empirical research that suggests a strong link. In both cases one can imagine a tradeoff between loyalty and flexibility. It could well be that loyalty is more important in some sectors (those that change little, but depend on lots of tacit knowledge perhaps) and flexibility in others (those that change fast and can quickly train new workers).

7.4 Institutional Change

Though our understanding of the range of good institutions is far less precise than it could be, it is still important to dwell at length on how countries might move in the direction of better institutions. In general we know very little about why good institutions develop in some places but not others (Greif 6). Clague (1997) argues that some institutional reforms – such as those that support macroeconomic stability – can be made quickly and generate immediate political rewards, while others – such as rooting out corruption – take longer and may provide little political reward. More generally, we might expect that different institutions develop in different ways. Different theories of institutional change may fit some institutional trajectories better than others.

We will evaluate in turn the insights generated by several disciplines regarding institutional change, and then discuss how these might be integrated.

7.4.1 Economics Approaches

7.4.1.1 Functionalist

Common within economic theory, this (rational choice) approach assumes that institutions are developed to serve particular purposes. The effects of institutions largely reflect the intent of their creators. The theory predicts that institutions should be steadily improved through time. The observed persistence of seemingly sub-optimal institutions must then be attributed to the costs of institutional change. Often, this is done by appealing to the importance of complementary cultural norms: these cannot be changed by decree. Yet such an appeal challenges the basic assumptions of the theory, for if institutions rely on culture, and culture cannot (easily) be changed purposely, then it is not clear how institutional change can be guided rationally (Greif 2006, 154). Mahoney (2000, 518-9), a political scientist, is skeptical that rational choice guides institutional change: unlike in markets it is hard to analyze the costs and benefits of different institutions, and agents often lack the incentive to do so. One might at least hope that humans can rationally evaluate the effects of institutional changes after the fact – such an argument blends into evolutionary theorizing (below) regarding the selection environment for institutional mutations. Since an institution may serve multiple roles the trade-offs between improvements in one direction and costs elsewhere may not be obvious, even after the fact. Moreover if we are not sure of the causes of growth how can we imagine that agents achieve the growth maximizing institution? Socio-logists Swedberg and Granovetter (2001, 15) are even harsher in their judgment of an approach that assumes that institutions are efficient and represent the revealed preferences of those that designed them, rather than examining in context why actors acted as they did.

A more pragmatic objection is that it is not obvious why rational individuals would work toward institutional improvement. Institutional innovation, like tech-nological innovation, takes a lot of time and effort. Rational individuals might be expected to free ride on the efforts of others to change institutions. If all are ratio-nal, nobody may bother to pursue change. Of course an individual may stand to benefit from institutional change enough to warrant effort. But if the individual benefits of institutional change loom large in the process, then concerns arise about whether individuals seek to guide institutional change in a direction that serves them at the expense of the wider society. These concerns have been addressed more directly by non-economists (see below). We can note here that the assump-tion of rationality might be maintained if economists were more willing to embrace altruistic motives: an altruistic individual might devote effort to institutional changes they thought would benefit society.

7.4.1.2 New Versus Old Institutionalism

Economists often distinguish between an old institutionalism popular early in the twentieth century and a new institutionalism that emerged in the last decades of that century.[10] Economists paid little attention to institutions in the middle decades of the twentieth century. Old institutionalists tended to see institutional change as unintentional; new institutionalists have tended (though not always) to evoke intentionality. New institutionalism tends to rely on rational choice, while old institutionalism saw itself as an alternative. The old was often descriptive/empirical while the new is very theoretical. The old often stressed group decisions while the new focuses on individuals. The new often stresses the optimality of particular institutions, while the old stressed that different institutions suited diff-erent contexts to such a degree that it seemed that any imaginable institution was acceptable in the right circumstances. The old institutionalism stressed pragmatic

---

[10] Clague (1997) identifies five branches of new institutional economics: transaction costs, prop-erty rights, imperfect information, collective action, and the evolution of rules and norms.

experimentation over the pretence that ideal institutions could be specified in advance. Several economists have suggested that the two approaches could and should be integrated along each of these dimensions. In particular, new institutionalists have been urged to recognize the limits of rationality in an uncertain process such as institutional change.

7.4.2 Economic History

7.4.2.1 Evolutionary Approaches

Common within economic history (and 'old institutionalism' in economics), this approach emphasizes the imperfect foresight of agents. Institutional changes can be treated as random mutations. Any improvement through time can be attributed to the working of the selection environment. North (2005, 169) notes that within an evolutionary perspective competition between different institutions encourages both progress and the ability to cope with change. While the original innovation may be random, others may copy a mutation that seems to work elsewhere. However, since institutions operate in a web and depend on culture, what is best depends on context (163). Persistence of suboptimal institutions can be attributed to a lack of improving mutations. In the absence of such mutations institutions that once served society well may be maintained even though they are no longer well suited to changing circumstances.

7.4.2.2 A Middle Ground

One way in which a middle path can be sought between the extreme assumptions attributed to the two approaches above (perfect foresight or no foresight) is to imagine that economic agents feel their way toward institutions that successfully serve certain purposes. Needless to say some theorists within both traditions have attempted to relax extreme assumptions and move toward such a middle ground. Traders for example may develop institutions that facilitate trade: these can be said to 'work' when not only does trade occur but it is characterized by very few negative surprises: contracts are rarely broken, theft of property rarely occurs, in other words other agents generally act as they are expected to. Game theory has been used by Greif (2006) and others to describe such a process.

There is obviously an equilibrium element to this sort of theorizing – agents strive toward an institution that serves a particular goal, and stop when successful. An institution is sustained in this equilibrium because the actions of each individual support it and reflect the expectations of other individuals. A process of institutional change may nevertheless be imagined. Most obviously, exogenous shocks can force agents to develop new institutions. But we can also imagine endogenous change: successful trading relationships might increase the wealth of the agents involved, and cause them to change their goals. Or agents may at first develop an institution that works, but not particularly well, and struggle through time to improve it (see below).[11]

Agents in such a scenario need not be assumed to be either perfectly fore-sighted or entirely without foresight. They will purposely experiment with institutions, but will not flawlessly imagine in advance the exact effects any institution will have. In particular, their foresight will likely be limited by the complementary role of culture: institutions only work if individuals act in accord with them. Yet cultural attitudes, unlike institutions, cannot be decreed. Intuition can/should be invoked here to explain how individuals may guess at appropriate behaviors and institutions when no rational model exists that can guide them.

Institutions depend not just on culture but on other institutions. The penalties imagined in stock market regulation must be consistent with more general laws. Since different institutions are determined within different organizations through different processes, agents considering changes in one institution cannot be confi-dent of the direction of change in others. Caution is again a useful guide, though at times it may be necessary to respond to real or expected changes in other institu-tions. Complexes of mutually dependent institutions may be particularly difficult to change.

Agents may never sit back and rationally compare existing institutions with some ideal: even if they do recognize some shortcomings in the existing institu-tions they may be hesitant to induce change because of their lack of perfect foresight. A seemingly superior institution may fail because supporting cultural elements do not materialize. Agents may also be wary of the costs of mastering a new institutional structure such that they know how to behave within it (Rothstein 1998, 152). Institutional change will only occur if the benefits appear to be huge or (more likely) if the existing institution is no longer serving its purpose(s) very well. In the latter case, institutional change may be sudden if the previous institu-tion fails suddenly, or more gradual if agents perceive that their institution is increasingly unsuited to the environment. Agents, in other words, should respect tradition, but consider rejecting this in particular situations.

Importantly, when institutional change is pursued agents have a powerful incentive to move in small steps. While a large institutional change may fail because of a lack of cultural support, a small change in institutions can largely rely on

---

[11] Sabel and Zeitlin (1997) thus urge scholars past the Schumpeterian dichotomy between agents maximizing within a particular institution or trying to change the institution: agents characteristi-cally do both simultaneously. Moreover they stress that agents often have a better idea of insti-tutional possibilities than we might think. But they stress (14-5) that agents had imperfect foresight, and thus often did not have a strong preference for one option. They thus faced the problem that choosing one path might foreclose others [That is they appreciated path depend-ence].

(small changes in) existing cultural elements. Note that one cannot even be confident that institutions that work elsewhere can be imported into a society with quite different institutions and culture – as the attempts of Russia to suddenly adopt certain Western institutions attests.[12] Nevertheless, if an institution fails suddenly a search for alternative role models is likely – as when Turkey adopted a host of Western institutions after the fall of the Ottoman Empire (Greif, 195).

The course of institutional change may be constrained by the past in other ways. As noted above, even the goals of humans reflect culture. And thus if we allow some scope for decision-making based on process/virtue, the culture of a society will influence what individuals imagine to be institutional advance. Likewise, individuals operating within a previous institutional structure will have developed rules of thumb on how to behave (which may be subconscious and thus embodied in intuition).[13] Greif (203) emphasizes that learning is relative to particular institutions, but individuals are likely to extend what they think they have learned into quite different environments. These rules of thumb will still provide some guidance to the individual during the period of uncertainty associated with institutional change. (Greif, 166, mentions limited attention and habit as other sources of path dependence).

7.4.2.3 A Non-equilibrium Approach?

Institutions must work in order to survive. But one should not then jump to the assumption that they must work *flawlessly* in order to survive. And this assumption is embedded in theories of institutions that treat these as equilibrium phenomena. Yet a casual glance at the institutions of developed countries suggests otherwise. Are our property rights protections ideal? No; crime still occurs, contracts are not always enforced, and one's enjoyment of property can be interfered with by the noise and pollution generated by others. Has corruption been eradicated? No; though in most (but not all) developed countries it is rare enough to be newsworthy (when exposed). Institutions, it might be concluded, must serve some purpose(s) or they would not survive, but will not generally achieve any societal purpose flawlessly.

---

[12] Greif (165 and elsewhere) notes that game theory often generates multiple equilibria: there may be more than one combination of rules and culture that solve a particular economic problem. He thus turns a widely-perceived failing of game theory (economists like theories that generate unique equilibria) into an asset in explaining path dependence in institutional change. Readers may judge how much this concept adds to their understanding.

[13] Cross-sectional statistical analyses suggest that countries that were colonies of Britain and France were more likely to have protection of property rights and the rule of law than were former colonies of Spain or Portugal (Greif, 6). Countries were more likely to sustain these good colonial inheritances if they were peaceful and not in economic distress at the time of independence (Greif 6).

This is especially the case given that societies have multiple and conflicting goals. Developed countries need property rights but also transport infrastructure. Yet every landowner along the route of a new highway or rail link may try to extract the full value of the entire road when selling their land. The solution applied almost universally – though to the horror of some of the more fierce advocates of property rights – is eminent domain, which allows governments to force the sale of land needed for public improvements. More generally, property taxes both fund government expenditures and ensure that valuable land is put to valuable uses: if you own land in a city centre you will have to develop it in order to pay the taxes.

Within this sort of quasi-equilibrium understanding of institutions, a further mechanism for institutional change emerges: purposive attempts to make an existing institution better. Such quasi-equilibria fit well within evolutionary approaches: mutations can be guided by a desire to improve institutions. The scope and merit of particular mutations will depend on the limited foresight of agents. The shape of the selection environment will be important: if mutations that serve societal purposes are selected, we can anticipate a process of institutional improvement. If the selection environment is heavily biased toward particular special interests this result is less likely – but not impossible: democracy emerged in most developed countries as the powerful came to see advantages in extending the franchise.

The policy implications for less developed countries are many:

- We should not expect or demand perfection, but should support even small moves toward better institutions.
- We should stress changes in selection environments. Democracies might be expected to select (and propose) beneficial mutations more often than autocracies (though autocracies devoted to growth as in East Asia can do well). (See below).
- Given the interdependence among institutions, and between institutions and culture, we should appreciate that institutions must be shaped to fit their environment.
- Since one purpose of institutions in less developed countries is to impress foreign investors and donors, we should look beyond the formal nature of rules to whether these are enforced. This insight, happily, is generally appreciated in empirical analysis (see above) and the result usually found is that it is the 'quality' of institutions rather than their form that influences growth.

7.4.2.4 Path Dependence

If institutional change is constrained by the shape of past institutions, then we may see path dependence.[14] Path dependence occurs when there is no one inevitable outcome of a historical process. Path dependence is ubiquitous in the short run, for clearly our decisions today are shaped by our circumstances, but in the long run some (especially economists) wonder if there is some strong tendency toward optimal institutions. Alternatively Mahoney (537-8) argues that given the complexity of any chain of events one can find path-dependence of any outcome if one looks hard enough and far back enough for conditioning events that theory does not predict. Other economists, and especially economic historians, have sought to explain path dependent outcomes, and the term has traveled from economic history to other social sciences (Mahoney 2000, 507).[15] One line of explanation involves arguments for continuing to move in particular directions once an original contingent decision is made: in other words it involves theorization of movement in a particular direction. But path dependent processes may be directionless: the only requirement is that the outcome observed today would have been different if a different decision had been made in the distant past. Indeed, it is often observed historically that a change in one direction invites a reaction in the opposite direction (an observation that should give pause to anyone pursuing institutional change). Tracing such a causal chain through history requires a careful set of related causal arguments.

A couple of examples may be useful here. James (2006) has examined the curious (to British/American eyes) case of large family firms in Continental Europe in which hundreds (or more) family members share ownership of a particular firm. He explains this institution in two ways. First, the Napoleonic Code insisted on partible inheritance, and thus firm owners had to pass their assets fairly equally to all children. Before corporation laws were introduced late in the nineteenth century these had no ability to sell their 'shares.' The second argument suggests that in an environment of political instability and limited protection of property rights, family firms had advantages in terms of networking (the families were strategic in marriage choices) and also a commitment to permanence. Surprisingly, perhaps, family firms are found to perform as well as other firms even in the twentieth century, and perhaps outperform them in sectors with limited capital requirements

---

[14] Kuran (2000) argues that the Islamic Middle East could not break away from a constellation of institutions that served it well in the year 1000 but were inimical to modern economic growth: lack of the corporate form was supported by an inheritance law that required fragmentation of wealth holdings; provision of public services was limited by a reliance on private charities, but these though also a means of sheltering wealth from inheritance rules could not make the leap to the corporate form; given the small scale of industry, sophisticated banking institutions did not develop – these would in any case have required incorporation.

[15] Sociologists add arguments involving power [those who benefit from institutions support these], legitimacy, and functionalism – note that different arguments suggest different ways in which path dependence might be reversed – Thelen 1999 (509).

(for family firms may be shy of borrowing) and in which reputation for quality and service are important. James notes that there has been a resurgence in family firms at the end of the twentieth century and conjectures that the uncertainties (and importance of brand identification) associated with globalization may again be supportive of this institution not just in Europe but in much of the world. This is a good example of path dependence (and of the case study approach in economic history), for dramatic differences in industrial structure in modern developed countries can be traced to contingent differences in economic environment centuries ago. And it has policy implications, for economists in the United States or Britain can too easily presume that corporations are the unique best way to organize a large economic undertaking.

Hall and Soskice (2001) argue from a (interdisciplinary) business history perspective that continental countries rely more on cooperation (between firms and with workers) than Anglo-Saxon firms.[16] There is no difference in overall economic performance, but there are differences in innovation strategies (see above). Cooperative countries tend to have fewer hours worked and more equal income distributions. A German firm may react to an appreciation in its currency by sacrificing profits in order to maintain market share, while a British firm does the opposite: the former does not want to layoff workers and can rely on patience among its financers, while the latter worries less about layoffs but fears punishment by stock markets. This example shows that there are complementarities between quite different institutions: labor loyalty is aided by patient capital. One also sees more general rather than industry-specific education in market-reliant countries, and more hierarchical as opposed to consensual firm decision-making; they suggest that strong states may be unable to make credible commitments to firms or workers unless these are organized nationally to exert power. .

7.4.3 Sociological Institutionalism

Sociologists have until very recently emphasized the effects of institutions (including their effects on the goals agents pursue), and devoted relatively little attention to their evolution. This situation reflected a broader emphasis within sociology on causal influences from society to individuals rather than the reverse. Yet sociologists have long doubted that observed institutions were necessarily efficient.

Following Randall Collins, Mahoney (2000, 517) identifies four broad types of sociological analysis of institutions:

- Utilitarian: an institution is reproduced by rational cost-benefit analysis, and is changed either when the situation changes or the agents learn new information

---

[16] Alternatives to the large corporation were possible in American history, including networks of smaller firms, but governments supported large corporations institutionally (Perrow 2004).

- Functional: an institution is reproduced because it serves some societal function, and changes only when an exogenous shock changes those needs.[17]
- Power: an institution is reproduced because powerful actors support it, and changes when the power balance in society shifts
- Legitimation: an institution is reproduced because agents believe it to be just or appropriate, and changes when values change. Institutions may in turn shape values, but only if the institution is seen to be legitimate.

The first two of these overlap with the approach of economists, while the latter two involve quite different emphases. Note that Mahoney draws on examples of detailed historical case studies to justify and explain each type of approach.

Mahoney notes that while path dependence is used in economic history to explain inefficient outcomes, it can be used in sociology to explain also limited functionality [though this seems a lot like inefficiency], limited legitimacy, or unanticipated changes in power relationships (as when private corporations became centres of power rivaling the governments that facilitated their creation).

Swedberg and Granovetter (2001, 7-8) argue that the new economic sociology has made its most significant contributions by applying social network ideas (see below), organizational sociology, or the sociology of culture. That is, sociologists contribute to our understanding of institutional change by looking at how the networks in which agents operate determine possibilities, how organizations operate, or how culture influences decisions. Within our typology of theories, these three approaches respectively privilege relationship agency, group agency, and the role of attitudes, all elements that tend to be missing from economic analysis. The main concepts in these analyses are 'social embeddedness' and 'social construction of reality'. Unlike many social science concepts that are dangerously vague, these can be easily understood in terms of theoretical arguments: 'economic acts are embedded in (that is, influence and are influenced by) social relationships and culture,' and 'our acts are conditioned by the meanings we attach to events.'[18] While Swedberg and Granovetter recognize that the latter idea in particular requires much further development, it is at least fairly straightforward to comprehend the broad thrust of the argument.

The organizational approach guides sociologists to recognize conflicting motives within organizations (workers connected through stable employment relations can develop complex mechanisms for shirking), but even moreso to stress how organizations operate in an environment of other organizations and institutions. Thus whereas the business historian Chandler emphasized the supposed internal efficiency of the large multi-division corporation, economic sociologists

---

[17] Functionalist theories often do not explain how an institution is created (see chapter 3).

[18] Importantly, while the term 'embeddedness' is borrowed from the work of Karl Polanyi, the new economic sociology disagrees with his argument that modern economic relations are no longer embedded; it is argued that Polanyi exaggerated the difference between modern and pre-modern societies. However, Polanyi's argument that reciprocity and redistribution are alternatives to market exchange relationships is maintained (Swedberg and Granovetter, 10-12)

emphasize how such firms interacted with others, and how financial and other institutions paved the way for the rise of the large corporation (7).[19]

The social construction approach guides not only an emphasis on the role of culture but a skepticism that institutions are the objective realities that they seem. Rather a way of doing something thickens and hardens over time until it seems natural. One cannot understand an institution without looking at its history (17). This bears some similarity with approaches in economic history, but relies much less on equilibrium. Note that this approach suggests that institutions can generate to some extent supportive changes in cultural attitudes (but the failed efforts of Communist China to generate collective attitudes through collective institutions suggest that there are limits to this approach).

Dobbin (2004) takes a slightly different approach to both Mahoney and Swedberg and Granovetter. He argues that sociological interest in economic issues resurged in the 1980s as it became obvious that countries with quite different institutions were achieving similar levels of economic success. Many sociologists then began to apply their theories of (religious, ritual, and so on) behavior to economic behavior. Dobbin emphasizes four key sociological approaches to the study of the economy. One emphasize networks (as above),[20] and another makes the general point that widely held ideas influence behavior (again this was presaged above).

The third approach stresses political institutions. Unlike political scientists, sociologists emphasize how political institutions shape cultural attitudes as institutions come to be seen as right and natural (that is, how they are legitimated).[21] Perrow (2004) thus argues that the large corporation came to dominate the American economy because a relatively weak federal government in the late nineteenth century served the interests of big business: not only was it easy to establish a limited liability corporation, but limited liability was denied to small private companies. As large corporations came to dominate the American economy (to a much larger extent than in most European countries, and even in industries with no significant economies of scale), this came to be seen as the natural state of affairs. Gao (2004) alternatively argues that in Japan government bureaucrats were powerful and

---

[19] Chandler had suggested that economic growth was driven by large corporations, but Cassis (1997) argues from European experience that growth does not depend on increased size of businesses. Some justify large corporations in terms of hypothesized advantages in innovation, and others argue that they must reflect the beneficial outcome of an evolutionary struggle, while others see them as only the outcome of favorable treatment by the American government. Note that the empirical analysis of economists finds large multi-divisional firms no more efficient than much smaller firms in many industries.

[20] Haveman and Keister (2004) argue that savings and loan institutions in California benefit from proximity to other S&Ls with different specialties: they can refer customers to each other, and jointly offer a broad package of financial services.

[21] There is a longstanding tradition of studying 'political culture.' While the term has often been vaguely defined in the past, there is now mounting survey evidence from various countries of particular attitudes. Yet there has been little theorization of whether there are (as seems likely) many sets of values conducive to democracy (Dalton, 1998, 341).

wished to copy German business groups; this state of affairs also came to be seen as natural.

The fourth approach emphasizes institutional mimicry: one society or group or organization often copies institutions that work well for others. Notably, this need not involve a rational assessment of why the institution works, but merely a desire to do what the successful do. One unfortunate effect is fads, as when several American investment banks established foreign branches in the 1960s, only to withdraw these in the 1970s. More seriously, most corporations engaged in poorly conceived exercises in downsizing in the 1990s, and found that they needed to restore middle management soon after. Swedberg (2004) argues that commercial law looks quite similar across countries today because the laws of the earliest modern economies were copied by those striving to catch up. The obvious lesson is that we should not assume that widely observed institutions are optimal. Dobbin also notes that the internal dynamic sketched previously and this external dynamic are in tension: as we have had cause to stress above borrowed institutions often do not work well in a new environment.

7.4.4 An Insight from Anthropology

Anthropologists have tended to stress uniqueness of historical processes rather than seek generalizations. Yet some generalizations emerge: 'those institutions that surround the organization of work will have the greatest tendency to converge, since they are most closely determined by technology' (Parry 2005, 142). Otherwise, differences in culture will suggest differences in institutions. Anthropologists have tended to stress causal influences of culture much more than causal influences on culture (when they make causal arguments). They would thus tend to me more skeptical than sociologists or economists that institutions can shape culture. But there is an increasing appreciation that cultures do evolve through time in response to (especially technological) changes. There is also a longstanding appreciation that cultures evolve due to cross-cultural contact, though the tendency has been to stress the more obvious negative effects on community cohesion than the possible influence on institutional change or economic growth.

7.4.5 Institutions and Psychology

Seabright (2004) argues that division of labor in human societies requires that we trust complete strangers. It thus depends on institutions that build on the human ability to calculate costs and benefits, and the human tendency to reciprocity. Less fortunately division of labor builds on and reinforces tunnel vision, by which humans convince themselves of the importance of their little piece of reality while downplaying the rest. Notably, Seabright seeks to overcome academic tunnel vision via integration.

North (2005) notes that we cannot understand institutional change [among other things] without first understanding how humans make sense of their world. He notes that the rationality assumption blinds us to the fact that we often design poor institutions because we misunderstand reality (5). The accuracy of beliefs is limited by our imperfect perceptions and/or the uncertainty that abounds around us. We can reduce uncertainty by learning, developing new knowledge, constraining our options through institutions (so that we can better know how others will behave) or by developing beliefs. [If these are not accurate it seems we will only have the appearance of reduced uncertainty]. Learning involves the development of new classifications and the use of heuristics. Since we build on schemas developed as children, these classifications and heuristics are naturally socially embedded (25). One advantage of cultural diversity then is that we will have a range of thought patterns with which to cope with change (42-3). The degree to which people deviate from self-interested rationality differs across societies (46-7). Cultures in turn evolve in response to circumstances, and thus history matters. We generally do not try to deal with uncertainty rationally but work from analogy and imagine patterns where none exist (25). In sum, psychology guides us to appreciate that we are not always guided rationally, but are influenced by culture, and develop flawed guidelines for action.

7.4.6 Politics and Institutions

'Political scientists doing exciting work on economic policy have tended to draw basic insights from Douglass North [the economic historian], who attributes the persistence of economically inefficient institutions to their usefulness to rulers' (Geddes 2002, 360). Thus reforms are opposed not by those who will suffer from them but those who benefit from existing rules: state owned enterprises allow politicians to reward friends (and disguise unemployment), corruption funds political campaigns, and so on. While they may borrow from economic history, political scientists are much more likely to stress issues of power and capability.

The old institutionalism in political science (before 1950s) focused on describing institutions and eschewed theorizing. The new institutionalism is theoretical, and examines primarily how institutions shape political outcomes. Several strands can be identified (Peters 1998):

- A normative approach stressing how institutions depend on supportive norms. This in turn drew on organizational analysis, though the latter tends to emphasize different norms in different parts of an organization. The normative approach emphasizes collective decision-making.
- A rational choice approach.

- Historical institutionalism which stresses path dependent processes. This reflects a desire in the 1960s to bring 'the state back in' to political science, but moves past simplistic conceptions of the state to focus on particular institutions of governance. Various case studies (often comparative) have shown that political institutions shape policies (such as differences in welfare provision). There is a danger, though, of these arguments being hard to refute unless careful comparisons are made.
- Social institutionalism which addresses such themes as corporatism, networks, and interest group behavior. Increasingly, these investigations seek to identify patterns of interactions among organizations.
- Structural institutionalism: For example, how do parliamentary systems differ in behavior from presidential systems?

7.4.6.1 Supportive Norms (Legitimation Again)

As the war on drugs attests, institutional decrees may have limited effect if the decree is widely seen as illegitimate. If individuals anticipate that others will ignore the decree, they are guided to do so as well. The state (or other organization issuing a decree to its members) may try to penalize offenders, but will likely face difficulties here: penalizing a large segment of the population may be impractical, while harshly penalizing only those who are easily caught may seem unjust.[22]

A particular decree is more likely to be seen as legitimate if the body issuing it is seen as legitimate (and vice versa: those who disdain the war on drugs often disdain the police and courts in other contexts as a result).[23] Decrees may be followed in some circumstances out of fear of punishment alone (but then only if someone else may be looking who does not share one's hostility to this particular authority), but are much more likely to be followed if the issuing authority is thought to have the right and indeed responsibility to issue such decrees. Seen in this light, the efforts of authoritarian rulers past (the divine right of kings in Europe and heavenly mandate in China) and present to legitimize their rule is not just mindless propaganda but important for the functioning of the state (Greif 2006, 147-8). Since power and legitimacy may be mutually reinforcing – a state that has no power is unlikely to be seen as legitimate – the legitimacy of any organization, or any decree, will depend in large part on the ability of the organization to reward those who obey and punish those who decline.

---

[22] While we will not stress it here, political institutions reflect economic reality to an important degree. Diamond (1997) describes how the different economic possibilities of different Polynesian Islands resulted in large differences in political (and social) structure.

[23] Rawls, responding to critiques of his path-breaking work in political philosophy, now recognizes that what is considered just will be shaped by political institutions. One cannot determine from outside what is legitimate. This does not mean that political philosophy might not place some limits on what should be seen as legitimate.

The implications for economic growth are obvious and profound. Governments that lack legitimacy will be unable to establish viable economic institutions. In some circumstances, the value of such institutions may be so obvious that they are accepted anyway. But complex economic institutions are likely to be abused and/or ignored.

This is especially important because of the role of government intentions. When Rodrik (2005, 990) analyses 83 cases of 'growth acceleration' (sustained increases in growth rates of at least 2 percent for eight years), he finds that these often reflect changes in the stated goals of government policy rather than obvious changes in particular policies or institutions (which often came later). However, growth rates often fall again unless institutions do change. Legitimacy is important, but has to be utilized to good ends.

7.4.6.2 Rational Choice

Rational choice analyses of political decisions show that the power of agenda-setting is important. Case studies of various sorts have been performed. Oregon school boards set referendum questions on school taxes, and thus target the maximum the median voter will accept (given a default option of reversion to 1911 levels). 'Often apparently minor [such as procedural rules in Congress], micro-level details have a dramatic effect on outcomes' (174). Differences in electoral systems have systematic effects on policies, and those creating such systems are observed to bias them in their favor (Weingast 1998, 182).

Weingast argues that constitutions will survive best if they provide incentives to political leaders to maintain them. That is, they must reflect political compromises that all powerful groups find it useful to uphold. This allows the society to move away from autocracy in which a ruler serves one group at the expense of others (that group must be convinced that it cannot resume its dominant status).

The economists Acemoglu, Johnson, and Robinson (2005) also stress power relations in their (rational) explanation of institutional choice. In societies where power is widely distributed, and there are checks on the exercise of power by any one person or group, protection of property is likely (especially if property is not easy to expropriate). Importantly such protection is credible, for the government can be seen as devoted to property protection. If a small elite or autocrat rules, they cannot make a credible commitment, for expropriation is always a viable option. Nor can they be convinced to give up their power in return for the promise of future rewards as society becomes more productive, for the new government need not honor its promises. The powerful may cede power if fearful of revolution, and confident that they will not be completely dispossessed. This will be unlikely if income is very unequally distributed, for then expropriation will be an attractive option to the masses. The authors stress a distinction between the legal power associated with political institutions, and the de facto power associated with economic and military resources: political institutions are only viable if they are acceptable to those with the power to overturn them. Thus economic elites may stifle political changes that would support economic growth, because there is no way for them to ensure their future prosperity (especially in relative terms) within a new economic regime.[24]

7.4.6.3 Historical Institutionalism

While rational choice scholars see institutions as equilibrium responses to collective action problems, historical institutionalists 'see institutions as the developing products of struggle among unequal actors.' Rather than focusing on one institution they tend to look at interactions among these (Pierson and Skocpol 2002, 706). Moreover, historical institutionalists are suspicious of functional explanations, in large part because actors creating institutions are often focused on short-run rather than long-run effects; but also because of the unintended effects of institutional change (708). Because of path dependence, institutions will rarely resemble an optimal solution to any problem (709). Historical institutionalists recognize the importance of context and are careful to define the spatial and temporal range of applicability of their causal arguments (711).

Thelen (2002) celebrates historical institutionalism for the historical analysis of the formation of institutions and the institutional analysis of their effects (373). She later (381) emphasizes (following Pierson and others) that historical analysis needs to look beyond final choices to how choice sets were determined: historians study how businesses shaped social security legislation while ignoring the fact that most would have preferred no legislation. And in analyzing coalitions one must look at the role of individuals in shaping winning coalitions, and thus appreciate that different outcomes were possible (382). In general, Thelen argues that historical institutionalism at its best carefully analyzes an interacting set of path dependent causal interactions rather than overemphasizing just one causal argument.

Historical institutionalism has tended to stress political institutions (and has looked in detail, for example, at the sources and effects of political revolutions), but has at times studied economic institutions. Thelen (2002) cites Huber and Stephens (2001) as an example of the advantages of the historical institutional perspective. They combine quantitative cross-sectional analysis with detailed comparative case studies in an analysis of the welfare state. They argue for the importance of a long-term perspective: in the short-run individual decisions tend to be emphasized rather than the structural determinants (states, parties, markets) of choice sets. They suggest path dependence: once social democratic institutions were in place for decades in Sweden firms developed strategies based on these.

---

[24] Their empirical work has been criticized on the grounds that one cannot distinguish their argument empirically from one that gives causal force to their instrumental variables; their argument is preferred because it is plausible, and because it is presented in terms of a mathematical model and statistical tests.

Business leaders did not even try to move toward firm-level bargaining. Moreover, centralized bargaining had weeded out 'low wage sectors' and thus there were few employers of cheap labor to complain about wage compression. This last point provides an example of a broader and important argument for careful historical analysis: the losers in one round of negotiations may not survive to influence the next rounds.

Thelen (2002) also identifies two modern streams in the study of business-labor relations. Both react to a previous over-emphasis on labor. One looks at how business and labor 'cross-class coalitions' shape institutions, and thus sees institutions as the result of compromises among politically powerful actors. The other examines how employers coordinate their behavior, and thus focuses on the coordinating role of institutions, and how these shape firm preferences (373). Thelen argues that these approaches need to be integrated, for one cannot fully appreciate the effects of institutions in isolation from their causes, and vice versa. But both can be applauded for stressing how coalitions are formed and interact with institutions.

7.4.6.4 Structural (and Social) Institutionalism

Theories of the development of political institutions stress either a 'good' story in which citizens collectively pursue such institutions out of a recognition of common interests, or a 'bad' story in which the powerful impose these sorts of institutions in their own interest (though in each case the institution is structured to encourage legitimacy) (Rothstein, 1998, 133-4 argues that there is truth in both). In any case political science largely seeks to explain and evaluate the wide variations in institutional form observed in the world: democratic versus authoritarian, centralized versus federal, meritorious versus nepotistic bureaucracy, proportional versus majoritarian elections, and so on.

Structural and social institutionalism both emphasize the interactions between institutions and individuals. Institutions determine who are legitimate actors, the number of actors, the ordering of action, and to a large extent what information actors will have about others (Rothstein, 146). In more sociological approaches they also influence actor preferences. An actor designated as a judge acts differently than one designated as social worker (148). Institutions designed with a mistaken impression of preferences will serve some interests more than others (148).

Rothstein (149) draws special attention to Ostrom (1990). How can common property be managed collectively without state sanctions? A political institution in which actors are called upon to justify their behavior diverts them from self-interest and guides them toward following social norms of collective responsibility. This result accords with experimental results that agents communicating with each other are more likely to cooperate. Rothstein also talks of Putnam's analysis of northern versus southern Italy: involvement in voluntary associations in the north causes individuals to see not just their own self-interest and also to trust others (see social capital in chapter 9).[25]

One source of institutional stability is that those with power relevant to an institution may resist changes that might challenge their power. One source of institutional change is self-interested actors seeking to enhance their own power. History is full of miscalculations where the new institutions do not enhance the agent's power. Structural institutionalists are wary then of arguments for rational development of institutions, though they accept the idea of purposeful institutional change: agents try to advance certain goals but do not know the full effects of their actions and thus often make mistakes.

7.4.7 Business History

Hall and Soskice (2001) argue that firm behavior should lie at the centre of any examination of institutions in market economies. They identify three approaches to institutions common in the business history literature. One asks how governments can create institutions which enhance firm performance. A second focuses more narrowly on government-business-labor cooperation, and stresses the necessity of broad labor (and business) organizations. A third focuses on the role of institutions in generating trust and/or skill acquisition. Hall and Soskice suggest that each has merit but that each fails to emphasize the strategic behavior of firms. That is, they talk of how governments can exercise power, influence norms, or create incentives/constraints, but should instead talk of conditioning strategic behavior (later the authors note that influencing institutions themselves is one form of strategic behavior). Firms need to behave strategically in their interactions not only with other firms but with workers (including how these are trained, motivated, and bargained with). These arguments are especially notable in light of our discussion of business history in chapter 5: this has often focused on the internal workings of firms to the exclusion of the broader institutional environment. It would seem that as some business historians have moved to look at the broader institutional environment they have distanced themselves too much from the study of firm behavior.

---

[25] While Olson's research warns us that some sorts of group cohesion can be bad, if groups fight over the spoils, Olson (2000) argues that poor countries are poor because of bad governance, that this in turn reflects the exercise of power, and that it is difficult for citizens to organize to pursue good governance.

7.4.8 Integrating These Approaches

The value of integrating (some of) these approaches has occasionally been appreciated in the literature. Thelen (1997, 370) notes that it is common to identify three broad types of institutionalism: rational choice, historical [political science], and sociological, but these overlap and can be complementary: rational choice theorists can appreciate historical circumstances while historical institutionalists can think more about why actors do what they do; all can recognize the role of norms in supporting institutions. She notes that it is mistaken but common to accuse rational choice analysis of theory without empirics and historical institutionalism of details without generalizations (372) – though indeed the latter pursue midrange theory with less generalizability than rational choice. Historical institutionalism usually starts from a historical question of why different societies behave differently (is thus comparative) while rational choice tries to explain seeming deviations from rational behavior (374). These approaches can be combined. In this section, we will extend Thelen's integrative impulse across a wider set of institutional theories; we will also use our classifications of phenomena and theory types to identify a wider range of sources of difference across theories.

The wide range of approaches surveyed above is potentially complementary, at least once some extreme assumptions are pruned from some of them. As noted above, institutions are likely not the result of either perfect foresight or no foresight at all. So then the question is empirical as to what extent agents know what they are doing, and thus the institutions created serve the purposes intended. Rational choice approaches in economics stress foresight and functionalism, as do rational choice approaches in political science and functionalism in sociology. Social utilitarianism in sociology argues that agents are purposeful, but does not necessarily assume that they have good foresight. Scholars within all of these traditions relax assumptions of perfect foresight. At the other extreme, evolutionary analyses can assume that institutional mutations are random, but often do not. Game theoretic analyses assume that agents feel their way toward institutional solutions that work. While this is usually done in an equilibrium framework, this element can be relaxed so that institutional change is viewed as a (perhaps) never-finished project.

Whether equilibrium is assumed or not (but especially if it is not) path dependence becomes possible and can be used to explain in part a variety of types of suboptimal outcomes of historical processes. Path dependent processes are important not just in economic history, but in historical institutionalism in political science, where interactions among a variety of institutions (including influences of political on economic institutions), and among agents of unequal power generate path dependent processes. The objection to path dependence comes only from rational choice scholars who assume optimal outcomes.

Once we move away from assumptions that institutions are purposely designed to serve societal goals, scope is created for a variety of causal arguments. Most obviously, the relative power of different agents comes into play. Power is stressed both in sociology and political science, but also by economists such as Knight or Acemoglu. And economic historians have a long tradition of appreciating the role of power (in for example analyses of the feudal system). Political scientists, it was noted, tend to tell both good stories of purposeful pursuit of beneficial institutional change and bad stories of the exercise of power; these are likely complementary explanations rather than substitutes.

As noted above, the exercise of power is often obscured from view: those exercising power generally wish not to encourage an angry reaction and thus pretend to have other motives. Analyses of power, then, are entirely compatible with analyses of legitimation. Both sociologists and political scientists speak of legitimation. But as game theory analysis of institutional change suggests, cultural attitudes are not easy to change purposefully. Scholars can usefully investigate, then, the degree to which processes of legitimation serve the interests of the powerful, or have a momentum of their own. Social constructionism provides one useful hypothesis here: that institutions solidify over time into a form that comes to seem natural. While this result should not be assumed, the implied two-way interaction between culture and institutions accords well with the insights of other approaches such as game theory. The broader social embeddedness approach encourages the study of links between culture, society, and institutions. Another sociological hypothesis is that political institutions themselves shape which other institutions are viewed as legitimate. Both could well capture important aspects of legitimation.

Sociological treatment of 'ideas' encourages a broader exploration of the influence of culture on institutions. If culture is not shaped entirely by the powerful, then cultural values may exert a range of influences on which institutions are thought desirable. The normative approach in political science is similar. The 'ideas' approach is particularly unique in emphasizing the role that social science might play in establishing the desirability of certain institutions. The seeming reticence of other social scientists to engage this line of argument is remarkable.

Campbell (1998, 377) discusses how both historical institutionalism (as practiced by political scientists and political sociologists) and organizational institutionalism (of the sociology of organizations) have both studied how ideas (as opposed to self-interest) influence institutions, but in different ways. These approaches are only rarely compared (usually to stress the advantages of one), and while synthesis is urged on occasion it has not been pursued. Historical institutionalism emphasizes the constraints imposed by both institutions and culture ('underlying normative structures') while organizational institutionalism emphasizes cognitive as opposed to normative constraints (378). Campbell urges us to see ideas and interests as complements that reinforce each other rather than attempt to ask which is most important (379). Historical institutionalists have indeed found that ideas matter – political actors are often observed to pursue ideas that do not serve their self-interest – but that 'the power of ideas depends largely on how much support they receive from political parties, unions, the business community, and influential political and intellectual elites and how much institutional access these actors have to critical policy-making arenas' (379)[26] The tradition of the field encouraged such an emphasis on institutional constraints, but some authors came to appreciate that cultural constraints mattered too: ideas were more likely to be accepted that fit with norms and values. But they did not go further and discuss how policy-makers deliberately frame ideas in order to convince other policy-makers and the public of the appropriateness of certain policies, and thus how the existing menu of ideas is purposely built upon and extended to achieve certain results (380). Again it would be useful (as some have) to recognize how political actors purposely try to ground favored policies in these general cultural under-standings (and how, in particular, as Mary Douglas has argued, they can creatively mix different cultural elements). Organizational institutionalism has thus moved farther than historical institutionalism in appreciating policy creativity (383), though Campbell criticizes them for focusing 'almost exclusively on the unin-tended effects of largely 'taken-for-granted ideas' (398). He closes by critiquing those who argue that only interests matter or only ideas matter: it is the successful framing of ideas by interests that matters. If so this integrative insight can be used to understand how political leaders and perhaps international organizations can creatively build support for growth-enhancing institutions across quite different cultural settings.

Network analysis in sociology argues that agents are constrained by their net-works: institutional change is only possible if supported actively by a sufficient network. Such an approach needs to look at the resources that different network members bring, and is thus compatible with an emphasis on power. The business-labor analyses in political science can be seen as a particular approach to network analysis, looking at how particular coalitions, whether within or across groups, were formed and able to achieve change. Organizational institutionalism in soci-ology alternatively examines the different motives of agents within an organiza-tion. [More general treatments of social capital and social structure will be addressed in chapter 9, but it is notable that these are not central to treatments of institutional change in any discipline.]

Historical institutionalism is not alone in stressing the causal links between institutions. Both structural institutionalism and social institutionalism emphasize the effects of certain sorts of institutions on others. The degree to which a parti-cular institution depends on others, and also on particular cultural values, has an important implication for a key policy issue: how fast institutions should be changed. In transitional economies economists have often urged rapid change (toward Western institutions), but these new institutions have often functioned less well than was hoped. Rapid change may sometimes occur for pragmatic reasons: there is a popular desire for change at a moment in time, and leaders fear that this 'window of opportunity' will close if they do not act fast. On the other hand, slower

---

[26] These insights are based on case studies, such as of how different types of Keynesianism were applied in different countries because of the different opportunities for influence faced by econo-mists.

changes allow policy-makers both to feel their way to complementary changes in institutions, and also to encourage supportive changes in cultural attitudes.

Structural and social institutionalism, along with rational choice theory, also guides us to appreciate that individuals can play an important role in institutional change. Yet the insights of psychology as to how individuals conceive the world around them have only tentatively been incorporated into theories of how individuals pursue institutional change. In addition to cultural influences, theorists need to appreciate that limited foresight is generated by the limitations of human cognition and perception. Since individuals learn by gradually adjusting their schemas, it may be easier to achieve certain sorts of attitudinal changes than others.

The sociological approach of mimicry is the only one of those discussed that emphasizes how institutional ideas flow across societies. But such flows are regularly appreciated by analyses in economic history and historical institutionalism. Various approaches to institutional change warn us that a borrowed institution may not work well within a different institutional and cultural environment.

Thelen's (1997) main argument is that scholars cannot understand change without also understanding stability. That is, one needs to understand the previous situation (and its reproduction and feedback mechanisms) before fundamental change became possible (399) [Thus stated, the argument presumes the existence of equilibria punctuated by innovations, but the argument holds even if we think of periods of relative stability]. Both the coordination emphasized by rational choice theory and the shared cultural understandings of sociological institutionalism allow us to understand continuity better than change (386). Historical institutionalism on the other hand invokes sunk costs and vested interests, and thus is good at identifying critical junctures that send countries on different trajectories, but worse at explaining continuity. Again it would seem that different approaches could usefully be combined.

The various theories thus address links from each of the major categories of phenomena in Table 1 with the exception of the non-human environment (and the two psychological categories are little addressed). The treatment of cultural and social phenomena tends as everywhere to be too broad and diffuse, and needs to more carefully focus on particular cultural and social elements. Beyond this observation there are no obvious missing variables from the set of theories as a whole. But each theory on its own omits much that is potentially of interest.

In terms of theory types, different theories emphasize individuals (rational choice), relationships (game theory, networks), groups (legitimation, cultural and social arguments), and non-intentional agents (historical institutionalism's emphasis on interactions among institutions). There are hopeful signs of increased flexibility within theories on this point: while rational choice used to stress individuals and historical institutionalism stressed groups, both increasingly relate the behaviors of aggregates like unions to those of members (Thelen 1997, 378). Theories of institutional change naturally stress actions (more rarely passive reaction in some evolutionary and historical approaches), but some note the intermediate role of ideas or values. Rational decision-making is mentioned most explicitly, but game theory and evolutionary approaches often refer to an intuitive groping for improvement. Structural institutionalism emphasizes how decision-making processes or rules influence outcomes, but at the level of political institutions rather than individual agents. Organizational institutionalism in sociology stresses the role of routine in behavior. Legitimation approaches have a central place for virtue-based decisions. Path dependent theories have an obvious place for traditions, though agents need not argue explicitly from tradition in order to generate path dependent outcomes. Rational choice and game theory analyses stress equilibria (but not necessarily), but most other approaches embrace dynamic or stochastic outcomes.[27] In terms of theory types, then, the major omission is in terms of decision-making: more explicit attention to intuitive and traditional, and especially virtue and rule based decisions would be useful.

How can we know which theories or causal links are the most important – and whether the relative importance varies by time or place or type of institution? The empirical evidence collected in support of each theory is strong enough, arguably, to urge the dismissal of the extreme arguments noted above. Legions of political scientists and sociologists and economic historians have been fooling themselves if assumptions of perfect foresight or functionalism are entirely correct. The debate regarding path dependence is more subtle: while it is clear that path dependence is important over some time periods the question of whether optimal institutions are inevitably selected in the end is hard to establish uncontrovertibly, though the diversity of economic institutions in countries of similar levels of development suggests otherwise.

The theories surveyed above are only rarely explicitly tested against each other. Variables from various theories are often thrown in the same regression, but this practice generates huge questions regarding the appropriateness of the functional form. Case studies are generally pursued from a particular theoretical perspective. And thus the relative importance of theories is very hard to judge. Explicit comparison is a challenging task for researchers – for it forces them to master more than one theory. The discussion above has hopefully helped to clarify the essence of different theories (though some are very broad in compass). Comparison should ideally be open-minded; when theories are compared at present it is often with the intent of showing the advantages of one. Still this practice is better than no comparison at all, for scholars arguing concretely for different theories can usefully identify the strengths and weaknesses of each.

---

[27] Thelen (1997, 384) argues that a key difference between rational choice and historical institutionalism is the former's continued emphasis on equilibria and the latter's emphasis on change.

7.4.9 Democracy

We have focused above on economic institutions. But we have noted more than once that these depend in turn on political institutions. Moreover discussions of legitimacy raise questions of what sort of government is best able to support good economic institutions. The obvious question to ask at this historical moment (when democratization is spreading through much of the world) is whether democracy encourages growth.

Lane and Ersson (1997, 89-91) identify three broad types of theory regarding the effect of democracy on growth. Conflict theories suggest that distributional wrangling may deter democracies from a focus on growth: in new democracies governments may be too weak to make tough decisions; later on special interests may be too strong. Compatibility theories note that democracies provide property rights and civil rights which are conducive to growth; they also encourage a sense of equality (but do not push redistribution too far) and strive toward equal access to education. Skeptical approaches doubt that the link is strong one way or the other and expect that other causal links are much more important. Each of these merits further discussion.

In the 1970s it was argued that bureaucratic-authoritarian regimes (with technocratic rulers such as after military coups in South America) emerged because of the stresses of economic development: mass industrialization required forced savings and the suppression of labor unions. A few counterexamples such as India or pre-coup Brazil established that industrialization could be accommodated by democracy. Still, the general idea that authoritarianism responds to stresses difficult for democracy to cope with has survived. Lately, however, Bermeo (2002) has shown that the degree of popular discontent is often exaggerated by the elite groups that benefit from authoritarian regimes – both in interwar Europe and after (Kohli 2002, 96-9). And those who had previously argued for the inevitability of authoritarianism in poor countries have struggled to explain the recent wave of democratization. Kohli (102) notes that we need to carefully consider the quality of democracy in such analyses. It could be that democracy is able to support economic growth best within certain institutional configurations and/or cultural attitudes.

Democracy generally makes more credible commitments to property rights, for interfering with property rights (except perhaps the rights of a minority) tends to be electorally unpopular. But some autocrats have managed to make credible commitments to protect property. Autocrats not fearing overthrow (or alternatively those wary of overthrow and seeking to curry favor) may be able to convince their population that they benefit more from encouraging economic activity than from arbitrary confiscation (but an autocrat that has a weak hold on power may always be tempted to steal and run). Still, Douglass North has long argued that England after the Glorious Revolution of the seventeenth century was able to make more credible commitments to protect property precisely because of the enhanced power of a diverse body of property owners in Parliament (Snowdon 2002, 8).

Are there other effects of democracy, and might these work in opposite directions? Sen notes that famine is never observed in multiparty democracies (Snowdon 41). Stiglitz (in Snowdon 404) hails democracy for increasing access to information. Clague (1997) remarks along these lines that reformers in the former Soviet Union did not know what effects their reforms had. Political scientists, though, have long worried whether citizens in democracies have enough access to information to make sound electoral decisions. There is a danger, especially in poor countries, that elite groups are able to manipulate legislators and/or bureaucrats, and thus a benevolent autocrat may be able to achieve better outcomes.

What is the empirical evidence? There appears to be an empirical correlation in both directions between democracy and growth, but with obvious exceptions (such as China).[28] Chang (2002) reminds us that democracy emerged slowly in the present developed countries, and that these had very flawed democracies at best (limited franchise, open balloting, corruption) when they were as poor as present less developed countries.[29] While democracy should be applauded, we should not be surprised if it takes time to take root (138).

Kohli (2004, 20) argues that the literature on whether democracy aids development is necessarily inconclusive. Authoritarian states differ dramatically (and democracies may) in terms of how much power they possess and how well they wield it. Scholars should first ask more detailed questions about whether certain types of democratic institutions are better than certain types of autocratic institutions; they should also recognize that extraneous factors, such as the quality of leadership, may be hugely important. Political scientists have studied in some detail whether the type of democracy matters.[30] There is some evidence that parliamentary systems and corporatist arrangements enhance democratic stability on average, but little sense of how robust these results are: many political scientists were thus wary of advising constitution writers in new democracies. Durlauf, Johnson, and Temple (2005, 656) report several studies that have obtained mixed results with respect to civil liberties and political rights, and a couple of studies

---

[28] Democracy has limited effect on growth in cross-section, partly because democracy has good (transparency) and bad (slow reaction) effects, but also because democracy is correlated with high income [which should only be a problem if converging], good institutions, and education: effects are difficult to disentangle (Aron, 124).

[29] However, economic historians have found that European city states controlled democratically were more productive, due to less fear of confiscation.

[30] Political scientists interested in developing countries ignored questions of democratic governance until the recent wave of democratization; they focused instead on relationships between authoritarian regimes and economic elites (Geddes 2002, 343). They now instead apply theories and methods used to study developed country democracies: they investigate the evolution of parties, voting behavior, public opinion, the diverse effects of diverse institutions, and the development of an independent judiciary (344-5). Geddes recounts research on the political effects of different electoral systems on the number and type of parties, and also discussions of the role of presidents versus legislatures, but does not relate these to economic outcomes.

that have found positive significant effects of judicial independence or constraints on executive power. These early empirical results must be viewed as highly speculative, especially until complemented by detailed case studies.[31]

Does growth in turn encourage democracy? Until the democratization wave of recent decades, democracy was heavily concentrated in the richest countries (with some exceptions such as India). Katznelson and Miller (2002, 18) argue that recent research broadly supports earlier analyses that suggested that democracy 'is premised on certain socioeconomic requisites.' Others are more skeptical. Political scientists have drawn on but also critiqued the idea that stable democracy flows from a certain level of economic development (such that a large middle class is created). This is thought not to be sufficient and likely not necessary, but certainly important (Kohli 2002, 92). Recent analyses suggest it is not just a middle class that is important: a 'commercialized' agriculture removes anti-democratic impulses, and a mobilized working force is essential to the extension of democracy (100). Other works stress non-economic forces (sometimes as substitutes, other times as complements), such as political parties and leaders. One possibility is that the transition to democracy depends on contingent factors such as leadership[32] but its sustainability depends on the level of economic development. On the whole advanced economies with income equality and stable party structures seem most supportive of democracy (103).

Where do democracies come from? According to Acemoglu and Robinson (2005), who use a mixture of formal models and case study illustration, democracies emerge when the previous elite fears revolution more than it fears ceding some power. This is unlikely if incomes are severely unequal, for then democracies are likely to redistribute, especially if wealth is easily seized. However, other models have been developed to explain democratization in countries which did not face the threat of revolution: elites may cede power because they are dissatisfied with the level of public goods provision (and cannot raise taxes unilaterally without encouraging public hostility), or they may gradually expand the franchise because successive median voters see advantages in doing so (Bertocchi 2006). The latter argument, it should be noted, relies on unforeseen consequences: I imagine it is safe to let people a little poorer than me vote, only to find that they then let even poorer people vote.

Last but not least we should not neglect the personal dimension. Democracies work best when created or led by the right people. While it widely accepted that

---

[31] Decentralization is a popular idea, and it makes sense to place governance decisions at the level with the right incentives and accountability. However, many poor countries [and some rich countries?] lack the structures of local accountability that would prevent local political elites from serving only themselves. Decentralization must then be coupled with mobilization of people to participate in governance (Bardhan 2002).

[32] Wood (2006) argues that the leaders of the American Revolution were infused with a gentlemanly ideal of rising above self-interest to pursue the public good. Yet the democracy they created encouraged the pursuit of self-interest. They each recognized this change in attitudes and felt out of place in later life.

the common good can only be served if leaders are not entirely selfish (and the idea of intrinsic motivation suggests that it is possible for politicians to eschew opportunities to cheat), both economists and political scientists have stressed the creation of institutions that limit selfishness rather than the selection of un-selfish leaders. But political legitimacy depends on making good choices in this respect (Besley 2005). Besley suggests that democracy is more likely than either heredity or lot to select leaders that are both competent and other-oriented. As to how democracies can best select good leaders, he talks about institutional incentives (such as lowering opportunities for graft and increasing opportunities for doing good), making politics attractive financially and otherwise taking selection away from small groups that might share in graft. One might imagine that such institutions are more likely if democracies are created by individuals who are themselves other-oriented.[33]

---

[33] Diamond (1997) speculates on the role of individuals in world history. Clearly some individuals have mattered: Christ, Lenin, Alexander. Thomas Carlyle argued that 'Universal history, the history of what man has accomplished in this world, is at bottom the history of the Great Men who have worked here.' However, Bismarck replied that 'The statesman's task is to hear God's footsteps marching through history, and to try to catch on his coattails as he marches past.' I have always envisioned history as a large boulder rolling down a hill. All of us nudge it a little, but none very far. I also think that it is easier to do harm than good in the world. Vandalism and hooliganism are just two easy ways that one can leave a negative mark on the world. And a politician determined to leave a legacy is more likely to do something grandly stupid than farsighted. If so, we should be wary of relying too much on any one leader to promote growth.

8 The Causes of Economic Growth: Cultural and Social Determinants

8.1 Culture

8.1.1 Culture and Institutions

It is noteworthy at the outset that the theories of institutional change referred to in chapter 7 almost all had some role for culture. This insight accords with casual empiricism: we all know, for example, that laws against littering or even certain illegal drugs are almost impossible to enforce if many members of society view them as illegitimate. Yet while economists and economic historians admit the importance of culture in this way, they tend to stop short of explicit cultural analysis. Greif (2006, 8, 19-20), for example, not only recognizes that we must understand why rules are enforced and obeyed, and cannot thus simply study the development of formal rules in isolation, but goes so far as to define 'institution' as a complementary complex of formal rules (what we and most others would call institutions) and cultural elements.[1] The main reason why institutional change is slow and path dependent is that institutions depend on 'poorly understood and often unintentional processes of socialization, internalization, learning and experimentation;' these processes include beliefs and ethical attitudes (190). When agents are forced to engage in institutional change, cultural norms guide them as to which of many possible new equilibria they should move toward (129-33). Yet he worries that cultural elements are largely unobservable, and despairs of cultural explanations for this reason: since ad hoc appeals to unobservable cultural elements can explain everything they explain nothing (2006, xv). He thus focuses his analysis almost entirely on the observable formal rules: when these seem to work supporting cultural values and beliefs must be in place. When he makes specific reference to particular beliefs these tend to be beliefs derivative of the institution itself such as a belief that kings will respect the institution of private property.

---

[1] Greif notes that different disciplines define institutions differently: as rules, as norms, as functional solutions to particular problems. He urges the integration of these definitions. From our holistic perspective, this is best done not by conflating quite distinct phenomena but by capturing through different causal links both the influence of culture on institutions and the role of institutions in solving particular problems. Greif's own wish that different definitions be viewed as complements (40) is best achieved in this manner. Greif's definition encourages an emphasis on culture over other causal influences on/of institutions, while inviting us to treat the culture-institutions nexus as a black box.

R. Szostak, *The Causes of Economic Growth,*
DOI: 10.1007/978-3-540-92282-7_8, © Springer-Verlag Berlin Heidelberg 2009

Many political scientists also define institutions so broadly as to include culture. But if a concept is defined too broadly it becomes meaningless. Most political scientists, while generally favoring a narrower definition in terms of formal rules, have appreciated that these formal rules matter only if followed. One popular strategy is to refer to 'standard operating procedures' which need not be written down (Rothstein, 146). Again the challenge has been to identify such cultural elements. [Anthropologists would then encourage us to explore the meaning attached to these procedures: why do people come to follow them?]

North (2005) argues that we need to understand the relationship between institutions and culture. For example, how did perceptions change in the Soviet Union of how well their institutions worked? He cites Greif on how we get different institutions in Christian versus Islamic worlds because of differential emphasis on individuals versus collectives (136). Yet one sees quite different institutional forms between Japan, South Korea, and Taiwan despite sharing Confucian culture. Likewise in Europe one sees great diversity. One thus needs to be careful in attributing differences in institutions directly to culture. (Likewise, though, it is hard to explain such differences in terms of economic factors alone). The differences can perhaps best be traced to path-dependent political processes, with these in turn influenced by culture and economic circumstances at the points in time when major decisions were made.

The old institutionalism in economics stressed cultural influences. Indeed some would define the old institutionalism in this way: the diversity of institutions was ascribed to cultural diversity. Development economists in the early postwar period borrowed old institutionalist ideas to understand the variety of institutions and cultures they faced. But there was an inevitable reaction among economists against treatments of culture that left no space for individual choice. In particular, economists objected to the idea that individuals in some societies lacked the impulse to better their economic position. Yet as we have stressed many times in this book one can embrace both individual and group-level decision-making: economists need not jettison considerations of culture in order to maintain a place for individual decisions.

Finally, there is an obvious direct link between culture and institutions. Formal institutions at times represent the codification of cultural values. An informal injunction against murder in a small group may become formalized as the group grows in size and complexity. At other times, though, institutions may conflict with certain values, as when formal property rights are established in a community that previously relied on communal resource allocations. In such a situation, we can expect the formal institution to be undermined unless cultural attitudes change.

8.1.2 The Nature of Culture

Greif does speculate on the nature of culture. He notes that, as with institutions, cultural attitudes will only be maintained if they 'work': if they allow individuals to accurately predict how others will behave.[2] If this is not the case – if norms favor honesty but people often cheat – either the norm or the behavior will be encouraged to change. Anthropologists reach a broadly similar conclusion, though they do not express it in terms of individuals: anthropologists would instead stress that a shared culture is essential to deep and constructive social interaction.

One might imagine that only a narrow range of cultural attitudes will serve human purposes. However, the goals that humans emphasize are themselves shaped by culture. A society may be governed by a sadistic religion which demands enormous sacrifices from individuals: it will survive if it allows individuals to predict/understand the behavior of others, and if they cannot imagine a better world (Greif 2006, 137). Anthropologists have often gloried in the cultural diversity of the world, and have often posited that any culture that supported social cohesion was possible.

If human goals are themselves influenced by culture, then no social science theory can serve to constrain the range of possible cultural attitudes. Only human psychology can do so. We need not review here in detail the longstanding debate between cultural anthropologists – who argued that the human mind was a blank slate on which any cultural element could be written – and psychologists who sought to describe 'basic human nature.' Evolutionary psychologists in particular have argued that human psychology places limits on the range of possible cultural attributes (Szostak 2003b). As particular cultural elements are described below, we can reflect on their compatibility with human psychology.

As noted in chapter 5, anthropologists have tended to take a holistic approach in their ethnographic work. This approach has supported a common belief that cultures are monolithic: that they are a system of interacting elements with important emergent properties. Emergent properties of systems of causal links are certainly possible, but these should neither be assumed nor ignored. Szostak (2003b) was skeptical that cultures were (much) characterized by emergent properties that could not be appreciated in terms of particular attitudes and beliefs. One could thus identify any particular culture at any point in time in terms of the attitudes, beliefs, and practices listed under culture in Table 2.1. If cultures were truly monolithic, it would be hard to understand the simple fact that individuals within any society differ in terms of particular attitudes, beliefs, and practices (though a central tendency can usually be identified for the society as a whole). It would also be hard to understand how cultures often evolve slowly through time. To be sure,

---

[2] Though he does not stress this, this argument provides an insight into the problems faced by members of indigenous societies as these come in contact with more developed societies: members of their own society no longer behave predictably, and thus they no longer know how they themselves should best behave.

cultural elements are causally related, and thus change in one element may encourage change in others, but such relationships can be understood in terms of causal links. This argument is important for the purpose of this book (and indeed for any project in which cultural elements might play an important causal role). If cultures are viewed as monolithic, then causal analysis tends to occur at a very broad level: 'Confucian' culture is castigated when certain Asian economies perform poorly, and celebrated when they do well. A more disaggregated approach allows the investigation of causal links between particular cultural elements and particular economic or political phenomena. It also importantly allows an appreciation of how particular cultures change over time, including how they may change in response to changes in economic challenges and opportunities.

Yet I should stress here that I am taking a position that disagrees at least in degree with that taken by most anthropologists. If I am mistaken, then analysis at the level of individual causal linkages, while still useful, may tell us much less about the economic influence of culture than I would hope. There may be a much more important role for analysis at the level of cultural aggregates than I imagine. If so, I would urge much greater clarity with respect to emergent properties themselves: what exactly are the emergent properties of cultures and what are the precise mechanisms by which they affect each of the proximate causes of growth?

8.1.3 Cultural Change

Richerson and Boyd (2005) discuss how cultures evolve (and co-evolve with genes).[3] They argue that culture interacts with human psychology to generate behavior; economists and psychologists tend to ignore culture, while sociologists and anthropologists ignore basic psychology (4). Culture exists because it can adapt to environmental change faster than genes (7). Culture is only useful though to the extent that the environment changes slowly enough for it to catch up (118). That is, culture must have elements of stability in order to serve its purpose. Humans are thus selected both to imitate and to innovate. When the environment changes (or even when it does not), successful innovators will be copied (12).[4] This must mean that in addition to a general predisposition to imitate those around us we have a particular tendency to imitate the most successful (hence the value of celebrity endorsements) (124).

---

[3] The approach can potentially explain genetic selection for altruism: communities with cultural values that support group cohesion might provide an environment in which genetic selection for altruism could occur (see chapter 6). Language capability and lactose tolerance are two genetic traits that could only have been selected after cultures evolved in certain directions.

[4] Anthropologists, again, would tend not to stress the role of individuals in shaping culture. Yet anthropologists, especially in the past, have been more interested in describing cultures at a point in time (and often assuming that traditional cultures had changed little through time) than describing how these evolve.

The core argument in evolutionary psychology is that human genes evolved during the millennia that humanity operated as hunters and gatherers; genes have had little time to evolve further in the few millennia since some humans adopted settled agriculture. We might for example have been selected to be more aggressive than is ideal in a modern urban environment. It is tempting to extend this argument to the cultural realm: inappropriate cultural attitudes may reflect the co-evolution of genes and culture in hunter-gatherer times. But cultures have evolved considerably over the last millennia. Richerson and Boyd (2005) thus disagree with those who argue that observed modern cultural maladaptations reflect primarily the fact that genes and culture co-evolved in hunter-gatherer communities.[5] They also note that cultural evolution is not necessarily constrained by natural selection. We are selected to learn from not just our parents but others as well, and thus fitness-reducing elements can be adopted by a group and not weeded out by natural selection. Of particular importance, cultural elements that serve the elite at the expense of others may survive due to the tendency to imitate the successful.[6] They urge the identification of more precise mechanisms of cultural evolution (such as how prestige is determined), and of how different mechanisms interact.

Cognitive science (and most social sciences) tells us that people form habits. If these are widely shared, they will appear as unified culture (say, a common language). Within traditional cultures anthropologists suspect that most/all cultural elements are universally shared. Yet traditional cultures do not shun personal autonomy, and thus considerable scope for individual differences likely remains even there. If cultural elements are communicated less consistently we will see much greater cultural diversity. This diversity will itself be a source of change as individuals choose among alternative cultural elements. Thus cultural change needs to be comprehended at the individual level.[7] Cultures evolve as more and more individuals within a society choose (perhaps subconsciously) a different attitude or belief or practice. We will not see completely identical cultural elements in any two individuals: even when the same behavior is exhibited (such as prayer) this may be done for different reasons and to different effect (Turner 2002, 2-3).

---

[5] At the end of chapter 6 the authors have a couple of enigmatic pages about how modern complex societies require efforts at coordination that our loyalties to small groups prepare us poorly for. Modern bureaucracies are able to mimic smaller groups at different levels of the hierarchy: they can thus pretend to an egalitarian form of decision-making. Some of the failures of bureaucracies to do what they are told can then be attributed to humans not being designed for such complex hierarchies. They also note that our selection for loyalty to small groups has a natural side effect of encouraging undesirable cross-group hostility.

[6] They also explain the modern preference for small families (which reduces genetic fitness at the individual level) in terms of a search for prestige (170-7). We will see below, when we discuss population, that there are much simpler explanations of the demographic transition. One danger in the evolutionary psychology literature is that theoretical speculation is not always supported by careful argument and evidence.

[7] Turner notes (14) as I do that cultures are thus ensembles of distinct cultural elements. There is no essence of a particular culture. Again, this belief depends on there not being significant emergent properties of culture.

8.1.4 Culture and Growth

Interwar writers such as Gramsci (within the Marxian tradition) and Polanyi had emphasized the causal influence of culture on political and economic phenolmena, but in the postwar world sociologists and political scientists pursued this line of argument much more than economists (Guiso, Sapienza, and Zingales 2006).[8] Economists did not need another variable in their models, especially one that was hard to measure. The profession was suspicious of cultural explanations because these were often vague, because too many possible causal links might exist, and because it was hard to test these conjectures statistically. In the last decades the availability of better data and techniques has induced some economists to study culture. One popular approach is to look at whether membership in particular ethnic or religious groups affects economic outcomes. The advantage of this approach is that such memberships are easily measured and are also largely inherited: this overcomes the possible concern that any correlation between culture and economy reflects causation in the other direction. Both internationally and within countries, ethnic and religious differences do generate different economic outcomes [though within countries, studies of immigrants suggest that these will lessen over time]. Moreover these differences are correlated with different values and beliefs (trust, social mobility, fairness, hard work, fertility, thrift) in both regressions and experiments. Yet such studies can only be suggestive of links between such values and economic growth, and these links are hard to establish statistically.[9] After all, the success of certain groups might be explained in terms of networking or discrimination, and differences in values might then reflect rather than cause their economic success: disadvantaged groups that feel cut off from most economic opportunities will be less likely to embrace the value of hard work.

For present purposes the most telling sentence in the survey provided by Guiso Sapienza, and Zingales is the mention in passing at the very end of their article (and the provision of only one citation) of the wealth of field work in other disciplines

---

[8] 'Within a generation or so after the Second World War mainstream economists had abandoned serious attempts at cultural explanation' (Jones, 2006, 255). Jones concurs that the main reason was that non-cultural variables were more mathematically tractable; he notes that cultural explanations were not uncommon in nineteenth century economics.

[9] In the following survey article, McCleary and Barro look more closely at religion. They find that belief in heaven/hell is positively correlated with economic growth, but religious service attendance is negatively correlated. Belief apparently encourages some growth-oriented behaviors such as hard work or thrift, while attendance seemingly detracts from economic activity (and thus the longstanding belief that religions were important for networking is not generally true). [a couple of caveats: they discuss at length how religions differ in whether they think access to heaven depends on behavior in this life but do not include this important distinction in their regressions; as for networking this may be particularly important among minority religions whereas they focus on majority religions.] Islam is an exception, perhaps for political reasons. They also note that increased income does seem to cause a reduction in religious belief, though this secularization trend is slow and uneven. Research they note is only just beginning on looking at how religions influence economic growth through particular values.

that shows links between culture and economy. Given the difficulty in separating causal influences statistically, economists would benefit from a greater familiarity with insights from other methods.[10]

Economic historians have dealt with culture much longer and more extensively than economists. Some economic historians have stressed the role of culture. Landes (1998, and elsewhere) is perhaps the strongest proponent: he argues that values such as thrift, honesty, tolerance, and hard work are highly conducive to economic growth. 'If we learn anything from the history of economic development, it is that culture makes all the difference' (1998, 516). Why else would expatriate minorities thwarted by bad governments at home succeed as entrepreneurs abroad? Alternatively, Jones (2006) is highly skeptical. While theoretically he appreciates that culture both influences and is influenced by the economy, he emphasizes the latter effect, especially in the long run. He notes that mere decades ago Confucianism was widely seen as a major obstacle to economic growth, for it lacked the stress on individualism of Protestantism. After the East Asian miracle Confucianism is widely hailed for encouraging trust and hard work. Jones argues that unchanging culture cannot be the key explanatory variable when lengthy stagnation is followed by rapid growth. Jones predicts that as more countries develop economically, cultural explanations will fade away as it will no longer be plausible to identify the religions of each with Protestantism. Jones (256) also suggests that one source of the decline of development economics was that it had emphasized culture but that the rise of East Asia showed that culture was malleable. But one might instead argue that the lesson to draw from history is to focus on particular cultural elements rather than broad cultural amalgams such as the Protestant ethic or the Confucian way.

Jones urges analysts to appreciate that economic opportunities and challenges can encourage cultural changes which in turn facilitate growth. And who can deny that economic growth has induced dramatic cultural changes in both developed and developing economies in recent decades? Thus when we observe a hardworking or trusting society that is growing rapidly, it may well be that people reacted to economic opportunities by working harder or developing institutions that encouraged trust. The link from institutions to culture should be stressed. Jones argues that the tendency of Chinese businesspeople to focus on personal relationships rather than formal contracts may reflect not cultural propensity but the environments of weak property rights in which they operated both in China and as minorities in Southeast Asia (168-70).[11] Jones would thus suggest that some/all of

---

[10] While economists underemphasize the degree of cultural embeddedness of economic activity, anthropologists tend to exaggerate this. This at least is the judgment of the anthropologist Gudeman (2001, 19), who cites the sociologist Granovetter.

[11] Immigrants from countries with poor financial institutions are found to be less likely to invest in stock markets (Guiso, Sapienza, and Zingales, 2006). Lal (140-1) attributes the success of Chinese family enterprise to the move from mass production to flexible production; he argues it is only possible within a Western institutional structure. [But as Jones notes they have little recourse to legal institutions.]

the different cultural attitudes associated empirically with ethnic/religious groups will dissipate over time as economies converge.[12] But Jones appreciates that culture does not respond quickly to economic change. While thus skeptical of cultural explanations over the long run he does appreciate that culture can influence economic outcomes at least in the short term. Recall from chapter 3 a concern that formal growth theory emphasizes long run equilibria and thus may steer attention away from the dynamic process of generating and sustaining growth. We must be careful here as elsewhere of not missing important early components of a growth process: a country with unhelpful cultural attitudes may have difficulty generating the economic opportunities that will in turn encourage cultural change. Moreover we should not casually assume that even in the long run cultures will always adapt in ways supportive of economic growth: economic growth is, after all, not the sole purpose of human existence. Since we have seen above that economic convergence hardly ensures institutional convergence, we might well suspect that considerable cultural diversity is also possible.

Reflecting on the East Asian experience, Jones (259) provides a valuable methodological warning: cultural arguments must be justified by comparisons across many cases. It is too easy to compare a couple of economies, identify differences in culture, and argue that these were the source of differences in economic performance. Only by comparing many economies can one overcome spurious correlations. It is also important to appreciate variations within culture (32), especially given that minority groups often play a disproportionate role in economic growth.

The economist Sachs (2005, 316-7) also notes how easy it is to exaggerate the role of culture. Japan, China, Ireland, Spain and now the Islamic world (Bangladesh and Malaysia have impressive growth records) have each been criticized in turn for bad culture before experiencing rapid growth. He notes though that economic growth in its early stages might have encouraged cultural change. Sachs also warns of the dangers of stereotyping: surveys of values often paint a quite different picture of the cultures of other societies than casual empiricism suggests.

These warnings should not discourage us from investigating possible links between culture and growth. They should guide us to be careful in identifying specific causal linkages, and to worry about feedback effects from growth to culture. They also guide us to be careful in measuring cultural elements, and of leaping from observed correlations to causal arguments. Both internationally and regionally within countries there appear to be correlations between certain cultural values and economic performance (trust and respect are good, obedience is bad). Reverse causation cannot be entirely ruled out, but should not be assumed.[13]

---

[12] Jones (178) notes that values such as thrift and hard work are less widely observed in the West than they were in the nineteenth century: he predicts a similar value shift in other societies as they grow. If so this provides a cultural argument for convergence.

[13] The economist Acemoglu uses instrumental variables such as literacy rates in previous generations to control for reverse causation. His results have been criticized, though, because such variables may in fact have a direct impact on growth.

The sociologist Beckert (2002) provides a compelling overview of the need for socio-cultural analysis of economic decisions. Economic theory itself suggests limits to the exercise of rationality in two common circumstances.[14] The first is when cooperation among agents is required, in which case economic calculations depend on culturally conditioned expectations regarding the behavior of others. The second is when uncertainty is present: if actors cannot rationally attach probabilities to the results that their actions might produce, they must rely on various mental rules to guide behavior. While individuals will differ in these, there will also be cultural influences (and cooperation in the face of uncertainty would depend on similar mental rules). He devotes particular attention to the uncertainty associated with innovation, and notes that this will reduce the level of investment in innovation below the societal optimum, but that this effect can be alleviated by culture. Notably, when Beckert lists the key elements of the mental representations that guide economic behavior, these are precisely the 'schemas' identified in Table 2.1: views of self, understanding of causal relationships, and expectations of the behaviors of others. Szostak (2003b) outlined various ways in which culture influences schema formation.

Beckert urges sociologists to focus on examining the social influences on those economic decisions for which rationality is particularly problematic. This recommendation would have the effect of strengthening the value of the research in each discipline to the other. He also urges sociologists to move away from references to 'irrationality' but rather to identify specific strategies engaged by actors when strictly rational calculation is not feasible. This advice is similar to the advice of Newell (2007) to find common ground between economists' rationality and sociologists' irrationality by thinking of a continuum between the two. While Beckert does not attempt to classify these non-strictly-rational[15] strategies, he makes frequent reference to following routines[16] and following cultural guidelines – including respect for widely-shared values, and less frequent mention of intuition, and thus his analysis is consistent with the elucidation of the five-types of decision-making

---

[14] In addition to these major circumstances of cultural influence Beckert also recognizes occasions of intentional non-rationality – when altruism deflects actors from maximizing according to self-interest – and non-intention – when various cognitive limitations or cultural biases influence rational calculations, given that humans do not have the time or cognitive capacity to carefully evaluate every decision.

[15] Beckert in distinguishing himself from the emphasis of other sociologists on irrationality strives to emphasize the 'rationality' of other decision-making strategies. In this book these can be seen as reasoned but non-rational strategies. Note that semantic confusion between narrow and broad uses of the word 'rational' contribute to misunderstanding between sociologists and economists.

[16] In this he follows the small European tradition in economic sociology. Swedberg (2005) recounts the work of Luc Boltanski who discusses how economic actors develop conventions as part of efforts to coordinate economic action – these conventions consist of a few standard ways of thinking about reality, and thus justify certain actions. Note that while such routines may be selected evolutionarily, they may fail to adapt to changed circumstances and may thus provide undeserved levels of confidence.

in chapter 3. Beckert argues that no sociological theory is perfect, but leans toward the structuration theory of Giddens, because this allows for actors to influence cultural expectations at the same time as they are influenced by these. Actors thus exercise some reflexivity in attaching meaning to circumstances (Durkheim and Parson had instead tended toward a 'normative determinism' in which individual actions did not in turn shape norms). The implication here is critical: *we should be wary of cultural explanations that do not engage the question of how values are shaped by individual behavior.* This outlook is of course complementary to that outlined by Greif above. [It is, though, at odds with the tendency in anthropology to downplay the role of individuals – but also to emphasize stability rather than change.] Beckert hypothesizes that in developed economies people expect a gradual evolution in attitudes whereas in traditional economies people do not: if so, one challenge of development is embracing cultural change without threatening cultural stability.

Sociologists more generally stress that economic actions are invested with meaning, and cannot be separated from agents' pursuit of power, status, approval, and sociability (Swedberg and Granovetter, 8). The anthropologist Gudeman (2001, 4) likewise stresses that one cannot understand how real markets work without looking at how individual actors invest these with meaning.[17] The work of sociologists and anthropologists should guide us not just to appreciate the range of cultural elements that might have an economic impact but the range of economic activities these might affect. This suggests that the statistical analyses of economists need to be supplemented with careful comparative case studies of particular sorts of economic decisions.

Care must still be taken in drawing lessons from comparative case studies of the links from culture to economic performance, because there are so many variables interacting (Keating, Loughlin, and Deschouwer 2003, 181). But these authors nevertheless think that their eight cases show that: a shared cultural identity is good for a region, but only if this is open and porous [that is, there are strong bonds within but many bridges outside; see social capital below]. The right balance between identity and openness is hard to identify or achieve. Internal ties should be strong enough for trust, but not so strong that the government cannot abandon failed enterprises (182). Successful regions point to myths of past successes by their groups (182). They also modernize tradition so that the culture evolves even while it is celebrated (183). Leaders have scope then to shape identity (184-5). Regional governments encourage a sense of identity (183). This study shows the potential of careful comparative analysis. Nevertheless, the results must be viewed as tentative until many similar studies are performed.

---

[17] The literary theorist Baudrillard's conception of hyper-reality also suggests that culture and economy are intertwined (Throsby 2001, 11).

8.1.5 Which Values?

8.1.5.1 A Range of Values?

It was argued in chapter 7 that a fairly wide range of institutions seems to be capable of supporting economic growth. This argument reflects the institutional diversity observed among successful economies. Arguably the cultural diversity among developed countries – at least for some cultural values – is even greater. Several authors have thus argued that quite different values may serve growth equally well.

Blim suggests that economists believe there is one best value set for capitalist societies (2005, 307), and endeavors to show that there are diverse cultural attitudes across successful capitalist societies. Modernization theory in sociology had suggested that certain values, such as attitudes toward achievement, were essential for economic growth (308). More recently Fukuyama has stressed trust and Harrison has urged future orientation, work effort, frugality, education, merit, trust, honesty, justice/fairness, dispersed authority, and secularism (309). Blim criticizes both for arguing from correlation without demonstrating the causal links between these values and growth. Blim devotes several pages to detailing differences in institutions across modern economies (including poor economies), and then argues that these both reflect and support value differences. Different emphases on individual versus community are reflected in lifetime employment in Japan and huge executive salaries in the United States. Differences in the relative importance of competition versus cooperation are reflected in different approaches to labor/management relations (316). Attitudes toward equality are reflected in taxing and spending and also in affirmative action policies. Yet Blim is careful not to suggest that the range of cultural values compatible with growth is infinite; indeed he goes so far as to suggest that values completely incompatible with capitalism will have been weeded out everywhere by now (315). Given the miserable economic performance of some countries in recent decades, this seems a questionable assertion. Blim can also be criticized for focusing exclusively on the culture/economy nexus. For example he cites Malaysia as an example of a country pursuing affirmative action for cultural reasons. One could instead argue that this reflected instead the political power of ethnic Malays. More generally Blim seems guilty of arguing from correlation himself, even while criticizing others for this practice.

Hefner (1998) also suggests from an anthropological perspective that a range of cultural attitudes are conducive to economic growth. Growth has not been associated with secularization or individualism, especially in the Islamic world. He examines East Asia, and suggests that trust within paternalistic relationships is more common there. As with Blim we can worry that Hefner argues from correlation and ignores political influences. We have seen above that paternalistic business relationships in Asia may reflect the (previous) absence of secure property rights.

Nevertheless, it is hard to travel through the developed world without suspecting that these authors are correct that a huge variation in cultural elements is compatible with growth. Yet we should be careful of assuming that this result applies equally to all values. It may be that the obvious differences in cuisine and attitudes toward politeness and relationships are less important for economic performance than other values and practices.

8.1.5.2 Trust

Trust is the cultural attitude most examined by economists (but even it has received far less attention from even institutional economists than from sociologists or business schools). In part this reflects its obvious theoretical importance in facilitating economic transactions: agents that trust each other can contract much more easily than agents who do not. It is prohibitively expensive to contract for all possible outcomes (not to mention enforcing a complex agreement legally); contracting is easier if shared values will guide consensus in evaluating unforeseen developments. Yet the emphasis on trust also reflects the ease with which trust can be treated in mathematical game theoretic models as the probability that other agents act as one expects.

Some transactions will occur even in societies without trust. We can imagine that trust becomes more important as the level of uncertainty rises. Long-distance trade requires more trust than local trade. Trade involving goods and services where quality is hard to measure requires more trust. Importantly for present purposes, contracts involving the future require more trust than spot transactions. And growth as we have seen depends on a host of future-oriented activities involving multiple agents.

Statistically, measures of trust in a society seem to be associated with economic growth, and also with the degree of entrepreneurship in a society (it is plausibly conjectured that entrepreneurship is more appealing in a trusting society). Societies characterized by ethnic homogeneity and income equality are more likely to exhibit trust, though democratic institutions and rights guarantees can erode the suspicion inherent in ethnic differences (Snowdon 2002, 99).

Ironically but importantly, cultural embrace of the naked self-interest often assumed by economists may destroy the trust on which exchange depends. The sociologist Granovetter (2002) notes that trust means being confident that another will act against selfish incentives (for we need no trust that another will act selfishly). Some economists try to rationalize trust by referring to repeated interactions (either within a relationship or group) or perhaps appealing to evolutionary mechanisms. Individuals behave in a trustworthy manner only because a reputation for trustworthiness is more beneficial than cheating. But it seems clear that trust extends into situations where others might benefit from cheating, and thus that it reflects in important ways a form of self-respect that can trump narrow self-interest. Economists (and economic historians such as Greif) tend when speaking of trust to try to align this with self-interest, while sociologists argue that it is especially important when it trumps self-interest. These approaches may be complementary and may be important in different situations.

Modern societies may rely more on Granovetter's sort of trust than traditional societies, for the latter can rely on close monitoring of behavior within kin and community. That is, behaving in a trustworthy manner is personally beneficial in a society where one regularly interacts only with the same small group, but is less so when one has infrequent interactions with many people. However, societies moving from a kin-based to a less personal form of exchange may struggle to generate the necessary degree of trust. Marx and Tonnies both wrote at great length in the nineteenth century about this important transformation, the latter speaking of a shift from community to society.

Business historians have argued that trust is particularly important in a changing world. In order for networks of entrepreneurs to respond to new opportunities (and yet cope with uncertainty), they need to trust each other not only to respond to surprises honorably (rather than seizing opportunities to renegotiate) but not to steal freshly-trained workers or new ideas (Sabel and Zeitlin 1997, 21). Each foregoes opportunities to take advantage in expectation of not being abused in turn (by many others). If actors saw themselves as the selfish calculators of neoclassical theory, this trust would be impossible. Trust in practice is sustained in part by recourse to arbitration when it is thought opportunistic behavior had occurred (24), and also by collective institutions for training and research (25).

Can agents behave in a credibly trustworthy fashion in order to achieve the economic benefits of trust? Economists and economic historians applying game theory analysis imply that this is the case. But Offe (1998, 686-7) stresses that norms of promise-keeping and property-respecting serve economic efficiency as a 'latent' function: were they entirely justified on efficiency grounds evasion would be common. That is, an agent thought to be strategically acting in a trustworthy way will not in fact be trusted.

As noted in chapter 5, some sociologists have struggled to explain social stability (while others have instead stressed change). The idea of trust is thus potentially of central importance in sociological analysis. If individuals can come to trust others then the result is cooperation rather than theft and stealing. The danger of course is that sociologists are then tempted to assume rather than establish trust.

As noted above, cultural values will only survive if they serve to predict behavior. This is especially important with respect to trust: this value will only be respected if individuals usually find that others behave in a trustworthy fashion. No society is perfectly trustworthy, and thus no individual should blindly trust others. As the term 'confidence game' attests, fraud and embezzlement are only possible in situations of trust. But a high degree of trust will still be both possible and advantageous if cheating is rare.

Trust is not just a cultural value but also a characteristic of relationships. One can trust particular individuals more than strangers if those individuals continually act in a trustworthy fashion. Such relationship-level trust may still be much easier to establish in a society that values trust, but may also be possible within non-trusting societies and across societies. Trust then can usefully be examined as a property of networks (chapter 9). And the economic implication is profound: agents will prefer if possible to contract with those they know. Buyers and sellers generally establish stable relationships, and thus it can be hard for a new actor to break in (Granovetter 2002). This natural human tendency slows the establishment of better trading relationships, and the flow of new ideas. Again, agents will be more willing to deal with strangers in a society characterized by trust.

8.1.5.3 Other 'Good' Values?

A variety of other cultural influences have begun to receive empirical treatment. Thrift is strongly associated with higher levels of saving (though it is hard to show that this result is not due to institutions: opportunities for saving may generate thriftiness). Attitudes toward redistribution influence public policies toward redistribution (which may in turn affect growth). And a belief in autonomous individuals and egalitarianism is associated with the rule of law (Guiso, Sapienza, and Zingales 2006).

Various other cultural attitudes have received theoretical treatment. The debate regarding individualism versus collective responsibility was touched on above. Landes (1998) hails the value of scientific rationality over superstition. Societies that value increases in incomes both individually and collectively will arguably grow faster (though individuals willing to cheat in order to earn will decrease the level of trust). Without shared norms of fairness, our natural tendency to exaggerate what we deserve might prevent many mutually beneficial contracts. As noted above, Harrison has urged future orientation, work effort, frugality, education, merit, trust, honesty, justice/fairness, dispersed authority, and secularism (Blim, 309). John Stuart Mill, the nineteenth century economist, stressed attitudes to work, time preference, and risk aversion, and urged an 'ethology' of how these differed across time and place; this project is still in its infancy.

Marketization

The anthropologist Gudeman (2001, 10) notes that farmers in traditional societies use a variety of traditional measures for such things as the amount of labor expended on various tasks, or amounts of various crops, and so on. That is, there is no obvious common standard (like money) for comparing across these. He appreciates that commensurability is a matter of degree: even western societies do not put a price on love. But some societies monetize much more than others. And thus in some societies culture plays a much bigger role in placing value on certain activities and outcomes (and the role of rational calculation is reduced). And while marketization may be important for encouraging growth, the possibility that it leaves some feeling devalued must be appreciated. GDP statistics will give a poor measure of change in well-being in such a situation, and may be a poor predictor of future potential if some people give up on the possibility of meaningful lives.

Sharing

Poor communities generally have an ethic of sharing so that unlucky members do not fall below subsistence; this can limit economic incentives.[18] Merchants in such societies are often viewed as challenging cultural norms, and there is a general belief that they earn 'too much.' Szostak (2003b) outlined four inherent models of exchange: authority (where an authority figure orders exchanges), equality (where goods are distributed equally), community sharing (where goods are distributed in accord with cultural values), and market exchange. All cultures sanction these in different contexts. Thus culture may prohibit markets for people (or body parts) or land or religious objects. If culture limits markets for land, labor, or goods, then opportunities for economic growth will be constrained. Sharing, though, can have good effects (as can redistribution by authority) in limiting the risks faced by individuals, and may thus encourage them to undertake certain risky activities such as innovation and investment. Communities thus need not exalt markets in all situations but should seek the best balance.

Ethics

The economic historian and methodologist McCloskey (2006) has treated the 'ethical' bases of economic growth in some detail. Her main point is that economists tend to stress the virtue of prudence when they speak of rational decision-making. However, economic success requires that prudence be balanced by other virtues such as love; without these the trust referred to above is impossible. Game theorists have shown that strategic interaction works only when there is a shared understanding of the rules of the game; we need and observe economic actors expecting altruism, fairness, and justice (ch. 8). Societies that engage in honorable exchange prosper while those that steal from each other fail (8-9). As such, the correct virtues both encourage and are encouraged by modern economic growth.

---

[18] The historian E.P. Thompson coined the term 'moral economy' to describe how (English) peasants had an idea that one should not profit at the expense of basic needs, and thus attacked merchant holdings of grain if prices were too high or grain was being exported during a time of scarcity. Note here that the very idea of markets for land and labor cannot emerge unless a society sets aside the idea that every person has the right to some land to grow food.

Unfortunately, McCloskey in her determination to defend modern capitalism tends to gloss over the common ethical lapses of businesspeople (and neglects the important question of whether corporate managers' fiduciary duty to shareholders limits their ability to act ethically; see Szostak 2005a). One must thus view her arguments about the virtues associated with modern business behavior with some skepticism: but I would celebrate the assertion that there can and should be virtues associated with business.[19]

Achievement and Work Effort

McClelland's work on achievement motivation has been criticized both empirically and theoretically. In particular, we must worry about feedback effects: people seeing few opportunities for economic advance decide not to make this a life focus. Yet we should not dismiss the possibility of autonomous effects of culture either. Different societies may well value different activities. Historians have often attributed economic success to a desire to succeed (both at individual and collective levels).

Economic historian Gregory Clark has compared work effort across countries for both the nineteenth and twentieth centuries, and found that this differs markedly: indeed differences in work effort explain why nations with lower wages were not able to out-compete Britain on world markets.[20] And Clark attributes these differences to cultural pressure: workers feared that increased effort would result in job losses.

Tastes

Economists have generally assumed tastes as given, both for practical convenience and because it frees the discipline from the ethical question of whether people want what they should want (and thus whether consumption adds to well-being). Yet of course tastes are influenced by culture (and advertising). Local tastes can affect the size and shape of markets for local producers. Do local consumers prefer local products? Do they prefer variety, or is mass production possible? Economic historians have suggested that North Americans were particularly open to mass produced goods in the nineteenth century. If so, both the shape and speed of economic growth were likely affected.

---

[19] McCloskey is also guilty of elevating virtue analysis above other equally valid forms of ethical evaluation. She is particularly critical of Kantian ethics and utilitarianism. Szostak (2005) argued that these and other approaches to ethical analysis should be seen as complements.

[20] Such arguments are generally not framed in terms of comparative advantage: low wages will only encourage trade if they have a much greater impact on costs in some sectors than others.

8.1.6 Culture as Economic Asset

Some localities have used cultural characteristics as a draw for tourists or to boost the export markets for cultural products. Notably, the cultural characteristics emphasized in these endeavors tend to be quite different from the cultural characteristics engaged above – and thus it is particularly important not to confuse the two types of culture/economy links. Here, cultural expressions like cuisine and dance loom large but also values associated with sociability (or in some cases attachment to tradition). Various authors in Kockel (2002) engage such efforts. Their anthropological concern is with how the integrity of local cultures can be maintained rather than with identifying the types of cultural element most conducive to success. Can a society inundated with tourists maintain an authentic culture that attracts them, and if so under what conditions? Is the sanitizing result of packaged cultural performances almost inevitable, as the locals adopt cultural values from tourists? Multiple authors discuss languages: tourists like to be able to communicate and thus encourage disuse of local languages; the authors argue/ assume that language maintenance is essential to cultural integrity (even, notably, in the case of Ireland). The importance of power relations is stressed. There is scope for much careful study of this type of culture/economy link.

8.1.7 Cultural Capital

Throsby (2001, 46) moves back and forth between a definition of culture as values and culture as art. He thus defines cultural capital as partly tangible (works of art) and intangible (beliefs and values). This is quite different from Pierre Bourdieu, who coined the term and for whom cultural capital was the mastery of high status culture by an individual (48). Cultural capital at the societal level can influence economic efficiency (through values such as trust), equity (by influencing institutions), and objectives such as growth (as opposed to other goals) (63).

The vague and conflicting definitions of cultural capital do not encourage careful scholarly analysis. The term may have some value in stressing the importance of culture in economic growth. But in understanding that link scholars are best advised to pursue a variety of carefully defined causal links.[21]

8.1.8 Cultural Influences on Politics

Jones (2006, 256) bemoans the interest in cultural explanations of East Asia's choice of good policies. He suggests we just focus on what the good policies are. But an examination of culture not only helps us to understand how other countries might move toward better policies. Culture is actually a component of those better

---

[21] A similar argument is made with respect to social capital below.

policies. A country can have rules against corruption but these will be ineffective without supportive cultural attitudes. Lal (1998, 16-7) argues that culture has its greatest economic impact via politics: how rapacious the government is. And as noted above governments that lack legitimacy will not be able to mobilize people, and may indeed be especially fearful of change. We must thus keep culture in mind when we turn to the broad question of the role of government in economic growth in chapter 11.

8.2 Entrepreneurship

One in twenty-five contemporary Americans can be described as entrepreneurs, and there are many chairs of entrepreneurial studies in business schools, but the field of study is fragmented. 'Surveys describe the field as organized by camps, where the lack of cross-level and cross-disciplinary interaction tend to obscure the overall picture of what gives rise to entrepreneurship. Many commentaries on the field have called for an increase in the quality, interdisciplinary nature, and development of unifying schemes to integrate diverse pieces of research on entrepreneurship' (Thornton, 1999, 20).

Swedberg (2000) surveys the treatment of entrepreneurship across the social sciences. There has been relatively little research in economics for the simple reason that the idea of entrepreneurship fits poorly with economic models. Joseph Schumpeter was the main exception. He viewed entrepreneurs as introducing novelty, and thus they lay at the core of his idea of growth as 'creative destruction' (see chapter 9). Novelty emerged through new combinations of existing knowledge. He stressed five types of entrepreneurship: introducing a new product, introducing a new process, opening a new market, developing new sources of inputs, or developing a new organizational form (though he stressed the industry rather than firm level here). Swedberg queries his omission of financial innovation (15-6). Schumpeter emphasized psychological over economic motives: the will to succeed, will to power, and satisfaction from accomplishment (16). In later writings Schumpeter stressed that organizations could be entrepreneurs. He also emphasized the role of intuition over rational calculation. Swedberg wonders if this is true; the best approach may be to recognize that intuition and rationality interact in innovative processes. Schumpeter also stressed the need to overcome resistance to change (46).

Minority traditions in economics, such as old institutionalism and the German historical school, spoke about entrepreneurs, but even some mainstream economists like Arrow and Baumol addressed the topic (22).[22] Knight stressed that

---

[22] Entrepreneurs will focus on rent-seeking if the institutional structure encourages this over valuable innovations. Snowdon (101) praises Baumol for thus updating Schumpeter: he notes but does not stress that economic historians had long made this argument.

entrepreneurs deal with uncertainty as opposed to risk: that is, they act where the probabilities of future success cannot be estimated. Kirzner identified entrepreneurship with alertness to opportunity, and treated entrepreneurial profits as a return to ability. Mises emphasized the financial motives for entrepreneurship, and worried that public suspicion of profits would discourage entrepreneurs (19-20). One point often stressed when economists do study the topic is that entrepreneurs often fail. Yet both those who fail and others learn from these mistakes. As with technological innovation, excessive optimism may be critical for entrepreneurship. Individual entrepreneurs also need to rise above failure (23).

Swedberg (2000, 24) argues that the non-economic literature on entrepreneurship is less theoretically coherent, but more practically oriented. The business literature often stresses the relentless pursuit of opportunities regardless of resources (23). Kanter urges firms to encourage new ideas, provide resources to those with ideas, and forgive failures (31). It is increasingly felt that entrepreneurship can be taught (to at least some extent): managers should look out for changes in markets and industrial structure, new knowledge, demographic changes, changes in attitudes and more generally the unexpected. Employees should be encouraged also to look for opportunities. The business literature emphasizes the importance of persuading others of one's good ideas. Entrepreneurs in large firms face quite different challenges in this respect from those in small firms (162-3)

Sociologists have devoted even less attention to entrepreneurship. Weber was the key exception. He emphasized the role of charisma, though he felt this was of lesser importance in contemporary society where entrepreneurs had to act through firms. [It can not be stressed too much, though, that entrepreneurs can only succeed by convincing many others to share their optimism – this may be easier in societies that believe in progress.] His famous work on the Protestant ethic largely discussed how societies came to appreciate entrepreneurship (25-8).

Sociologists have made a variety of theoretical arguments. Lipset has argued that the 'Puritan' culture in many parts of the United States was more conducive to entrepreneurship than the Iberian culture of South America (48). There is a large literature on ethnic entrepreneurship that stresses the importance of networks. Burt has argued that entrepreneurship results when one has networks that connect otherwise unconnected agents (like buyers and sellers). He argues that opportunity is likely more important than motivation: when a clear path to success exists, only the least motivated will not pursue it (Lipset might agree with this sentiment). And a non-redundant network will naturally cause one to think of how to act entrepreneurially between agents otherwise unconnected. Granovetter has stressed that entrepreneurs need the trust of others, but can be hindered by cultural expectations of sharing (29-30). They will operate best in an environment with just the right amount of de-coupling of economic interaction from social interaction: where there is enough cohesion for trust but no suspicion of individual gain. Historically, the entrepreneurial task was often accomplished by minority groups with strong internal ties but limited external links; it is not clear if this balance can be created purposefully (165).

Some sociologists have looked at the creation of entrepreneurial opportunities (that is, the demand for entrepreneurs), and have emphasized variously the attitude of existing firms toward spinoffs (one quarter of new firms in the United states are spinoffs), the activity of the professions, government policy, the development of markets, and technological innovation (Thornton 1999, 20). Following in the tradition of Weber, others have stressed the supply of entrepreneurship as the intersection of personality and culture. The supply side analyses have been criticized for monocausalism and non-rigorous methods, and the demand side for a lack of a theory of action; they also differ in a micro versus macro perspective; both should be integrated (Thornton 22). One problem (36) is that there is no set methodology for linking micro and macro; those that do so often use data at only one level.

Economic sociologists have worried about both the cultural and institutional sources of entrepreneurship. There has been a heated debate as to whether entrepreneurs are more likely to come from marginalized groups (squeezed out of other opportunities for success and with an identity of difference and desire to succeed) or dominant (access to resources through networks). There has been no empirical resolution to this debate. Institutions matter because entrepreneurs need supportive networks and are affected by patent laws, antitrust laws, and so on. Swedberg and Granovetter (12-3) follow Schumpeter in seeing entrepreneurship primarily in network terms. An entrepreneur succeeds by linking others with complementary interests (such as buyers and sellers). Nevertheless entrepreneurship is observed across countries with quite different institutions.

The economics discipline has tended to assume that economic opportunities are automatically taken up, and thus has largely avoided questions of entrepreneurship. But once it is appreciated that firms are necessary to solve a variety of coordination problems, it naturally becomes of interest how readily firms are formed to pursue these opportunities. And since firms always operate in networks, a related question involves whether a new firm can easily enter such a network. Granovetter (1995) argues that social divisions, and especially lack of trust (see above), often make both forming firms and operating in networks difficult or impossible.

There is even less study of entrepreneurs in anthropology. Barth (like Merton in sociology) worried about how entrepreneurs might threaten basic values. He stressed a form of entrepreneurship that involved joining different spheres of communal action (such as making a political donation to achieve an economic benefit). More generally, anthropologists have stressed the need to understand local culture in order to identify opportunities: when can credit be extended?, what are accepted approaches to bargaining? Swedberg wonders if big firms need to be as careful here as small firms (280). Though Swedberg does not make the point, the combination of this insight with the cultural entrepreneurship of sociologists raises the question of whether entrepreneurs can change cultural attitudes so that entrepreneurship is encouraged. This question can in turn be related to the arguments encountered above about how culture and institutions have to be changed in response to new generations of technology.

Swedberg says little about political science. Kohli (2004, 370) was struck by the importance of having a sizeable body of indigenous entrepreneurs. He notes that at least some of the differences across countries might be traced to their colonial experience. But countries that gained independence with lots of entrepreneurs differ quite a bit in performance. And independent states have pursued policies that encouraged entrepreneurship in some places and discouraged it in others. His main objection to the literature on entrepreneurship, though, is that he thinks entrepreneurship is more likely a result or a symbol of industrial growth, rather than a cause.

Studies in psychology have identified theoretically a range of entrepreneurial personality characteristics: independence, problem-solving style, flexibility, creativity, self-esteem, and endurance. Social psychology has looked at the role of cultural attitudes in fostering entrepreneurship. Famously McClelland argued for the importance of achievement motivation: different societies encourage achievement of different types and to different degrees. His claims are now thought to be exaggerated, but not without merit (Swedberg, 33-4). Given the importance of networking in successful entrepreneurship, extroversion and persuasiveness may also be important. The empirical efforts of psychologists to identify personality traits conducive to entrepreneurship produced mixed results and have largely been abandoned (but Thornton, 36 still urges us to build on insights involving achievement, risk-taking, and locus of control). One problem was failure to distinguish direction of causation: do opportunities generate entrepreneurial behavior? Also, different types of enterprise likely require different types of entrepreneur.

Economic history may have paid more attention to the issue than any other field. Economic historians have long debated the empirical importance of entrepreneurship: when we see one society being more entrepreneurial than another, is it because there are more entrepreneurs or more entrepreneurial opportunities? Economic historians have often proven skeptical of cultural explanations of entrepreneurship, but more willing to engage institutional barriers. For example, it may be that family firms encourage greater caution among firm leaders than do corporations. Or perhaps entrepreneurs are attracted into government or religion rather than business in some societies.

When Landes (1998) lists his 'ideal prerequisites for growth' all five largely operate through the supply and effectiveness of entrepreneurship:

- Environment which fosters initiative, competition, emulation
- Job selection on merit [Note that entrepreneurship can happen within organizations too.]
- Financial rewards for effort/enterprise
- Full exposure to existing technology
- Education.

This vast literature is in some ways easy to integrate: as elsewhere in this book most of the theoretical arguments are potentially complementary. Both institutions and culture may act to shape both whether entrepreneurial personalities are more common, and whether such people have access to necessary networks. Yet the lack of sound empirical work – and especially work that distinguishes among different types of entrepreneurship – makes it very difficult to decide which causal influences are most important. Indeed, the very question of whether societal differences in entrepreneurial activity reflect primarily differences in entrepreneurship or in opportunities remains to be resolved. It is unlikely that major opportunities will be missed even in conservative societies, but no society seizes all opportunities: thus small differences in entrepreneurship may have a large cumulative effect.

8.3 Social Capital

Pierre Bourdieu defined social capital for an individual as the size of the networks one can mobilize and the capital (he identified as many as twelve types, including cultural capital) of all network members. The political scientist Putnam popularized the idea in 2000. The idea has since become popular in sociology and business studies, and among some economists and historians.[23] The World Bank has a social capital discussion group.

'One problem with the analysis of social capital is that it is ill-defined, with different authors attributing different meanings to the concept'; it is often defined tautologically in terms of its outcomes and then is 'observed' whenever outcomes are good (Durlauf, 1999, 2). He suggests defining it as 'the influence which the characteristics and behaviors of one's reference groups has on one's assessments of alternative courses of behavior.' There are three types of definition (Durlauf and Fafchamps 2005). The worst indeed invites tautology (and ignores the reality that bad outcomes are possible) by defining social capital solely in terms of results. The second stresses cultural values such as trust. The third emphasizes networks and perhaps organizations. These last two definitions can be combined: networks generate generally beneficial outcomes by encouraging trust. Note that in identifying social capital with networks, such a definition establishes that social capital is conceptually quite distinct from physical or human capital which are primarily attached to individuals.

Lin (2001, 26) also worries about sloppy usage of the term which ignores its embeddedness in relationships. Social capital should not be identified (at least exclusively) with cultural elements such as trust. Nor should it be defined tautologically in terms of its results as Coleman and others have (28). Rather social capital must refer only to resources embedded in social networks that can be mobilized for useful ends (24). Despite urging clarity of definition, Lin is vague on exactly what sorts of network resources are critical to social capital: 'valued goods in

---

[23] Laird (2006) applied social science and management studies in her analysis of the effects of social capital on individual and group success across three centuries of American history.

a society which maintain or promote self-interest' (55). At some times but not others it seems that values such as trust can be included as resources.

The general approach of this book is to break vague and complex terminology into its constituent parts wherever possible. Trust was discussed at length above, and networks will be addressed at length in chapter 9. Literatures that focus on these are on the whole more useful than the literature on social capital. Nevertheless, due to the popularity of the term, this section addresses key elements of the social capital literature.

8.3.1 Effects of Social Capital

Some authors emphasize the benefits to individuals of social capital, and others the social benefits; Lin and most scholars recognize both types of effects (26). Social capital has four key effects on individuals: it provides information, it can affect the actions of others in desirable ways, it gives one 'social credentials,' and it reinforces identity and recognition (19-20). With respect to information, Burt (in Swedberg 2000) stresses that for all economic opportunities (including job openings) there will be multiple contenders with similar skills and resources; social capital is critical in determining who gets the opportunity. Networks are valuable only if you can trust the information you get from others, and especially if you get it before others.

Durlauf and Fafchamps (2005) argue that social capital works in three ways at the societal level. It aids information sharing on diverse matters such as entrepreneurial opportunities, job markets, other markets, technology, reputations (so that cheaters are punished), and relative effort within teams. Second, group identity encourages altruism. Altruism in turn overcomes strategic problems, and thus allows cooperation when otherwise fears of the selfish behavior of others would prevent this. Group identity also encourages mimicry: students work harder if it is clear that parents care about education. Third is coordination through leadership. Leaders can encourage good behavior and punish cheaters.

Institutions can substitute for social capital in all of these ways. The relative advantage of social capital versus institutions likely varies by circumstance. Institutions may be superior when groups are large and complex. But institutions and social capital can also be complements. Political scientists often worry that social capital is only seen as a substitute for institutions. But it is easier for a government to collect taxes when it is trusted and viewed as legitimate. Public goods are also superior in societies with social capital. Schools work better when parents cooperate and are active. In poor countries, public goods may be provided informally through networks.

In general, social capital may be more important in poor countries. Poor villagers complain to Woolcock (1998) of the fact that people cannot be trusted: landlords exploit loans and employment, teachers and doctors fail to show up, local elites take aid money, police torture innocents (there are even fake aid workers that take their money) (152) There are similar problems of distrust in transition economies. Putnam has complained nevertheless that development policy focuses on human and financial capital exclusively while ignoring social capital (154).[24]

It was noted above that social capital is often defined tautologically. One side effect of this practice is that the literature tends to view social capital as only generating good outcomes. But of course networks and trust can be employed to negative ends. Social capital provides advantages to some individuals and groups relative to others. As Mancur Olson has stressed, cohesive groups may work to increase their share of the economic pie at the expense of others and of economic growth. Szreter (2002, 577) argues that good outcomes are most likely when there are lots of bridging links between groups of identity rather than bonding links within (575-6): these groups can then cooperate in the pursuit of societal goals. Szreter argues that we will only see lots of bridging and respectful forms of linking when there is general ideological and political support for the state, and a sense that the state has a positive role to play (612). But this analysis seems to assume that social capital is directed only to political ends; why would agents not link for economic or social purposes?

8.3.2 Sources of Social Capital

Different theorists have stressed different mechanisms for generating social capital. The rational choice sociologist Coleman has argued that individuals can purposefully create social capital. Putnam has argued conversely that the economic and political benefits of social capital emerge primarily as side effects of connections pursued for other reasons.

The connection between social capital and institutions was addressed above. If these are substitutes, then the creation of formal institutions to replace informal provision of various services may decrease the amount of social capital in a society. If they are primarily complements the opposite may occur. It might be anticipated that some institutions are more likely to be complements than others.

It was suggested above that social capital may be especially important in poor countries. It may also be harder to generate. Sharp social divisions, whether ethnic, class, family,[25] or gender, will limit social capital. Poverty and the lack of a social

---

[24] Woolcock describes the literature on comparative institutions of development: this speaks of difficulties in forming integrated bureaucracies to serve complex economies. These need to be autonomous to be fair but need to be connected in order to provide needed services. Woolcock (177) cites the Soviet Union and India as examples of strong bureaucracies decoupled from societal needs. He urges stronger ties to business leaders. But this approach is criticized for tending to ignore group differences within societies and not generating clear policy advice.

[25] Banfield in Italy noted that too-strong attachments to family or narrow community discouraged achievement, geographic mobility, or amicable interaction with outsiders. Granovetter and Swedberg (12-3) observe that entrepreneurs often only succeed after migrating away from

safety net will discourage trust. So too will a failure to maintain the rule of law. The success of microfinance institutions, which rely heavily on peer pressure, suggests that social capital can be generated in poor countries. Governments might then be urged to fight discrimination in order to lessen social divisions.

How can individuals best increase their social capital? Lin reminds us that 'bridges' between groups are very important for some purposes (but not others) (27). Individuals close to bridges will have more social capital, and the value of bridges depends on how different the groups are (69-77). Individuals in lower groups have much to gain by bridging to higher groups. Lin does not explain why those in more prestigious groups wish to bridge downward; these too will benefit from access to information they cannot obtain within their own group.

8.3.3 Limitations to Empirical Analysis

Durlauf and Fafchamps (2005) conclude that much of the social capital literature is flawed, and that it makes exaggerated claims beyond what the evidence supports. Interestingly, they advocate more qualitative case study research on how social capital works in practice, though they expect this to inform later statistical analysis. Vagueness in definition has limited research effectiveness but has encouraged use of the term in many disciplines. The authors stress the study of informal networks, partly as these are easier to measure than culture. Since these can substitute for formal institutions in sharing information and supporting rules of conduct, empirical work needs to control for institutions but generally does not. Research should move away from social capital in general to specific aspects of this (in part as no variable can serve as a proxy for social capital in general). Regressions are generally not grounded in a clear theoretical understanding of how social capital works.[26] There 'simply do not exist any available data or methodology that can allow an assessment of the broad claims of the sort one finds in the social capital literature' (1691). The exaggerated claims of Putnam and others risk destroying a valuable research endeavor.

Empirically, there may be no way of evading the problem of tautology when measuring social capital. Having a friend that knows of a job opportunity is only valuable if one is looking for a job. To be sure, the same problem exists in the measurement of physical capital (see chapter 6). But the measurement of social capital seems likely to face the same problem as the evaluation of entrepreneurship: one may perceive a lack of social capital when there is instead a lack of opportunities for the exercise of social capital.

---

expectations such as that they will employ family members. Woolcock (172) thus urges crosscutting links across networks (which requires that members are autonomous enough to have strong external linkages), and attributes problems in Russia and Africa to lack of these.

[26] Durlauf, Johnson, and Temple (2005, 658) list a dozen empirical studies that have included different social capital variables: with a couple of notable exceptions these found positive and significant results.

8.3.4 Scholarly Biases Favoring Social Capital

Fine (2001) argues that, despite Bourdieu's intentions, social capital has become primarily a component of economic imperialism, utilized when straightforward applications of rational choice theory are unacceptable. Social capital thus captures what is left out of other types of capital, and provides a means for dealing with the informational imperfections allowed by mainstream economic theory (194). There are many competing definitions and measurements; like globalization it means different things to different people and is used to explain everything (190). It has tended, though, to stress civil society and thus abstracts away from power, politics, social divisions, and economic relationships (Bourdieu's emphasis on social distinctions has been left behind) (191). The right embraces social capital because it takes analysis away from the state; the left likes it because it stresses collective action and values [like cultural theory]; in practice it preaches cooperation while leaving markets unfettered and encourages self-help for the poor (196).

While Fine may exaggerate, the acceptance of the term by many economists is puzzling given its loose definition. Indeed, Arrow and Solow have argued that social capital is not really capital at all; Ostrom has pointed out that it depreciates with disuse, not use; is hard to measure; and is also hard to purposely invest in. Arrow argues further that it does not involve deliberate sacrifice of present for future (Throsby 2001, 49). Why then do some economists celebrate the term rather than focus on networks and trust, if not because social capital lends the appearance if not the reality of a straightforward extension of economic analysis? Development economists have been especially attracted to the term, perhaps because they are trying to reinvent their field along lines that appear less exceptional to other economists.

Fevre (2003, 210-1) criticizes social capital as an example of how sociologists try to mimic (rather than critique) economic concepts. Sociologists are then guilty of only celebrating how social capital supports growth, without appreciating how growth may erode social capital. While Fukuyama has suggested that humans are innately guided to reconstitute social capital, Fevre doubts that this is the case.

8.4 Community Development

Among disadvantaged groups, both in poor countries and rich countries, economic growth may depend on 'community development:' members of the community need to come together in order to identify strategies that enhance economic growth prospects directly or indirectly (by improving education, health, legal, or a host of other institutions and policies).[27] Community development involves

---

[27] Stiglitz (2006, 51-3) urges the importance of community involvement in development. Communities often provide important public goods like irrigation systems. While corruption may

strengthening civil society (through strengthening both links within the community and its interaction with sources of academic and professional advice) in order to prioritize the actions and perspectives of these communities in addressing the development of social/economic/environmental policies. It thus involves empowerment: strengthening the capacity of both individuals and community-level institutions. Community development, like economic growth itself, is best pursued in an interdisciplinary manner. This is in part because community development challenges are usually complex, and thus require input from a variety of academic disciplines and professions. The diversity of insights also gives communities a freedom of choice that they lack if presented with only one discipline-grounded policy option. Moreover, there is a synergy between cross-disciplinary integration and the integration of community insights with academic/professional insights: both types of integration depend on respect, forging a common vocabulary, and seeking a whole that is greater than its parts. Community activists often need to oppose entrenched interests, just as interdisciplinarians must at times confront the entrenched authority of disciplines. The advantages and challenges of inter-disciplinary community development are discussed in detail in Butterfield and Korazim-Körösy (2007). [28]

8.5 Population

Concerns regarding population growth have decreased markedly in recent decades. In large part this reflects the fact that fertility rates have fallen dramatically in most poor countries. Population growth should thus cease across most of the world (with the important exceptions of several Islamic countries) by the middle of this century. Economists generally explain declining fertility in terms of changing economic conditions: urbanization (no work for kids on the farm) and public pensions (do not need to be supported by children in old age) decrease the benefits of having children, improved medicine increases confidence that one's children will survive, and increased educational expectations and women's work outside the home increase the costs of children. Sociologists are more likely to

---

still occur in some cases, local communities have a strong incentive to limit this. The World Bank now makes small loans to local communities, allowing these to decide the best use of funds. More generally the World Bank recognizes that development projects of all sorts work best with community involvement.

[28] The book talks a great deal about how the academic understandings of social scientists and humanists can be integrated with the professional insights of social workers and other professions. Professional training is generally interdisciplinary, but often not self-consciously so, and one of the thrusts of the discourse on interdisciplinary theory and practice is and should be a discussion of how professional training could be improved by interrogating the nature of interdisciplinarity itself.

stress power relations within the family. Women bear most of the costs of children, and play a bigger role in family decision-making when they are educated and work outside the home.

It is also no longer assumed that moderate population growth has a negative impact on economic growth. Among contemporary countries, population growth of less than about 2 percent per year appears uncorrelated with economic growth rates. Population growth above 2 percent per year does seem negatively correlated with economic growth. Temple (1999) surveys research and concludes that the effect of population growth on economic growth is minimal. Theoretically, population growth affects economic growth in a variety of ways:

- It increases market size. Recent growth models often assume positive scale effects.
- It discourages saving as parents feed and clothe multiple children.
- It forces 'capital widening' as public (schools, hospitals) and private capital is spread across more bodies instead of increasing the capital/labor ratio.
- In some countries it places pressure on a limited resource base. Note that this is an effect of population size rather than growth rate.
- Historically, Boserup and others have argued that it was population pressure that encouraged humanity to first engage in settled agriculture, and thereafter change agricultural practices in ways that increased both work effort and output. A positive link between population pressure and technological innovation is still posited by some.

In the developed world, many countries are projected to soon experience population decline. While not uncommon in human history, this has not been observed on a wide scale outside of wartime since modern economic growth began. As with population growth, the net effects may be minimal. One concern is that an increasing proportion of the population will be retired (but a decreasing proportion will be children). There may be difficulties in transferring sufficient resources from those of working age. If so, increased immigration may provide a solution.[29]

---

[29] The economic effects of immigration are often misunderstood: immigrants have a slight if any negative impact on unemployment rates, since they often take jobs local residents do not want while buying goods and services locally; most but not all immigrant groups approach indigenous average incomes within a couple of generations. Opponents of immigration often focus exclusively on the effects on the home country, while supporters often emphasize the benefits to migrants themselves. The migration of the poor from poor to rich countries can potentially make the individual and both countries better off; the migration of skilled workers may have a detrimental effect on the exporting country. Decisions about migration should balance domestic and international concerns, perhaps by seeking levels of migration that maximize global welfare (where the cultural and political effects of migration should be evaluated along with the economic). If rich countries benefit at the expense of poor countries, a compensatory transfer of funds is called for. Immigration also generates cultural challenges: while beyond the scope of this book, these might best be handled by both respecting diversity and a common set of values.

8.6 Health

The economic historian Robert Fogel has argued in many publications that much of the economic growth in nineteenth century Europe reflected improvements in health. As nutrition increased, and disease incidence fell, people were enabled to work much harder. Arora (2001) attributes about a third of economic growth to improvements in health. Fogel suggests that people in many poor countries today do not get enough calories to be able to put in a full day's work (and he made this claim years before global price rises in 2008 pushed millions more into this situation). Others have argued that even the poorest countries could provide this minimal level of nutrition.

Calculations of the social return to various sorts of foreign aid often find that interventions with respect to nutrition and disease have the highest returns. Putting iodine in salt or iron in flour solves pressing nutritional needs at little cost. The United Nations calculates that malnutrition is the greatest single contributor to disease. Bacterial pneumonia can be combated with 25 cents in antibiotics, and polio vaccine costs $15 per child. $2 billion could cut in half the number of people without access to clean water. In some countries nearly half of children under five are undernourished enough to cause stunting. AIDS medications are considerably more expensive, but many lives could be saved if these were provided at cost in less developed countries. Still, Banerjee and Duflo (2005) note that while some health interventions provide very high social returns the average return is not extremely high. This suggests that health expenditures can usefully be reoriented, but also augmented.

8.7 Social Structure

The area of greatest consensus across disciplines is in the realm of social structure. Not only do all disciplines appreciate that social divisions – primarily ethnic and class differences, but also gender and family divisions – can have negative economic and political effects, but writers in each discipline show how in at least some instances these negative effects are of enormous importance.

Easterly (2002, ch. 10) summarizes economic analysis on the issue. While the government of a society with a shared culture may decide to pursue economic growth, in a divided society politics focuses on the division of the pie among groups. A united but corrupt government may still have some interest in growth – for this will enhance its own future income stream. But a government that is a coalition of competing interests will reward each of these with some special privilege. Since by definition each group suffers only a fraction of the cost of their particular advantage (say, access to foreign exchange at the official exchange rate), they naturally pursue such benefits at the expense of general well-being.

If, instead, one minority group holds power, it will likely focus its energies on redistributing income from others rather than encouraging aggregate growth. If it is recognized that some government policy needs to be changed – say the budget deficit needs to be trimmed – each group delays acting in the hope that another will bear the brunt of the cost of change.

These arguments apply to ethnic divisions, but also to class divisions (though economists tend to avoid the word 'class'[30] and speak of highly unequal income distributions). If a society is characterized by a small group of very rich, and a large group of very poor, the rich will act to maintain their power. They may limit the ability of the poor to start businesses or otherwise participate in economic life. More directly, they will not fund general education, for literate peasants are more likely to demand political change. If the mass of poor does obtain power, it will likely focus on redistribution, but such redistributive policies may destroy incentives to invest. (Easterly, it should be stressed, does recommend some sorts of redistribution, but structured so that incentives to work and invest are maintained).

Landes (1998) stresses a further problem with social divisions of any type. Efficiency in both the economy and polity depends on the best people being chosen for important jobs. The discrimination that tends to characterize divided countries assures that the most talented do not get the best jobs. In governments especially key jobs are handed out as rewards to particular groups. Laird (2006) worries that the early literature on 'social capital' focused a lot on how different groups had differential access to networks and thus women and minorities were often limited in their economic contribution, but that the more recent social capital literature has ceased to concentrate on the fact that different groups have different access to social capital.

Arguments that social conflicts are bad for economic development need to engage how people interpret social divisions and the institutions available for reacting. Otherwise Switzerland's success or the waves of strikes in Japan in the 1950s are mysterious. In the first case an obviously divided society has forged a common identity; in the latter a seemingly homogenous society engaged in open conflict. Institutional responses that might encourage a sense of common identity include welfare, lifetime employment, and affirmative action, but each of these may also raise concerns that some groups benefit at the expense of others. In any case, it seems that it is possible but difficult to alleviate social divisions (and/or their effects) institutionally.

---

[30] This in large part reflects methodological individualism. Economists are skeptical that amorphous groupings like a 'working class' can act in concert. Notably, many sociologists now also doubt the importance of class: increased occupational diversity, cross-generational mobility, and two-income families have all served to lessen the sense of class identity in contemporary society, and thus the value of class as an analytical unit.

8.7.1 Inequality

Why did Canada and the United States fare so much better than the rest of the New World? The question has long intrigued economic historians. Inheriting institutions from Britain was likely part of the story (a line of argument I myself pursued in 1991b), but cannot on its own explain the disappointing performance of former British colonies in the Caribbean. A more powerful explanation focuses on income inequality. Nations characterized by less inequality in 1800 grew much faster over the next two centuries. Nations with a narrow elite possessing both economic and political power (whether due to economic circumstances such as the importance of plantations, or because Spanish colonies tended to be governed through elites) tended to see institutions that served the elite rather than economic growth.[31] Though more detailed research is necessary, this story seems plausible and accords with the data we have on inequality (Sokoloff and Engerman 2004).

Acemoglu et al. (2001) established the following correlations: European settlement rates in their colonies (in turn correlated negatively with mortality rates) was correlated with institutional quality; institutional quality at independence is correlated with institutional quality now; and this institutional quality is correlated with growth (They thus hope to overcome the reverse causation problem that afflicts other studies of institutions and growth). This analysis is consistent with both the institutional inheritance and income inequality stories. In colonies with limited European settlement, narrow elites tended to rule.

Most empirical studies on modern economies find that inequality is bad for growth (Perotti 1996). Equal societies have less need for redistribution, and less social instability. But economists have tended to ignore concerns with the degree to which elites pervert decision-making. They have tended instead to stress the ill effects of certain redistributive policies. Temple (1999) is skeptical empirically, though, of arguments that pressures for redistribution limit growth.[32]

Inequality may serve to increase savings rates, for the rich save more than the poor. It may thus be associated with higher levels of investment in physical capital. However, inequality likely reduces investment in human capital. Human capital must be associated with a body, and the poor are generally not able to borrow in order to finance their education. Inequality may also encourage increased fertility, but empirically this link seems small.

Inequality can be viewed positively to the extent that it reflects differences in effort, ability, and experience. If however differences are seen to reflect primarily differences in access to physical or human capital, location, or even luck, the system

---

[31] Kohli (2004, 369) feels that landowning classes ceased to be politically powerful, even in poor countries, in the twentieth century; the military and the state itself were the key actors.

[32] While income distributions differ across time and space, the share of labor income in GDP varies little over space and hardly at all over time. Keynes thought this stability a miracle and Solow wondered if it were a mirage. It is especially surprising given the increased importance of human capital (whose share must have increased while the share of raw labor decreased).

may be perceived to be unfair. It may be thought that effort is not rewarded appropriately or that upward mobility is impossible.

Simon Kuznets famously posited that inequality would rise at first as poor countries developed (as at first small numbers gained high paying jobs in the modern sector) but would later fall. Kuznets noted at the time that this 'Kuznets curve' was based on very limited empirical evidence. It now seems that many countries have achieved growth without rising levels of inequality. Yet the Kuznets curve is still widely referred to – perhaps because it allows countries experiencing rising inequality to be optimistic about the future. Lane and Ersson (1997; ch. 9) argue that poor countries face a choice between equity and growth, but it would seem that in fact countries can have both.

Why do people not vote to redistribute more? While appeals to privilege or nationalism (fascism) may have worked in the past, inequality can only be justified politically today by the belief that some degree of inequality is necessary for the financial incentives essential to growth. It is hard to evaluate the ideal balance between equity and incentives. The poor avoid massive redistribution for fear that the system may collapse (but also perhaps because of a human tendency to exaggerate how well they are doing relatively) while the rich support some redistribution because they recognize the system must seem to be fair (Szostak 2005a discusses the ethics of redistribution). Poor countries today often redistribute primarily through health and education policies that also encourage growth.

8.7.2 Ethnic Divisions

Easterly provides case study evidence of the malign effects of ethnic divisions on growth. Successive Ghanaian governments destroyed cocoa exports by taxing these out of existence: the cocoa was grown by the Ashanti which were only briefly associated with government. There are also compelling statistical correlations. The East Asian success stories were generally characterized by almost complete ethnic homogeneity and also very equal income distributions [Easterly does not discuss Malaysia, where a political compromise ensures that the three main ethnic groups each share in economic growth]. Sub-Saharan Africa is characterized by ethnic diversity within nations (Botswana, a recent success story, being a notable exception). As noted above, Latin American countries were/are characterized by severely unequal income distributions. In many countries, these income differentials are associated with ethnic differences: black and indigenous groups are poorer than whites. Even in the United States, provision of public services such as education (and also welfare) is lowest in districts characterized by racial diversity: it seems that rich whites are unwilling to spend much on educating members of other groups.

Linguistic diversity is highest in sub-Saharan Africa (and New Guinea), and lowest in East Asia. Linguistic differences serve to harden ethnic boundaries, and limit the possibility of cross-group networking. They can also have a directly negative impact on schooling, when one group insists that others be educated in its language (or compromise is achieved on a colonial language that few children master). Moreover school texts can be difficult to obtain in minority languages.

Whenever there are ethnic divisions in a society, these are imperfectly correlated with class/occupational differences (though these correlations evolve). These correlations in part reflect networks. In many cases they reflect stereotyping and discrimination. They may also reflect different cultural attitudes. While it is easy to exaggerate its importance, there can be a 'culture of poverty' whereby disadvantaged groups come to reject the cultural value of hard work or saving (Eriksen 2005). Eriksen discusses Creoles in Mauritius: their culture places little emphasis on helping each other whereas other ethnic groups in Mauritius are characterized by strong networks.

What about ethnic entrepreneurship? Economic historians have a limited understanding of why some persecuted groups achieve economic success but not others. The trust that exists in some groups is obviously helpful (but may be a result rather than cause of economic success), especially in places with limited contract enforcement. A rebellious disposition may be directed toward innovation, but not always.

Geddes (2002) warns us not to take ethnic divisions as given. Individuals (at least in most societies) have choices about where to identify themselves. They also decide whether to feel mistreated or threatened by other groups, and how to respond. She argues that this focus on malleability characterizes modern political science research (361). She notes that most ethnic groups manage to cohabit peacefully, and thus occurrences of violence or secession need to be explained in terms of more than just ethnic differences (361-2). Violence and secession are most likely when credible guarantees of non-persecution are not possible. Voting systems (in particular the size of constituencies) also influence the relative importance of ethnicity in voter choice. Small groups may choose to assimilate while larger groups jostle for power. She applauds Laitin's (1998) study of Russian minorities in other ex-Soviet republics for using content analysis, surveys, interviews, and observation to establish comparatively that individuals respond rationally to their situations in revising their identities (364-5).

Easterly suggests some policies that can minimize the negative effect of ethnic diversity or unequal income distributions. An independent central bank can, as in developed countries, resist the temptation to inflate away the size of government debt. Democracy can provide a useful forum for achieving compromises among groups [sadly, though, democracy did not protect the Ghanaian cocoa farmers] Redistributive policies that maintain economic incentives can slowly expand the size of the middle class; countries with large middle classes are on average more democratic and pursue better policies. Various policy reforms that he would advocate in any case – removing exchange controls, and reducing bureaucratic red tape – also serve to limit opportunities for corruption. He argues that it is important to move past simply advocating these better institutions to recognizing 'the incentives that government officials face in polarized societies as the root of bad policies' (279). Note that good policies then serve the complementary goal of reducing social tensions.

8.7.3 Gender

'In general, the best clue to a nation's growth and development potential is the status and role of women' (Landes 1998, 413). Not only is a country deprived of much labor and talent if women are excluded from economic and political spheres, but the achievement motivation of men is limited (and the birth rate may be excessive). Still it must seem that much growth occurred in the past in male-dominated societies. Gender equity is thus not necessary for growth. There may nevertheless be a beneficial mutual causation between growth and emancipation.

Feminists have argued that the role of women is often under-appreciated by both scholars and policy-makers. Household labor is undervalued relative to market-oriented work. Models of household production ignore internal negotiations and power relationships.[33] Women with the power to make their own economic decisions can be very important in the development process. They are also less likely to have large numbers of children, and more likely perhaps to encourage children to get an education. One of the reasons that microfinance has proven so successful is that women proved to have both untapped entrepreneurial capabilities and the social capacity to employ peer pressure to ensure loans were repaid.

8.7.4 Family Structure

The extended family structures that characterize many poor countries are often criticized for limiting economic incentives. If successful family members are expected to share much of their income, they may be much less willing to work hard.[34] On the other hand individuals may be more willing to take certain risks if confident of family support. The empirical importance of these links is debated. The strength of feedback effects is unclear: as societies move above subsistence, there may be a strong tendency for the emphasis on sharing within extended families to dissipate.

---

[33] The household economics of Becker has been criticized by anthropologists and sociologists for ignoring the power relations within families. The preferences of women and children are under-represented in decisions about work and consumption. Different outcomes will result from different power structures and bargaining possibilities within the household.

[34] Anthropologists report that those earning money often complain about such demands. They may react by spending money on big houses that they are not expected to share. Or they may challenge norms of sharing, with unfortunate consequences for the less fortunate (Ortiz 2005).

9 Causal Arguments Under-studied in the Literature

This step is an important one for the interdisciplinarian, especially with respect to economic growth. As noted more than once in this book, disciplines often fail to connect their conversations with those in other disciplines. There is thus much value in the interdisciplinarian pointing out how researchers in different disciplines might more usefully interact. Such advice often follows from the analysis in chapters 6 through 8 and 10. When pursuing those steps we often suggest useful directions for research. For presentational purposes, then, much of the work of chapter 9 is reported elsewhere. In this chapter we focus on a couple of areas of potentially major importance where research to date has been very limited.

How can the researcher identify that which has not been studied? In some cases, previous researchers will have identified missing pieces. However, to rely exclusively on the existing literature would carry the danger that the interdisciplinarian would continue to ignore that which has already been ignored. The strategy recommended here draws instead on the classifications of phenomena and theory types from steps 2 and 3. Have any causal links or theory types received much less attention than they deserve?[1]

In terms of phenomena, there is a surprising omission within the economics category itself. The process of economic growth is rarely discussed with reference to what sort of goods and services are actually produced. Growth, that is, is implicitly considered to comprise 'more of the same.' Yet we saw in chapter 2 that growth generally involves the introduction of new goods or services. There has been some attention to the broad issue of the shift in resources from agriculture to industry to services that is associated with economic growth. But the more detailed study of the shifting importance of particular goods and services – and thus of firms and sectors of the economy – has been very rare.

In terms of theory types, there has been limited application of relationship analysis – with the exception of game theory. Yet network analysis has been applied to a host of other questions across the social sciences. It makes sense, then, to discuss how network analysis might be applied to the study of economic growth.

---

[1] One question to ask is whether non-academic insight fills these gaps? (Szostak 2002, 111). I confess to not having read widely in the non-academic literature. Most of this provides highly simplistic and selective overviews of the growth process.

R. Szostak, *The Causes of Economic Growth*,
DOI: 10.1007/978-3-540-92282-7_9, © Springer-Verlag Berlin Heidelberg 2009

9.1 Sectoral Interactions

One link within the economy category leaps out as having been little studied: the role of different goods and services (and thus firms and industries/sectors) in the growth process. Solow (2005, 4) in reflecting on the past half century of growth theorizing, argues that at the start 'one would have expected much more work on multi-sector growth models than there has been.' This is especially puzzling given that the growth accounting exercises of the 1980s found changes in the sectoral composition of output to be an important source of growth: resources shifted from sectors with low productivity to sectors with higher productivity.[2]

The development of endogenous growth theory might have encouraged economists to pay more attention to this issue. Endogenous growth theories have moved away from assumptions of perfect competition inherent in neoclassical growth models to recognize that firms innovate in order to earn monopoly profits. This theoretical innovation might have been expected to encourage much greater investigation of the rise and fall of firms and industries. It has indeed encouraged an appreciation that firms pursue diverse strategies, but little effort to understand how firms and industries interact. A possible explanation is simply that it is hard to model imperfect competition in a general equilibrium framework.

Economic history provides a much greater puzzle. Economic historians have indeed explored developments (especially technology, but also output growth more generally) in particular sectors. They have often at least implicitly assumed that some sectors are more important for growth than others. Oddly, such an approach is extremely important in research focused on the period preceding the twentieth century, but is eclipsed almost entirely by macroeconomic analysis of the interwar period and policy analysis for the postwar period.[3] Even for earlier periods this sectoral analysis has been almost entirely internalist in orientation, and cross-sectoral links have only rarely been explored.

Growth is not something that happens magically at the level of entire economies: it is simply measured at that level.[4] Growth always occurs faster in some

---

[2] Some of the growth attributed to investment or education may also reflect the fact that these facilitate sectoral shifts. Bruton (1997, 49) notes that levels of labor productivity and returns to capital vary across sectors, because of divergent historical trends (though economic theory assumes otherwise). At the macro level the ideas of aggregate demand and supply can be very misleading, because neither labor nor capital can quickly move between sectors; we must thus look at how demand operates sectorally (72). A productivity increase in one sector will have limited effects on the economy if monopoly power prevents prices from falling or if workers absorb the entire productivity advance through wage increases (rather than increased employment) (85).

[3] It is thus a challenge to follow the same topics through a textbook-like treatment, as in Szostak (2001). There is little research on policy for the earlier periods and exceedingly little sectoral analysis for later periods.

[4] Simon Kuznets, the pioneer of national income accounting, had stressed the rise and fall of industries. Since mature industries could not continue to expand output, new industries were needed in order to have continued growth. That is, new sectors are critical for the third type of

sectors than others; indeed, growth is almost always associated with the *decline* of particular sectors.[5] At the level of firms or enterprises, this is almost necessarily the case: the dramatic rise of some firms is mirrored by the disappearance of others. 'In short, a theory of decline in economic activities is an integral part of any useful theory of economic growth ... economic growth is never a steady advance, with all activities expanding at the same rate, as the prominent, aggregative theories of economic growth would have us accept' (Metcalfe 2006, 114).

The performance of the aggregate economy is thus the weighted sum of the performance of its components (interactions are discussed below). Why do economists imagine that the growth process can be comprehended exclusively at the aggregate level?[6] Economists (over-) emphasize the equilibrating mechanisms in an economy: if many workers lose their jobs in one sector or firm, wages should fall so as to create jobs for them elsewhere (while dramatic growth in one sector or firm should push up wages and draw workers from elsewhere). Economists thus tend to explain sluggish growth or persistent unemployment in terms of labor market rigidities that impede this equilibrating mechanism. In reality, though, these equilibrating mechanisms are sluggish at best. Even in the depths of the Depression real wages did not fall. At the best of times frictional unemployment (as workers look for job) and structural unemployment (as workers have the wrong skills or location) can be expected. The relative stability that characterizes most modern economies most of the time thus reflects the fact that there are rarely lots of declining sectors without the contemporaneous existence of expanding sectors that can absorb displaced workers.

Economists accustomed to thinking in terms of equilibrating mechanisms may immediately imagine that sectors only decline because of the rise of others: they decline because they cannot either afford the higher wage rates generated by the rise of other sectors or compete with them for consumers' expenditures. While these connections surely exist (see below), the rise and decline of sectors can generally be explained better in technological than in economic terms (and other causal forces, such as changes in tastes or government regulations are important in particular cases). Nor should the fact that sectors interact cause us to ignore the internal dynamics of different sectors. There is thus no guarantee that there will always be a rough balance between rising and declining sectors.

While the equilibrating mechanisms emphasized by economic theory may be weak, we should not completely neglect the idea of other sorts of strong connections across sectors. Walt Rostow famously argued in the 1960s that periods of

---

growth identified in chapter 2. Mowery and Rosenberg (1998) concur, but note that we do get innovation and even new products in mature industries, often with transfers from others.

[5] It may thus be that growth is positively correlated with the variance in sectoral growth rates. I am not aware of any empirical investigation of such a link.

[6] The fact that economics has treated growth as a subset of macroeconomic theory, with its emphasis on broad aggregate variables, may be part of the reason. Macroeconomists have only begun recently to explore the sectoral nature of business cycles.

rapid economic growth were always driven by a small number of 'leading sectors': these through linkage effects induced growth in many other sectors. Railroads, for example, not only stimulated growth in the sectors that used them for transport but induced growth directly in iron, timber, and locomotive production. This bold claim has not fared well empirically: railroads likely had a less revolutionary impact on economic growth than Rostow imagined (though those who have estimated these effects have assumed away potentially important types of dynamic effect; see Szostak 1991a). But that does not mean that some sectors at some times may have an impact on growth far beyond their share of GDP. It could well be, for example, that computers are finally having a major impact on productivity statistics; yet computer production itself is small relative to total GDP. Sectors may play a leading role two main ways: by creating demand for the products of others, or by encouraging productivity advances in other sectors. Staple theory (see chapter 6) can inform the former type of effect. Endogenous growth theory, with its emphasis on technological spillovers, could inspire the latter, but has led to very little sectoral analysis.

Notably, business analysts in making predictions about future growth prospects (at least in the medium term) tend to focus precisely on the potential for new technologies to cause certain sectors to expand. They at least implicitly imagine that the broader economy will benefit. They do not speak of equilibrating mechanisms but rather presume that several growing sectors will translate naturally into aggregate economic growth.

Conversely, the rise of one sector or firm may have negative effects on others. Joseph Schumpeter, the economist and economic historian, had pioneered the use of the phrase 'creative destruction' early in the twentieth century to refer to the success of some firms/sectors at the expense of others. He had appreciated that technological innovation in particular could not be modeled in an equilibrium fashion. Rather an evolutionary approach was required. Entrepreneurs pursued a variety of strategies; some of these would be very successful, and would have a negative impact on some competitors. These negative effects might be experienced by other firms in the same sector, or by other sectors producing substitute goods (as the birth of the automobile hurt carriage producers). There may well be equilibrating forces at work, but economists need also to appreciate the forces driving us away from equilibrium. Schumpeter's advice has been largely ignored (Rosenberg 2000).

It is often observed that firms hang on in declining sectors (or in the face of damaging competition from firms in their own sector). That is, firms that would not think of entering do not immediately shut down. Their capital costs are sunk, and thus they need worry only about covering variable costs such as wages and materials. They may even suffer losses for a while in the hopes that their fortunes will recover. This tendency to hang on may cause productivity to rise less rapidly than it otherwise would, but has the benefit of limiting unemployment.

The political implications of the above analysis should not be neglected. If growth always involves the decline of some sectors or firms, then politicians may always be tempted to interfere. This may be one reason that extensive social safety nets are not observed empirically to impede growth: they may serve to deflect the political demands for support of declining sectors.

In sum, we cannot expect to fully understand economic growth without studying this at the level of sectors and firms. While tantalizing hypotheses abound, we still know relatively little about how sectors both develop and interact at different times and places. On the one hand, we must appreciate that sectors/firms have internal dynamics, and that the equilibrating mechanisms posited by economists may be too weak to guarantee full employment. On the other hand we must appreciate that other types of cross-sectoral linkage – technological spillovers, direct demand linkages, and the development of goods that substitute for existing goods – may be hugely important in the process of economic growth. Individual sectors may be much more important than their share of GDP might suggest.

9.1.1 Technology and Sectoral Interactions

The role of technology in creative destruction deserves to be emphasized. It is not essential to the process. Firms in particular may displace others through success in marketing, or through increases in efficiency of production or distribution. Even sectors may rise and fall due to changes in taste or infrastructure. Yet as Schumpeter emphasized it is indeed technological innovation that most often generates creative destruction.[7]

It is also important to appreciate that technological innovation does not always cause creative destruction. Process innovation in particular can cause some sectors to expand output without requiring that others contract in absolute terms. Product innovation on its own, if it causes one sector to expand, will lead to contraction elsewhere unless unemployed resources are put to use. Product innovation combined with process innovation may allow society to have more of one thing without producing less of another.

The most powerful sort of creative destruction occurs when a new good or service substitutes for an old good or service. Notably, endogenous growth models sometimes assume substitutability and sometimes assume the opposite. In the real world, both types of product innovation occur, and thus these two approaches need somehow to be integrated (Gancia and Ziliboti 2005, 114).

We have seen in chapter 6 that technological innovation does not occur smoothly through time. Rather innovations cluster. Creative destruction is thus not a smooth process through time, but occurs quite unevenly. Freeman and Louca (2001) argue that there is generally some unemployment (and often labor strife)

---

[7] Unfortunately, Schumpeter imagined an unnecessarily large distinction between the act of inventing (creating a technologically feasible idea) and innovating (making this idea profitable). The entrepreneur thus took ideas 'off the shelf.' In practice, invention and innovation are linked.

during this period of transition. That is, they doubt that equilibrating mechanisms work quickly enough to prevent unemployment. They also argue that aggregate profit rates rise at first but then fall (2001, 336-40). One can appreciate the plausibility of this analysis without necessarily accepting the idea of regular long waves in economic activity (which they posit). The relationship between innovation, fluctuations, and growth will be further explored in chapter 10.

Creative destruction itself may influence the rate of innovation. Verdoorn's Law says that innovation occurs fastest in growing industries. They have profits to devote to research, and investment in new plant complements innovation. Firms will likely be battling for market share as the sector grows. On the other hand, economic historians note that sectors forced into decline often innovate to survive. The classic case is the wooden sailing ship which was much improved in the nineteenth century in the face of competition from steamships.[8]

While it is easy to hypothesize links between innovation and creative destruction, little empirical work has been done to clarify how strong these links are or how they differ across time and place.

9.1.2 Catching the Wave

Once it is understood that growth occurs at the sectoral level, it makes sense to ask how growth plays out internationally. Do poor countries have a better chance of catching up in new sectors? Indeed is there a danger of falling behind if they specialize in sectors in decline?

Follower countries may find it easier to catch up in relatively new industries. For those countries that experienced modern economic growth for the first time in the last decades of the nineteenth century (the 'third generation' of industrializers), it may have been easier to catch up in areas of the Second Industrial Revolution like electrification or internal combustion than in older areas like textiles, for the simple reason that even advanced countries were struggling to master these new technologies. Italy, for example, moved quickly into both electricity generation and automobile production (though it did not ignore textiles). Japan adopted electrification very early, though this largely followed development in textiles. Note though that Japan had trouble at first keeping up with the rate of innovation in electronics, and thus had to import successive innovations. Gerschenkron famously argued that the third generation of developers emphasized heavy industry, but this empirical observation may simply reflect the advances in steel-making technology in the 1860s.

A related hypothesis is that different countries may be better suited to different technological epochs. Italy had vast hydro-electric potential but little coal. Britain,

---

[8] However, declining sectors will not be attractive to bright young people. This limits the likelihood of these sectors being innovative.

which grew relatively slowly in this period, had the opposite natural endowment. Nor are natural resources all that matters: Germany's technical educational system was particularly well-suited to the Second Industrial Revolution. Follower nations may also benefit from not having developed an institutional structure better suited to the older technology (as when politicians interfered with British electrification?). To what extent can we explain the success of some countries with respect to industry-specific as opposed to general pre-conditions? That is, to what extent was Italy's success in the late nineteenth century due to its hydro-electric potential rather than its more general capability to absorb foreign technology? If the former, then countries hoping to catch up at the present time might usefully ask what are the characteristics conducive to success in areas of the so-called 'third industrial revolution' such as microelectronics, biotechnology, and nanotechnology.[9]

Some questions: Did new industries play a disproportionate role in economic growth in these countries? If so, how were they linked to the wider economy? Did they act to some extent as leading sectors? If so, did they do so primarily by demanding inputs from other sectors or by generating technological spillovers? Did different sectors have different effects?: electrical products may naturally generate technological spillovers. When thinking in terms of technology, we should include an appreciation of the impact on education and training. Automobiles because of their engineering requirements likely fostered skills useful for many industries.

On the other hand, poor countries may simply lack the research potential (a form of social capability; see chapter 6) that is required to leap to the latest technology. Certainly some old industries such as textiles seem to play an important role in the early development of most economies.[10] Perhaps some combination of the two strategies is called for: building an industrial economy by slowly catching up in traditional sectors but eventually being able to leap to the latest technology. If so, the question deserves to be asked if these countries then 'skip' involvement in certain sectors that were important for economies that developed earlier.

9.1.3 Firms

Microeconomic theory has emphasized a fairly static form of competition: firms that achieve the lowest costs of production given existing technologies survive. This form of competition is important in sectors where technology evolves slowly.

---

[9] Of course the opportunities available in the nineteenth century need not be duplicated today. Chandler and Hikino (1997) have suggested that existing firms have dominated more recent technological developments (he ignores information technology here it seems), and thus it has been harder for follower nations to catch up in these.

[10] Evans (1995, 7-8) talks about how textiles were able to generate more growth in eighteenth century Britain than in twentieth century India, automobiles more in the United States than later in Brazil. More generally, Evans, a sociologist, stresses the advantages of dynamic comparative advantage, and finding a niche where productivity growth is rapid.

But a more dynamic form of competition dominates in sectors where technology changes rapidly. There some firms are able to reap high profits and expanded market share through successful innovation.

Firms pursue different research strategies. Some may spend less on research, and emphasize efficiency and marketing. They may hope to borrow new technologies from others (this depends on both their access to intellectual property and their ability to adopt and improve upon new ideas). Since firms pursue different strategies, they will possess a unique knowledge base at any point in time, and this conditions their searches for new technologies (Bruton, 66).[11] Economic theory tends to assume that firms are similar.

Population ecology in sociology talks of how new organizational forms evolve. In the early stage of a new sector, entry is easy but failure common. Later entrants may have easier access to finance but will generally need to identify a niche in order to compete with firms already in place (Swedberg 2000, 163-4). There is a tendency for the number of firms to fall over time. As firms identify different market niches, their research and other strategies are oriented toward those niches. Yet technological innovation has unforeseen effects, and so firms may enter or establish new niches as a result of innovation.

Chandler (2005) argues that successful innovators and close followers strive to place barriers to new entry. They develop organizational capabilities for international production and marketing but also for ongoing improvements in products and processes. As is common in his work and that of other business historians, he focuses on internal firm strategies, and pays little attention to the socio-institutional environment in which these are pursued (whereas economic theory focuses on relations between firms and ignores what happens within them). The institutional structure in which firms operate – corporate governance, patent policy, competition rules – will shape their ability to restrict entry.

The sociologist White (2002) attempts to integrate the study of firms and the study of markets. He argues that firms collectively construct markets (loosely what we have been calling sectors): it comes to be recognized by them and by others that they produce a set of similar but qualitatively distinct goods. Firms move strategically in pursuit of quality/cost niches, some of which allow greater profits than others. A pecking order results. He thus criticizes the separation of studies of markets and firms, because the latter constitute the former. Different types of market emerge depending on how the ratio of quality to cost varies with output. He criticizes economists for modeling how imperfect competition might work, but not how firms would feel their way to particular quality/output/price points (which requires modeling firm interactions), and also how markets themselves develop through interaction with other markets. He notes that competitive markets emerge when consumers discriminate little by quality. The spread of best-practice

---

[11] Decisions need to be made about the size of the R&D budget, its division among major categories (and perhaps divisions), key objectives, and particular projects; decisions also have to be made about managerial strategies such as the balance between autonomy and control.

techniques or institutions across firms lessens diversity, but this is limited by firm routines and tacit learning processes. Though White develops a quite complex set of models, this work must be seen as at best a very tentative step toward understanding how firms interact. And it says very little about how these interactions might generate growth.

Economic growth occurs when firms (or governmental bodies) expand their output. The analysis above suggests that we need to understand both intra-firm and inter-firm dynamics, and place these in institutional context. This will involve the much greater integration of disciplinary insights than has occurred to date. A new synthesis should likely embrace the following elements:

- Firms are creatures of routine (a point famously made by Nelson and Winter decades ago). Even their research operations will tend to be routinized. There is thus a tendency among existing firms to emphasize a regular stream of small innovations. Firms have trouble coping with major changes. It may be hard to change one firm routine without disrupting others. We thus often see firm exit and entry in the face of major changes.
- Firms should identify core competencies.[12] These will often though not always involve unique technological capabilities. They will almost always reflect organizational elements. If a firm produces many goods or services these should each draw upon its core competencies.
- Firms and their core competencies evolve in a path dependent manner through time. They respond to changes in external environment, but as noted above generally respond slowly and imperfectly and with unforeseen consequences.
- Firms need to succeed in several realms: production, distribution, finance, marketing, and innovation among them. It is dangerous for scholars to focus on any one of these in isolation.
- Firms who excel at innovation more than in other areas may do well when technology changes rapidly, but be overtaken thereafter.
- Firms operate in an environment of uncertainty, and can thus not rely exclusively on rational decision-making.
- Firms operate through networks of internal and external relationships. Elements of organizational culture such as trust and loyalty are thus important to a firm's success.
- Various firm characteristics will be influenced by its technology. If the technology has many applications, the firm may produce many products or services. If the technology changes rapidly, the firm may prefer flexibility in production: it may contract out production to multiple suppliers.

---

[12] Just a couple of decades ago, firms were urged to diversify in order to reduce risk: if one of their product lines suffered from creative destruction, profits could be maintained by others. This benefit should not be neglected, but is generally felt today to be outweighed by the advantages of management focusing on core competencies. Note that to some extent this shift in priorities reflects an orientation toward the long term.

9.2 Networks

Social network analysis has blossomed across many fields since the 1980s (Galaskiewicz and Wasserman 1994). The defining element of network analysis is its focus on relationships. It generally employs survey methods. It has found that many important social activities occur within networks. It thus assumes that actors are interdependent, and that resources of various types (goods, money, information, support) flow through networks. Networks are seen to endure through time. Network research occurs at the level of interactions of two to a handful of people, as well as in terms of larger networks; the bridge between these approaches is an appreciation that large networks are a combination of smaller networks. Networks in turn interact with institutions. Notably the chapters in Galaskiewicz and Wasserman (1994) span several disciplines – sociology, psychology, anthropology, management science, and political science – but not economics.

Networks are a third way of organizing economic activity, along with the markets and hierarchy (within organizations) that economists have stressed until recently. Yet economists are just beginning to appreciate the possibilities of network analysis. The few that employ network analysis tend to stress a static analysis of how these work rather than looking at how networks evolve. This limits their understanding of how networks might influence economic growth. Scholars in other disciplines have applied network analysis much more to questions of social or political interaction than to economic questions. This section begins by discussing how network analysis might inform scholarly understanding of each of the proximate causes of economic growth. It then proceeds to examine some of the advantages and challenges of network analysis.

9.2.1 Networks and Technological Innovation

Decades ago, historians of technology often celebrated the heroic innovator. Historians now appreciate that innovation is far from the lonely activity that popular conceptions of innovation often imply. Successful innovators have always been involved in conversations with others: exchanging information of a technical nature with other innovators and/or skilled artisans in particular, but also learning about the needs of a particular industry from owners or workers and perhaps obtaining financing from interested parties. These various sorts of networking are now formalized within industrial research laboratories (though much innovation, and especially radical innovation, still occurs outside of them) but have always been important in the history of innovation.

Networks of firms in innovation were viewed as exceptional until recent decades but have become common. The reason seems to be that such networks are able to bring together an even wider range of skills and perspectives. It is now appreciated that such networks were more important historically than had previously been thought. Such networks combine elements of cooperation with elements of competition, but we know little about what the best balance is or how this is achieved. There is evidence that networks become more productive over time as personal ties are strengthened, but also that unchanging networks can ossify (Powell and Grodal 2005).

Why do some countries innovate more than others? One possible source of differences in innovative success, and perhaps even innovative activity, is differences in the nature of networks across countries. If it is easier to gain relevant information through networks in one country than another, we would expect to see more successful innovative activity in the first country.[13] We might reasonably anticipate that people would be less likely to engage in innovative activity in the latter country in recognition of the difficulties involved.

Do networks differ across countries? It would be useful to compare the network relationships of innovators in different countries. But a general appreciation of the nature of all types of networks in different countries may also be valuable. One of the key insights of network analysis is that 'weak links' – occasional conversations between individuals who primarily operate within different groups – are of critical importance. The strong links that exist within groups are largely redundant in terms of information flows: one hears the same thing from many people. Weak links give one access to novel information. In a country in which a social gulf exists between entrepreneurs and the educated (who may possess important technical knowledge necessary for innovation) or between ethnic groups involved in distinct but related economic activities, or between workers and managers, it will likely be much more difficult to put together the body of diverse information necessary for successful innovation. While this hypothesis is plausible, it needs to be tested empirically, and network analysis provides the obvious means of doing so.

Different types of innovation likely have different network requirements. Incremental improvements to an existing technology may require only small networks of workers and engineers. More radical innovations likely depend on broader networks (involving many weak links) for they generally involve the integration of previously separate pieces of information. Strong within-group links should not be neglected: an organization may only be able to successfully develop or adopt complex new technology if many individuals work closely together. There may also be important differences between, say, the networks involved in chemical innovations and those involved in mechanical innovations. While not couched in the terminology of network analysis, the work of Mowery and Rosenberg (1998) indeed suggests that this is the case. Network analysis can thus shed light not only on why some countries are more innovative than others in

---

[13] 'If individual B is surrounded by neighbors A and C who can verify his work, and C is similarly surrounded by neighbors B and D, and so on, the world of useful knowledge reaches an equilibrium in which science as a whole can be trusted even by those who are not themselves part of it' (Mokyr 2005, 1121). Meeus and Faber (2006) find that networks of firms increase both innovation and diffusion (though they note that these results are often assumed).

general but also why some countries excel in particular types of innovation. And thus network analysis could assist policy-makers in both poor and rich countries in identifying the sorts of research most likely to succeed.

9.2.2 Investment in Physical Capital

Investment is often naively viewed as a function only of the availability of both investment opportunities and a well-functioning financial system that channels financial resources to promising opportunities. But the entrepreneur will often have personal ties to financers, and will have to convince financers (who are often acting informally outside of the institutional structure, even in developed countries) of their access to the suppliers, workers, and markets on which the success of the investment depends. Successful businesses rely not just on accurate perceptions of market possibilities but on complex interactions with suppliers of materials and services on the one hand and customers on the other. While economic historians have correctly stressed the importance of property rights in supporting economic activity, in practice businesspeople see recourse to the courts as the last resort in contract enforcement. They appreciate that it is impossible to contract for every foreseeable outcome, and prefer informal negotiation should one party have difficulty living up to the terms of a contract. Trust and reputation thus become crucial elements in the conduct of business. Investment in turn, then, is heavily embedded in networks, and one can well imagine that investment will be both more voluminous and better targeted in societies with broad networks such that agents with access to diverse bodies of information are in contact and trust each other.[14]

Banerjee and Duflo (2005) note that rates of return to investment vary considerably across projects within poor countries. Surely one key reason is that some agents have access only to limited networks: they may have to rely on too little capital to realize economies of scale, they may have difficulties obtaining inputs or disposing of outputs, and they may be less well treated by government bureaucrats. Well developed financial institutions can compensate to some extent for deficiencies in networks by channeling funds toward entrepreneurs with good ideas but limited finances, and thus less dispersion in rates of return is observed in developed countries. Still, even in developed countries some agents are able to achieve much better returns than others because of network opportunities.

In order for networks of entrepreneurs to respond to new opportunities, they need to trust each other not only to respond to surprises honorably (rather than trying to re-negotiate every time an unforeseen event increases their bargaining power), but not to steal freshly-trained workers or new ideas from those they

---

[14] Laird (2006), a business historian, traces entrepreneurial success since the time of Benjamin Franklin and argues that this has generally depended more on the networks in which the successful were embedded than on their unique talents or energy.

interact with (Sabel and Zeitlin 1997, 21). Each foregoes opportunities to take advantage in expectation of not being abused in turn (by many actors). If actors saw themselves as the selfish calculators of neoclassical theory, this trust would be impossible (unless frequent interactions with the same agent were so important as to outweigh the benefit of taking advantage). While trust is determined primarily by networks and culture, it can be supported by institutions. Trust was observed to be sustained in part by recourse to arbitration and also by collective institutions for training and research (1997, 24-5).

As with technological innovation, there is scope for both comparative research on entrepreneurial[15] networks across countries, and for more general comparisons of network possibilities. In particular, business deals will be harder in countries characterized by distrust within or across groups.

9.2.3 Investment in Human Capital

Easterly (2002) makes an important social network argument: that the poor have limited incentive to gain education because they are linked to other poor people. There are increasing returns to education such that one educated person is more productive when in contact with other educated people. Education in poor societies will only succeed if there is a possibility of networking with other educated people. It may be that the Internet will prove important here in allowing the poor to have access to a wider conversation (assuming they have some access to the technology). But the more obvious solution is the generation of cross-class networks so that ambitious but poor children have a reasonable hope of benefiting from educational attainment.

9.2.4 Institutional Change

How does institutional change occur? It is a political act and political acts involve networking. Political scientists have studied the role of networks in politics, but tend to emphasize the effects on particular policies rather than on the institutional

---

[15] The word 'entrepreneur' is used purposely here. Economists and economic historians have long been wary of the term: unsuccessful economic performance can all too easily be attributed to a lack of entrepreneurship when the problem may have instead been an absence of investment opportunities. Sociologists have used network analysis to study entrepreneurship, and the approach holds considerable promise of allowing careful empirical research of entrepreneurship. Swedberg and Granovetter (2001, 12-3) follow Schumpeter in seeing entrepreneurship in network terms. An entrepreneur succeeds by linking others with complementary interests (such as buyers and sellers). Thornton (1999, 20) cites Burt on the value of a non-redundant network (weak links): entrepreneurs need to be linked to diverse agents. See chapter 8.

environment itself. Nor have they tended to investigate the question of under what circumstances efficiency-enhancing outcomes will result. One hypothesis suggests itself: societies characterized by lots of links between groups will be more likely to develop institutions that benefit all. That is, the same sort of weak links that may support technological innovation and investment may also be crucial for the creation of institutions that serve the needs of society well.[16] In the absence of such links, each group uses its political influence to generate institutions that serve group interests. But much work needs to be done to establish whether this hypothesis is correct and under what circumstances.

Different communities of scholars have applied network analysis to institutional change in different ways (see chapter 7). Network analysis in sociology argues that agents are constrained by their networks: institutional change is only possible if supported actively by a sufficient network. Such an approach guides researchers to look at the resources that different network members bring, and is thus compatible with an emphasis on power. The business-labor analyses in political science can be seen as a particular approach to network analysis, looking at how particular coalitions, whether within or across groups, were formed and able to achieve change. Organizational institutionalism in sociology alternatively examines the different motives of agents within an organization.

Finally, it should be noted that networks can to some extent substitute for institutions. As implied by the above discourse, networks of trust may be able to successfully transact business even in environments where courts are unreliable or corrupt (though they will likely perform even better when recourse to courts is possible). Networks are likely more important within informal economies (black markets) than formal economies. But it would be a grave error if economists too readily jettisoned their newly-recovered interest in institutions in favor of an exclusive focus on networks. Scholars need to establish to what extent networks can substitute for institutions, and this result likely varies by type of institution. Financial institutions may (or not – the Grameen Bank relies on local networks to provide credit to poor people in poor countries) be much harder to mimic informally than is contract enforcement.[17] It must also be appreciated that networks and institutions are complements as well as substitutes: the court system can only serve as the recourse of last resort if it is not overburdened by its case load, and

---

[16] As we saw above when we addressed social capital, scholars too often assume that networks have only good outcomes. The many books of Mancur Olson serve as an important reminder that this is not the case. Olson argued that strongly integrated groups would focus on obtaining a larger share of the economic (and political) 'pie' even at the expense of limiting the rate of economic growth in society (see Szreter 2002). Though Olson's work has been controversial, it supports the conjecture here that links across groups may be of crucial importance in generating beneficial societal outcomes.

[17] This sort of research presupposes a careful categorization of 'types of institution'. This classification should be functional – in terms of the functions that different institutions play – rather than in terms of their form. This was the approach taken in chapter 6.

this in turn depends on most conflicts being settled informally.[18] Institutions that require people from different groups to work together may be able to forge the weak links essential to many types of societally beneficial networking.

9.2.5 Trade

As noted above, success in business depends on networking. This is most obviously the case with respect to trade. Since businesspeople rely on trust and reputation rather than the courts for contract enforcement, trade will be more voluminous within and across countries where networks of trust and reputational information are robust.[19] In studying trade it is important to examine both internal and external trade networks. External trade usually depends on internal trade: goods must first be produced and moved to a port before they can be shipped abroad. But then links between businesspeople in different countries become important. One important consideration here may be the existence of dispersed ethnic groups: much of the trade of China (and Israel, and to a lesser extent India) passes through the hands of ethnically related residents of other countries.[20]

9.2.6 Other Links

Advocates of network analysis tend to stress the ubiquity of networks. We can here only briefly list some of the other links prominent in the literature. It is often argued that networks spread social values, and thus that understanding cultural change requires network analysis. Network analysis may also prove essential in evaluating how advances in communications technology affect economic relations: how do people network online as opposed to face-to-face? Our understanding

---

[18] Durlauf and Fafchamps (2005) hail the [complementary] ease of taxing and spending when governments are trusted/legitimate (and also note that propaganda works best when combined with coercion). There is also a sociological literature on how bureaucracies need to be properly networked to economic actors: sensitive to their needs but not captured by their interests. This literature has not yet produced clear policy advice.

[19] Jones (2002, 46) argues that the rule of law allowed European commerce to move away from personal networks. Greif tells a slightly different story in which the much earlier development of non-kin-based institutions set the stage for later institutional developments. In any case, we can expect kin and personal relationships to be more important when property rights are insecure (see family firms in chapter 6).

[20] We should also note here the argument made in chapter 6 that regional clusters of economic activity, which may be of critical importance for both trade and growth, likely reflect at least in part the importance of networking. Regional clusters likely reflect both networks and agglomerative economies, with their relative importance varying by locale. Indeed the Saxenian (1996) analysis suggests that networks were more important in Silicon Valley than Boston.

of the relationships between firms, and of worker behavior within firms, can also be enhanced through network analysis. For example, there is much research on how outside directors (that is, those not involved in firm management) coddle executives. Labor markets reflect networking in a variety of ways, as friends follow friends, friends hire friends, and decisions about unionization follow the advice of friends. Strong networks sometimes encourage and sometimes discourage job satisfaction. To date, though, there has been little exploration of the effects of networks on firms' production decisions or on work effort.

A new literature in industrial economics and business studies stresses firm networks. Firms are observed to stress core competencies and thus rely increasingly on other firms for the performance of non-core functions. Firms also pursue subcontracting as a source of flexibility (but generally maintain control of marketing and distribution to preserve brand identity). There is a sense that links with suppliers are becoming tighter so that firms can better ensure quality and innovation. Strategic alliances to pursue innovation also became common in the 1980s.

9.2.7 Advantages and Challenges of Network Analysis

Network analysis is not the only, but is certainly one of the most important, areas of scholarly research in which a gap exists between research programs in economics and elsewhere. The task of the interdisciplinarian in such a circumstance is to suggest ways in which the gap might be bridged. Scholars of interdisciplinarity tend to emphasize the quite different circumstance in which different disciplines study the same question and reach different results (or at least emphasize different facets of a common puzzle).[21] Yet interdisciplinary research has much to offer when gaps exist as well, for scholars in each discipline may be unaware of the potential for fruitful links with scholars in other disciplines.

It is notable that network analysis provides an important justification for interdisciplinarity itself. As recognized above, one of the key insights of network analysis is that 'weak links' – occasional conversations between individuals who primarily operate within different groups – are of critical importance. Interdisciplinary conversations are weak links: they allow scholars from different disciplines to gain information unavailable within disciplinary networks. While interdisciplinary networking is not easy – it takes time to fully appreciate the conversation under way in a different discipline (though one does not have to master an entire discipline in order to appreciate a particular disciplinary conversation) – the informational advantage it provides may be huge.

---

[21] Sociologists of finance stress networks of interaction, while anthropologists emphasize cultural influences. Sociologists note that networks are maintained by norms of reciprocity. Anthropologists think it important to understand how these emerge (Maurer 2005).

A typology of theory types was developed in chapter 3. One dimension of that typology examined the type of agency. Economists are methodological individualists for the most part, while other social scientists have tended to favor relationship or group agency. Network analysis presumes the importance of (systems of) relationships. Economists have not entirely eschewed relationship analysis: game theory stresses relationships, albeit a very constrained sort of relationships. One of the advantages of introducing network analysis to economics, then, is that relationship analysis provides a markedly different perspective from individual-level analysis. While game theory establishes a limited precedent in this respect, some resistance to a further move away from methodological individualism may nevertheless be anticipated.

Network analysis may also imply flexibility with respect to the common assumption of rationality in human behavior. This is not necessarily the case: sociologists such as Coleman have emphasized how agents may rationally construct a network. Other analysts such as Putnam have conversely argued that the economic (and political) roles of networks are generally a side-effect of relationships pursued for social reasons. Granovetter (2002) takes a middle position, arguing that there are limits to the degree one can instrumentally structure one's network in order to achieve desired outcomes: important information often only flows as a side effect of relationships pursued for non-instrumental reasons. Of course, one could still invoke rationality (with unintended spillovers as in technological innovation), but economists have tended to shy away from speaking of rationality with respect to goals such as friendship. And perhaps for good reason: human relationships likely depend as much or more on intuitive impulses as on rational calculation.

Economists may be attracted to formal network analysis, for its equations and diagrams are modes of expression with which economists are familiar. The data for empirical work often comes from surveys; while economists have in the past voiced some skepticism of surveys, the profession is increasingly open to the use of at least quantifiable survey results (as in relying on surveys for estimates of institutional quality to use in cross-country growth regressions; chapter 7). Yet empirical network analysis works best when quantitative and qualitative approaches to particular case studies are blended. Network analysis in other disciplines has tended to emphasize the influences of the social context in which a certain network operates. Network analysis at its best requires a range of detailed knowledge of the case in question that is generally not required for most empirical research in economics. Economic history may prove a more hospitable venue for network analysis, for detailed case studies have long been an integral part of the field.[22]

It would be undesirable to leave through omission the incorrect assumption that network analysis is something that economists and others can simply take 'off the shelf' and apply to economic growth. Network analysis has been widely applied for only a couple of decades, and many questions remain regarding both theory

[22] Greif (2006) has studied the institutional nature of trading networks during the Middle Ages, though he only rarely employs network analysis.

and method. It was noted above that the important question of what resources are embedded in networks has yet to be clarified.[23] This question leads to an even more central query of how exactly networks function: why does one member of a network pass information or other resources to another? The fact that most network theory casually sidesteps this question does not diminish its importance. The most obvious answer is that agents do so in anticipation of being rewarded in return (with information, but perhaps also with affection, power, status, and so on). There is a related question of how agents can be confident of the veracity of the information they receive: along with the importance of reputational effects some scholars have stressed the value of 'redundant' links so that one receives the same information from multiple sources. If these expectations regarding veracity could be precisely identified for each piece of information transferred, networks would dissolve into market exchange: an agent could contract to provide something in return for something else. The advantage of networks is that they can handle a diverse body of information and other resources, and cope quickly with unantici-pated developments. The challenge for economists is that networks must thus rely on cultural expectations of fairness rather than careful calculations of profitable trades. We have seen above that even market exchange depends on networks and fairness; informal flows of resources through networks must deviate even further from rational calculation of advantage.[24] The precise type of decision-making that characterizes different sorts of networks should thus be a focus of study.

---

[23] The work of Foa and others on resource theory still provides a useful starting point. Whereas economists have tended to try to monetize all elements of a utility function, Foa has long stressed that it is difficult to trade one sort of resource for another: one cannot buy love, for example. See Foa and Foa (1980).

[24] Dolfsma, van der Eijk, and Jolink (2005) discuss this question, and suggest that networks are best conceived in terms of gift exchange: we give to others in the expectation of an unspecified form of reciprocation, and rely on cultural norms to ensure that reciprocation is appropriate in both kind and amount. Amitai Etzioni in many works has studied how values such as fairness underpin economic interactions.

10 Emergent Properties of the System of Causal Links

Emergent properties are outcomes of complex systems of interaction that are not easily understood in terms of the behaviors of individual components of the system. The idea is perhaps most readily comprehended in the natural sciences: life forms have behaviors that cannot be understood in terms of any of the chemicals that together constitute that life form. Emergent properties are often surprising: if chemicals could think they would be amazed at the behaviors of the life forms they constitute. In the social world, individuals may interact in ways that generate results that no individual wants or expects. Emergent properties emerge when there are differences among the constituent elements of the system, and when interactions generate both positive and negative feedbacks. This chapter discusses two possible emergent properties of systems of economic interaction: first poverty traps and then business cycles.

10.1 Aggregate Growth Dynamics: Is There a Poverty Trap?

It should first be noted here that growth itself can be conceived as an emergent property of microeconomic processes that stimulate investment and innovation (Metcalfe 2006, 107-8). Whereas standard economic theory examines these microeconomic processes in an equilibrium framework, Metcalfe notes that these mechanisms within capitalist economies are both self-stabilizing and self-transforming: markets are reasonably stable [although see below] but change is endemic. Despite the usual aggregate stability, uncertainty is everywhere.

Nevertheless, the study of growth has generally proceeded in terms of specific causal linkages rather than emergent properties. Scholars in all disciplines have attempted to identify causal influences on either growth itself or the proximate causes of growth. One potential exception to this approach is in the literature on 'poverty traps' where it is suggested that there may be some mechanism(s) that keep poor countries poor. Yet we shall see that even this literature emphasizes particular causal relationships for the most part.

We can begin by contrasting two visions of growth. One vision is guardedly optimistic: growth will follow if rates of investment (including in human capital) and innovation are increased (assuming that innovations are appropriate to the economy in question). Those who share this vision can then differ in their evaluation of how, and how difficult it is, to increase investment and innovation (or education or infrastructure or trade). The other vision is pessimistic: there are mechanisms that tend to keep poor countries poor. Advocates of this pessimistic vision

R. Szostak, *The Causes of Economic Growth*,
DOI: 10.1007/978-3-540-92282-7_10, © Springer-Verlag Berlin Heidelberg 2009

have nothing as simple as an aggregate production function with which to illustrate their arguments. A variety of arguments have been proposed at various times:

- Political elites in poor countries will be bribed or coerced to pursue the interests of rich countries. And rich countries, or at least multinational corporations based in rich countries, want to keep poor countries poor. We can critique the latter argument: the West has clearly benefited rather than suffered as East Asia has developed (though some workers may have lost their jobs as a result). Developed countries do not depend on the labor of poor countries: trade with such countries accounts for only 5 percent or so of rich country GDP, and thus a tripling of wages in the poorest countries would at most cost rich countries the equivalent of a couple of years worth of economic growth. This is not a trivial amount, to be sure, but hardly the bedrock of Western prosperity. While poor countries have often been governed badly, the most obvious beneficiaries of corruption are locals rather than foreigners, though it can hardly be doubted that foreign governments and companies take advantage of weak governments. Unless rich country governments are completely in the pockets of multinationals one would think that the interest of rich countries in world peace, if not social justice, would encourage some effort to support growth elsewhere (though perhaps not as strongly as during the Cold War). It is worth noting that multinationals are generally observed to pay wages above the local average in less developed countries, a result which certainly suggests they are not wedded to the idea of everlasting poverty. Moreover, Woo-Cummings (1999, 23) makes the interesting argument that it was the very dependence of East Asian countries on the United States both economically and militarily that encouraged popular support for the focus on economic growth as an objective.
- It is more common these days to criticize the elites of poor countries for pursuing self-interest. A small and rich elite amidst widespread poverty may limit, for example, education in order to preserve power (see chapter 9).
- Corrupt institutions enhance the incentive to corruption, for people come to expect corrupt behavior.
- Poor countries are too poor to generate the necessary saving. If this were an eternal law, no country could ever have developed. Nevertheless, it is true that the poorest countries cannot save much, and thus one might expect sluggish growth at best. Endogenous growth models can, with certain assumptions, generate a poverty trap in which growth never occurs because of low savings (Gylfason 1999, 79-80). If so, foreign aid or foreign investment may be of particular importance. Alternatively, governments may force saving by taxing resources from the poor and investing these.
- Low saving rates may also reflect limited opportunities for investment – which may be the case in a largely agricultural country serving local markets. Pursuing exports may be a solution in this case (Bhagwati in Snowdon, 229).
- However, the poor will have difficulty borrowing because they have no collateral. Improved property rights may be helpful in this respect.

- Growth in its initial stages requires a 'big push.' Investors want to serve a mass market, but this can only exist once enough jobs have been created. Somehow this process needs to begin with a mutually reinforcing surge of investment and employment. This idea was very popular in development economics in the 1960s, but has declined in popularity. Still, the emphasis on 'spillovers' within endogenous growth theory has created an opening for the re-consideration of the possibility that there are 'positive externalities' within the modern sector (Gylfason 1999, 81). The earliest investment in modern industry may be the hardest to induce. Sachs (2005) has recently revived the 'big push' argument. He conjectures that there is an increasing return to investment at low levels of development (especially with respect to infrastructure): a half-finished highway (or one only open part of the year) or an electricity generation scheme subject to frequent blackouts is much less useful than fully-functioning systems.
- Easterly (2002): stresses complementarities between different technologies (like internet and PC). This generates increasing returns to investment. There are also complementarities between advanced technology, skilled labor, and capital (and between one skilled worker and others), and thus these tend to flow to high technology areas (unless the technology can flow to them). It may thus be necessary to kick-start the process in poor countries.
- Complementarities between old technologies, or network effects, may lock in inefficient technologies, preventing the adoption of better technologies (on this and other points see Azariadis and Stachurski 2005)
- Rodrik (2005) notes that spillovers in learning about foreign technologies may be important, and thus independent efforts to do so undersupplied
- Terms of trade can be conjectured theoretically to move against the exports of less developed countries. In other words it takes more tons of raw materials to buy a certain quantity/quality mix of manufactured goods. Empirically, though, there has been no obvious trend over the last several decades.
- Cultural elements reflective of poverty – such as income sharing among extended families – may limit personal ambition, and act directly to discourage change (Azariadis and Stachurski 2005)
- In some countries rapid population growth exacerbates some of the above problems. Population growth tends to fall with economic development. Note, though, that extensive growth – growth in total output – has been the most common case in human history, and is conjectured by some to set the stage for intensive – per-capita income – growth.

One powerful counter-argument is that the present developed countries were once poor, and thus must have evaded this sort of poverty trap. Yet at least some of the above arguments suggest that the economic and/or political circumstances facing less developed countries today are particularly inauspicious. More troubling for the pessimistic cause is that even the poorest countries experienced significant economic growth in the 1950s and 1960s (Latin America grew by 2.9 percent per year in the 1960s and 1970s and Africa by 2.3 percent), though stagnation has since ensued in Africa and parts of Latin America. Fully a quarter (26 of 102) of the countries in the sample assembled by Durlauf, Johnson, and Temple (2005) has grown less than 60 percent (or less than 1.5 percent per year) since 1960. It is notable in this respect that the world distribution of incomes by country is bi-polar: there are several countries with average incomes well above $10,000, and many with average incomes below $1500, but almost none between $5000 and $10,000. Likewise, one can identify a set of countries which have stagnated in recent decades while another group has grown fast. Azariadis and Stachurski (2005) conclude from this statistical reality that poverty traps are not impossible to break out of, but can be difficult: they note that many African countries have followed the sorts of policies recommended by economists but remain poor.

The average growth rate of less developed countries 1960-2000 of 2.3 percent compares favorably with the 1.3 percent recorded by Britain 1820-1870 or 1.8 percent in the United States 1870-1914, but not with the 2.7 percent recorded by developed countries 1960-2000 (Rodrik 2005). Still, less developed countries generally experienced rapid advance in literacy, infant mortality, and life expectancy during this period. We must be careful, then, of holding countries to too high a standard of growth: we should perhaps accept even sluggish growth as evidence against the existence of a poverty trap.

Sachs (2005), while arguing for the existence of poverty traps, also refers to a development ladder whereby countries can move through various stages (such as the export of labor-intensive manufactured goods) in a self-reinforcing process. That is, once a country breaks out of a poverty trap, it can enter sustained growth. Many African countries, though, seem to have been on such a ladder in the 1960s and fell again into a poverty trap through poor governance coupled with population growth. Sachs argues that one sixth of the world's population is in a poverty trap, but can be removed through aid (18-9). Indeed aid allocations within the range of previous promises could eradicate extreme poverty by financing fertilizers, water, health, education, power, and transport investments (30-5).[1]

Jones (2002, 7-8) provides an even longer view of economic growth. Since human population has been growing through most of human history without humanity descending into deeper poverty, extensive growth – growth in GDP at the same rate as growth in population – must have been endemic in human history. In early history, extensive growth might be accomplished through simply expanding into new lands. In more recent millennia even extensive growth would require increases in the productivity of land (and/or compensating increases in the productivity of labor or capital). Extensive growth, that is, must reflect similar causes as intensive growth. Jones and many other scholars also suggest that there was a trend of slight increases in per capita GDP over the last millennia [with occasional setbacks]. Rather than seeking to explain economic growth, Jones urges us to be

---

[1] He performs detailed calculations on 288-306, and argues that the United States could finance this effort alone by merely reinstating tax cuts for those with incomes over half a million dollars.

surprised that the transition from extensive to (fast) intensive growth was not more common in human history. He suggests that the explanation for the general lack of rapid intensive growth is largely political: institutions severely limited levels of innovation and investment. Jones' observation that extensive, and likely even mildly intensive, growth is widely observed in human history, lends some support to the optimistic point of view.

10.1.1 Convergence

One important contemporary variant of the optimist outlook is the idea of convergence. The convergence hypothesis suggests that poor countries should grow faster than rich countries for one of two reasons:[2]

- Poor countries have a lower capital to labor ratio, and thus the return to investment should be higher in poor countries (The justification is the simple idea of diminishing marginal returns to capital: giving a worker one machine to work with makes the worker much more productive, while further additions to the capital stock by the same amount increase output by lesser and lesser amounts). As a result investment in poor countries has a greater impact on output. We might also anticipate capital flows toward poor countries in response to the higher return. This line of argument is often associated with the neoclassical growth models of the 1960s though it is not inconsistent with endogenous growth theory. Capital flows from rich to poor countries have been much smaller than neoclassical growth models predict.
- Poor countries have less advanced technology. While developed countries can only improve their technology by the expensive process of research and development poor countries can potentially borrow more advanced technology from other countries. This line of argument is most strongly associated with endogenous growth models, though it was widely appreciated before these emerged.

In the aftermath of the development of endogenous growth models, a great deal of empirical research was performed regarding convergence. This research was also inspired by the development of better data on the growth experience of a wide range of countries. The simplest analyses are cross-section regressions where growth rates (usually since 1960) are regressed against level of per capita GDP at the start of the period. More complex analyses include a host of other variables

---

[2] Temple (1999) notes a third possible reason: factor price equalization through trade liberalization. That is, trade theory suggests that wage rates and interest rates should converge across countries as trade expands. In practice, factor price equalization occurs very little in the world, perhaps because trade flows are not in fact driven by comparative advantage (see chapter 7).

thought to influence economic growth. Such regressions thus examine both convergence and the importance of other factors (including sometimes political and social variables that can be quantified): many of the empirical results reported elsewhere in this book flow from such regressions.

What are the results of these regressions?:

- There has not been overall convergence among countries in the postwar period. While some poor countries have become rich, many others have stagnated. Note that there has not been divergence on average either, but a rough balance between convergence and divergence.
- However, if one weights countries by population in such regressions, and thus looks at convergence in terms of people rather than countries, one does find significant convergence. The reason is simple: China and more recently India, the two most populous nations in the world, have grown more rapidly than the developed world, while a number of small countries in Africa and elsewhere have not. The future performance of China and India will have a major impact on whether optimists or pessimists are correct.
- If one looks just at members of the OECD one also finds convergence in the postwar period: several countries in Europe have largely caught up to the United States and Canada, while the poorest countries in Europe (Ireland being the standout here) have grown much faster than their richer neighbors. There is a selection problem in such analysis: if one samples only those countries presently defined as 'rich' one must find that those that were previously poor must have grown faster than those thought to be rich decades ago. Yet the fact that convergence is seen strongly within Europe in recent decades suggests that there is some force leading to convergence at least among similar countries. The policies of the European Union may be partly responsible for this convergence, but seem unlikely to be the sole cause.

Scholars have naturally turned their attention to factors that may limit convergence, and have argued that countries need a certain ill-defined 'social capability' in order to absorb the investment and/or technology that drives convergence. There is a danger of tautological reasoning here, for countries that fail to grow are then assumed to lack the capability to do so. It is necessary to carefully identify the elements of social capability. Infrastructure, financial institutions, and good governance are most often mentioned. For technology flows, a local research capability is likely crucial. If Chandler the business historian is correct, then managerial capability to establish the necessary organizational structure may be a key part of social capability.

The social capability argument presents an opening for pessimists to suggest that there are mechanisms preventing the poorest of countries from developing. Such a debate can of course not be decided unless we strive to more carefully identify the elements of social capability and examine the barriers to achieving this (or alternatively wait a couple of centuries and see what happens in Africa).

Some of the regressions above serve to identify variables that help to explain why certain countries fail to converge. But it is common practice to insert a 'dummy variable' for Africa, which is almost always found to be important: that is, for reasons that economists have yet to uncover, African countries on average perform less well than economist models predict.

It is also important to look at economic history. In the nineteenth and early twentieth centuries, divergence was dominant. It is thought that in 1800 the richest countries in the world may have had average incomes only three or four times those of the poorest countries. By 1913 the gap was 10:1 and by 1950 26:1. Those ratios today are 40 to 1 or 60 to 1 (if one compares the very richest and very poorest country). It is thus obvious that convergence is not an inexorable force in human history (Snowdon, 50).[3]

10.1.2 Common Ground Between Optimists and Pessimists

In terms of the three strategies for dealing with differences in interdisciplinary insight (see chapter 6) it is clear that this difference is not merely semantic: pessimists and optimists are talking about the same thing and reaching different conclusions. Do these hypotheses have different ranges of applicability? It must seem that many of the world's poor countries have achieved impressive rates of economic growth in recent decades, and thus better fit the optimistic outlook. Sub-Saharan Africa might better fit the pessimist scenario, though again it must be recalled that these countries often grew rapidly in the 1960s. Is there some mechanism that ensures that at least some poor countries remain poor? This leads to the third question: could one achieve common ground by changing some assumptions in one or the other perspective? Indeed one could. If one strips away the determination to identify without doubt the future course of history, each perspective supports and depends upon a set of causal arguments. It is entirely possible that all of these have some empirical merit, and thus whether a country grows or not depends on which causal forces operate most strongly. And such a common ground can indeed be seen in the writings of both camps: when optimists bemoan what they see as surmountable barriers (but barriers nevertheless) to economic growth, and when pessimists suggest (generally dramatic) changes to the way the world operates. We can thus usefully progress to looking at particular causal arguments in turn. We can hope that any growth-inducing strategies we can identify should be embraced by both optimists and pessimists, though pessimists will often doubt that these will be 'good enough.' We must not, though, lose sight of emergent

---

[3] The present status of less developed countries looks less bleak if one turns from GDP to the United Nations' Human Development Indicator. This includes GDP but also measures of literacy and life expectancy. Less developed countries still look bad, but not by as wide a margin. In HDI terms they are better off than Europe in 1870 (Snowdon 2002, 19).

properties only visible in a system of links: pessimists in particular generally refer to a complex of (not always well specified) forces that work together. Notably, though, the optimist/pessimist debate has generally emphasized particular causal arguments rather than an appeal to emergent properties.

Still we must appreciate that these differing views are not just academic disputes. Optimists recommend a variety of growth-inducing strategies (and argue that poor countries can develop much as rich countries have). Pessimists must instead speak of radical change – either some sort of global revolution or some sort of 'big push' package of reforms for poor countries. If they imagine that such programs are feasible, pessimists can in fact be very optimistic about the future: Sachs (2005) thus speaks of erasing poverty in our lifetimes.

10.1.3 The Poor are Different

This book has analyzed economic growth largely as a general process, and purported to provide insights applicable to growth processes everywhere. Yet it has also valued idiographic research. And at many points it has noted that growth processes will differ much across countries, and thus that the best policies will also differ across countries. The analysis above suggests further that there may be common challenges faced by the poorest of countries. The field of development economics is largely predicated on such a belief.

Hollis Chenery tried to stress the various structural changes associated with development: as countries move toward $1000 average income, savings and investment rates rise, capital inflows fall, tax rates and government spending rise, education spending increases a little but enrollment a lot, there is a shift from primary to secondary production and then services, exports rise but primary exports fall and service exports rise, urbanization occurs, and birth and death rates fall. Poor countries, it must seem, both should and do pursue a different set of policies. Yet we must again be careful: poor countries still have differences and a country may well be advised to follow a different path from the average identified by Chenery.

10.2 Macroeconomics and Growth

There is obviously not the space here to completely rehash the entire field of macroeconomics (the study of business cycles) – especially as this field has tended to be even less interdisciplinary in orientation[4] than the study of growth. But it is

---

[4] One exception involves discussions of a 'political business cycle' that might result from increased government spending before elections. Recent research suggests that politics does influence macroeconomic performance but not as much as older political business cycle theories suggested (Alt and Alesina 1998, 663).

useful to stress that the present practice in economics whereby 'growth' is a sub-topic in macroeconomics is almost exactly backwards. Business cycles are a reflection of growth processes much more than a cause of these. In a world without growth, economic theory would point toward an equilibrium in which every agent knew exactly what other agents would do, and thus consumption, investment, and employment would cease fluctuating. Of course, one might posit sources of 'change' that generate cycles but not growth – such as the 'harvest cycles' of pre-industrial times – but the fact remains that without growth business cycles would be much less severe. It is the changes wrought by economic growth that drive business cycles. The simple fact that business cycles are an 'emergent property' of the system of causal links driving economic growth should lie at the heart of macroeconomic theorizing but does not.

This book has argued for a conception of growth that involves the complex interaction of myriad causal links. The fact that business cycles are an emergent property of the growth process does not mean that cycles in turn do not affect growth rates. 'The short run and its uncertainties affect the long run through the volume of investment and research expenditure, for instance, and the growth forces in the economy probably influence the frequency and amplitude of short run fluctuations' (Solow 2005, 5). Given the two-way connection between growth and fluctuations, and the fact that growth theory has until recently been taught only in courses on macroeconomics, one might have expected the two types of theory to be closely linked. But growth theories have tended to emphasize the 'supply' side: the supply of investment or innovation. Most macroeconomic theories have stressed fluctuations on the demand side: why do consumers and/or investors wish to decrease their spending at times? Macroeconomic theory has also paid less attention to technology, institutions, and culture than has growth theory. On the other hand, the recent emphasis on expectations within macroeconomic theory might usefully be incorporated into growth theory. The discussion that follows is based on the reasonable premise, shared by many macroeconomic and growth theorists, that these two types of theory should be integrated in order to enhance our understanding of both growth and fluctuations.

10.2.1 The Medium Term

The discussion regarding the integration of the two types of theory often focuses these days on the idea of a 'medium term' (Solow 2005, 5). Blanchard (2000, 1403-4) notes that the traditional distinction between short term business cycles and long term growth is misguided. There is an important medium term of a couple of decades in length which 'appear to involve different shocks from those generating business cycles – changes in the pace or nature of technological progress, demographic evolutions, or in the case of Eastern Europe, dramatic changes in institutions.' I made a similar argument in Szostak (1995): The Great Depression was not just a really bad couple of business cycles. Yet both economists and economic historians have tried to understand it through macroeconomic analysis.

There is some recognition among economists that business cycles differ through the medium term: they are shorter and less severe during medium term upswings. In other words, business cycles are less problematic when growth is fastest. This result may seem unsurprising but is not obvious theoretically. If it is accepted that growth involves the cross-sectoral shift of resources, then one might expect higher rates of unemployment during periods of rapid growth. If though growth is associated with an abundance of growing sectors relative to declining sectors then the observed result would be expected (see chapter 9 for a discussion of the sectoral nature of growth). While a minority of macroeconomists has begun to investigate the medium term, it must seem that economic historians and others could contribute much to this enterprise.

10.2.2 Long Waves

Another literature that has tried to connect growth and cycles is the 'long wave' literature. This idea, first developed by Kondratiev a century ago, hypothesizes that there are regular long cycles in economic activity. Long waves are generally posited to be about a half century in length. Long wave theory is at present out of vogue – interest in long waves tends to peak during periods of poor economic performance such as the 1930s and 1970s. Long wave theory is challenged on both empirical and theoretical grounds. Empirically, there has only been enough time to observe a handful of such cycles during modern economic growth, and the shocks that the world economy has received from such events as the two World Wars complicate the identification of cycles. If one thinks there have been a handful of cycles empirically, these might have been generated by such exogenous shocks. Theoretically it is wondered what causal mechanisms could drive regular cycles of such a length.

Elsewhere in this book when systems theories of any type have been engaged, the strategy taken has been to carefully engage the posited causal links but be wary of the assumption that some sort of regularity or stability necessarily emerges from the system of such links. This was also the attitude taken in Szostak (1995) regarding long wave theory. It is clear that economies perform much better in some decades than others, and thus theories explaining upswings and downswings longer than standard business cycles seem valuable. But one does not have to accept regular cycles in order to borrow certain causal linkages emphasized in long wave theory.

Technological innovation has been stressed in many long wave theories. We saw in chapter 6 how the development of a general purpose technology might lead to a period of above-average economic performance. The GPT literature tends to assume that GPTs emerge irregularly through time. But it is not difficult to posit sources of regularity. Innovators might, for example, turn their attention from incremental innovation toward the development of the next GPT as the opportunities for incremental innovation decline. Since innovators tend to specialize, such an argument is more readily applied to a particular type of technology than to innovation as a whole. Or one might include an economic linkage: as the opportunities for incremental innovation peter out economic activity declines; different theorists have posited that radical innovations are more likely either in the depth of depression (when society is ready to countenance radical change) or at the start of the next upswing.[5]

Other long wave theorists talk of cycles in resource prices, investment rates, or credit availability. The capital goods sector and infrastructure are often stressed. These theories are sometimes combined with technological explanations: profits and consumption patterns may both reflect and drive trends in innovation.

Importantly, long wave theorists (like scholars of the medium term) often argue that business cycles are different during long wave upswings versus downswings. Recessions are usually milder during upswings.[6] There is some evidence that the experience of the Great Depression, in which real wages actually rose (and thus likely exacerbated problems of unemployment), is not atypical of periods of economic stagnation.

We have discussed investment and technological innovation at length in chapter 6, and will address infrastructure in chapter 11, and need not rehash those discussions here. We will not say much about resource prices: there is a great deal of empirical doubt regarding any regular cycle in these, and very few scholars hold to this explanation. There may nevertheless be scope for further research. We have not had cause elsewhere to talk much about how aggregate supply and demand might interact in generating growth, and will do so below. While many of these various feedback effects are plausible, one can still reasonably doubt that any/all of them are strong enough to generate regular long waves.

Long wave theory can be considered pessimistic in positing regular periods of very poor economic performance, or optimistic in positing inevitable recovery from these. In any case, long wave theorists suggest that the mechanisms driving

---

[5] Long cycle theorists and others have posited that innovative activity fluctuates with economic cycles. Forrester has argued that innovation is most likely in business cycle upswings: people are too pessimistic during downturns and too complacent during booms. Alternatively, Mensch (1979) argued that depressions encouraged radical thinking. Kleinknecht (1987) notes that research expenditure did not surge during the Depression, but there may have been a shift toward radical innovation (but this hard to define and measure). All of these approaches tend to abstract away from the technological opportunities at any point in time. While innovations do tend to clump historically, they do not seem to do so at any particular point in the cycle.

[6] There is also cross-section evidence that countries experiencing more rapid productivity growth experience less severe cycles. One possibility is that innovation generates many investment opportunities (and/or keeps expectations high). In North America, some of the postwar experience can be attributed to demography: the entry of the baby boom into the job market in the 1970s increased both the scope and volatility of unemployment as younger workers are more likely to move in and out of employment than are the middle aged.

cconomies toward equilibrium are much weaker than macroeconomic theory tends to posit. This may be the most important insight to be taken from this literature. We will return to this point when discussing technology below.

10.2.3 Implications of Growth Theory for Fluctuations

This book focuses on the causes of growth rather than the consequences. A brief exception is made here. Since it will be argued that cycles exert some feedback effects on growth below, it makes sense to discuss briefly how growth generates cycles. More importantly, in understanding the causes of growth it is important to understand how growth occurs through time. The argument here is that growth is inextricably associated with fluctuations in both the short and medium (and perhaps long wave) terms. As we saw in chapter 3 growth theories tend to assume/predict much greater stability in the growth process than is ever observed. This section will discuss why the growth process is never so smooth.

Economists have sought to explain business cycles in two broad ways: they have sometimes searched for endogenous business cycles (that is upswings generate downswings and vice versa), and at others sought propagation mechanisms for exogenous shocks. Methodological concerns often favored the latter, for the former requires the use of non-linear relationships. Shocks could be monetary, political, or technological. Models pursue one or the other strategy when both may be important. Expectations can be important in both approaches. If we rely on shocks then we would not see cycles in an unchanging world. If expectations are important within endogenous cycles, then again cycles should be virtually non-existent in an unchanging world (for then there is no reason for expectations to change).

10.2.3.1 Technology and Cycles

If business cycles are an emergent property of the growth process, then a logical place to begin theorizing about cycles would be with the proximate causes of growth. Business cycle theory has tended to emphasize fluctuations in investment (and/or consumption) but has rarely engaged technological innovation. Real Business Cycle theory was an exception. It posited a link between productivity growth and unemployment that depended on workers choosing not to work for a while if they expected real wages to rise in future. Not surprisingly, it proved difficult to empirically support the idea that unemployment rates responded to annual changes of a couple of percent in productivity. Our discussion in chapter 6 leads us to identify two other problems with the approach. Productivity advance occurs for reasons other than technological innovation (including institutional change, but in the short run the cycle itself affects measured productivity rates if one assumes that the least productive workers are laid off first in a recession). And the theory dealt only with process innovation while ignoring product innovation. Despite these glaring weaknesses in conceptualization, the failure of Real Business Cycle theory seems to have soured the profession on technological explanations of fluctuations (e.g. Blanchard 2000, 1388). The growing interest in the 'medium term' may serve to revive this interest.

If technological innovation is the main driver of economic growth, but we appreciate that innovation occurs unevenly through time, it does not seem unreasonable to expect that innovation might also affect or even drive at least medium term fluctuations. Our discussion in chapter 6 focused on how innovation affects economic performance in the long run. The business press focuses instead on how innovation might affect economic prospects in the short and medium term. It is thus doubly surprising that economic theorists have not paid more attention to the link between innovation and cycles.

The distinction between product and process innovation is particularly important here. In general, product innovation can be expected to have a positive effect on investment, consumption, and thus unemployment. Process innovation may also stimulate investment but it will generally decrease consumption expenditure and employment in the short/medium term (the effect depends on the elasticity of demand: do consumers end up spending less or more on a product as the price falls?) (see Szostak 1995).[7] Woirol (1996) concurs that process innovation tends to decrease employment, while product innovation has the reverse effect. Labor markets will be especially slow to adjust if prices are sticky or skills not transferable. Woirol notes that there was a literature on technological unemployment during the 1930s and on structural unemployment in the 1960s, but in both cases (some) economists only examined this possible connection after the idea emerged in public debate, and most economists ignored both the theory and empirics, especially as the downturns ended. 'There was a distinct feeling, especially in the structural debates, that those challenging the accepted view were acting somehow outside the accepted normal course of professional behavior' (11). Woirol appreciates that the link is hard to establish empirically because product and process innovation are hard to measure, and the effects in short, medium, and long run are different; effects also differ by sector. Nevertheless he suggests that the main barrier to acceptance of the link was 'a strongly held professional belief' in equilibrating mechanisms (144).[8] That is, real wage rates should simply fall until full employment is restored. As noted above, though, the historical experience of lengthy periods (especially the Great Depression) of poor economic performance should

---

[7] Process innovation will generally be deflationary (though firms are often slow to lower prices). Product innovation is trickier, because its effect on aggregate prices depends both on how the new products enter the measurements and to what extent they complement or substitute for other goods. New products generally require investment (as does much process innovation), and investment is inflationary (since investment goods are not included in the calculations, but the income earned in capital goods industries is spent on consumption).

[8] Those who critiqued structural arguments in the 1960s usually attacked straw men rather than the more subtle arguments of proponents of the idea (142).

lead us to expect that equilibrating mechanisms are less powerful than generally thought. Vivarelli (1995) argued that economic stability is the usual result only because there is generally a rough balance between product and process innovation. Szostak (1995) argued that the Great Depression was largely due to an imbalance between product and process innovation.[9] Christopher Freeman and Carlota Perez have in many places also stressed that the general stability observed in economies reflects not the power of equilibrating mechanisms but a rough balance between declining and growing sectors; they attribute sectoral growth and decline in turn largely to technology. If these various authors are correct then economic stability (such as it is) reflects not so much the power of equilibrating mechanisms but the fact that the expansionary effect of product innovation in the short/medium term usually balances the contractionary effect of process innovation. If only process innovation occurs we should expect unemployment; if only product innovation productivity will fail to rise.

It should be stressed immediately that process innovation is contractionary only in the short/medium term. Over the long run, process innovation is a critical component of the productivity advance on which long-term growth is predicated. But if as we shall suggest below cycles themselves influence growth processes, then growth theorists should not ignore the negative short/medium term effect. Nor should they ignore the implication that growth occurs most smoothly when there is both product and process innovation.

10.2.3.2 Sectoral Interactions

In chapter 9 it was argued that the rise and fall of both sectors and firms was an integral part of the growth process. That is, growth is not just the happy production of more by everyone but always involves also the production of less by some agents. It should hardly be surprising that this sort of cross-firm and cross-sector instability is somehow related to the temporal fluctuations studied here. Macroeconomic theory would generally predict that workers would flow quickly from declining firms/industries toward those that are growing. Pasinetti (1981), among others, had argued for weak links across sectors, and that thus differences in technology and demand growth across sectors ensured that equilibrium and balanced growth were unlikely. Classical economists also often posited that sectoral imbalances would generate aggregate unemployment (Kates 1998). In the last decades a handful of macroeconomists have begun to study the possibility that sectoral

---

[9] Could the Depression happen again? The analysis here suggests that the answer depends on how balanced product and process innovation are through time. This is not a question that economic theory itself has much to say about. Szostak (1995) argued that the unfortunate interwar time path of innovation reflected the confluence of developments in the GPTs associated with the Second Industrial Revolution of the 1880s, and perhaps also the tendency of industrial research laboratories to stress process innovation at the time. As the research enterprise becomes more diversified, such an imbalance between product and process innovation becomes less likely.

interactions generate unemployment: this emerging research agenda marks a major shift from the previous emphasis on a handful of aggregate variables.

In the previous section it was argued that an aggregate imbalance between product and process innovation could generate fluctuations. Here it is suggested that a mere sectoral imbalance can generate unemployment. If many sectors are declining but few are growing unemployment will result. Moreover, even if there are growing sectors that can absorb workers from declining sectors, this will not happen overnight. Workers will face many barriers – location, training, and informational most obviously – in moving, and thus a smooth transition is unlikely.

When Real Business Cycle theories were criticized above it was noted that cycles themselves generate fluctuations in productivity. It was suggested that the least productive workers might be let go in a recession, and thus measured productivity might rise. There is also evidence that the least productive firms are more likely to go out of business. Schumpeter thus famously argued that even severe downturns like the Depression served a necessary cleansing function for the economy: otherwise weak firms might stumble on for years. It is also possible that 'good' firms, forced to restrict output in a recession, may be more likely to introduce productivity enhancements at that time. Productivity growth, like economic growth, does not occur everywhere, but much of it occurs when high-productivity firms/sectors expand while low productivity sectors/firms disappear. Recessions may accelerate this transition. If so, this would be an important feedback effect from cycles to growth. But Blanchard (2000) reports that recessions also destroy some firms that should survive, and thus the net effect of cleansing is unclear.

10.2.3.3 Savings and Investment

Keynes focused the attention of macroeconomic theorists on why the amount that people might wish to save could differ from the amount of desired investment. Savings decisions will reflect to a significant extent one's expectations regarding the future. Investment decisions are even-more future oriented. But they also depend on the rate of innovation: investment is often called forth because new technology (both product and process) often must be embodied in new equipment. Desired savings are most likely to exceed desired investment then if expectations of future growth falter, and/or the rate of innovation falls. Note that a declining rate of innovation might itself lead to low expectations.

10.2.3.4 An Insight from Economic Anthropology

Some economic anthropologists – notably the classic work of Sahlins (1974) – argued that the forces of supply and demand did not determine prices in premodern economies. But their own analysis shows that prices would eventually adjust if there was a serious disjunction between supply and demand. Thus what they actually succeeded in doing was explaining price stickiness. Networks of individuals engaged in exchange acted to keep prices stable if possible, for then each actor could predict the behavior of others. Price changes disrupted the network, and forced each actor to reach new expectations of others (Swedberg and Granovetter 13). Notably price stickiness is the *bete noire* of macroeconomic analysis in economics. Macroeconomists are generally only able to generate business cycles in their models by assuming that prices do not adjust automatically to shocks, for if prices (including wages) did adjust instantaneously negative economic shocks should be accommodated by a fall in (some) real wages rather than unemployment. But microeconomics, the theory of individual markets, has long assumed that prices do adjust very quickly. Macroeconomists have sought in recent decades to establish micro-foundations for macroeconomic arguments, but without any obvious increase in our understanding of the macro-economy (Blinder in Snowdon 2002 thus suggests that we know that prices are sticky – even if we cannot explain this result – and should proceed with modeling the effects of this). Economic sociology/anthropology provides an explanation of price stickiness that bears a striking resemblance to economic analyses of institutional change: actors resist change because of the period of uncertainty necessarily involved in change.

10.2.4 Implications of Macroeconomic Theory for Growth

10.2.4.1 The Lucas Critique

Robert Lucas famously suggested that the parameters in macroeconomic models were not stable when policies changed. If a government ran a deficit, for example, individuals might increase their savings rate in order to pay anticipated future taxes. The critique had an important policy implication: that government policies might be less effective than imagined because individuals would adjust their spending habits in a direction opposite to that desired by the government. We can leave aside for now the question of whether the critique was as quantitatively relevant to policy debates as was often claimed. For our purposes, the important insight is this: if countries differ in policies or institutions or indeed in a host of other ways, they may exhibit quite different parameters (savings rates for example), and these will likely change through time. Care should be taken in using any model, especially one derived from analysis of other countries, to predict the quantitative effect of any change in policy.

The argument made here reinforces that made elsewhere that we should be focused on studying individual causal links in detail rather than only trying to estimate multi-equation models. The latter are not without insight. Just as Lucas would advise macroeconomists to ask where the saving rate parameter came from, and thus how other variables might affect it, growth theorists must ask how each variable in their models might be affected by a host of others.

10.2.4.2 Volatility and Growth

There have been some cross-section regression analyses of the effect of business cycle volatility on growth. The empirical results are diverse and not robust to changes in model specification. This result may well reflect the simple fact that different sources/types of volatility – changes in policy, trends in technology – have different effects. If cycles are different during medium term (or long wave) upswings as opposed to downswings, regressions that lump the two types of recession together are likely to generate weak results. Also, these regressions tend to focus only on short-term effects on productivity; theoretically one might posit longer-term effects.

Theoretically, though, it is not hard to imagine a variety of links between fluctuations and growth. We have already encountered an important positive link: that recessions may weed out weak firms and sectors. We also discussed above the possibility that certain types of innovation may be more likely during economic downturns or upswings (but should also appreciate that volatility itself must at times also discourage innovation).[10]

On the negative side we can first note that lengthy periods of unemployment lower GDP below what it could have been if resources were fully employed. If some of those resources could be diverted to the production of useful (private or public) capital, then the long-term trend in the capital/labor ratio might be raised (Unless the act of diversion somehow discouraged an equal amount of future investment). Likewise, if the unemployed would have saved from employment earnings, there will be less capital available for future investment. Also, to the extent that learning-by-doing is an important component of productivity advance, then any reduction in output reduces economic growth.

The level of investment is also affected by interest rates. As noted in chapter 6, central banks focused on business cycles may often be guilty of raising interest rates more than necessary in order to restrain inflation: this may serve to lower the long-term trend in investment, and thus economic growth. It is worth noting that before Keynes wrote in the 1930s economists tended to urge low interest rates to foster growth, but now economists think primarily in terms of stabilizing business cycles. Solow has urged the use of fiscal policy (government spending and taxation) rather than monetary (interest rate) policy in booms so that it is government spending rather than private investment that contracts. Tax increases that are clearly temporary might cause consumption rather than investment to fall. If these taxes were used to finance government expenditure during the next recession, the

---

[10] Bruton (1997) argues that reducing unemployment increases the incentive to develop labor-saving technology.

government would not have to borrow. The fear that government borrowing crowds out private investment by pushing up interest rates could then be side-stepped.

The hardest link to establish is possibly the most important: cycles affect expectations. Investors (and innovators) must worry that a future recession will cause their otherwise sensible investment plans to become unprofitable.[11] If growth were smooth, investors could rely upon a steadily expanding aggregate market. If investors need to borrow, they may find that banks are unwilling to lend if they fear a severe economic downturn. It is not clear how important these cyclically-related expectations are. Investors have a host of other things to worry about: the future paths of technology, institutions, tastes, and competitor behavior. Szostak (1995) suggested that these might loom much larger in individual decision-making than concerns about macroeconomic stability (and thus that any investor worries in 1929 reflected the lack of new product innovation rather than monetary stringency). But fears regarding cycles may nevertheless cause some dampening of the long-term trend in investment.

10.2.4.3 The Demand Side in Growth

As noted above, macroeconomic theory has tended to emphasize the demand side, while growth theory has tended to stress the supply side. The discussion of expectations just above should remind us that the two are linked. Investors and innovators will be less likely to invest and innovate if they fear an economic downturn. Endogenous growth theory, in making the rate of innovation endogenous to economic variables, potentially brings the demand side into growth theory. But it is economic historians that have pursued this line of argument the farthest.

George Grantham has in many publications argued that it was demand growth that stimulated productivity growth in agriculture in early modern Europe. Farmers near (growing) cities or with easy access to water transport worked harder and developed new techniques (that tended to increase both output and effort required) in response to market signals. Szostak (1991a) discussed how increased market (and raw material) access as a result of transport improvements encouraged the development of the modern factory and a host of technological innovations during the Industrial Revolution.

If individuals do not anticipate growth in demand, they may well feel that working harder, investing, or innovating can only result in unemployment for them or their friends. In discussing culture in chapter 8, this sort of mental outlook was addressed. These sorts of cultural attitudes are one alleged source of 'poverty traps' (above). Once one breaks out of such a trap, then a virtuous cycle can

---

[11] Durlauf, Johnson, and Temple (2005, 574) note that it is common to observe double-digit drops in output in poor countries, though such downturns are almost nonexistent in postwar developed countries. This might cause investment rates to be much lower in poor countries.

emerge: innovation and investment and hard work stimulate growth in demand, and expectations of demand growth stimulate more investment and innovation and effort. But if for some reason stagnation sets in it may be hard to get this virtuous cycle going. The Grantham and Szostak analyses suggest that shifts in demand toward certain localities or sectors may start the process. Still, foreign aid programs have often hoped that an infusion of money could kick-start a growth process, but these hopes have generally been dashed – though perhaps because flows were small and mismanaged.

Bruton (1997, 73-4) argues that the focus of macroeconomic policy, especially in poor countries, should be on encouraging demand for labor (he appreciates that policy-makers should also avoid both high inflation and imbalances of foreign payments). This not only reduces unemployment but encourages good entrepreneurial expectations (especially in sectors that might otherwise saturate markets), lowers barriers to the adoption of labor-saving technology, and encourages the search for labor-saving technology.

The demand side was touched upon also when the differences between product and process innovation were outlined in chapter 6. If only process innovation ever occurred, the population might soon tire of more of the same stuff. Demand keeps up with supply only because an ever wider range of goods and services is produced. If not for this expansion in demand, process innovation would have developed and diffused more slowly. But of course product innovation is not the only stimulus to demand. Government spending, efforts at redistribution, and changes in tastes may also be important.[12]

While much more needs to be done, the point to stress here is that increases in demand may (under at least some circumstances) stimulate increases in supply. Moreover increases in supply cannot long be sustained unless matched by increases in demand. Economists tend to think in terms of equilibrium between supply and demand. With respect to economic growth, the question is not one of static equilibrium but how to ensure that supply and demand expand at similar rates. We could better achieve this goal if we better understood how supply and demand influence each other.

10.2.4.4 Inflation

Double-digit inflation adds a great deal of uncertainty to investment decisions. It also increases transactions costs: one cannot so easily specify a future delivery price (a point long stressed by old institutionalist economists). It also shifts the reward structure away from investment in real economic activities toward financial speculation. The size of the financial sector is observed to grow during periods of high inflation. The costs are even more severe when coupled with limits

---

[12] Cornwall and Cornwall (2001) maintain that institutions encouraged demand growth in the 1950s and 1960s but not thereafter.

on nominal interest rates. If inflation is 40 percent but nominal interest rates are capped at 10 percent, putting money in a savings account is a very bad idea: one will lose 30 percent of the value of one's funds every year. This, needless to say, creates a powerful disincentive to saving.

Empirical studies suggest lowering inflation from 50 percent to 5 percent increases growth by 1-2 percent (Gylfason 85-95). The case studies in Rodrik (2003) also serve to highlight the advantages of keeping inflation under control. Temple (1999) is more cautious, noting that a few outliers drive most empirical results that inflation lowers growth. But this result again suggests that the problem is very high rates of inflation.

Some economic theories suggest a possible positive impact of inflation: workers may be fooled by rising nominal wages into taking jobs that they would previously have rejected, even though the increased wages are matched by increasing prices and thus the real wage is unchanged. It is doubtful that the unemployed can be urged into employment by small changes in perceived wage rates. They may not respond to even sizeable increases in wage rates, and are unlikely to be unaware of rapid increases in price levels.

A more likely positive effect of mild levels of inflation is that it facilitates economic restructuring. If workers' wages reflect their productivity, then workers will wish to move toward firms/sectors in which productivity is highest. As we have seen, productivity growth tends to occur unevenly across sectors. Wage rates should thus grow at different rates as well. Workers tend to bargain over nominal rates rather than real rates, and will often accept no nominal increase when prices are rising, but would reject a nominal decrease when prices are stable (even though the effect on their real wage is identical in the two cases). Moderate inflation then makes it easier for wages to adjust in order to reflect differences in productivity growth rates.

A further argument for not interfering with moderate levels of inflation is that estimated inflation rates are likely higher than they should be. It is hard for statisticians to cope with improvements in product quality, but we know as consumers that the quality of many of the things we buy has improved over time. If we pay a higher price for a better quality good, the higher price may reflect the improved quality rather than just inflation. Economists have worried about this a great deal in recent years, and methods of calculating inflation have been adjusted, but an upward bias is still suspected.

Economists sometimes worry about deflation as well. The Great Depression was a time of rapid deflation, and this likely contributed to the severity of the Depression, as deflation encouraged money hoarding over investment. The much lower levels of deflation observed in the late nineteenth century (likely driven by technological innovation) had little or no negative consequences. The lower level of deflation then than in the 1930s may reflect a greater incidence of counteracting product innovation. In any case the lesson seems to be that, as with inflation, moderate levels of deflation are not dangerous.

11 Integrating Diverse Views of the Role of Government

A first path to common ground involves simply rejecting the exclusionary practices of various disciplines. When economists theorize that growth is entirely endogenous to a few variables, we can simply object that various political, social, cultural, and technological factors have a major role to play (as many economists themselves appreciate). Likewise when cultural studies specialists imagine that culture is the prime moving force in human history we can suggest that other phenomena also exert important influences, even on culture itself. With such a simple stratagem we can find that different theories can be treated as complements even though their advocates view them as substitutes.

While this first effort is invaluable, interdisciplinary analysis is not so simple, especially in human science. Human science theories often reach substantively different conclusions. That is, the logic of the theories, not just those variables assumed to be unimportant, lead to different conclusions. In such cases, we need to ask why these differing conclusions are reached, and then whether relatively minor adjustments to the assumptions of these theories can allow us to achieve common ground (Szostak 2002, 115). This step has for presentational reasons often been combined with the preceding steps: we spent a great deal of effort, for example, integrating different theories of institutional change in chapter 7.

In the study of economic growth, it is the vexed question of the role of government that excites the most controversy. This broad issue has been touched upon at many points in the preceding chapters. This chapter integrates diverse arguments regarding the role of government.

11.1 The Role of Government

Economists often emphasize in their theories and particularly their policy prescriptions a limited role for government. This is justified in terms of both microeconomics and macroeconomics. The microeconomic argument is that markets coordinate economic activity better than governments, and especially than corrupt or inept governments. The macroeconomic argument is that financial stability (important especially for encouraging investment, but also trade), depends on reasonably balanced budgets: countries with limited tax revenues should be wary of borrowing in order to finance increased expenditures. Concerns about how taxes distort economic decisions and may act to decrease work effort can discourage such governments from raising taxes, even when they possess the administrative capability. Foreign aid may solve some of the fiscal problem, but cannot solve the microeconomic problem. In addition economists often apply their assumptions of

R. Szostak, *The Causes of Economic Growth*,
DOI: 10.1007/978-3-540-92282-7_11, © Springer-Verlag Berlin Heidelberg 2009

selfish behavior to government bureaucrats, and thus expect that these may twist rules to their own benefit or be captured by private interests.

McCloskey (2006) makes an ethical argument for stressing market exchange over government. Businesspeople are forced to behave ethically in order to do business, while politicians and bureaucrats have much greater freedom to abuse power. The evidence that McCloskey provides is transparently biased: the ethical lapses of businesspeople are readily forgiven (including their corruption of government officials), whereas the efforts of many public servants to do well are simply ignored. There is an important point nevertheless: that competitive pressures can provide an antidote to both dishonesty and sloth. Yet businesspeople still can often reap greater financial rewards from unethical behavior than most bureaucrats. Social scientists have provided little empirical evidence of the relative balance of ethical versus unethical behavior in the private versus public sphere.

Development economists and theorists from other disciplines have imagined a much greater role for government. They have worried that markets on their own may act to keep poor countries poor (see chapter 10). Within countries as well, market exchange may generate a very high level of income inequality. Markets themselves are subject to a range of distortions: monopolies charge prices that are higher than is socially optimal, pollution and congestion are ignored by markets, and public goods such as police forces or roads (and maybe technological innovation) are undersupplied if left to markets alone. Markets may also deal poorly with major changes that require coordinated action by many agents: in such cases government imposition of common standards and regulations or even government coordination of complementary investments may be necessary. It is argued that the historical record points to active rather than passive behavior by the governments of the present developed countries when they were in the early stages of growth.

Most of the analysis of the limitations of both markets and governments has focused on issues of economic efficiency rather than growth. An emphasis on growth may yield different conclusions: a monopoly that plows profits into research is bad in a static sense but perhaps not bad for growth. Since theories of growth are less developed than theories of static efficiency, history may in many cases provide our best guide as to which works best.

The obvious stratagem here is to recognize that neither governments nor markets are perfect, and then see which is 'less bad' in a particular circumstance.[1] Few on either side would likely object to such a principle, though it is rarely applied in practice. Joseph Stiglitz has devoted much of his distinguished career to urging such a balanced perspective on economists, and noting that the best balance will vary across time and place (Snowdon 2002, 6).

---

[1] Clague (1997) argues that the new institutional economics can take scholars past the ideological 'markets versus government' debate. It appreciates that markets depend on institutional support, but also that institutions suffer from individuals twisting those institutions to serve their own purposes. Thus in determining whether to rely on governments, markets, or a mixture of both in a particular situation, scholars should look at the difficulties of establishing and maintaining appropriate institutions for each.

11.1.1 The Washington Consensus

The Washington Consensus was for many years the guiding set of principles used by the World Bank and International Monetary Fund (IMF) in their dealings with less developed countries. Rodrik (2005) lists the original elements of the package – fiscal discipline, reorientation of public expenditure, tax reform, interest rate liberalization, unified and competitive exchange rates, trade liberalization, openness to direct foreign investment, privatization, deregulation, and secure property rights; and also several ideas that have later been added: corporate governance reform, anti-corruption, flexible labor markets, adherence to World Trade Organization discipline, adherence to international financial codes and standards, prudent capital account opening, independent central banks with inflation targeting, social safety nets, and targeted poverty reduction. This package of policies shares a preference for markets over government interventions (except for the last two add-ons which respond to complaints about the emphasis on market processes). Ideological debate treats elements of the package as either good or bad. Our analysis in this book suggests that whether a policy is good or bad depends on circumstances: are government or market imperfections likely to be greater?

Rodrik (2005) notes that the Asian tigers when developing each violated key elements of the consensus: Taiwan and South Korea did not deregulate their trade or financial systems until the 1980s and Korea was very hostile to foreign investment. Both pursued a variety of industrial policies.[2] East Asian corporate governance is widely accused of cronyism. East Asia more generally enforced below market interest rates and restricted foreign entry of financial firms: this may have encouraged financial stability, greater care in monitoring borrowers, and greater effort to mobilize deposits. China has had dramatic growth despite appending a market system to an institutional structure of a planned economy (and with limited private property protection and endemic corruption). On the other hand, many Latin American (and to a lesser extent African) countries have [albeit recently] undertaken many of the Washington Consensus reforms, but have had disappointing results. Rodrik concludes that we should focus not on specific policies but on the broader common elements in growth success: 'a semblance or property rights, sound money, fiscal solvency, market-oriented incentives' (978). China, for example, allowed farmers to sell above-quota surplus at market prices: this provided market incentives while maintaining government supplies; and they gave credible

---

[2] Stiglitz also argues that East Asian governments invested heavily in transport and education (at all levels), encouraged saving, did not pick winners but recognized spillovers and thus encouraged innovation in some sectors (networking), required foreign investors (if allowed) to provide technology and training, developed a safety net and reduced inequality, and had limited short-term capital flows till the 1990s. Latin America instead followed the Washington Consensus and failed. Rodrik himself has a paper on how the active (and carefully implemented) industrial policy pursued by East Asian countries (subsidies, public ownership of upstream producers, investment guarantees) may make sense if scale economies and inter-industry linkages are both present, for then the social return to investment is higher than the private (980-1).

property rights to village corporations. Rodrik warns that these institutions like others may have been accidental, may or may not have been of critical importance, and may perform poorly in other settings (984).

With respect even to fiscal solvency and sound money, Rodrik (2006, 975) is cautious. While extreme policies can cripple growth prospects, moderate deficits or inflation or trade restrictions need not do so. The World Bank should not insist on complete orthodoxy but only warn against extreme behaviors.

Stiglitz (in Snowdon 2002, 391) notes that his skepticism of the Washington Consensus came from a career examining various market imperfections – and thus a fear that economists would over-generalize the usefulness of competitive models. He was particularly concerned that poor countries lacked the institutions – say, corporate governance, or well functioning capital markets that provide information to potential investors – assumed implicitly in economic theories. Stiglitz and others were successful in moving the IMF and World Bank toward a 'post-Washington Consensus' that looks more favorably upon government involvement. Yet Fine (2001) argues that the Stiglitz-inspired post-Washington Consensus, while it has opened up room for state intervention, nevertheless limits intervention to areas of informational asymmetry recognized by mainstream theory. It thus may still favor markets in situations where governments could better support growth.

One negative impact on growth can be readily identified. In practice, the Washington Consensus as applied often neglected the important roles that governments have to play: taxes were to be reduced so far that governments could maintain neither infrastructure nor institutions. The biggest single change in the policy of the IMF and World Bank has been to place more emphasis on the provision of public services.

The Washington Consensus has been criticized for misguided application as well as misguided goals. Easterly (2002) discusses how in the 1980s the IMF and World Bank failed to police the conditions supposedly attached to their loans. The IMF threatened to not renew loans if receiving governments failed to comply with IMF directives. In part due to bureaucratic empire building within these organizations, these threats were almost never exercised despite widespread non-compliance. There were also many ways that countries could pretend to comply: they could for example achieve the appearance of a balanced budget by shifting revenues or expenses between years (or selling assets well below market prices). There was also a perverse incentive in tying loans to promises to improve policies: a country that actually fully accepted the desired policies would no longer be eligible for loans. The result was a cycle of failed promises.

The Washington Consensus, then, can be accused of both misplaced goals and faulty implementation. The first can only be repaired through a more nuanced understanding of the good and bad effects that governments can exert on economic growth. The second depends both on better understanding and on changing bureaucratic structures. Note that the deserved unpopularity of the Washington Consensus makes it very easy for governments to complain about IMF policies, even when these are aimed at laudable goals such as reducing corruption or waste.

11.1.2 Property Rights

Even the most market-oriented economist recognizes that governments should provide 'property rights': a legal code and police and courts that protect individuals from having their property taken by either other individuals or the government. This legal system also serves to enforce contracts, and thus facilitates both internal and external trade. To be sure, private individuals have often combined historically to create systems of property rights in the absence of government, but it seems unlikely that a complex modern economy could function in such a fashion.

Indeed, it is often forgotten just how complicated and expensive the institutional structure of the modern economy has become. The ugly transition from communism to capitalism in the former Soviet Union highlighted the necessity of detailed stock market regulations and a legal system able and willing to enforce these. Economists urging 'lean government' must be careful of trimming it so much that such basic but costly services are provided. On the other hand, some of the poorest countries in the world may be unable to provide such institutions. What should be done then? Encourage local companies to list on foreign stock exchanges (as many Southeast Asian companies did in the wake of the 1997 financial crisis) – an option available only to large companies? Allow local poorly regulated stock markets, and suffer the occasional scandal? Encourage bank finance rather than stock markets (noting that banks play a much larger role in Japan and Germany than they do in Britain and the United States)? Encourage family capitalism and personal relationships among entrepreneurs? Such questions can only be answered on a case-by-case basis: note that the best answer may change quickly as the country develops.

11.1.3 Public Ownership

What goods and services should be provided publicly and what should be provided privately?[3] Private ownership succeeds best in competitive environments in which consumers can readily evaluate the quality of the goods and services provided. Government ownership is often pursued in the case of natural monopolies such as water and sewer systems (where it would be prohibitively expensive to lay more than one set of pipes). Public goods (see below), in which those who do not pay also benefit (such as police protection) are often also provided publicly. Government provision is often favored in cases such as medical care where it is hard to observe the quality of service (as frequent scandals in elder-care facilities attest). The question then arises as to whether government bureaucracies necessarily

---

[3] Sachs (2005, 252-3) lists five reasons for public provision: public goods concerns (see below), natural monopoly, non-rival outcomes in scientific research, concerns with fairness, and to help the poorest.

provide quality. Whether services are provided publicly or privately, third-party regulation (and inspection) of quality seems to be necessary. Finally, governments often provide services such as education or health care for distributional reasons.

In all cases where governments provide a good or service, it is possible that a regulated private firm could do so. But then the question arises of why such enterprises would be superior. It is hard for governments to structure appropriate incentives for such firms. If private firms cut their costs, the government may be tempted to regulate a lower price. The firm may then reasonably devote more effort to lobbying for beneficial regulation than cutting costs. As noted above, unless quality is rigorously monitored, these firms may cut corners in order to cut costs. It is sometimes argued that private firms can achieve greater work effort from employees, but it is not clear why large private bureaucracies need function better in this respect than public bureaucracies. Private firms may be insulated from political interference more than public bureaucracies – but this is an argument for arms-length public corporations rather than privatization. It is sometimes possible for private firms to compete to provide public services (school buses, garbage pickup); in such cases competitive pressures may yield lower cost provision of a service. Again, though, concerns with quality of service arise: school buses in my city fail safety inspections far too often.

Even in competitive environments the modern corporation with diffuse ownership faces the same agency problems as public enterprises. How can managers be inspired to act in the interests of shareholders when these exercise very limited managerial control? Takeovers in the United States or bank oversight elsewhere are costly means of disciplining managers. There is no clear evidence that public firms are less efficient than private firms when one adjusts for the different sectors (and thus government regulation and market structure) in which the two types of firms operate (Bardhan and Romer 1992).

In chapter 10 we discussed the possibility that weak firms might be weeded out during economic downturns. It is possible that the cleansing effect of economic fluctuations is less powerful with public enterprises. Politicians may prefer losing money to losing votes. And public firms need not face the possibility of bankruptcy. But government expenditures are often slashed in downturns.

Governments may at times shrink from the capital investment necessary to provide good services. But this is not an argument for privatization unless governments have poorer credit ratings than private companies. Governments should be at least as willing to bear risk as a private company. Some would argue that governments have less capacity for making sound investment decisions, but there is little empirical evidence on this question.

The historical experience of privatization suggests that this is not always beneficial. Privatization makes sense when competition is possible, but need be no improvement if a private monopoly either gouges consumers or becomes bloated under government regulation. The sense that public companies were inefficient in the 1970s reflects in part the fact that governments prevented such companies from shedding workers or raising prices. Lower profit rates before that time also reflected efforts to decrease prices. Public enterprises in Britain and France experienced rapid productivity growth in the 1980s once freed of government interference. On the other hand, some private enterprises have been showered with government subsidies to expand employment (Toninelli 2000).

11.1.4 Public Spending and Taxes, Federalism

Interestingly, there is no cross-country correlation between tax rates and growth. Easterly (234-5) argues that this may reflect widespread tax evasion in poor countries: the official tax rate thus has little meaning. It may also reflect the simple fact that much government expenditure is growth-enhancing.

Lindert (2004) argues that there is likewise no correlation between public spending and growth. He suggests that this is because governments that spend a lot are more careful about how they tax and also more careful of incentive effects when spending. They tax consumption rather than capital (and thus do not discourage saving). They especially tax 'bads' such as liquor and tobacco. And they avoid means-testing of benefits which discourages work (because those who get a job lose many of their benefits). They are more open to trade (perhaps because this is easier politically when a safety net is in place to aid displaced workers).[4]

I argued (1991a) that Britain's success during the Industrial Revolution of the eighteenth century was in large part due to a decentralized decision-making structure: local people could secure Parliamentary authority to proceed with a road or waterway improvement. Lindert (2004) has suggested that decentralization may also have encouraged Continental efforts at education in the next century when some regions favored this more than others (though later on centralized states ensured education spread to other regions). Theoretically, it is argued that local governments do a better job of providing services because of local expertise, local political responsiveness, and different needs by region. If so it is troubling that contemporary poor countries are more centralized than rich countries.

Obviously, we would benefit from a more detailed understanding. What are the effects of particular taxes and particular types of spending on growth? What factors encourage countries to tax and spend in different ways? We have good reason to believe that some types of spending have good effects and others have bad effects (otherwise high-spending countries would consistently over- or under-perform low-spending countries), but we have limited guidance on which is which. Likewise, some types of taxation likely have lesser impact on growth than others.

---

[4] Lindert also wonders why social spending is higher in some countries than others. For political reasons redistribution is most likely in jurisdictions where it is less needed. The spread of the vote encourages social spending, as does increases in average income. Ethnic homogeneity and social mobility have been important factors postwar in encouraging social spending.

11.1.5 Public Goods

Property rights are hardly the only public good provided by developed country governments. Public goods are defined in economic theory as goods (or services) that by their very nature provide benefits to individuals who do not pay for them. If I hire a security guard to stand in front of my house, he will deter crime for my neighbors as well. If police services were provided privately, they would be undersupplied because many individuals would hope to obtain the benefits without shouldering the costs. Police forces, fire trucks, and parks tend thus to be provided collectively in developed countries. We should thus not limit the role of government in less developed countries such that public goods cannot be provided.

Much of the expenditure of developed countries is devoted to quasi-public goods. Education likely has spillover effects: economically, one literate and numerate person will be better able to create jobs for others, and the value of being literate to any one person depends on how many others one can communicate with. On the other hand much of the benefit to education is private, and thus individuals or families might be expected to pay much of the cost. This debate has played out noisily with regard to university tuition in developed countries in recent decades, but the arguments can be extended to primary and secondary education, especially in poor countries struggling to provide these services. The obvious cost of insisting on private finance is that the poorest children are excluded: this raises questions of equity as well as limiting the economic potential of the country.

Transport infrastructure is also a quasi-public good. Toll roads are quite possible, and have existed for millennia (at least in the form of toll bridges). But the cost of collecting tolls is not small, and thus is generally infeasible for local roads. These at least then are usually provided publicly. Even when tolls are feasible there is often an economic cost of imposing them: potential users will be discouraged even when they would benefit more from using the road than the congestion and maintenance costs they might impose.

Empirical work in developed countries can be divided into two groups: some studies find that public capital (such as roads) has a huge impact on growth, while other studies suggest a limited effect. The latter result might simply indicate that these countries are already close to the optimal level of public infrastructure.[5]

Many governments in less developed countries fail to provide the most basic public infrastructure. Roads are poor or nonexistent, power blackouts are frequent (even in oil-rich Nigeria 92 percent of industrial enterprises have backup generators because of the blackouts), and irrigation systems are allowed to silt up through lack of maintenance. In fully one third of less developed countries, the waiting list for a telephone line is at least six years (happily, individuals in these

---

[5] Mosk (2001) argues that strategic and coordinated investment in infrastructure was the prime mover in early Japanese economic development. Unfortunately he at times defines the word so broadly that it subsumes the whole social and political order, but at other times stresses education, transport, and so on.

countries are often now able to leap to cell phone technology).[6] Various studies suggest that the social rate of return to investments in these areas is as high as 16-18 percent (Easterly 232-4). These estimates are likely too low for they do not capture the more dynamic effects of encouraging private investment.

Jones (2006, 131) applauds the argument recently made by Lindert that in the earliest stages of economic development European countries needed to focus on property rights but later they needed to develop systems of education. This transition is important, for governments move from having just a permissive role in economic growth to playing a positive role. Jones and Lindert, though, neglect the earlier importance of transport infrastructure, and thus a positive role for governments much earlier in the development process. While private provision of both education and transportation is both possible and often observed, extension of these services to the entire population generally involves some sort of public provision.[7] Moreover, governments have a critical regulatory role to play in ensuring that roads are built where needed and that schools provide a quality education.

In sum, a variety of public and quasi-public goods need to be provided in both developed and underdeveloped countries. Notably, these tend not only to encourage economic growth but enhance people's lives directly in important ways: a healthy and literate individual who can move freely without fear has an infinitely greater set of options in life than an illiterate and sick peasant bound to their village and with limited defense against the actions of others. The experience of developed countries suggests that these should be publicly provided if possible, but that private financing is to be preferred (at least temporarily) to no provision at all.

11.1.5.1 Education

Empirical studies at the level of individuals tend to find a very high social rate of return to educational expenditures. As with return to physical capital, Banerjee and Duflo (2005) find that the rate of return varies considerably by agent. Since the economic return to education depends in large part on how many other educated people one can interact with, we might anticipate even higher returns at the aggregate level: that is, there should be increasing returns to education. Yet when spending and economic performance are compared across countries, little correlation is found. The latter result may in part reflect the fact that some countries have over-educated their population: India has long had a host of unemployed or

---

[6] Nigeria raised $570 million auctioning mobile phone licenses – so infrastructure does not have to hurt government budgets. A World Bank study found a strong correlation between access to telephones and average incomes.

[7] The turnpikes and waterways of the Industrial Revolution were provided privately. Yet it was an odd sort of private provision. All men of substance in a locality would subscribe to a turnpike trust. These were rarely if ever profitable. So these trusts (and most river improvement companies) might best be seen as quasi-public bodies that used social pressure to 'tax' the rich for improvements that would benefit all. See Szostak (1991).

under-employed university graduates. In other words, education is only valuable economically to the extent that the educated are able to apply their human capital produc-
tively. The result may also reflect the simple fact that educational quality is not a
simple function of money spent or even attendance levels.[8] Temple (1999) notes that
these studies also face problems of data, lags, and possible feedback effects.

Easterly makes the same arguments about investment in human capital as he
does about investment in physical capital (chapter 9): human capital is complementary to other proximate causes. He adds an incentive argument: students can
be compelled to attend school but are unlikely to apply themselves if there are few
opportunities to apply this knowledge (This argument neglects the non-economic
value of literacy and numeracy.) Easterly makes an important social network
argument: the poor have limited incentive to gain education because they are
linked to other poor people; education in poor societies may provide little economic advantage if there is little possibility of networking with other educated
people [the Internet may be important here]. Unfortunately, schools are often
poorly staffed and teachers often do not show up. Indeed teaching jobs often reflect government patronage rather than skills or devotion. Studies show that investments in teaching materials have a much higher return than hiring more teachers.

Economic history suggests that education has come to play a very important
role only since the nineteenth century. Even the British Industrial Revolution of
the eighteenth century occurred against a backdrop of widespread illiteracy and
almost no public education. (Even there an elite that was literate and numerate
may have been necessary for many types of innovation.) In the nineteenth century,
though, regions (Scandinavia, parts of Germany, and so on) that developed good
education systems grew much faster than those that did not.

Education has a strong complementarity with technology in the modern world:
most sorts of innovation require education in science or engineering to both create
and adopt. And both generally occur within organizations managed by individuals
with training in the social sciences or business. Easterly (ch.9) recognizes the
complementarity between education and technology, and that the importation of
advanced technology requires some minimum level of skills. Complex technologies often also require an educated workforce that can read instructions, perform
mathematical calculations, and so on. We might thus expect that the value of
education increases (usually) with technological complexity.

---

[8] The problems identified by Easterly in using enrollment data as a proxy for education reflect a
more general problem with quantitative performance indicators. Governments everywhere in the
world have in recent decades introduced such performance indicators. While the desire to
measure the effectiveness of government programs is laudable, the simple fact is that most/all
government services have important qualitative elements. The effects Easterly describes are
common: bureaucrats evaluated in terms of certain indicators focus on achieving those and nothing else: herding students into an empty classroom satisfies the indicators (just as teachers in
developed countries increasingly focus on teaching to standardized tests used to compare
schools). The lesson is obvious but hard to implement: government programs need to be evaluated in qualitative as well as quantitative ways. This can be done by expert panels, though with
some inevitable loss in objectivity.

Education has a variety of positive effects (at least theoretically):

• It increases worker productivity in a variety of settings and ways. Among other things, schools may accustom individuals to boring routine, following instructions, and being punctual.
• Specialized education supports the division of labor.
• Education may develop teamwork skills.
• Education improves the innovation and diffusion capabilities of scientists and entrepreneurs, and improves managerial capabilities (and thus among other things the quality of entrepreneurship). Education may, though, limit innovation, if it celebrates the past in a conservative fashion.
• Education is associated with decreased fertility and increased life expectancy. Both in part reflect learning about health issues. Educated women are more powerful, and likely use this power to restrict fertility.

Debates rage as to what is the best sort of educational system.[9] Many poor countries arguably lavish scarce resources on universities when they might obtain a higher social return to primary or secondary education. In the past the United States followed an egalitarian approach while other countries favored the training of an elite. Recent economic models suggest that these other school systems were shaped by elites in order to preserve elite status (Bertocchi 2006). The latter countries have tended to converge toward the United States, largely as the needs for literacy and numeracy have expanded. If these arguments are correct we could expect support within poor countries for public education to increase as growth proceeds. Social divisions of any sort naturally weaken the move toward universality. While developed and some East European countries provide very equitable access to education, educational inequalities are five times greater in countries such as Egypt, India, Pakistan, and Tunisia.

Kohli (2004, 371) [political scientist] argues that education is important in his case studies: the successful countries had much better educational systems. He recognizes that funding is not the whole story: educational funding is often misallocated in Nigeria. Yet Kohli's approach is to stress the different types of government that encourage education, rather than carefully identify the characteristics of a good system. He suggests that good governance will lead to good education, but this needs to be shown rather than assumed.

What about educational research itself? Do we know how to get the best outcomes from a given expenditure? Lagemann (2000) notes that educational research is and always has been poorly respected by both academics and policy-makers

---

[9] Technical education can be provided publicly, privately, by companies, or through apprenticeships. The move toward mass education changes the relationship between education and technology, but firms may be slow to redesign jobs to allow greater creativity. Little research has been done on a variety of issues: decentralization, educational content (tradeoff between acquisition of information and creativity), diversity of institutions and participants, adult access, and work-based learning (Meeus and Hage, ch. 17).

(232). This perception reinforces poor funding and low quality. It has moved 'away from close interaction with policy and practice and toward excessive quantification and scientism' (xi). Dewey in 1929 had already complained about the gap between theory and practice, and urged more interdisciplinary interaction, more philosophy, and less quantification (due to the importance of quality) (231). The lack of interdisciplinarity meant that research did not keep up with latest theories and methods in social science (234). Early research had a narrow focus on testing and tracking, and ignored group processes in favor of genetic arguments (235). One big problem with educational research is that it ignores context and thus fails for example to look for combined economic/social/geographic explanations of inner city school performance. Much research is both flawed and focused on trivialities (212). School boards and governments often find that the research they need – on whether a program works – has not been done (240). The record is not entirely bleak: there is strong evidence that numeracy and literacy are best mastered in small classes in the early grades, for example. But guidance on what to teach, when, and how is much less precise than it could be, given the size of the educational research establishment.

11.1.4.2 Transportation

Transportation is another area of developed government expenditure with a huge influence on economic growth. Despite its similarity in both respects to education, transportation has received much less attention in the literature.[10] Both the quantity and quality of transport infrastructure are harder to measure – or at least appear harder. Easterly has noted that measures like years of schooling or percentage of children in school can be quite misleading. With respect to roads, it is harder to establish whether a certain road supports wheeled vehicles year round, and whether the network of roads connects key economic areas. The spatial dimension complicates the mathematics in economic models immensely, whereas education can at least potentially be fed directly into aggregate production functions as human capital.

As with education, the sort of transport system necessary to support economic growth has changed over time. Paved highways and air service are now of central importance in developed countries. A century ago it was railroads. A century before that it was water transport (for bulky goods) and year-round gravel roads (for speedy and/or extensive transport). Technological innovation has been important in generating transport improvements throughout the period of modern economic

---

[10] Alfred Marshall, in the eighth edition of his *Principles of Economics,* argued that decreases in transport costs were the major factor in encouraging industrialization (674-5). Mathias (1983) argued that low transport costs were 'a vital condition for economic growth' because they encouraged regional specialization, division of labor, innovation, and economies of scale.

growth.[11] But institutions have also been critical. Road, water, and rail networks can only exist if governments or companies can expropriate land (with compensation), borrow money, and somehow finance continued maintenance.

Szostak (1991a) compared Britain's eighteenth-century transport network with that of France in some detail, and briefly showed how transport infrastructure was poorly developed in all other countries. I argued that Britain's lead over France was primarily due to institutional differences: promoters of British turnpikes, river improvements, and canals could obtain private acts of Parliament that gave them the important rights of incorporation (still rare at the time), eminent domain, to borrow, and to charge tolls (to pay off their debt and provide maintenance). The French government lavished funds on a few main roads, but failed to maintain even those. I then showed how Britain's superiority in transport encouraged both the rise of the modern factory and an increase in the rate of technological innovation. Entrepreneurs considering a factory could rely on delivery of raw materials and access to a wider market. Transport improvements encouraged regional specialization and urbanization, which in turn encouraged both factories and technological innovation. Improved information flows were also of critical importance to innovation (see chapter 9).

Pomeranz (2000, 184) in a book devoted to understanding why (and when) Europe has outperformed China economically discussed transport only rarely. Yet these brief discussions are supportive of the idea that a deficient transport system was at least one important source of Chinese economic backwardness. 'Many Chinese roads do seem to have been quite poor, despite adequate road-building knowledge' (184).[12] In his discussion of the Chinese financial system, he notes that this failed to support transport infrastructure. It seems that the Chinese national and regional governments also failed in this respect well into the nineteenth century. Pomeranz argues that the timber and rice trades were likely hurt by poor transport (185), and more generally that regional specialization [a key characteristic of the British Industrial Revolution] was limited by the deficiencies in the road network (247). Early in the book, he recognizes that Europe had better roads than China (33), but argues that China had superior water transport. In this he celebrates China's two very long rivers (Yellow and Yangtze), and the Grand Canal linking these. But these do not form a national network such as various rivers and canals did in Britain. Pomeranz recognizes that Chinese waterways provided limited access to Chinese coal resources, unlike British waterways (65-6, 184). He also appreciates that it was hard to move goods upstream on the rivers (247).

---

[11] Perez (2002, 14) provides a table listing the (largely transport) infrastructure associated with each technological revolution: turnpikes and canals; railways; steamships and telegraphs; roads and airports; digital communications.

[12] Notably, Japan was in much better shape. 'Although there was a surprising absence of wheeled traffic, early European travelers noted the excellence of the main highways and the extent of internal commerce' (Macpherson 1987, 29; he argues that Japanese urbanization required extensive transport infrastructure.

Sachs (2005, 57) stresses that most of today's poorest countries are landlocked and lack good transport. He talks more generally (59-60) about government failure to provide infrastructure, social services, property rights, and peace. There are often increasing returns to investment in public capital at low levels; he gives examples of how a road passable everywhere or at all seasons is many times better than a road often closed or with very poor sections. The main road from Uganda, Rwanda, and Burundi to the coast is often washed out and is slow at best, and transport costs are thus high (250). Peasants in isolated villages (and nearly half the world's population still resides in villages) have little incentive to increase their output, and manufacturers have limited access to best-practice techniques if it is hard for them to visit the next village or town.

Satellite photographs show a huge difference in the density of transport links between developed and less developed countries (Owen 1983, 6). This reflects a strong empirical correlation between GDP and the level of transport facilities. 'The lack of all-weather access is a prime factor in rural poverty' (Owen, xi). He stresses that movement of passengers should be considered as well as movement in freight (but usually is not) and may be of greater importance. (He talks about labor mobility and access to education; ch. 5) Teachers and doctors often refuse to serve villages without roads. 'Full- scale efforts to improve mobility, applying recent advances in technology and management, could thus be a key to overcoming the hunger and poverty that afflict more than half the people on earth' (17). Increased agricultural output often reflects increased movement of fertilizer (in India the areas with the best roads use more fertilizer). In India industrial firms hold large inventories because of the uncertainty of supply due to poor roads. 'Transportation, as a means to other ends, plays a catalytic role in the performance of all sectors of the economy ... Lack of mobility in low income countries imposes limits on the access to resources, the conduct of industry, the adoption of farming practices, the delivery of education, and the viability of the cities ... nothing can be done to address the multiple causes of poverty without first making the problems accessible and the remedies removable' (129).

Still, we must be careful in our choice of projects: there have been many wasteful transport projects. The complex nature of transport systems in developed countries indicates what is needed in less developed countries. India has at times worried that better roads will hurt the huge publicly-owned railway, but is belatedly financing a national highway network. Unfortunately it has been common for LDC governments to discriminate in favor of railways (Owen, ch. 6). Tariffs on imports limit car ownership and thus demand for good roads that would benefit trucks as well (99); car ownership stimulated road building in the United States (there were already 2.5 million cars in 1916) and Japan (one million in the mid-1950s) (Owen, 131).

To be sure, we would not wish to assert that transport improvements will always have a revolutionary impact on economic growth. It had often been thought that railroads had had a dramatic effect on economic growth in the middle decades of the nineteenth century. Economic historians showed that the direct impact of railroads in terms of cost reductions amounted to only a few percent of GDP in most countries (though in some areas, like parts of the prairies of North America or the Russian steppe, where canals were not a viable alternative, economic development would likely have been delayed until the arrival of internal combustion trucks). I have critiqued these analyses for ignoring dynamic causal linkages (Szostak 1991a): many investment decisions may have rested on this small differential in transport costs – or on the harder-to-measure improvements in speed and reliability associated with railroads.[13] I also with others have argued that the gains from earlier improvements – a decent all-weather road network, and system of navigable waterways – was likely greater than that associated with railroads. Indeed, the small effects found for railroads reflected the fact that roads and waterways could provide low cost transport alternatives.

In the 1960s, aid agencies financed railways in many parts of the world which never became economically viable, in part as the economics of bulk goods transport was shifting toward trucks at that time. Investments in roads would in many countries apparently provide a high return today. This will particularly be the case with respect to isolated villages that presently lack access to the outside world. In some of these cases, dramatic dynamic effects – expansion of agricultural output and development of industry – can be anticipated (though it may be hard to predict which villages will respond in this way). China, India, and several other developing countries have indeed been devoting massive sums to investments in transport (and other sorts of) infrastructure in recent years, and these investments may have played an important role in encouraging growth.

As noted above, empirical analyses in developed countries differ on the value of further transport improvements. Fernald (1999) finds that while road construction in the 1950s and 1960s in the United States had a powerful impact on industrial productivity, the marginal impact is today not particularly large because a good system is already in place. However, as problems of road and rail congestion and infrastructure deterioration emerge in many places, others would argue that there is still a very high return on certain sorts of transport investments in developed countries.

Transport projects have declined as a share of foreign aid. Sadly, given the expense of transport infrastructure, and the financial failure of some attempts to build railways in the 1960s, international aid agencies (excepting the World Bank) do relatively little in the area. The best balance between aid for transport, education, or health will vary by country of course (Sachs, 251-2). But a mix of different types of investment is generally called for (255-6). Foreign investment in infrastructure should also be encouraged in many countries.

---

[13] Freeman and Louca (2001, 35-7) make a similar point. They note that railways soon became a major component of GDP in advanced economies. Simon Ville has argued that in the case of transport social savings calculations suffered not only from their static nature but also ignored the benefits of increased speed, regularity, and reliability of service, and moreover assumed demand to be homogenous.

As with education, it is possible to have users pay for transport services. Nor is this just a theoretical possibility. My own earliest research suggested that the eighteenth century English Industrial Revolution was largely triggered by previous transport improvements and these were privately financed and paid for.[14] Owen (ch. 6) encourages the use of user fees, and especially tolls to ensure roads are built where most needed, and then maintained. Japan devoted much effort to toll highways in the 1950s; these soon became self-financing; South Korea has followed a similar strategy (111-3). There are successful toll roads in several Asian and Latin American countries. Charging tolls is not ideal. Some individuals who would otherwise benefit from traveling will not do so because the toll is too high. And if a merchant decides not to visit a remote village because of a toll, all those in the village who would have wished to buy the merchant's wares suffer as well. Yet if alternative sources of financing are not available, a toll road is much better than no road.[15] As with education, the debate in developed countries has largely been decided in favor of public provision: though toll roads and bridges exist in many jurisdictions, free and useful alternatives are usually provided.

11.1.6 Government Intent

Economists who favor market solutions will generally offer two main arguments against government provision of services. First, they will note that taxation imposes its own external costs (distortions, incentive effects), and that these may outweigh the limitations associated with private provision of public goods. The fact that taxation is not empirically correlated with growth (see above) suggests that this argument may be overstated. Second they will note that governments do not always spend funds wisely. Roads especially, but also schools and hospitals are often built in locations determined by political convenience rather than economic desirability. If individuals were paying directly for these services, providers would face a more direct incentive to provide them where most needed (though again the poorest would receive few services).

11.1.6.1 Motives

One of the naïve assumptions of early postwar development policy advice was that Third World governments would naturally have economic growth as their primary goal. How could one govern in an environment of poverty without devoting

---

[14] These investments are best seen as quasi-public. See note 7.

[15] India is contemplating hiring the poorest to work on infrastructure projects. Such 'food for work' schemes have been tried in the past, but often fail because of corruption. If the amount of money transferred to local governments is public knowledge the poor might monitor corruption.

every ounce of energy to alleviating that poverty? Sadly, Third World politicians proved to be shockingly self-interested at times. Economic historians should not have been surprised by this outcome. As argued by Jones (2002), governments throughout human history have actively limited economic growth by failing to protect property rights and restricting the potentially destabilizing effects of innovation or trade.[16] Of course, the world has changed in one important respect – before 1800 the very idea of sustained and rapid growth was hardly imagined and thus governments rarely even considered the costs of their policies in this regard. The point to stress here is that even governments aware of the possibilities of growth may not actively encourage this.

Why do governments act against growth? The obvious answer is that other goals intervene: defence, redistribution, environment, art, corruption; self-preservation. In some cases, elite groups may even derive a direct benefit from the poverty of others. The poor may provide less of a threat to their political power than would a rising middle class. Moreover, as we saw in chapter 1, happiness seems to depend on one's relative income, and thus policies that keep others poor may seem advantageous.

11.1.6.2 Corruption

The World Bank Institute estimates that corruption (the misuse of public office for private gain relative to some legal standard) absorbs about $3 trillion annually, or 3 percent of world GDP. In some countries the numbers are horrific: in Zaire, the Philippines, and Indonesia, deposed dictators had assets in the billions. The Turkish earthquake of 2004 was unnecessarily severe because contractors had bribed officials to evade building codes. Embezzlement of government funds in Angola amounts to at least three times the humanitarian aid received in 2001 (Svensson 2005).

There are various measures of corruption by nation, compiled from business surveys, institutional expert evaluations, and broad-based surveys (especially the UN survey on crime which asks about bribe incidence). These different measures are highly correlated (Svensson 2005) – though there is a danger that this may for some countries reflect a common misperception that poor countries are necessarily

---

[16] One persuasive argument for the relative economic success of Europe over the last millennia is political fragmentation (though this argument says nothing about the stagnation of fragmented India). Whereas the Chinese emperor could and did unilaterally ban trade or prohibit innovation, European governments were locked in military competition with each other. They thus had to worry that acts and actors banned in their realms might pop up elsewhere to their detriment. European governments did not consciously pursue economic growth but found it useful to support/allow innovation. And they found it useful to provide credible commitments to merchants in order to attract trade (and thus tax revenue). Indeed, European monarchs could make credible commitments to foreign traders precisely because they feared that these could take their business elsewhere; Chinese emperors could not inspire such confidence in their own merchants because nothing prevented them from becoming confiscatory at some point.

corrupt.[17] With few exceptions, the most corrupt countries are the poorest. Corruption is also correlated with low education (because a quality bureaucracy, and legal proceedings against corruption, requires literate and educated officials). It is correlated with lack of freedom of the press. It is correlated with the degree of government regulation. This might be a spurious correlation, given that corruption is measured by perceptions, though it likely captures opportunities for corruption. Svensson hypothesizes that culture, colonial history, and type/degree of democracy may also matter, but these connections have not been established empirically.

Is corruption negatively correlated with growth? Easterly argues for a strong correlation, but Svensson maintains that this is not so (though many think it); the correlation is not statistically significant. Yet this result largely reflects a couple of outliers such as China and Indonesia where rapid growth has occurred despite widespread corruption. There is a host of micro-level evidence on the costs in terms of public service provision and incentives to entrepreneurs. One could expect that corruption siphons funds from public services and discourages private investment. (Svensson reports on one school funding initiative in which only 20 percent of the funds reached the schools; corruption in that country accounted for 8 percent of costs of firms surveyed, and bribes seemed to be extorted according to a sense of the firm's ability to pay). Entrepreneurs may also choose costly forms of investment that allow them to flee future increases in bribes. And talent is diverted from productive use to bribe evasion. On the other hand, low levels of corruption might be seen in a more positive light: as an informal form of 'taxation' whereby civil servants in a poor society are enabled to earn a living (but there is a high transaction cost given that the size of a necessary bribe is not known, and corrupt promises are unenforceable in court). It can also be hoped that the most efficient firms are best able to pay bribes.

It could be that the connection between corruption and growth would appear stronger empirically if different types of corruption and their effects were identified. Easterly (239), for example, hypothesizes that centralized corruption (that is, corruption directed from the top) may be less harmful than decentralized corruption (where each bureaucrat tries to extort as much as possible). This argument reflects his treatment of social divisions more generally (chapter 8). Centralized corruption will not wish to choke off growth, but decentralized agents will ignore the effect of their actions on growth.

How should corruption be fought? The evidence on whether higher wages reduce corruption is mixed. Theoretically this result is most/only likely if there is punishment such as job loss for taking bribes. Replacing nepotism with merit in the bureaucracy may be more important. Easterly urges governments to reduce opportunities for corruption by withdrawing harmful regulations such as foreign exchange restrictions, reducing red tape, and enhancing the rule of law (see

---

[17] In particular, business people's subjective evaluations of corruption may be contaminated by their more general sense of how profitable it is to invest in a particular country (a measure one might expect to be correlated with growth).

chapter 7). Litigation is one avenue for fighting corruption in some countries. Increased public access to information is another: in Uganda when the government publicized disbursement data so that local people knew how much was allocated to their district schools received 80 percent of the funds. But locals need to organize against corruption, and information access is less useful with more complicated government programs. In some cases non-corrupt international firms can be hired (this is done by over 50 Less Developed Countries; see Svensson 2005).

The World Bank has in recent years threatened to withhold funds from countries that fail to fight corruption. Sachs (2005) worries that concerns regarding corruption provide too easy an excuse not to help. The challenge in such a policy is to identify the costs and benefits: how corrupt is a country?;[18] how easily can it reduce corruption?; are there mechanisms for ensuring that foreign aid reaches people in need despite corruption? It should be remembered that the present developed countries are not flawlessly non-corrupt today, and were more corrupt when poor. It makes sense to oppose corruption but not to hold countries to an unattainable standard.

11.2 The Developmental State

As we saw when discussing trade in chapter 6, economists tend to focus on identifying the best policies, while sociologists and political scientists are more likely to worry about whether governments have the capability to properly administer any policy. The economic historian Eric Jones has also suggested that we should just identify good policies and not worry why some countries have adopted these. But if a policy requires some discretion by politicians or bureaucrats then it will only work if these are guided by culture/nationalism to pursue growth rather than self-interest. In chapter 7 we saw that institutions depend on supportive cultural attitudes. This suggests that governments in some countries will be able to support institutions that would not succeed elsewhere. The literature on 'the developmental state' in political science and sociology explores the conditions under which a government is able to successfully encourage economic growth. To be sure, this literature tends to assume that a wide range of governmental interventions in the economy are beneficial. But its insights on what makes a government effective can potentially be integrated with a more nuanced appreciation of the best role for government.

---

[18] The World Bank publishes governance indicators: these address not just corruption but rule of law, voice, accountability, and other characteristics of governance. These indicators receive media attention and are used by the United States and other countries in aid allocations. But the data base is weak and the (arbitrary) weighting of different elements differs across time and place.

11.2.1 The Idea of the Developmental State

Political scientists engaged questions of economic development little in the early postwar period when (development) economists themselves encouraged state intervention. But as economists moved toward discouraging an active state role, political scientists reacted. Much of this research focused on East Asia and suggested that countries there had actively encouraged development, and in particular had fostered certain industries by both providing incentives and encouraging cooperation between state and private enterprises (Kohli 2002, 109-11). Chalmers Johnson coined the term 'developmental state' in 1982 in a study of the government agency MITI in Japan. The term has since become 'a shorthand for the seamless web of political, bureaucratic, and moneyed influences that structures life in capitalist Northeast Asia' (Woo-Cummings1999, 1). This is, of course, a vague definition that cries out for unpacking.[19] In practice most scholars focus on the nature of bureaucracy and/or political leadership, and how this is shaped by culture. Johnson had stressed the role that nationalism and a desire to catch up to the West (energized by wartime experiences and fear of future hostilities) played in allowing the government to focus on growth. The idea of the developmental state has since been applied to other Asian countries.

The World Bank and many economists have disagreed that the state played such a central role in economic development. They argue that the private market played a greater role in Japanese credit allocation than the state, that the sectors which the state promoted did no better than others, that the bureaucracy was responsive to legislative direction, and that at a global level industrial policy did more harm than good. Woo-Cummings appreciates that some of the policies hailed by Johnson were problematic: channeling funds to preferred firms invited cronyism, and in some cases led to over-expansion and government bailouts (12). It important to appreciate that France, India, and many Latin American countries also had nationalism and state intervention, but achieved much less impressive results. Yet if it is recognized that governments have any valuable role to play in economic growth, then arguments for the developmental state still have merit. And some of the policies stressed by Johnson, such as restraining worker wage demands, or keeping interest rates low, might be approved by even market-oriented scholars.

Kohli (2002) like Johnson celebrates states for a host of policies, not all of which may have in fact encouraged growth; certainly most economists would disdain some of them. Providing public infrastructure is generally a good idea, but directing credit to desired firms and sectors is a dangerous policy (though these governments were careful to reward only firms that were increasing productivity), as is allowing inflation to shift resources from agriculture to industry. Repressing

---

[19] Other authors use equally vague terms such as 'governed independence', 'governing the market', and 'dependent development' to define a particular pattern of government-business interaction. (Woo-Cummings 1999, 15).

labor demands can have both good effects (if profits are re-invested) and bad effects (as consumer demand is restrained). The value of tariffs and export subsidies is hotly debated (see chapter 6). Care must be taken not to assume that simply because a state wishes to pursue growth that every policy it pursues acts to achieve that goal. We would generally not attribute such sagacity to our own governments, and so should be wary of bestowing such praise on governments of other countries. Still, Kohli's argument that no state has experienced rapid growth while doing nothing fits with our discussion of the role of the state above, and suggests that at least some of these policies likely were important. Kohli appreciates that regressions by others find little (positive or negative) correlation between the amount of intervention and growth. Kohli attributes this to the fact that the quality of intervention is more important (377). This argument needs to be coupled with an appreciation that some types of intervention are better than others.

Kohli argues that private investors need help in dealing with capital scarcity, technological backwardness, rigidities in labor markets, and in order to confront the power of multinationals and foreign producers (Kohli, 377-8) Investors, he says, feel threatened by laissez-faire economic policies. Economists are generally skeptical of arguments that the state needs to play a guiding role in private investment. Yet endogenous growth theory in stressing increasing returns, spillovers, and complementarities provides an opening for such an analysis. Since the profit on any one investment depends on whether complementary investments are undertaken, governments can reduce uncertainty by credibly supporting investment in certain areas – the economist Rodrik has argued that this is what happened in Taiwan and South Korea (Vartiainen 206-7).[20] But it is crucial that the state be able and willing to discipline underachieving firms (this is most easily done when the country faces an external threat; Vartiainen, 219).

Economists, though often suspicious of the motives of politicians and bureaucrats, should be open to cultural and especially institutional innovations that cause these to try to encourage growth. Bureaucracies in East Asia tend to be meritocratic, while the Brazilian bureaucracy replaces tens of thousands of bureaucrats during regime changes. Japanese bureaucrats are selected by examination and only a dozen or so are changed with regime change. They thus have considerable autonomy. But the same might be said of India (Woo-Cummings, 13-14). Nor are East Asian governments without flaws. Crony capitalism is a reality, and Japan, South Korea, and other countries have been hit by scandals as huge sums moved both from bureaucracy to business but also from business to politicians (which suggests that bureaucrats could be interfered with by politicians). Businesses in both countries sought oligopolistic positions across a range of industries, and focused on market share. Woo-Cummings takes pains to distinguish these practices

---

[20] Lipsey (2001, 192-3) argues that while no industrial policy is preferable to bad policy, some good policies can be even better. While history is littered with failures, it also has many examples of success. He is skeptical of grand efforts to transform entire societies; these generally fail. But efforts to evaluate and accentuate a country's strengths are more likely to succeed.

from indiscriminate crony capitalism in Southeast Asia where the government was less focused on growth. But then it is not clear exactly how this difference was instantiated or how Southeast Asia later became growth oriented.

11.2.2 The Essence of the Developmental State

Kohli (2004, 2) concludes from his inductive comparative analysis of South Korea, Nigeria, India, and Brazil that the creation of effective states has generally preceded the 'emergence of industrializing economies'. He notes that comparisons across Less Developed Countries to identify best government attributes only became possible from the 1970s as differences in economic performance became obvious. Modernization and dependency theorists had previously focused on differences between poor and rich countries (2004, 5). There is still much to be done, therefore, in identifying precisely the key elements of success.

Evans, a sociologist, energized this literature in 1995. 'Sterile debates about "how much" states intervene have to be replaced with arguments about different kinds of involvement and their effects' (Evans 1995, 10). Developmental states need a meritocratic and professional bureaucracy. This bureaucracy needs to be embedded in society in order to obtain relevant information and ensure appropriate policy responses, but autonomous enough not to be captured by private interests (12). While ties to industrial capitalists are of greatest importance in the short run, the legitimacy of government will be questioned in the longer run (as these firms succeed) unless ties with labor and other groups are forged as well (17). This suspicion may appear early and derail developmental efforts, especially if the bureaucracy is corrupt.[21]

Scott (1998) provides a useful corrective to the idea that states will pursue enlightened policies. States everywhere wish to understand the societies they govern and naturally simplify in order to do so: traditional and complex land tenure systems are reduced to some standard form that is legally enforced [though of course there may be more purely economic motives for such changes]. Sometimes society does not change in response to the state's description of it, and then state policies can be wildly inappropriate. The worst disasters occur when a state is confident of its ability to undertake social engineering, has authoritarian powers, and does not face a civil society that actively protests its actions (4-5). Scott emphasizes the need to seriously engage local knowledge. By this logic there are likely severe limits to what states can know about any complex social process. And thus the best policy involves 'muddling through': trying reforms, judging how they work, and trying more, but never imagining one has the entire blueprint for success (327-8). One should plan on surprises, innovation, and reversibility

---

[21] Evans employed a comparative case study approach, reading government reports and interviewing bureaucrats in several countries.

(345). It is not clear that Asian governments were not often guilty of thinking they were too clever, but their close ties with business and focus on increased productivity and exports may have encouraged the sort of experimentation and policy revision that Scott would advocate.

Political scientists have explained sub-Saharan African failures not in terms of the type of intervention itself but the perversion of intervention by 'neo-patrimonial' elites so that these policies benefited elites rather than the wider society (Kohli 2002, 111). This tendency in turn has been attributed to the residue of colonialism, rapid population growth, and ethnic divisions (2002, 112). Many political scientists have focused on the nature of bureaucracy and argued [like Evans] that a professional and politically independent bureaucracy that cooperates with business is critical to success (2002, 112-3). Phrases like 'embedded autonomy' celebrate the state-business links, but also the insulation of the bureaucratic elite to minimize corruption (Kohli 2004, 7). But Kohli urges a complementary emphasis on the nature of governance and the motives of government leaders.

India is often seen as a failed developmental state. It too had a professional bureaucracy (with examinations for entry and promotion by merit), and a government that pursued economic development – though perhaps not as exclusively as was the case in East Asia. One should not be too harsh: India's growth rates in the 1950s and 1960s were higher than during colonial days (despite the disruption of partition) and comparable to many Latin American countries (without the fluctuations) and developed countries; they just look bad relative to East Asia. Moreover, some Indian states had very high growth rates. Nevertheless, the move toward liberalization in recent decades reflects a widespread belief that India had previously made some mistakes: too much red tape, too little openness to the world or pursuit of exports, and too little effort to ensure that only companies improving productivity were rewarded. There was also a great deal of low-level corruption (though not the high level scandals of Japan). Ironically, equity was a key governmental goal but the government was unable to achieve land reform or other sorts of redistribution as did East Asia. Nevertheless a fear of the side effects of capitalism encouraged state enterprise. A concern with self-reliance turned India from foreign trade and foreign investment. The government failed to provide public infrastructure (Herring 1999). Scholars can still debate whether India was hampered more by bad policies or a failure of government capability.

The developmental state approach can be criticized for too-often assuming that states are all-knowing and all-powerful, and thus ignoring the constraints exerted by other phenomena (Kohli 2002, 115). And Kohli worries that scholars have rejected dependency theory too thoroughly and could usefully consider the global forces acting on political elites. These arguments fit well with the general approach of this book: we can appreciate the effects of developmental states without ignoring other influences on both states and growth.

Rational choice scholars critique the developmental state literature for being atheoretical, methodologically flawed because it relies on too few cases, and noncumulative; Kohli responds that the field is cumulative and theoretical: it just differs in pursuing a less generalizable sort of theory, but also does not worry as much about establishing detailed microfoundations for theoretical arguments (2002, 114-5). As usual, there is some truth on both sides: more careful causal argumentation and a wider array of cases would be useful, but the case study approach in general has considerable merit in investigating how government leaders and bureaucrats behave.

11.2.3 Sources of the Developmental State

While it has usefully challenged economic orthodoxy, 'The statist literature on economic growth can be criticized for having a weak underlying theory, for focusing too much on bureaucratic and not on political variables, and for not asking why some regions of the developing world have ended up with developmental states, and others with predatory states' (Kohli 2002, 113-4). Kohli departs from the statist literature in two ways – by asking also how effective states emerge, and by looking beyond bureaucratic capability to the exercise of power by leaders. Kohli identifies three types of states (but is unhappy with his categorization): The first is neo-patrimonial in which personalistic leaders are not bound by norms or institutions, and office-holders see offices as opportunity for personal gain; this is coupled with poor-quality and corrupt bureaucracy. Such states at best pretend to pursue development, and pervert any development policies toward personal gain. Cohesive-capitalist states have several characteristics: growth is pursued as a priority (tied to national security), governments have close ties to business and control of labor (and thus are often authoritarian in political structure), and there is an effective bureaucracy. The third in-between category is fragmented-multiclass states: here there is a legitimate government and bureaucracy, and leaders need public support, but public authority rests on a broader class alliance and thus consensus on how to move forward is difficult to achieve; growth must thus compete with other priorities (7-11). Political competition limits the fragmented state's ability to raise taxes, cooperate with business, and restrain labor demands.

While categorization is an important step in scholarly analysis these categories lump together many elements without (at least yet) telling us what the connections between these are. Kohli notes that the second category has some similarities with fascism, and the 'fragmented' state seems more democratic, so we to some extent slide into the old argument that repressive states can develop faster. We need analysis at a more disaggregated level. We also need to understand why the other goals of the fragmented state are not compatible with growth. After all, Kohli himself (367) appreciates that states should also pursue as part of a development strategy goals such as poverty reduction, civil liberties, supporting agricultural advance, and allowing people to lead meaningful lives. Kohli recognizes that his categories are ideal types never precisely observed, and that comparative analysis must be performed in terms of more specific characteristics such as leadership goals, degree of centralization of public authority, downward penetration of public authority, 'political mobilization of the mobilized political society', scope of state intervention, and bureaucratic quality (12). Unfortunately, some of these characteristics seem pretty vague too.

How did different state types emerge? Kohli first notes that institutions usually evolve slowly through time, and thus we must pursue historical analysis. He stresses three key historical elements: experience of colonialism, nationalist movements, and role of the armed forces. Yet only in a few cases did the armed forces and especially nationalist movements change institutions inherited from colonialism dramatically. Thus colonial experience looms large. Colonial powers pursued different ideologies and goals in different places, and thus left behind the three different structures he has described above. Japan established a bureaucracy like its own in Korea, while the British in Nigeria ruled through local leaders. Latin America has had more time to recover from colonialism, but nevertheless some effects on institutions can still be seen (16-20). Surely, though, countries are not victims of their colonial history forever? Again we need to understand the mechanisms of the developmental state in more detail before we can suggest how other states might mimic its achievements.

11.2.4 Summing Up

Pempel (1999) thinks the idea of the developmental state has been useful in four ways: in stressing (though often excessively) political influences on growth, recognizing path dependence and the existence of multiple paths to success, noting (sometimes) that the state needs to pay heed to international market forces, and by providing a more optimistic outlook than dependency, modernization, or world systems theories, and many cultural arguments (140-4). It also has several weaknesses: it exaggerates the role and independence of bureaucracies, it does not tell us how the bureaucracy sets its goals or how/why these reflect national interest, does not place bureaucratic actions in context, and does not pay enough attention to the international conditions that the state reacts to (144-7). Pempel also lists four puzzles that remain unresolved: that the three Asian Tiger countries are quite different institutionally and have followed quite different strategies (149-52); these institutions and strategies changed in important ways through time (152-4), all three countries were big recipients of foreign aid – and thus there is an alternative causal mechanism that should not be ignored (155); and all three countries have managed to achieve growth with very equal income distributions – not what we would expect from top-down management (155).[22] This last point deserves

---

[22] Then he identifies several similarities: strong states; elimination of a landowning elite, meritocracy; dedication to growth but suspicious of big states; manipulate but respect market; limits to foreign direct investment, and close links to the United States (160); weak labor movements (167); ethnic homogeneity (168); good educational systems for decades and that emphasize tech-

emphasis given the stress placed by Kohli and others on how these states repressed labor demands: it may be important to distinguish the avoidance of labor strife (which can be very good for economic growth) from favoring profits over wages (a policy with both economic and political risks). Labor unrest can be an important source of uncertainty, so states can encourage investment by repressing labor conflict (Vartiainen 1999, 210).[23]

The literature on the developmental state can be seen as a substitute for the economist's stress on market solutions. Indeed, in the last two decades of the twentieth century scholarly debate often polarized around neo-liberal and statist perspectives. Kohli proposes a further act of integration: statist approaches are generally anti-market but one should see how states actively reinforce markets. Earlier in this chapter it was suggested that government intervention be evaluated on a case by case basis. The literature on the developmental state suggests that some governments may be able to pursue certain strategies that are unavailable to countries with a different cultural or institutional inheritance. We need a more nuanced understanding of which strategies have worked best for developmental states. We might then wonder if there are other workable strategies for countries with different culture or institutions.

To sum up, then, the literature on developmental states, while flawed, guides scholars to pay more attention to how and why states pursue policies that may encourage economic growth. And it guides us to look at both institutional inheritance and cultural attitudes in order to explain why some states are more willing and able to pursue growth. It often assumes that all observed policies were beneficial. These policies should neither be assumed to be good or bad but subjected to careful interdisciplinary analysis. And the literature generally emphasizes political influences on growth to the exclusion of other influences. These political influences can be appreciated as complementary to the variety of other causal forces examined in this book.

---

nical and business education, and educate girls (169); political dominance of one party (171). They rewarded successful exporters and penalized unsuccessful (173). Each had privileged access to the American market, which was for each by far the biggest export market; the United States did not insist on reciprocity until recently for strategic reasons (178).

[23] More generally only the state can suppress distributional conflicts so that agents can focus on growth.

12 Reflections on the Results of Integration

Several distinct sorts of reflection are called for. All are often eschewed by researchers anxious to publish their results as quickly as possible. In some ways interdisciplinary analysis should be inherently reflective: the interdisciplinarian has to ask what theories and methods and phenomena and disciplines to engage, and it is hard to perform such steps without thinking a little bit about why certain choices are made. It may thus be that an explicitly reflective step is *less* needed in integrative research than in specialized research. However, if interdisciplinarians will be successful in gaining the attention of specialized researchers they may have to be *more* reflective: about how to enter the specialized scholarly discourse in an interesting and persuasive manner, and thus how to address those elements of their own research that may cause concern among the intended audience.

12.1 Reflect on One's Own Biases

This step should be mandatory. A key guiding principle of interdisciplinary analysis is that no piece of scholarly research is perfect. If we accept that no scholarly method can guide a researcher flawlessly toward insight, then it follows that scholarly results may reflect researcher biases. This does not mean that results only reflect such biases, as some in the field of science studies have claimed. But it does mean that one way of evaluating the insights generated by research is to interrogate researcher biases. Since researchers have a unique insight into their own thought processes, they have a valuable role to play here. And thus an exercise such as the present one – where authors reflect on their own biases – should be performed as a matter of course. Of course researchers may be biased in their assessment of their own biases. Given the human tendency to mislead ourselves about our faults, others may also usefully identify researcher biases. But again the researcher has a unique insight into their own psychology, and can thus at the very least provide a starting point for readers as they reflect upon possible authorial biases. One powerful means of limiting authorial bias in reflecting on their own biases is to require the author to consult a lengthy list of potential biases. Authors may not consciously admit the possibility of certain biases unless guided to reflect upon them.

What might my own biases be? As should be clear by now, I believe in theoretical and methodological flexibility. I may thus be biased toward seeing some good in all approaches. Indeed, I do suspect that any idea pursued at length by some academic community must have some kernel of truth in it. But this need not prevent skepticism: I can appreciate that those who thought the world was flat were misguided while appreciating the value of the ways they amassed evidence in support of their hypothesis. I can and have thus disagreed with insights from many disciplines in this book.

Still, I can imagine that disciplinarians in reading this book – and perhaps especially my fellow economists – will readily imagine that I have been too harsh with respect to their discipline and too lenient in my treatment of others. And surely some of them will be right (but hopefully not to a considerable degree), though I know not which. At the same time some interdisciplinarians may worry that I have under-estimated the degree of conflict and/or terminological confusion across disciplines. I have perhaps been too eager to assume that I could translate disciplinary insights into common terminology. I was surprised but not at all displeased by the number of times that I was able to treat insights from different disciplines as complements in this book.

As for more specific biases (this list draws on the classification of biases in Szostak 2004):

- *Limitations of understanding:* The first source of bias a researcher should engage stems from the simple fact that all humans have limited perceptual and cognitive capabilities. As noted at the outset I could hardly be expected to have practitioner-level understanding of every theory and method covered in these pages. But this has not proven necessary. One can gain a very good understanding of the insights provided without being able to produce them. Of course a greater mastery would be necessary in order to pursue some of the further lines of inquiry I have suggested.

- *Responding to incentives:* Researchers may ask questions and even derive results that are guided by the incentive structure within their academic community. For better or worse, I have largely ignored academic incentives in my career. I have followed my curiosity wherever it led – and it has taken me on a wild ride through methodology (both economic and historical), interdisciplinary theory, ethics, policy analysis, sociology, information science, and beyond – and I have worried about publication later. I was urged early in my career to write what other economists wrote (articles full of equations) but the questions that interested me called for books full of words. This *hubris* has guided me down avenues that a more cautious scholar would have ignored. But it likely has had a cost in that I have paid less attention to persuasion and networking than I might have. I have had to consciously tailor my ideas to a variety of distinct audiences in the past, and thus hopefully have developed some skills in this respect (which the disciplinarian who has subconsciously absorbed the preferences of one academic community may lack), but have tended in my research to be more excited about convincing myself than about convincing others. For readers of this book, my bias has the advantage that I am generally willing to let my arguments stand on their own merits without a lot of rhetorical embellishment. For those who like to be led toward some artificially enhanced truth this may prove a source of frustration.

- *Historical Situatedness.* Despite my iconoclasm, I am, like any scholar, a prisoner of my times and especially of the scholarly debates in which I participate. All scholars (should) aspire to speak eternal truths, but all of us choose our questions and tailor our answers to fit the context of our conversations with others. This is perhaps most obvious in verbal interactions at conferences, but published work always somehow places one's research in the context of recent research by others. The fact that I participate in multiple scholarly communities may limit this source of bias, or may instead generate a congeries of conflicting biases. My involvement with the Association for Integrative Studies likely exerts the dominant influence on this work: I have long participated in discussions about how best to perform interdisciplinary research. These discussions have been guided by a belief that there is a best way, though this must be very flexible. Other scholarly communities (and even some in AIS) would shudder at the very thought of identifying best practices, especially for interdisciplinary scholarship. But I believe that one can have both structure and freedom, and that interdisciplinary studies needs some structure in order to dissuade scholars from superficial forms of interdisciplinary analysis. My path to self-conscious interdisciplinarity passed through the field of economic methodology where I reinforced my belief that there was no one best theory or method. This pluralism is, as noted elsewhere, the dominant but not unanimous belief in the field of economic methodology (and in philosophy of science) but not in the wider discipline of economics or in some other social sciences. My original field of economic history encourages greater theoretical and methodological flexibility than the economics mainstream. But at the time I earned my PhD in 1985 it very much stressed models and statistical analysis. I reacted against this narrowness, and fortunately for me the field proved just flexible enough in those early days of my career for me to survive. My acquaintance with the field of science studies has occurred at a time when the ideas outlined above – that scholarly results reflect some combination of the influence of scholarly biases and of external reality – had become current in the field. I would have found the field much more frustrating in earlier decades when first one and then the other was emphasized.
- *Institutional Home:* I teach in an economics department. As the only economic historian that we have these days (we need another, I keep saying), I largely get to teach only courses that interest me on economic growth and economic history. During a term as Associate Dean I created a couple of courses about interdisciplinarity in the Faculty of Arts that I also occasionally teach. Career and increment decisions are made at the faculty [college] level in my university, and thus it was possible to write without fear of penalty works that look more like what historians or sociologists do than what economists do. While my department cares about its place in international rankings that generally privilege a rather narrow type of economic publication, there are not yet any strong financial incentives in place in this direction (unlike for example the research assessment exercises of British universities). I thus face less pressure to conform

than most academics. Nevertheless I suspect I am still in many ways an economist in my outlook on life. I may, in particular, despite my efforts to classify theory types, still tend toward methodological individualism in my thought processes. I have striven to overcome such a bias in this book: some readers may think I have not striven hard enough, while some others may fear that I have striven too hard. Likewise, while I devote a whole chapter to emergent properties, I am undoubtedly more comfortable with well-defined causal arguments: my suspicion of the importance of emergent properties in the area of culture may (though I do not think so) reflect in part this inclination.

12.2 Reflect on Steps Omitted

Each of the twelve steps outlined in the introductory chapter has been performed in some way in this book. The most glaring deficiency noted along the way has been in step 4. The literature that could have been consulted is simply vast. I have described in some detail in chapter 4 itself the limitations of my search strategy. I can confess here that I likely could have been more systematic in my approach. At the same time there is some considerable value in practices such as randomly browsing the stacks, or allowing my own curiosity to guide me down particular avenues. I hope to have identified most of the relevant literatures (and their key strengths and weaknesses). I will confess again to the likelihood that I have missed many minority critiques within disciplines. I would think that this would be the main lacunae to be addressed in future research.

Step 11 will be performed very briefly in the next chapter. But this is not necessarily problematic. The focus here has been to integrate the existing literature. Interdisciplinary research, it has been argued, can proceed as normal science. That is, by following best-practice strategies, interdisciplinary researchers can build cumulatively on the works of others just as specialized researchers (ideally) do. If so, then it is no bad thing that the insights generated by one scholar be tested by others.

12.3 Reflect on the Weaknesses of the Theories and Methods Used in One's Comprehensive Vision

Given the complexity of the vision, and the range of theories and methods embraced, I can do little more than point back toward the analyses in chapters 3 and 6 through 11. No theory or method has escaped unscathed from the analysis in this book. As noted above, the author may be biased toward believing that there is some good and some bad in every theory and every method encountered.

13 Possible Tests of the Results of Integration

13.1 Empirical Tests

This book itself has been a test of the validity and usefulness of the 12-step process of interdisciplinary analysis. The next chapter will review in some detail the value of each step in that process. It will argue in particular that affirmative answers should be given to the following sorts of questions:

- Do we gain insight by looking at more phenomena than any one discipline generally encompasses?
- Do we gain insight by looking at more theories than any one discipline generally encompasses?
- Do we gain insight by looking at more methods than any one discipline generally encompasses?

This chapter will focus instead on how to test the various insights regarding economic growth derived in the preceding chapters. The analysis of preceding chapters has been pursued primarily along different causal links – but with attention as necessary to emergent properties. The book has not created some overarching grand theory or model, and has indeed argued that such an outcome is unlikely and probably undesirable. The results must thus for the most part be tested in pieces rather than in their entirety.

One of the key arguments of chapter 3 was that each theory surveyed has an as-yet-poorly-identified range of applicability. That is, each theory sheds useful light on some aspects of the economic growth process but not on others. Yet the scholarly urge toward over-generalization has meant that theories are often judged to be everywhere right or everywhere wrong. Theories should instead be tested in a very context-specific manner: does the particular theory shed light on a particular causal link?

An even more egregious error in standard scholarly practice is that theories are rarely explicitly tested against an alternative. It is generally easier to test a theory against no alternative – does the theory give us better insight than no theory at all? – and such tests are not totally valueless. But a much better test asks whether a particular theory explains some aspect of a causal relationship better than an alternative theory. If theory A seems to provide some sort of insight in the first sort of test, but it turns out that theory B explains everything captured by A and more (and/or seems to provide a more plausible explanation), then we should be wary of attributing any importance to theory A.

A more likely result is that theory A will explain some things better than theory B but not others. Even along a particular causal link, then, we should generally not search for the one best theory but rather for an amalgam of theories with overlapping explanatory power. In testing the various arguments highlighted in this book, then, the goal should not generally be to see whether particular insights were 'right' but whether they have been accorded too little or too much emphasis. Such a test may seem both more difficult and more arbitrary. Again, though, no method or piece of scholarly research is perfect, and thus no test of any hypothesis is perfect. Scholarly judgment always has to be exercised in determining how important a particular argument is.

One reason that theories are rarely tested against each other is that most scholars are intimately familiar with one theory (or at least one type of theory). The rewards for over-specialization in academia militate against the mastery of a wide range of theory. Interdisciplinarians may thus have to play an important role in testing one theory against another (though I would stress that this sort of test should characterize good disciplinary research as well). The discussion of the essence of different theories in chapter 3 provides a starting point from which scholars could identify the most promising theories to test against each other.

The next point to stress is that each method is biased toward the examination of certain theories. A test of one theory against another that relies upon only one method will almost certainly be biased. Multiple methods should be employed. If these generate different results, scholarly judgment needs to be exercised in choosing among the theories tested. Again, a likely result is that each theory has something to contribute to our understanding. And thus 'choosing' is in a sense a misnomer: the goal is generally to identify both the range of applicability and importance along each causal link of each theory. Economists may well survey the wealth of field work on the effects of culture, and think that it is only useful as a source of conjectures to test statistically. But statistical analysis is hardly foolproof, especially for variables that are hard to quantify.[1] The most powerful insights reported in this book – such as our nuanced understanding of the course of institutional change – reflect the results of a variety of methods.

13.2 A Holistic Test in Application

The only 'test' of the entire package of insights contained in this book occurs in the policy arena. Does a package of link-specific and nuanced analyses aid policy-makers? An important minority of economists – Sachs, Rodrik, and Easterly among them – have stressed the importance of tailoring policy advice to the particular circumstances of a country. They have appreciated that the growth process

---

[1] Bill Newell has argued that interdisciplinary analysis is best suited to complex issues, and these will involve non-linear relationships among some variables. Standard statistical analyses often fail to capture threshold effects (unless these are looked for) or cases where a small change sometimes results in a huge impact.

is complicated, and thus that different countries (and at different times) face different barriers and opportunities. The contribution of this book is to:

- Organize these diverse understandings around an exhaustive set of causal links (and emergent properties).
- Draw on the insights of diverse disciplines in outlining a more holistic and nuanced understanding of each link.
- Show how different theories and methods can be seen as complements rather than substitutes, and thus how different insights can be integrated.

Given the complexity of the growth process, it is easy for the most well-intentioned policy-maker to err. The most common sort of error is to neglect possible negative side-effects of any policy. Interdisciplinary analysis naturally tends to highlight the potential weaknesses of each theory or disciplinary perspective. Attention to the full range of causal relationships should further reduce the probability of this type of error. So too should an appreciation that the range of applicability of most theories is exaggerated. A second sort of error is to downplay the unique situation of a particular country. The difficulty faced by transition economies because they underestimated the difficulty of aping the institutions and growth processes of Western nations is just the most obvious example of such an error. Again a detailed appreciation of causal linkages and of the limitations of all theories provides the best antidote to this type of error. But at this point these are just authorial conjectures: the test would be whether real policy-makers find the approach and the insights this book provides to be useful.

14 Concluding Remarks

The final step in the interdisciplinary process involves communicating to multiple audiences the insights obtained through interdisciplinary analysis. If this step is not performed successfully, all previous steps will have been wasted. And this step requires a quite different skill set from most of the previous ones. The preceding analysis has largely proceeded through calm, careful, and introverted analysis; the last step requires a bit of flare and an extroverted disposition. One of the sad facts of academic life is that some who excel at analysis are miserable at communication, and their insights thus receive less attention than they deserve. Others are natural communicators. Interdisciplinarians, whatever their psychological profile, likely have to be more self-conscious about communication than disciplinarians: the latter can simply absorb their disciplinary perspective subconsciously and continue to do what seems to have worked for them in the past, while the former must think about how to speak to the language and interests of distinct audiences.

Often, different modes of communication are necessary for different audiences. The author of this book has in the past published across some dozen disciplines or interdisciplinary fields. He has also written pieces for a variety of more popular publications. In general, books are more likely than articles to be aimed at, and hopefully reach, multiple audiences. This book has been largely jargon-free, and should thus prove accessible to scholars across a wide range of disciplines as well as to those outside the academy interested in economic growth and/or interdisciplinary analysis.

A book must be not just accessible but of interest. Those interested in interdisciplinarity itself should be intrigued by this explicit test of a process for interdisciplinary analysis. Economists who study economic growth should appreciate the varied insights provided by other disciplines, while those in other disciplines should value the possible connections between their research and research on the proximate causes of economic growth. The word to be stressed here is *complementarity*. While disciplinary insights have occasionally conflicted in this book (but less often than in social science more generally), for the most part different disciplinary insights generate different emphases and thus combine to create a more nuanced understanding. More importantly, even when disciplinary insights do conflict, much that is good can generally be taken from each discipline such that a common ground can be constructed which integrates these elements. Interdisciplinarity should not be viewed as a threat to disciplinary research. Rather it identifies both weaknesses and possibilities with respect to existing research programs, and thus facilitates the pursuit of research questions that are of interest beyond the confines of any one discipline.

The book had two goals. One was to show how pursuing a process of interdisciplinary analysis could shed light on our collective understanding of economic growth. The other was to show the value in general of pursuing a logical process of interdisciplinary analysis. In neither case can the results be briefly summarized.

R. Szostak, *The Causes of Economic Growth*,
DOI: 10.1007/978-3-540-92282-7_14, © Springer-Verlag Berlin Heidelberg 2009

However, it is possible to point to how these goals were addressed in the course of the book.

14.1 Insights into Economic Growth

This book has not generated some bold new theory of economic growth. That was not its intent, though such an outcome may at times flow from interdisciplinary analysis. Interdisciplinarians in the earlier part of the twentieth century often pursued the ideal of some grand overarching theory of everything (notably within the 'Unity of science' movement); the lack of success in this direction encourages most contemporary interdisciplinarians to seek a more messy mélange of insights that collectively enhance understanding of complex issues (see Szostak 2003a). It may be that an author with more (or just different) imagination could pull more of the pieces together into some unified (if nuanced) theoretical vision. This book is indeed predicated on the belief that interdisciplinary analysis can proceed as 'normal science' – that is that each piece of interdisciplinary work need not yield some revolutionary insight (though it has more potential to do so than disciplinary work), but that successive pieces of research can build slowly toward enhanced understanding (Szostak 2007c). It is thus hoped that this work will inspire and inform further interdisciplinary investigations of economic growth.

Rodrik (2006, 974) celebrates the World Bank's *Economic Growth in the 1990s: Learning from a Decade of Reform* (2005) for its measured advice: 'There are no confident assertions here of what works and what doesn't – and no blueprint for policymakers to adopt. The emphasis is on the need for humility, for policy diversity, for selective and modest reforms, and for experimentation.' Later he worries that the United Nations Millennium Project assumes that we do indeed have such a blueprint. This book suggests that even the integration of our present state of understanding of economic growth does not yield such a blueprint. But it does yield an even broader set of insights that can be carefully applied by policymakers.

While this book may pave the way for exciting new syntheses, its main insight is that we should not expect our understanding of economic growth to be simple. Economic growth is generated by a wide array of causal links involving a host of economic and non-economic phenomena. There is no obvious reason why there should be some similarity across these diverse links. While they are clearly interrelated, and there are emergent properties of systems of links, it is nevertheless true that each causal link reflects a unique set of influences. The reader is invited to review the detailed analyses of causal links in chapters 6 through 11 with this thought in mind; the author certainly found each causal link to be unique in important ways. It must thus appear that our scholarly understanding of economic growth must always involve a host of largely independent link-specific analyses.

This point may seem obvious, and thus its importance is not fully appreciated. But it flies in the face of current academic practice in several important ways. Most obviously, economic analysis in particular, but also most studies in sociology and political science, do pursue some sort of integrated theoretical vision or mathematical model that attempts to capture the essence of the economic growth process. Too much of the literature pursues the false idol of the one true model, the one secret formula for achieving growth everywhere, anytime. Though endogenous growth models are hailed for encouraging a diverse body of research on economic growth, the fact remains that the economics profession had largely turned away from the study of growth for decades due to a sense that it lacked one overarching model on which to ground an analysis of economic growth. The Unified Growth Models that have recently become popular in the economics literature are a good (if perhaps somewhat extreme) example of this tendency: they hope to explain the entire course of growth over the last millennia within models containing a handful of variables. Such models may of course give us *some* insight into the growth process. Notably there are different Unified Growth Models that focus on different causal links: population growth, cultural change, institutions. Yet the presumption of the entire exercise is that these simple models capture much of what is important to know about economic growth. This book argues that a better guiding principle is that insights will not be all-encompassing, should be appreciated for illuminating one or a few causal links, and should not be presumed to provide 'the' answer.

The desire for one grand theory flows from another argument that is less obvious and thus more insidious: that scholarly understanding must be organized *theoretically.* This book has suggested instead that understanding should be organized in terms of causal links and emergent properties. The hardcore disciplinarian will respond negatively to the variety of detailed analyses provided in this book: they can instill greater order by simply ignoring theories and methods other than their own. But this book has striven toward an order that does not arbitrarily limit insight. Those who like simplistic arguments without caveats may prefer more order and less insight. But the cause of economic growth – and the billions of people who desperately need to experience more of this – is best served by privileging insight over other criteria.

The results of the detailed analyses of each causal link will not be reprised here. In each case, though, it was shown that insights from diverse theories, methods, and disciplines could usefully be integrated in order to generate more accurate and nuanced insights than could be generated by any one discipline. Again, the benefits of this sort of analysis can only be appreciated if scholars first jettison the misguided presumptions noted above that scholarly insight must be organized theoretically and/or that the goal of scholarly analysis of complex questions is some simple grand theory.

Social scientists are all too prone to assuming that their theories have wide generalizability. The causal link approach guides an appreciation that some theories tell us much more about some links than others. It also guides an appreciation that even along a particular link different theories may be more important in different circumstances. The approach taken here thus encourages social scientists toward an important task: identifying the range of applicability of different theories. This task will be better performed if we change our mindset away from the pursuit of one overarching theory, and then change the way we do empirical research.

Theory is privileged over empirics in most social sciences. Empirical analysis generally takes the form of 'testing' particular theories, often against no explicit alternative. Rule (1997) detailed the obvious dangers of this approach: that this empirical work would become useless when the theory went out of vogue, and that empirical evidence with no obvious implications for favored theory would simply be ignored. The latter concern is particularly apposite here. If one wants to believe that one's theory of population dynamics is *the* explanation of economic growth, then one naturally ignores evidence regarding culture or institutions or infrastructure. That is, the search for simple explanations *necessarily* guides one to ignore everything else. Only a mindset that explicitly embraces all sorts of empirical evidence allows one to embrace the true diversity of causes of economic growth.

Empirical analyses need not proceed exclusively in the form of theory-testing. There is much scope for a-theoretical investigations (such as certain sorts of VAR regressions but also much qualitative analysis) that are designed to let the data speak for themselves. Yet as Goethe long ago remarked every fact is already a theory: theory shapes how we interpret what we see. And thus openness to diverse theories provides the best guarantee that all relevant empirical evidence will be first appreciated and second evaluated accurately. Moreover, when empirical analysis does take the form of testing theories, good methodological practice has always urged the explicit testing of one theory against another. This simple guideline is ignored in practice because most scholars are only intimately familiar with one theory. Moreover we have seen that in testing one theory against another we should generally have recourse to multiple methods; most scholars tend to favor one or two methods.

Empirics become particularly important in the policy arena. Richard Jones, the classical economist, worried about the disjunction between formal theory and good policy. He noted that one could not rely exclusively on the theories of physics in building a machine, but would also need a set of more practical understandings.[1] Likewise economic policy required an understanding of both theory and practical matters. Two centuries of refinement of theory has not eliminated the need to go beyond theory either in building machines or in fashioning policy.

Those who favor theoretical generalizability will inevitably be hostile to path dependence. Nor is this a sin only committed by economists. Most sociologists, and even many historical sociologists, seek generalizations, and are thus suspicious of the value of path dependence research. They doubt that small events can

---

[1] However, all disciplines allocate more prestige to pure knowledge than to practical knowledge (Abbott 2005, 146). Refining core theory promises a better career path than confronting the messy details of reality.

have major effects (Mahoney 2000). For economists, the predilection toward generalizability was most clearly demonstrated in the unfortunate advice given to countries of Eastern Europe to quickly adapt Western institutions. Western policy followed the (politically attractive) strategy of urging a sudden adoption of Western institutions and policies, against the advice of others (including Stiglitz) who worried that good institutions had to build on the past and that it was dangerous to take some steps (such as privatization) before others (such as detailed stock market regulation) (Snowdon, 54). Those such as the Czech Republic that had had such institutions before World War II were able to do so much more smoothly than the former Soviet Union. 'All this now seems obvious but it wasn't obvious to too many people other than economic historians of Eastern Europe at the beginning of the 1990s' (Eichengreen, in Snowdon 2002, 304). Once the possibility of path dependence is accepted, an important policy implication follows: that the ideal policies for encouraging economic growth will differ across time and place, as these must be tailored to the particular path a country has taken to that point.

This policy implication in turn suggests an adjustment in the way in which we investigate the sources of economic growth. Economists have spent a great deal of time estimating aggregate production functions. They want to know what is the relative contribution to economic growth of investment, technological innovation, education, and so on. Such insights are important: a government wanting to foster growth, and wondering where to devote scarce resources, will necessarily be curious as to where the greatest sources of growth lie. Yet these relationships that economists estimate can hardly be stable. As the experience of the former Soviet Union attests, misplaced investment may have little impact on growth. And thus any connection between investment and growth holds only under institutional structures that do a good job of channeling investment in productive directions – a simple point that governments wishing to foster growth need to be aware of. Likewise, even endogenous growth theory highlights the complementarity of investment and innovation: new technology often needs to be embodied in new machinery. This insight suggests caution in trying to disentangle the effects of investment and innovation – and should point toward idiographic analyses of how these two processes interact in particular times and places. More generally, we should always ask ourselves how well any theoretical insight regarding the causes of growth might vary across time and place.

One lesson of this work is that we should not give advice to any country without looking carefully at its unique situation. What institutions has it inherited from the past? What is the fiscal capacity of its government? What is its infrastructure and education and health system like? Does the government have legitimacy? Does the culture favor hard work and thrift? The list of questions goes on. But the set of best policies depends very much on their answers.[2] 'While it is conceivable

---

[2] Easterly (2006) notes that the theory of second best in economics shows that in an imperfect world any one reform may not be beneficial. In other words, we need to appreciate under what precise circumstances a particular policy will have beneficial effects.

that there is an all-purpose universal theory and set of policies that would be good for promoting economic growth, it seems much more plausible that the appropriate growth policy will differ according to the situation ... Discussion of the theory and policy of economic growth seems at times remarkably insensitive to these distinctions' (Pritchett 1997, 15). Sachs (2005) has reached a similar conclusion, and recommends a diagnostic approach: one first identifies the major constraints impeding growth in a particular locale and works to alleviate these. In the words of Rodrik (2006, 976), 'different contexts require different solutions to solving common problems. Enhancing private investment incentives may require improving the security of property rights in one country but enhancing the financial sector in another.' This book moves past a necessarily inductive list of possible diagnoses to outline a more logical and potentially exhaustive list of relevant causal links. The various causal analyses in this book can aid in identifying what is 'missing' in a particular place, and also in identifying potential remedies.

In sum, this book has shown that:

- Economic growth is best understood in terms of diverse causal links and emergent properties.
- Each of these links and properties is best understood through interdisciplinary analysis. This in turn involves the integration of insights from different theories and methods.
- Different links are likely of different importance in different times and places, and thus optimal policies will likely differ too.

These three points imply a change in the *gestalt* with which scholars approach the study of economic growth. Indeed it has been argued here that these results can only be appreciated if scholars:

- Abandon misguided presumptions that scholarship should be organized theoretically, and or that the purpose is the development of simple grand theories.
- Appreciate the value of interdisciplinarity.
- Appreciate the value of theoretical and methodological flexibility.
- Appreciate that each theory has a particular range of applicability.
- Appreciate the value of synthesizing the widest array of empirical analysis within an organizing structure of causal links and emergent properties.

14.2 The Value of the Process for our Understanding of Growth

The two goals of the book were interdependent. We could only establish the value of interdisciplinary analysis for our understanding of economic growth by performing that analysis in a useful manner. In turn, the best evidence that the process is useful is that it yielded the results referred to in the previous section. Yet even flawed research strategies can yield useful insights: since no research is perfect, scholars would know nothing if not for our collective ability to use judgment in evaluating flawed research outcomes. It is thus useful to review here the importance of each step in the interdisciplinary research process for our understanding of economic growth.

Step 1

The scope for interdisciplinary analysis expands markedly when we move beyond studying the proximate causes of growth to ask why some countries innovate or trade or invest more than others. Economists – and far from all of these – have only recently extended their gaze beyond the proximate causes, and are held back in their advance by the difficulty of applying their usual theories and methods to non-economic phenomena such as culture. The importance of not arbitrarily constraining a guiding question along disciplinary lines could hardly be better illustrated.

Step 2

Once one moves beyond proximate causes, a dizzying array of possible influences presents itself. Given the natural penchant of humans to oversimplify (as North 2006 notes), and of scholars in particular to seek simplicity (see above), an antidote to oversimplification is essential. The wide-ranging discussion of possible causal factors in step 2 set the stage for the causal link analysis of later steps.

Moreover, the scholarly penchant for oversimplification encourages the reification of simple models with only a handful of variables. The causal link approach is only a feasible and attractive alternative if there is some logical format for organizing the diverse insights obtained in that manner. Moreover, such analyses must always seem somewhat *ad hoc* in the absence of an exhaustive classification of phenomena. The classification of phenomena in Table 2.1 overcomes both difficulties.

The final important advantage of the approach taken in step 2 is that it ensures terminological clarity. The act of classifying phenomena is simultaneously an act of defining each phenomenon carefully: identifying both what type of thing it is and what type of thing it is not. Sloppy or contested definitions are all too common in social scientific analysis, and these limit the rate of increase in academic understanding and particularly limit interdisciplinary analysis.

Step 3

Step 3 reviewed a wide range of theories and methods, and established that each had strengths for the study of growth that could compensate for weaknesses in others. No one theory or method was perfectly suited to the study of growth. The appreciation of these strengths and weaknesses was invaluable when disciplinary insights were evaluated in later steps. The analysis also served usefully to justify in advance the wide-ranging theoretical and methodological explorations of later chapters. For mainstream economists, the key message was that rational choice theorizing and statistical analysis need to be supplemented with other – for the most part *complementary* – theories and methods. Yet the exact same message was communicated to all other disciplines: these also are guilty of emphasizing a limited range of theory and method.

Chapter 3 did not simply set the stage for later analysis, but serves on its own as a guide to scholars pursuing interdisciplinary analysis of economic growth. Would-be interdisciplinarians need to understand the strengths and weaknesses of the theories and methods they draw upon (and also the disciplinary perspectives identified in step 4). Those of us trained in disciplines need to reflect from time to time on the potential value to our research agendas of the theories and methods used by others. More centrally, we should be able to appreciate the potential contribution of the research of others.

Step 4

Each discipline was shown to bring a unique perspective to the study of economic growth. The broad lesson to be learned from this step is that scholars in each discipline are at present encouraged to look in some directions and eschew others. The fact that different disciplines have different perspectives suggests that – as was the case with theory and method – integrating across disciplines will alleviate the biases that afflict any one discipline. More practically, the perspectives identified in step 5 also proved quite useful in later steps when disciplinary insights were evaluated.

Some scholars imagine that disciplinary conversations are *incommensurate*: that only a sociologist can understand what sociologists are saying. Our discussion of disciplinary perspectives suggests that there may be some truth in this conjecture. An outsider may not fully understand why a sociologist asks a particular question, uses a word in a particular way (indeed may not fully appreciate how a word is being defined), or celebrates a particular result. Yet an interdisciplinarian must hope that a fair degree of cross-disciplinary understanding is possible. The performance of steps 6 through 9 in this book suggests that this is indeed the case. Precisely by keeping in mind different disciplinary perspectives (and the strengths and weaknesses of different theories), we were able to evaluate and integrate insights from different disciplines. While some may celebrate disciplinary perspective as a barrier to interdisciplinarity this book suggests instead that appreciating disciplinary perspectives allows us to communicate across disciplinary boundaries.

It has been said of the world's cultures that they are united in xenophobia: each manages to think that it is somehow better than the others. The same is true of disciplines. It is hardly surprising that scholars who have devoted several years of their life to the mastery of a particular discipline would tend to think that their discipline has some special access to human understanding. Such attitudes are a major barrier to interdisciplinary understanding. In particular the arguments for theoretical and methodological diversity developed in step 3 are too easily ignored by disciplinarians simply because they assume the superiority of their own theory and method. The analysis in step 4 may encourage xenophobia by identifying weaknesses in other disciplines, but should mainly serve to counteract this by showing that all disciplines have both strengths and weaknesses.

Gerald Graff has in many works bemoaned the tendency of social scientists in both research and teaching to be unaware of the conflicts that exist between different disciplines (and students, he notes, compartmentalize knowledge, and thus do not appreciate that different professors tell different stories). This book will have accomplished much if it has brought such conflicts into the open (not just between disciplines but between theories as well), and also identified when conflicts are real as opposed to semantic.[3] But we have tried to take an additional step and construct common ground.

Step 5

The literature survey is one of the more problematic steps in interdisciplinary analysis, for scholars must necessarily choose works from literatures with which they lack familiarity. The strategy of moving from general to more focused works is useful, but hardly eliminates the danger of excluding important works through ignorance. The scholar also faces needless confusion in identifying relevant literatures because of the way library catalogues are constructed. Until a better classification system is developed (see Szostak 2007b), there is no perfect strategy for overcoming this problem, though useful strategies include consulting both thesauri and scholars in other disciplines.

---

[3] Some interdisciplinarians may worry that we have somehow under-estimated the degree of conflict. We have often suggested that disciplinary insights can be viewed as complements. Even then, it has generally been necessary to relax disciplinary assumptions that 'only our phenomena matter.'

Given these difficulties, it is likely of particular importance that interdisciplinary scholars be explicit about their search strategy. This work has been broad in scope, and thus the author had to curtail exploration of each causal link addressed. The book relies heavily on insights from more general works such as handbooks and texts. This likely means that minority viewpoints within all disciplines have been under-represented.[4] These can be especially useful to the evaluative task of the interdisciplinarian. Interdisciplinary scholars (or indeed disciplinary scholars) wishing to build upon the work of this book are urged to delve more deeply into the specialist literatures than it has been possible to do here.

Step 6

Steps 6 through 9 were particularly difficult to separate in practice. Nevertheless, they are logically distinct. The evaluative step is of obvious importance. Yet it is sometimes nevertheless subsumed under the heading of 'creating common ground' in treatments of interdisciplinary analysis. There is then a danger that disciplinary insights are only critiqued when they disagree. This book has sought to evaluate disciplinary insights even when only one discipline has addressed a particular question. Interdisciplinarians, like disciplinarians, should be familiar with strategies of critical thinking in evaluating the works of others (and indeed their own). Yet the point that should be stressed here is that interdisciplinarity itself suggests some powerful strategies for evaluation. As an example I reprise here one paragraph from the discussion of investment in section 6.2:

> This adjustment in our understanding of the relationship between investment and growth is entirely in accord with the strategies for interdisciplinary analysis outlined above: growth accounting regressions naturally omit many variables that condition this relationship; the structure of those regressions does not allow for independent variables to act in concert; the approach reflects a disciplinary tendency to identify supposedly enduring causal relationships without careful concern for the set of conditions in which these might hold; and the growth accounting analyses thus represent a widespread tendency in scholarship to assume greater generality for one's results than they deserve. The approach, it might be noted, also reflects the simplistic view of growth as "more of the same stuff" critiqued in chapter 2. It should be stressed that appropriate caveats were often included in the original analyses, but were forgotten as these works were cited. This practice of forgetting caveats is common across disciplines. While economists thus strove to identify *the* relationship between investment and growth, economic historians (and development economists) were driven by their interest in diverse times and places to show that no such fixed relationship exists.

---

[4] I may have given special attention to one type of minority viewpoint: scholars in other disciplines who focus on economic issues and may thus have absorbed some of the perspective of economists.

Similar conclusions were drawn throughout chapters 6 through 8 (and also in chapters 9, 10, and 11). The interdisciplinarian, armed with a handful of key questions to ask of any research result, can readily appreciate some of the likely weaknesses of any particular body of research. The careful interdisciplinarian will not stop there, but apply critical thinking tools, search out critiques from within the discipline, and when possible identify conflicts with insights from other disciplines. These strategies too were illustrated at several points in chapters 6 through 11.

Step 7

The identification of gaps in scholarly understanding is always a critical step in interdisciplinary analysis. It has been particularly important in the case of economic growth, for scholars of networks or culture or business cycles have only rarely addressed questions of economic growth (and vice versa), and even much of the literature on technology and institutions is oriented toward quite different questions. One of the main purposes of this book has been to identify areas where future research is needed, and generally to suggest some ways in which this might be pursued:

- The relationship between growth and economic fluctuations needs to be re-conceived: fluctuations are a result more than a cause of growth, and both to a large degree reflect trends in technological innovation and institutional change.
- Likewise the relationship between growth and the rise and fall of sectors and firms needs greater attention. Growth is never just 'more of the same' but involves losers as well as winners. Political resistance to growth often flows from this simple but oft-ignored fact.
- The effects of culture on economic growth will only be understood if scholars of culture are more careful of their terminology and methods than has been the case in the past. Careful definition of the various components of culture is the first obvious step that needs to be taken. Nevertheless, economists are in error when they suggest that only statistical analysis should be employed in this domain. Nor does the study of culture lend itself flawlessly to rational choice analysis, given that culture operates through a quite different sort of decision-making.
- Network theorists need to more directly address questions related to growth: what sorts of networks encourage what sorts of innovation, trade, or institutions? This may be the easiest gap to fill for these questions are not dissimilar from those addressed at present in the field, and at least some of the methods employed in network analysis will seem familiar to economists interested in economic growth.

Step 8

We have addressed the issue of the relationship between growth and business cycles above. The other possible type of emergent property addressed concerned poverty traps. Is there any general tendency for poor countries to 'catch up,' or are there powerful forces keeping them poor? The analysis in chapter 10 suggested that neither view is entirely correct: there are causal forces working in both directions. This suggests at least the possibility that the right set of policies can encourage rapid growth in the poorest countries.

Step 9

The result of integration cannot be tidy. Yet scientific progress often involves the complicated clarification of simple theories. Thus Kohli (2002, 94) on Skocpol's incorporation of the idea of weak states into predominantly economic explanations of political revolutions: 'Just as Weber had pluralized Marx's economic argument and made it much more broadly applicable and attractive – though by the same account, also less parsimonious – Skocpol pluralized Moore, or made the analysis more multivariate, for the study of grand revolutions.' The author became fatigued as he recounted one after another highly generalized and over-simplified account. Those that have not yet been critiqued and clarified will inevitably suffer this fate. Time after time, writers of survey articles encouraged the exploration of further causal links. This book hopes to accelerate the process of moving toward nuanced and complex understandings. It might even encourage scholars engaging new questions to omit entirely the step of excessive oversimplification in order to appreciate relevant interactions from the outset.

Step 10

Scholars should, but rarely do, reflect on their own biases. Interdisciplinarians, grounding their research in an appreciation of the ubiquity of disciplinary and other scholarly biases, have less excuse for ignoring their own inherent biases. Since this book aims in part to highlight the value of interdisciplinary research in general and a particular process for interdisciplinary research in particular, the author's biases in favor of both should be emphasized. I am also biased toward seeing value in diverse theories, methods, and disciplines. The reader should assure themselves that arguments in favor of such positions are supported by the evidence provided. More generally I have necessarily commented on many areas of research in which I lack any particular expertise, and thus the reader should recognize ignorance as another potential source of authorial error.

I should stress that I do not believe myself to be any more biased than the typical scholar; I am simply more willing to confess. Indeed I believe that my willingness to engage in self-reflection reduces the effect of bias on my work. I believe that this sort of self-reflection should be an integral part of all scholarly research. Scholars too often cling to an inaccurate belief that scientific investigation can be free of bias (often because of a mistaken belief that 'their' method is bias free); scholarship will be enhanced if scholars instead face up to the inevitability of bias; only then can they act consciously to reduce it.

Step 11

The analysis above has provided a test of the twelve-step process for interdisciplinary analysis. It has argued that each step proved useful in enhancing our understanding of economic growth. To test the process as a whole one needs to ask how useful was the understanding gained as a result of the entire process (keeping in mind, of course, that none of the steps, and especially not the literature survey, could be pursued in complete detail).

The book has argued for an approach to growth that stresses a complex mélange of insights rather than one comprehensive theory or model. There cannot then be one simple empirical test of the entire complex of understandings. Individual insights can be tested in further empirical research. Since each insight draws on different theory types, they should be tested using multiple theories.

The best test of the entire complex of understanding lies in the policy arena: can policy-makers be aided by the body of link-based analyses generated here? Policy-makers are often given advice that reflects an advisor's expertise with respect to a subset of the relevant causal arguments. This book should serve as an antidote to this sort of bias in policy-making.

References

Abbott, A. (2005) *Chaos of disciplines*. Chicago: University of Chicago Press.

Acemoglu, D., & Robinson, J.A. (2005) *Economic origins of dictatorship and democracy*. New York: Cambridge University Press.

Acemoglu, D., Johnson, S., & Robinson, J.A. (2005) Institutions as a fundamental cause of long-run growth. In P. Aghion & S.N. Durlauf (Eds.), *Handbook of economic growth* (pp. 385-472). Amsterdam: Elsevier North-Holland.

Acemoglu, D., Johnson, S., Robinson, J.A. (2001) The Colonial origins of comparative development: an empirical investigation. *American Economic Review* 91(5), 1369-1401.

Aghion, P., & Howitt, P. (1998) *Endogenous growth theory*. Cambridge MA: MIT Press.

Alesina, A., Spolaore, E., & Wacziarg, R. (2005) Trade, growth, and the size of countries. In P. Aghion & S.N. Durlauf (Eds.), *Handbook of economic growth* (pp. 1499-1542). Amsterdam: Elsevier North-Holland.

Alt, J.E., & Alesina, A. (1998) Political economy: an overview. In R. Goodin & H. Klingemann (Eds.), *A New Handbook of Political Science* (pp. 645-74). Oxford: Oxford University Press.

Altman, M. (2002) Staple theory and export-led growth: constructing differential growth. *Australian Economic History Review* 43(3), 230-55.

Altman, M. (2001) *Worker satisfaction and economic performance: microfoundations of success and failure*. Armonk NY: ME Sharpe.

Amatori, F., & Jones, G. (Eds.) (2003) *Business history around the world*. Cambridge: Cambridge University Press.

Antonelli, C. (1999) *The microdynamics of technological change*. London: Routledge.

Applbaum, K. (2005) The anthropology of markets. In J.G. Carrier (Ed.), *A Handbook of economic anthropology* (pp. 275-89). Cheltenham: Edward Elgar.

Aron, J. (2000) Growth and institutions: a review of the evidence. *World Bank Research Observer* 15(1), 99-135.

Arora, S. (2001) Health, human productivity, and long-term economic growth. *Journal of Economic History* 61(3), 699-749.

Arthur, B. (2000) Cognition: the black box of economics. In David Colander (Ed.), *The complexity vision and the teaching of economics*. Cheltenham: Edward Elgar.

Ausubel, J.H. (1997) The liberation of the environment. In J.H. Ausubel & H.D. Langford (Eds.), *Technological trajectories and the human environment*. Washington: National Academies Press.

Azariadis, C., & Stachurski, J. (2005) Poverty traps. In P. Aghion & S.N. Durlauf (Eds.), *Handbook of economic growth* (pp. 295-384). Amsterdam: Elsevier North-Holland.

Banerjee, A., & Duflo, E. (2005) Growth theory through the lens of development economics. In P. Aghion & S.N. Durlauf (Eds.), *Handbook of economic growth* (pp. 473-552). Amsterdam: Elsevier North-Holland.

Bardhan, P. (2002) Decentralization of government and development. *Journal of Economic Perspectives* 16(4), 185-205.

Bardhan, P., Roemer, J.E. (1992) Market socialism: a case for rejuvenation. *Journal of Economic Perspectives* 6(3), 101-16.

Baumol, W.J. (2000) What Marshall didn't know: on the Twentieth Century's contributions to economics. *Quarterly Journal of Economics* 115(1), 1-44.

Beckert, J. (2002) *Beyond the market: the social foundations of economic efficiency*. Princeton: Princeton University Press.

Bermeo, N. (2002) *Ordinary people in extraordinary times: citizens and the collapse of democracy*. Princeton: Princeton University Press.

Bernstein, W.J. (2004) *The birth of prosperity*. New York: McGraw-Hill.

Bertocchi, G. (2006) Growth, history, and institutions. In N. Salvadori (Ed.), *Economic growth and distribution: on the nature and causes of the wealth of nations* (pp. 331-49). Cheltenham: Edward Elgar.

Besley, T. (2005) Political selection. *Journal of Economic Perspectives* 19(3), 43-60.

Blanchard, O. (2000) What do we know about macroeconomics that Fisher and Wicksell did not? *Quarterly Journal of Economics* 115(4), 1375-1409.

Blaug, M. (1997) Ugly currents in modern economics. *Options Politiques* 18(17), 3-8.

Blim, M. (2005) Culture and economy. In J.G. Carrier (Ed.), *A handbook of economic anthropology* (pp. 306-22). Cheltenham: Edward Elgar.

Bowles, S. & Gintis, H. (forthcoming) *A Cooperative Species: Human Reciprocity and its Evolution.*

Brock, W.A., & Taylor, M.S. (2005) Economic growth and the environment: a review of theory and empirics. In P. Aghion & S.N. Durlauf (Eds.), *Handbook of economic growth* (pp.1749-1821). Amsterdam: Elsevier North-Holland.

Bruland, K., & Mowery, D.C. (2005) Innovation through time. In J. Fagerberg, D.C. Mowery, & R.R. Nelson (Eds.), *The Oxford handbook of innovation* (pp. 349-79). Oxford: Oxford University Press.

Bruton, H.J. (1997) *On the search for well-being.* Ann Arbor: University of Michigan Press.

Bunge, M. (1998) *Social science under debate.* Toronto: University of Toronto Press.

Burke, P. (2005) *History and social theory,* 2nd Edition. Ithaca: Cornell University Press.

Butterfield, A.K.J. & Korazim-Korosy, Y. (2007) *Interdisciplinary community development: international perspectives.* New York: Howarth Press.

Cameron, C.M., & Morton, R. (2002) Formal theory meets data. In I. Katznelson & H.V. Miller (Eds.), *Political science: state of the discipline* (pp. 784-804). New York: Norton.

Campbell, J.L. (1998) Institutional analysis and the role of ideas in political economy. *Theory and Society* 27: 377-409.

Carrier, J.G. (2005) Introduction. In J.G. Carrier (Ed.), *A handbook of economic anthropology* (pp. 1-9). Cheltenham: Edward Elgar.

Cassis, Y. (1997) *Big business: the European experience in the Twentieth Century.* New York: Oxford University Press.

Chaminade, C., & Edquist, C. (2006) From theory to practice: the use of the systems of innovation approach in innovation policy. In J. Hage & M.T.H. Meeus (Eds.), *Innovation, science, and institutional change: a research handbook* (pp. 141-60). Oxford: Oxford University Press.

Chandler, A.D. (2005) *Shaping the industrial century: the remarkable story of the modern chemical and pharmaceutical industries.* Cambridge MA: Harvard University Press.

Chandler, A.D., & Hikino, T. (1997) The large industrial enterprise and the dynamics of economic growth. In A. Chandler, F. Amatori, & T. Hikino (Eds.), *Big business and the wealth of nations.* Cambridge: Cambridge University Press.

Chang, H. (2002) *Kicking away the ladder: development strategy in historical perspective.* London: Anthem.

Clague, C. (1997) *Institutions and economic development.* Baltimore: Johns Hopkins University Press.

Cohen, J.H., & Dannhauser, N. (2002) *Economic development: an anthropological approach.* Walnut creek CA: Altamira Press.

Cohen, J.D. (2005) The vulcanization of the human brain: a neural perspective on interactions between cognition and emotion. *Journal of Economic Perspectives* 19(4), 3-24.

Colander, D. (2000) Complexity in the teaching of economics. In D. Colander (Ed.), *The complexity vision and the teaching of economics.* Cheltenham: Edward Elgar.

Colander, D. (2000b) New millennium economics: how did it get this way, and what way is it? *Journal of Economic Perspectives* 14(1), 121-32.

Coleman, W. (2002) *Economics and its enemies.* Houndsmill: Palgrave McMillan.

Collier, P., Gunning, J.W. (1999) Explaining African economic performance. *Journal of Economic Literature* 37(1), 64-112.

Cornwall, J., & Cornwall, W. (2001) *Capitalist development in the Twentieth Century: an evolutionary-Keynesian approach.* Cambridge: Cambridge University Press.

Daley-Harris, S., & Awibo, A. (Eds.) (2006) *More pathways out of poverty.* Bloomfield CT: Kumarian Press.

Dalton, R.J. (1998) Comparative politics: micro-behavioral perspectives. In R. Goodin & H. Klingemann (Eds.), *A new handbook of political science* (pp. 336-52). Oxford: Oxford University Press.

Damanpour, F., & Aravind, D. (2006) Product and process innovations: a review of organizational and environmental determinants. In J. Hage & M.T.H. Meeus (Eds.), *Innovation, science, and institutional change: a research handbook* (pp. 38-66). Oxford: Oxford University Press.

Diamond, J. (1997) *Guns, germs, and steel: the fates of human societies.* New York: Norton.

Dobbin, F. (2001) Why the economy reflects the polity: early rail policy in Britain, France, and the United States. In M. Granovetter & R. Swedberg (Eds.), *The sociology of economic life* (pp. 401-24). Boulder CO: Westview Press.

Dobbin, F. (2004) Introduction: the sociology of the economy. In F. Dobbin (Ed.), *The sociology of the economy.* New York: Russell Sage Foundation.

Dobres, M., & Hoffman, C.R. (1999) *The social dynamics of technology.* Washington: Smithsonian Institution Press.

Dogan, M. (1998) Political science and the other social sciences. In R. Goodin & H. Klingemann (Eds.), *A new handbook of political science* (pp. 50-96). Oxford: Oxford University Press.

Dogan, M., & Pahre, R. (1990) *Creative marginality: innovation at the intersection of social sciences.* Boulder CO: Westview.

Dolfsma, W.A., Eijk, A.R. van der & Jolink, A. (2005). No black box and no black hole: from social capital to gift exchange. Unpublished research paper.

Douthwaite, R. (1999) *How economic growth has enriched the few, impoverished the many, and endangered the planet.* Dublin: Lilliput Press.

Durkheim, E. (1984) *The division of labor in society.* London: Macmillan.

Durlauf, S. (1999) The case against 'social capital' *Focus* 20, 1-5.

Durlauf, S. & Fafchamps, M. (2005) Social capital. In P. Aghion & S. Durlauf (Eds.), *Handbook of economic growth* (pp.1639-1722). Amsterdam: Elsevier North-Holland.

Durlauf, S., Johnson, P.A., & Temple, J.R.W. (2005) Growth econometrics. In P. Aghion & S. Durlauf (Eds.), *Handbook of economic growth* (pp. 555-677). Amsterdam: Elsevier North-Holland.

Eades, J.S. (2005) Anthropology, political economy, and world-systems theory. In J.G. Carrier (Ed.), *A handbook of economic anthropology* (pp. 26-40). Cheltenham: Edward Elgar.

Easterlin, R.E. (1996) *Growth triumphant: the Twenty-First Century in historical perspective.* Ann Arbor: University of Michigan Press.

Easterlin, R.E. (2004) *The reluctant economist: perspectives on economics, economic history, and demography.* New York: Cambridge University Press.

Easterly, W. (2002) *The elusive quest for growth: economist's adventures and misadventures in the Tropics.* Cambridge: MIT Press.

Easterly, W. (2006) The big push déjà vu: a review of Jeffrey Sachs' 'The end of poverty: economic possibilities for our time.' *Journal of Economic Literature* 44(1), 96-105.

Edquist, C. (2005) Systems of innovation: perspectives and challenges. In J. Fagerberg, D.C. Mowery, & R.R. Nelson (Eds.) *The Oxford handbook of innovation* (pp. 181-208). Oxford: Oxford University Press.

Ellis, R.D. (1998) *Just results: ethical foundations for policy analysis.* Washington: Georgetown University Press.

Elster, J. (1993) *Political psychology.* Cambridge: Cambridge University Press.

Epstein, S.R. (2000) *Freedom and growth: the rise of states and markets in Europe 1300-1750.* London: Routledge.

Eriksen, T.H. (2005) Economies of ethnicity. In J.G. Carrier (Ed.), *A handbook of economic anthropology* (pp. 353-69). Cheltenham: Edward Elgar.

Evans, P. (1995) *Embedded autonomy: states and industrial transformation.* Princeton: Princeton University Press.

Evans, P., & Wurster, T.N. (1999) *Blown to bits: how the new economics of information transforms strategy.* Cambridge: Harvard Business School Press.

Fagerberg, J. (2005) Innovation: a guide to the literature. In J. Fagerberg, D.C. Mowery, & R.R. Nelson (Eds.), *The Oxford handbook of innovation* (pp. 1-26). Oxford: Oxford University Press.

Fehr, E., Tyran, J.-R. (2005) Individual irrationality and aggregate outcomes. *Journal of Economic Perspectives* 19(4), 43-66.

Fernald, J.G. (1999) Roads to prosperity?: assessing the link between public capital and productivity, *American Economic Review* 89(3), 619-38.

Fevre, R. (2003) *The new sociology of economic behavior.* London: Sage.

Fine, B. (2001) *Social capital versus social theory: political economy and social science at the turn of the millennium.* London: Routledge.

Foa, E. & U. (1980) Resource theory: interpersonal behavior as exchange. In K.J. Gergen, M.S. Greenberg, R.H. Willis (Eds.), *Social exchange: advances in theory and research.* New York: Plenum.

Fogel, R.W. (2004) *The escape from hunger and premature death, 1700-2100: Europe, America, and the Third World.* Cambridge: Cambridge University Press.

Freeman, C., & Louca, F. (2001) *As time goes by.* Oxford: Oxford University Press.

Frey, B.S. (1997) *Not just for the money.* Cheltenham: Elgar.

Galaskiewicz, J., & Wasserman, S. (1994) Introduction: advances in the social and behavioral sciences from social network analysis. In J. Galaskiewicz & S. Wasserman (Eds.), *Advances in social network analysis: research in the social and behavioral sciences* (pp. xi-xvii). Thousand Oaks: Sage.

Gallopin, G.C., Funtowicz, S., O'Connor, M., Ravetz, J. (2001) Science for the twenty-first century: from social contract to the scientific core *International Journal of Social Science* 16(8): 219-29.

Gancia, G., & Zilibotti, F. (2005) Horizontal innovation in the theory of growth and development. In P. Aghion & S. Durlauf (Eds.), *Handbook of economic growth* (pp. 111-170). Amsterdam: Elsevier North-Holland.

Gao, B. (2004) The State and the associational order of the economy: the institutionalization of cartels and trade associations in Japan, 1931 to 1945. In F. Dobbin (Ed.), *The sociology of the economy.* New York: Russell Sage Foundation.

Gasper, D. (2004) Building bridges and nurturing a complex ecology of ideas. In AK Girhi (Ed.), *Creative social research.* Lanham: Lexington.

Geddes, B. (2002) The great transformation in the study of politics in developing countries. In I. Katznelson, & H.V. Miller (Eds.), *Political science: state of the discipline* (pp. 342-70). New York: Norton.

Gerschenkron, A. (1962) *Economic backwardness in historical perspective.* Cambridge: Harvard University Press.

Gilfillan, S.C. (1935) [1970] *The sociology of invention.* Cambridge MA: Harvard University Press.

Goodin, R.E., & Klingemann, H.-D. (1998) Political science: the discipline. In R. Goodin & H. Klingemann (Eds.), *A new handbook of political science* (pp. 3-49). Oxford: Oxford University Press.

Goodwin, N., Nelson, J.A., Ackerman, F., & Weisskopf, T. (2005) *Microeconomics in context.* Boston: Houghton Mifflin.

Graff, G. (1992) *Beyond the culture wars: how teaching the conflicts can revitalize American education.* New York: Norton.

Granovetter, M. (1995) Coase revisited: business groups in the modern economy *Industrial and Corporate Change* 4(1), 93-130. Reprinted in M. Granovetter & R. Swedberg (Eds.), *The sociology of economic life* (pp. 327-56). Boulder CO: Westview Press.

Granovetter, M. (2001) Economic action and social structure: the problem of embeddedness. In M. Granovetter & R. Swedberg (Eds.), *The sociology of economic life* (pp. 51-76). Boulder CO: Westview Press.

Granovetter, M. (2002) A theoretical agenda for economic sociology. In M.F. Guillen, R. Collins, P. England, & M. Meyer (Eds.), *The new economic sociology: developments in an emerging field* (pp. 35-60). New York: Russell Sage Foundation.

Green, D.P., & Gerber, A.S. (2002) Reclaiming the Experimental Tradition in Political Science. In I. Katznelson & H.V. Miller (Eds.), *Political science: state of the discipline* (pp. 805-32). New York: Norton.

Greif, A. (2006) *Institutions and the path to the modern economy: lessons from medieval trade.* Cambridge: Cambridge University Press.

Grossman, G.M., Helpman, E. (1994) Endogenous innovation in the theory of growth. *Journal of Economic Perspectives* 8(1), 23-44.

Grübler, A. (1997) *Technological trajectories and the human environment.* Washington DC: National Academy Press.

Gudeman, Stephen (2001) *Anthropology of economy.* Oxford: Blackwell.

Guillen, M.F. (2003) The economic sociology of markets, industries, and firms. *Theory and Society* 32(4), 505-15.

Guiso, L., Spienza, P., Zingales, L. (2006) Does culture affect economic outcomes? *Journal of Economic Perspectives* 20(2), 23-48.

Gylfason, T. (1999) *Principles of economic growth.* Oxford: Oxford University Press.

Hage, J., & Meeus, M.T.H. (2006) Conclusion. In J. Hage, & M.T.H. Meeus (Eds.), *Innovation, science, and institutional change: a research handbook* (pp. 545-59). Oxford: Oxford University Press.

Hall, B. (2005) Innovation and diffusion. In J. Fagerberg, D.C. Mowery, & R.R. Nelson (Eds.) *The Oxford handbook of innovation* (pp. 459-84). Oxford: Oxford University Press.

Hall, D.J., & Hall, I. (1996) *Practical social research: project work in the community.* Basingstoke UK: Macmillan.

Hall, P.A., & Soskice, D. (2001) *Varieties of capitalism: the institutional foundations of comparative advantage.* Oxford: Oxford University Press.

Harrigan, J. (1997) Technology, factor supplies, and international specialization; estimating the neoclassical model. *American Economic Review* 87(2), 475-95.

Hausman, D. (1992) *The inexact and separate science of economics.* Cambridge: Cambridge University Press.

Haveman, H.A., & Keister, L.A. (2004) The effects of domain overlap and non-overlap on organizational performance, growth, and survival. In F. Dobbin (Ed.), *The sociology of the economy.* New York: Russell Sage Foundation.

Hayek, F. (1956) The dilemma of specialization. In L. White (Ed.), *The state of the social sciences.* Chicago: University of Chicago Press.

Heckman, J. (2000) Causal parameters and policy analysis in economics: a Twentieth Century perspective. *Quarterly Journal of Economics* 114(1), 45-97.

Hefner, R. (Ed.) (1998) *Market cultures: society and morality in the new Asian capitalisms.* Boulder CO: Westview Press.

Herring, R.J. (1999) Embedded particularism: India's failed developmental state. In M. Woo-Cumings (Ed.), *The developmental state* (pp. 306-34). Ithaca: Cornell University Press.

Hodgson, G. (2001) *How economics forgot history: the problems of historical specificity in social science.* New York: Routledge.

Hodgson, G. (1999) *Evolution and institutions: on evolutionary economics and the evolution of economics.* Cheltenham: Edward Elgar.

Huber, E., & Stevens, J.D. (2001) *Development and crisis of the welfare state: parties and policies in world markets.* Chicago: University of Chicago Press.

James, H. (2006) *Family capitalism.* Cambridge: Harvard University Press.

Jones, E.L. (2002) *The record of economic development.* Cheltenham: Edward Elgar.

Jones, E.L. (2006) *Cultures merging: a historical and economic critique of culture.* Princeton: Princeton University Press.

Jovanovic, B., & Rousseau, P.L. (2005) General purpose technologies. In P. Aghion & S. Durlauf (Eds.), *Handbook of economic growth* (pp. 1181-1223). Amsterdam: Elsevier North-Holland.

Kates, S. (1998) *Say's Law and the Keynesian revolution.* Cheltenham: Edward Elgar.

Katznelson, I., & Miller, H.V. (2002) American political science: the discipline's state and the state of the discipline' in I. Katznelson & H.V. Miller (Eds.), *Political science: state of the discipline* (pp. 1-26). New York: Norton.

Keating, M., Loughlin, J., & Deschouwer, K. (2003) *Culture, institutions, and economic development: a study of eight European regions.* Cheltenham: Edward Elgar.

Keller, W. (2004) International technological diffusion. *Journal of Economic Literature* 42(3), 752-82.

Kitcher, P. (1993) *The advancement of science.* New York: Oxford University Press.

Kleinknecht, A. (1987) *Innovation patterns in crisis and prosperity: Schumpeter's long cycle reconsidered.* London: Macmillan.

Kockel, U. (2002) Culture and economy: a brief introduction. In U. Kockel (Ed.), *Culture and economy: contemporary perspectives* (pp. 1-10). Aldershot: Ashgate.

Kohli, A. (2002) State, society, and development. In I. Katznelson & H.V. Miller (Eds.), *Political science: state of the discipline* (pp. 84-117). New York: Norton.

Kohli, A. (2004) *State directed development: political power and industrialisation in the global periphery.* Cambridge: Cambridge University Press.

Krieger, M.H. (1997) *Doing physics: how physicists take hold of the world.* Bloomington: University of Indiana Press.

Krugman, P. (1995) *Development, geography, and economic theory.* Cambridge MA: MIT Press.

Kuran, T. (2000) Why the Middle East is economically underdeveloped: historical mechanisms of institutional stagnation. *Journal of Economic Perspectives* 18(3), 71-90.

Lagemann, E.C. (2000) *An elusive science: the troubling history of education research.* Chicago: University of Chicago Press.

Laird, P.W. (2006) *Pull: networking and success since Benjamin Franklin.* Cambridge MA: Harvard University Press.

Laitin, D. (1998) *Identity in formation: the Russian-speaking population in the near-abroad.* Ithaca: Cornell University Press.

Lal, D. (1998) *Unintended consequences: the impact of factor endowments, culture and politics on long term economic development.* Cambridge MA: MIT Press.

Lam, A. (2005) Organizational innovation. In J. Fagerberg, D.C. Mowery, & R.R. Nelson (Eds.), *The Oxford handbook of innovation* (pp. 115-47). Oxford: Oxford University Press.

Landes, D. (2004) *The unbound Prometheus.* 2nd (Ed.) New York: Cambridge University Press.

Landes, D. (1998) *The wealth and poverty of nations.* New York: Norton.

Lane, J.-E., & Ersson, S. (1997) *Comparative political economy: a developmental approach.* 2nd Ed. London: Pinter.

Larrain, J. (1998) *Theories of development.* Cambridge: Polity.

Larsson, M. (2004) *The limits of business development and economic growth.* New York: Palgrave.

Lau, L.J. (1996) The sources of long term economic growth. In R. Landau, T. Taylor & G. Wright (Eds.), *The mosaic of economic growth.* Stanford University Press.

Lawson, T. (2003) *Reorienting economics.* London: Routledge.

Lawson, T. (1997) *Economics and reality.* London: Routledge.

Lederman, D., & Maloney, W.F. (Eds.) (2006) *Natural resources: neither curse nor destiny.* Stanford: Stanford University Press.

Lemonnier, P. (1992) *Elements for an anthropology of technology.* Ann Arbor: Museum of Anthropology.

Levine, R. (2005) Finance and growth: theory and evidence. In P. Aghion & S.N. Durlauf (Eds.), *Handbook of economic growth* (pp. 865-934). Amsterdam: Elsevier North-Holland.

Lewis, D. (2005) Anthropology and development: the uneasy relationship. In J.G. Carrier (Ed.), *A handbook of economic anthropology* (pp. 472-86). Cheltenham: Edward Elgar.

Lin, N. (2001) *Social capital: a theory of social structure and action.* Cambridge: Cambridge University Press.

Lindert, P.H. (2004) *Growing public: public spending and economic growth since the Eighteenth Century.* Cambridge: Cambridge University Press.

Lipsey, R.G. (2001) Successes and failures in the transformation of economics. *Journal of Economic Methodology* 8(2), 169-201.

Lipsey, R.G., Carlaw, K.I. & Bekar, C.T. (2006) *Economic transformations: general purpose technologies and long-term economic growth.* Oxford: Oxford University Press.

Loasby, B. J. (1999) *Knowledge, institutions, and evolution in economics.* London: Routledge.

Macpherson, W.J. (1987) *The economic development of Japan 1868-1941.* London: Macmillan.

Maddison, A. (2001) *The world economy: a millennial perspective.* Paris: OECD.

Mahoney, J. (2000) Path dependence in historical sociology *Theory and Society* 29: 507-48.

Manski, C.F. Economic analysis of social interactions *Journal of Economic Perspectives* 14(3), 115-36.

Marshall, A. (1920) *Principles of economics* 8th Ed. London: Macmillan.

Marx, K., & Engels, F. ([1848]1968) *The communist manifesto.* Hammondsworth: Penguin.

Mathias, P. (1983) *The first industrial nation.* 2nd Ed. London: Methuen.

Maurer, B. (2005) Finance. In J.G. Carrier (Ed.), *A handbook of economic anthropology* (pp. 176-93). Cheltenham: Edward Elgar.

McCleary, R.M., Barro, R. (2006) Religion and economy *Journal of Economic Perspectives* 20(2), 49-72.

McCloskey, D.N. (1998) *The rhetoric of economics.* 2nd Ed. Madison: University of Wisconsin Press.

McCloskey, D.N. (2006) *The bourgeois virtues: ethics for an age of commerce.* Chicago: University of Chicago Press.

McDonald, T.J. (1996) What do we do when we talk about history: the conversations of history and sociology. In T.J. McDonald (Ed.), *The historic turn in the human sciences* (pp. 91-118). Ann Arbor: University of Michigan Press.

McMichael, P. (2000) *Development and social change: a global perspective,* 2nd Ed. Thousand Oaks CA: Pine Forge Press.

Meeus, M.T.H., & Faber, J. (2006) Interorganizational relations and innovation: a review and a theoretical extension. In J. Hage & M.T.H. Meeus (Eds.), *Innovation, science, and institutional change: a research handbook* (pp. 67-87). Oxford: Oxford University Press.

Meeus, M.T.H. & Hage, J. (2006) Product and process innovation, scientific research, knowledge dynamics, and institutional change: an introduction. In J, Hage & M.T.H. Meeus (Eds.), *Innovation, science, and institutional change: a research handbook* (pp. 1-19). Oxford: Oxford University Press.

Mensch, G. (1979) *Stalemate in technology.* Cambridge MA: Ballinger.

Metcalfe, J.S. (2006) Innovation, competition, and enterprise: foundations for economic evolution in learning economies. In J. Hage & M.T.H. Meeus (Eds.), *Innovation, science, and institutional change: a research handbook* (pp. 105-21). Oxford: Oxford University Press.

Miller, R. (2008) *International Political Economy.* London: Routledge.

Moe, E. (2007) *Governance, growth, and global leadership: the role of the state in technological progress.* Burlington VT: Ashgate.

Mokyr, J. (1991) *The lever of riches.* Oxford: Oxford University Press.

Mokyr, J. (2002) *The gifts of Athena: historical origins of the knowledge economy.* Princeton: Princeton University Press.

Mokyr, J. (2005) Long-term economic growth and the history of technology. In P. Aghion & S.N. Durlauf (Eds.), *Handbook of Economic Growth* (pp. 1113-80). Amsterdam: Elsevier North-Holland.

Mosk, C. (2002) *Japanese industrial history: technology, urbanization, and economic growth.* Armonk NY: M.E. Sharpe.

Mowery, D. & Nelson, R. (1999) *Sources of industrial leadership.* New York: Cambridge University Press.

Mowery, D. & Rosenberg, N. (1998) *Paths of innovation.* Cambridge: Cambridge University Press.

Nee, V. (1998) Sources of the new institutionalism. In M.C. Brinton & V. Nee (Eds.), *The new institutionalism in sociology.* New York: Russell Sage Foundation.

Nelson, R., & Winter, S. (1982) *An evolutionary theory of economic change.* Cambridge MA: Harvard University Press.

Newell, W.H. (2001) A theory of interdisciplinary studies. *Issues in Integrative Studies* 19: 1-26.

Newell, W.H. (2007) Decision-making in interdisciplinary studies. In G. Morcol (Ed.), *Handbook of decision-making.* New York: Marcel Dekker Publishers.

North, D. (2005) *Understanding the process of economic change.* Princeton: Princeton University Press.

Nye, D.E. (2006) *Technology matters: questions to live with.* Cambridge: MIT Press.

Offe, C. (1998) Political economy: sociological perspectives. In R. Goodin & H. Klingemann (Eds.), *A new handbook of political science* (pp. 675-690). Oxford: Oxford University Press.

Offer, A. (2006) *The challenge of affluence.* Oxford: Oxford University Press.

Ogilvie, S. (2007) 'Whatever is, is right'?: Economic institutions in pre-industrial Europe *Economic History Review* 60(4), 649-84.

Olson, M. (2000) Big bills left on the sidewalk: why some nations are rich, and others poor. In M. Olson & S. Kahkonen (Eds.), *A Not-So-Dismal Science.* Oxford: Oxford University Press.

Ortiz, S. (2005) Decisions and choices: the rationality of economic actors. In J.G. Carrier (Ed.), *A handbook of economic anthropology* (pp. 59-77). Cheltenham: Edward Elgar.

Outhwaite, W. (2000) The philosophy of social science. In B.S. Turner (Ed.), *The Blackwell companion to social theory.* London: Blackwell.

Owen, W. (1983) *Transportation and world development.* New York: Random House.

Pallares-Burke, M.L. (Ed.) (2003) *The new history: confessions and conversations.* Cambridge UK: Polity.

Parry, J. (2005) Industrial work. In J.G. Carrier (Ed.), *A handbook of economic anthropology* (pp. 141-59). Cheltenham: Edward Elgar.

Pasinetti, L.L. (1981) *Structural change and economic growth: a theoretical essay on the dynamics of the wealth of nations.* Cambridge: Cambridge University Press.

Pempel, T.J. (1999) The developmental regime in a changing world economy. In M. Woo-Cumings (Ed.), *The developmental state* (pp. 137-81). Ithaca: Cornell University Press.

Perez, C. (2002) *Technological revolutions and financial capital: the dynamics of bubbles and golden ages.* Cheltenham: Edward Elgar.

Perotti, R. (1996) Growth, income distribution, and democracy: what the data say. *Journal of Economic Growth* 1: 149-87.

Perrow, C. (2004) Organizing America. In F. Dobbin (Ed.), *The sociology of the economy.* New York: Russell Sage Foundation.

Peters, B.G. (1998) Political institutions, old and new. In R. Goodin & H. Klingemann (Eds.), *A new handbook of political science* (pp. 205-22). Oxford: Oxford University Press.

Pierson, P., & Skocpol, T. (2002) Historical institutionalism in contemporary political science. In I. Katznelson & H.V. Miller (Eds.), *Political science: state of the discipline* (pp. 693-721). New York: Norton.

Pomeranz, K. (2000) *The great divergence: China, Europe, and the making of the modern world economy.* Princeton: Princeton University Press.

Powell, W.W., & Grodal, S. (2005) Networks of innovators. In J. Fagerberg, D.C. Mowery, & R.R. Nelson (Eds.) *The Oxford handbook of innovation* (pp. 56-85). Oxford: Oxford University Press.

Prasch, R. (2000) Integrating complexity into the teaching of macroeconomics. In D. Colander (Ed.), *The complexity vision and the teaching of economics.* Cheltenham: Edward Elgar.

Pritchett, L. (1997) Divergence big time. *Journal of Economic Perspectives* 11(3), 3-17.

Ragin, C. (2000) *Fuzzy set social science.* Chicago: University of Chicago Press.

Ragin, C., Berg-Schlosser, D., & DeMeur, G. (1998) Political science and the other social sciences. In R. Goodin & H. Klingemann (Eds.), *A new handbook of political science* (pp. 749-68). Oxford: Oxford University Press.

Ramaswamy, S. (2000) Development economics and complexity. In D. Colander (Ed.), *The complexity vision and the teaching of economics.* Cheltenham: Edward Elgar.

Repko, A. (2008) *Interdisciplinary research: process and theory.* Thousand Oaks: Sage.

Reuschmeyer, D. (2003). Can one or a few cases yield theoretical gain? In J.Mahoney & D. Reuschmeyer (Eds.), *Comparative historical analysis in the social sciences* (pp. 305-36). Cambridge: Cambridge University Press.

Richerson, P.J., & Boyd, R. (2005) *Not by genes alone: how culture transformed human evolution.* Chicago: University of Chicago Press.

Robotham, D. (2005) Political economy. In J.G. Carrier (Ed.), *A handbook of economic anthropology* (pp. 41-58). Cheltenham: Edward Elgar.

Rodrik, D. (2003) Introduction: what do we learn from country narratives? in D. Rodrik (Ed.), *In search of prosperity: analytic narratives on economic growth* (pp. 1-22). Princeton: Princeton University Press.

Rodrik, D. (2005) Growth strategies. In P. Aghion & S.N. Durlauf (Eds.), *Handbook of economic growth* (pp. 967-1014). Amsterdam: Elsevier North-Holland.

Rodrik, D. (2006) Goodbye Washington consensus, hello Washington confusion?: a review of the World Bank's 'Economic growth in the 1990s: learning from a decade of reform.' *Journal of Economic Literature* 44(4), 973-87.

Romer, P. (1994) The origins of endogenous growth. *Journal of Economic Perspectives* 8(1), 3-22.

Root-Bernstein, R. (1989) *Discovery.* Cambridge: Harvard University Press.

Rosenberg, N. (2000) *Schumpeter and the endogeneity of technology.* London: Routledge.

Rostow, W. W. (1960) *The stages of economic growth: a non-communist manifesto.* Cambridge: Cambridge University Press.

Rothstein, B. (1998) Political institutions: an overview. In R. Goodin & H. Klingemann (Eds.), *A new handbook of political science* (pp. 133-66). Oxford: Oxford University Press.

Rule, J.B. (1997) *Theory and progress in social science.* New York: Cambridge University Press.

Ruttan, V.W. (2000) *Imperialism and competition in anthropology, sociology, political science, and economics: a perspective from development economics.* Minneapolis: Economic Development Centre, University of Minnesota.

Sabel, C.F., & Zeitlin, J. (1997) Stories, strategies, structures: rethinking historical alternatives to mass production. In C.F. Sabel & J. Zeitlin (Eds.), *World of possibilities: flexibility and mass production in western industrialization.* New York: Cambridge University Press.

Sachs, J. (2005) *The end of poverty: how we can make it happen in our lifetime.* New York: Penguin.

Sahlins, M. (1974) *Stone age economics.* London: Tavistock Publications.

Samuels, W. (2004) Introduction. In W. Samuels et al (Eds.), *Essays on the history of economics* New York: Routledge.

Saxenian, A. (1996) Inside-out: regional networks and industrial adaptation in Silicon Valley and Route 128. *Cityscape: A Journal of Policy Development and Research* 2(2), 41-60; reprinted in M. Granovetter & R. Swedberg (Eds.), *The Sociology of Economic Life* (pp. 357-75). Boulder CO: Westview Press.

Scott, J.C. (1998) *Seeing like a state.* New Haven: Yale University Press.

Seabright, P. (2004) *The company of strangers: a natural history of economic life.* Princeton: Princeton University Press.

Shannon, T.R. (1992) *An introduction to the world-system perspective.* Boulder CO: Westview Press.

Snooks, G. (1998) *Longrun dynamics.* London: Macmillan.

Snowdon, B. (2002) *Conversations on growth, stability, and trade: a historical perspective.* Cheltenham: Edward Elgar.

Sokoloff, K.L., Engerman, S.L. (2004) Institutions, factor endowments, and paths of development in the New World, *Journal of Economic Perspectives* 14(3), 217-32.

Solow, R. (1956) A contribution to the theory of economic growth. *Quarterly Journal of Economics* 70(1), 65-94.

Solow, R. (1996) Perspectives on growth theory. *Journal of Economic Perspectives* 8(1), 45-54.

Solow, R. (1998) How did economics get that way, and what way did it get? In T. Bender & C.E. Schorske (Eds.), *American academic culture in transformation: fifty years, four disciplines.* Princeton: Princeton University Press.

Solow, R. (2000) Toward a macroeconomics of the medium run. *Journal of Economic Perspectives* 14(1), 151-8.

Solow, R. (2005) Reflections on growth theory. In P. Aghion & S.N. Durlauf (Eds.), *Handbook of economic growth* (pp. 1-10). Amsterdam: Elsevier North-Holland.

Stanley, T.D. (2001) Wheat from chaff: meta-analysis as quantitative literature review. *Journal of Economic Perspectives* 15(3), 185-92.

Stiglitz, J. (2000) The contributions of the economics of information to twentieth century economics. *Quarterly Journal of Economics* 115(4), 1441-78.

Stiglitz, J. (2006) *Making globalization work.* New York: Norton.

Strahler, A. (1992) *Understanding science.* Buffalo: Prometheus Books.

Svensson, J. (2005) Eight questions about corruption. *Journal of Economic Perspectives* 19(3), 19-42.

Swedberg, R. (2000) The social science view of entrepreneurship: introduction and practical implications. In R. Swedberg (Ed.), *Entrepreneurship: the social science view.* Oxford: Oxford University Press.

Swedberg, R. (2004) On legal institutions and their role in the economy. In F. Dobbin (Ed.), *The Sociology of the Economy.* New York: Russell Sage Foundation.

Swedberg, R. (2003) The case for an economic sociology of law. *Theory and Society* 32(1), 1-37.

Swedberg, R. (2005) Introduction. In R. Swedberg (Ed.), *New developments in economic sociology.* Cheltenham UK: Edward Elgar.

Swedberg, Richard, & Mark Granovetter (2001) Introduction to the second edition. In M. Granovetter & R. Swedberg (Eds.), *The sociology of economic life* (pp. 1-28). Boulder CO: Westview Press.

Szostak, R. (1989) The organization of work: the emergence of the factory revisited, *Journal of Economic Behavior and Organization,* 11(3): 343-58

Szostak, R. (1991a) *The role of transportation in the Industrial Revolution,* Montreal: McGill-Queen's University Press.

Szostak, R. (1991b) Institutional inheritance and early American industrialization *Research in Economic History,* Supplement, 287-308.

Szostak, R. (1995) *Technological innovation and the Great Depression.* Boulder CO: Westview Press.

Szostak, R. (2001) The domestic economy: an overview. In *Canada since Confederation: a history on CD-Rom* (90 msp.). Edmonton: Chinook Multimedia.

Szostak, R. (2002) How to do interdisciplinarity: integrating the debate, *Issues in Integrative Studies* 20, 103-22.

Szostak, R. (2003a) Classifying natural and social scientific theories. *Current Sociology* 51(1): 27-49.

Szostak, R. (2003b) *A schema for unifying human science: interdisciplinary perspectives on culture.* Selinsgrove PA: Susquehanna University Press.

Szostak, R. (2004) *Classifying science: phenomena, data, theory, method, practice.* Dordrecht: Springer.

Szostak, R. (2005a) *Unifying ethics.* Lanham MD: University Press of America.

Szostak, R. (2005b) Evaluating the historiography of the Great Depression: explanation or single-theory driven? *Journal of Economic Methodology* 12(1): 35-61.

Szostak, R. (2006) Economic history as it is and should be; toward an open, honest, methodologically flexible, theoretically diverse, interdisciplinary exploration of the causes and consequences of economic growth, *Journal of Socio-Economics,* 35(4): 727-50.

Szostak, R. (2007a) Modernism, postmodernism, and interdisciplinarity. *Issues in Integrative Studies* 25.

Szostak, R. (2007b) Interdisciplinarity and the classification of scholarly documents by phenomena, theories, and methods. In B. Rodriguez Bravo & L.A. Diez (Eds.), *Interdisciplinarity and transdisciplinarity in the organization of scientific knowledge: Actas del VIII Congreso ISKO-Espana* (pp. 469-77). Leon: University of Leon.

Szostak, R. (2007c) How and why to teach interdisciplinary research practice *Journal of Research Practice* 3(2), October.

Szostak, R. (2008a) Classification, interdisciplinarity, and the study of science. *Journal of Documentation*, 64(3), 319-32.

Szostak, R. (2008b) Classifying heterodoxy. *Journal of Philosophical Economics* 1(2): 97-126.

Szostak, R., & Gnoli, C. (2008) Classifying by phenomena, theories and methods: examples with focused social science theories. In C. Arsenault & J. Tennis (Eds.), *Culture and identity in knowledge organization,* proceedings of the 10th international ISKO conference (pp. 205-211). Würzburg: Ergon.

Szreter, S. (2002) The state of social capital: bringing back in power, politics, and history. *Theory and Society* 31(5), 573-621.

Temin, P. (1997) The Golden Age of European growth: a review essay *European Review of Economic History* 1: 127-49.

Temple, J. (1999) The new growth evidence. *Journal of Economic Literature* 37(1), 112-57.

Thaler, R.H. (2000) From homo economicus to homo sapiens *Journal of Economic Perspectives* 14(1), 133-41.

Thelen, K. (1997) Historical institutionalism in comparative politics. *Annual Review of Political Science* 2, 369-404.

Thelen, K. (2002) The political economy of business and labor in the developed democracies. In I. Katznelson & H.V. Miller (Eds.), *Political science: state of the discipline* (pp. 371-97). New York: Norton.

Thornton, P. (1999) The sociology of entrepreneurship. *Annual Review of Sociology* 25, 19-46.

Throsby, D. (2001) *Economics and culture.* Cambridge: Cambridge University Press.

Toninelli, P.A. (Ed.) (2000) *The rise and fall of state-owned enterprises in the western world.* Cambridge: Cambridge University Press.

Turner, S.P. (2002) *Brains/practices/relativism: social theory after cognitive science.* Chicago: University of Chicago Press.

Vartiainen, J. (1999) The economics of successful state intervention in industrial transformation. In M. Woo-Cumings (Ed.), *The developmental state* (pp. 200-34). Ithaca: Cornell University Press.

Vivarelli, M. (1995) *The economics of technology and unemployment.* Cheltenham: Elgar.

Weil, D.N. (2005) *Economic growth.* Boston: Addison-Wesley.

Weingast, B. (1998) Political institutions: rational choice perspectives. In R. Goodin & H. Klingemann (Eds.), *A new handbook of political science* (pp. 167-90). Oxford: Oxford University Press.

White, H.C. (2002) *Markets from networks: socioeconomic models of production.* Princeton: Princeton University Press.

Whitford, J. (2002) Pragmatism and the untenable dualism of means and ends: why rational choice theory does not deserve paradigmatic privileges. *Theory and Society* 31(3), 325-63.

Woirol, G.R. (1996) *The technological unemployment and structural unemployment debates.* Westport CT: Greenwood Press.

Woo-Cumings, M. (1999) Introduction: Chalmers Johnson and the politics of nationalism and development. In M. Woo-Cumings (Ed.), *The developmental state* (pp.1-31). Ithaca: Cornell University Press.

Wood, G. (2006) *Revolutionary character:what made the founders different.* NewYork: Penguin.

Woolcock, M. (1998) Social capital and economic development: toward a theoretical synthesis and policy framework *Theory and Society* 27(2), 151-208.

Index

Printed in the United States
148815LV00003B/1/P